Historic Gardens
and
Parks of Derbyshire

Challenging Landscapes, 1570–1920

Dianne Barre

WIND*gather*
PRESS

Windgather Press is an imprint of Oxbow Books

Published in the United Kingdom in 2017 by
OXBOW BOOKS
The Old Music Hall, 106–108 Cowley Road, Oxford, OX4 1JE

and in the United States by
OXBOW BOOKS
1950 Lawrence Road, Havertown, PA 19083

Paperback Edition: ISBN 978-1-911188-04-9
Digital Edition: ISBN 978-1-911188-05-6

A CIP record for this book is available from the British Library

Printed in Malta by Gutenberg Press Ltd

For a complete list of Windgather titles, please contact:

United Kingdom
Oxbow Books
telephone (01865) 241249
Fax (01865) 794449
Email: oxbow@oxbowbooks.com
www.oxbowbooks.com

United States of America
Oxbow Books
telephone (800) 791-9354
Fax (610) 853-9146
Email: queries@casemateacademic.com
www.casemateacademic.com/oxbow

Oxbow Books is part of the Casemate group

Front cover image: Anchor Church, oil painting (1745) by Thomas Smith of Derby.
Courtesy Derby Museum and Art Gallery and www.picturethepast.org.uk.
Inset: Vignette of Brookhill Hall, Pinxton, courtesy G. Laycock and www.picturethepast.
org.uk

Contents

Preface   v
Acknowledgements   vii

1.   Introduction: Derbyshire gardens 1570–1920   1

2.   The Enclosed Garden 1580–1700   13

3.   Early Eighteenth Century: From formal garden to *ferme ornée*   45

4.   Capability Brown and William Emes   72

5.   Late Eighteenth Century 1760–1800   94

6.   Caves, Hermitages and Grottos   119

7.   Early Nineteenth Century: Regency to early Victorian gardens   133

8.   The Early to Mid-Victorian Period: Reclamation, rockwork, conservatories   159

9.   A Victorian Miscellany, Including Designers from Loudon to Sitwell   180

10.   The Spas: Matlock Bath, Matlock Bank, Bakewell, Buxton, Derby, Ilkeston   199

11.   Edwardian Gardens   213

12.   A Miscellany of Gardeners and Nurserymen   237

Postscript: Three Modern Gardens   252
Bibliography   255

Preface

I had intended to write a comprehensive survey of Derbyshire's historic gardens and landscapes 1570–1920, but it was soon obvious that there were far too many for one book. So little by little the number was whittled down to a manageable 90 or so.

A major problem was the limited space available for important gardens such as Chatsworth, Kedleston, Melbourne and Renishaw. Fortunately their archive material has been researched already and information is available elsewhere, which allowed me to concentrate on other places. Therefore the space allotted is not necessarily in relation to the importance of a garden, but depends on accessibility, available archival material, and, to be truthful, what appealed to me. A chronological approach means that certain places appear in more than one chapter and full referencing is given. Interesting personalities soon appeared, with the result that local landscape gardeners, nurserymen and women, poets or just plain eccentrics receive as much attention as the famous Joseph Paxton or William Barron.

On reflection Derbyshire was a fool-hardy choice for someone who hates heights. I could never understand why the eighteenth-century tourist loved the frisson of terror, as nervously I struggled up precipitous tracks and drove round blind bends, trying not to look down a sheer drop, even if the view was exhilarating. Wherever possible I made a site visit and I am grateful for the help and welcome given by owners. Inevitably, once on site with a plan, there were more questions than answers.

Whenever possible I have quoted contemporary sources to reflect the spirit of the time, hence the copious use of poetry, book and newspaper extracts. The British Newspaper Archive is a fascinating source, and the local paper the *Derby Mercury* proved invaluable. I acknowledge with deep gratitude permission to quote from the totally addictive website www.britishnewspaperarchive.co.uk. All extracts from old newspapers are by permission of British Newspaper Archive and © The British Library Board.

A great disappointment has been the omission of several important estate plans and maps at the Derby Record Office because of the ever-increasing restrictions of copyright and the problem of locating copyright holders. Application for licensing 'Orphan Works' (those for which copyright holders are unknown or cannot be found), with the Intellectual Property Office is a daunting and time-consuming job. I gave up in despair towards the end, and have simply noted the Record Office accession number in the reference section.

On a more positive note this book is dedicated to Sue Gregory, friend and fellow garden history enthusiast, whose amazing knowledge of nineteenth-century gardeners, nurserymen and florists (among other topics) was generously shared, and who saved me from many errors with my over-enthusiasm in topics new to me.

Accessibility

Unless included below all other gardens described are not open to the public.

Rowtor Rocks, Anchor Caves and Dale Abbey, Swarkston Stand (Landmark Trust)

National Trust: Calke Abbey, Eyam, Hardwick Hall, Kedleston, Sudbury.

English Heritage: Bolsover Castle, Sutton Scarsdale.

Gardens privately owned but open regularly: Chatsworth House, Haddon Hall, Hopton Hall, Melbourne Hall, Renishaw Hall, Thornbridge Hall, Tissington Hall.

Public Parks: Alfreton Hall, Belper River Gardens, Buxton Pavilion Gardens, Derby Arboretum, Elvaston Castle, Markeaton Hall, Shipley Country Park.

Privately owned but open occasionally for charity: Locko Hall and Park Hall, Chesterfield.

Hotels: Breadsall, Cressbrook, Hassop, Newton Park, Ringwood, Risley, Willesley Castle.

Abbreviations

DRO	Derbyshire County Record Office
SRO	Staffordshire County Record Office
WRO	Warwickshire County Record Office
OS	Ordnance Survey map
DTT	Derby Daily Telegraph
DM	Derby Mercury
DTCH	Derbyshire Times and Chesterfield Herald
CL	Country Life
GC	Gardeners' Chronicle
JHCG	Journal of Horticulture and Cottage Gardener
Craven & Stanley	M. Craven and M. Stanley, The Derbyshire Country House, 2 vols. (Ashbourne, 2001)

Quotations after chapter headings are selected from Sir George Sitwell, *An Essay on the Making of Gardens* (1909). He seemed an apt choice for a book on Derbyshire gardens.

Acknowledgements

I acknowledge my debt to the two volumes of *The Derbyshire Country House* by Maxwell Craven and Michael Stanley, as shown by the number of times they are referenced. Anne Lawley, Paul Beattie, Becky Sheldon and Mark Smith at Derbyshire County Record Office, Matlock, showed great patience with my queries and requests for a mass of archival material. Archivists at Staffordshire Record Office and Nottingham University Manuscripts and Special Collections were similarly patient. Nick Thompson, www.picturethepast.org.uk was a tremendous help in providing pictures from the incomparable collection of historic images of Derbyshire and Nottinghamshire shown on this searchable, not-for-profit website. The site has over 100,000 pictures and is freely available for all to explore.

Thea Randall bravely proof-read the manuscript, corrected errors and suggested invaluable improvements. The National Trust provided certain images of their properties and kindly allowed use of my own. English Heritage (via Emma Weeks) allowed me to use my photographs of Bolsover and Sutton Scarsdale. Charles Boot, Hon. Richard Curzon, Sue Gregory, Philip Heath, Randle Knight, Helen Lawrence, Simon McCormack (National Trust) and Sir Andrew Walker-Okeover provided help and advice and Ray Conningham is thanked for his support during the five years of this project.

At properties I am greatly indebted to: James Cartland, Paul Winfield, Veronica Jones, N. Boys, Judith Wright, Nigel Webb, Craig Lynch, Carl Fisher, Nicholas Dumbell, Katherine Pryor, Eileen Swan, Jeremy Carter, Steve Biggins, Bill Cove, Mrs B. Hull-Bailey, Val Farren, Simon Baxter, Richard Merriman, Richard Fletcher, Richard Hatley, Jacqui Lomas, Thomas Chapman, Sarah and Dan Jones, Michael Harrison, Nicholas and Ollie Gerrish, Julian Scholefield, Lynette Prothero, John Stanfield, Peter and Linda Wiseman, Lauren Davies, Hon. Richard Curzon, Caroline Stanford, Stephen and Deborah Taylor, Mrs L. Palmer, Nina Grant, Mick Marshall, Lord Ralph Kerr, Gill Weston, Peter Marples, Adam and Lizzie Devey Smith, Moira Banks, David and Mrs Wakefield, Sir Andrew Walker-Okeover, Kim and Margaret Staniforth, Alice and Robert Shields, Mrs Alexandra Hayward, Chris Beevers, A. Bramall, Rona Davies, David Flanegan, Nicola Parkin, Richard Paine, John and Elizabeth Goodall, Sheagan Fradley, Kate Alcock, Simon Haslam, Michael Starsmore, Steve and Natalie Drury, R. Lucas, Joan Webb, Peter Jackson, David and Jo North, Jim and Emma Harrison, Nicky Dalton, Sir Richard FitzHerbert and Anne Allaway.

Finally, but by no means least, my grateful thanks to Oxbow Books for agreeing to publish my first solo book. Dr Julie Gardiner was wonderfully patient with my endless nervous queries, and Clare Litt, Mette Bundgaard and Tara Evans also provided guidance and support.

CHAPTER ONE

Introduction: Derbyshire gardens
1570–1920

The Garden maker is striving not for himself alone but for those who are to come after.

From the wide choice of gardens and parks in Derbyshire nearly 100 have been selected including many owned by established families, industrialists and businessmen. Both for the aristocratic Cavendishes and Curzons, and wealthy manufacturers such as the Arkwrights and Strutts, their pleasure grounds played a significant role in their social aspirations and social life. The latter acquired country estates having made their fortunes and became part of the establishment. Derbyshire is rich in minerals, coal, gritstone, alabaster, iron and lead, bringing wealth not only to entrepreneurs but also to established landowning families such as the Hunlokes, Mundys and Sitwells. This provides a very interesting mix of personalities, ambitions and challenges. However we start the story of Derbyshire gardens with a background miscellany.

Many country house gardens were based on a practical and down-to-earth emphasis on attractive productivity. So when Smalley Hall, a modest but attractive newly built country house, was offered to let in April 1764 with 'Land fitting for a Gentleman', the advert mentioned two fishponds, orchard and two gardens, 'wall'd with brick planted with the choicest fruit': that is ornamental utility.[1] In 1799 a property near Ashbourne was on the market and the auctioneer carefully mixed the appeal of the 'delightful prospect', with the suggestion that a nearby waterfall, 'near twenty feet high, and supplied by a fluent brook,' would be 'very advantageous to erect a manufactory thereon'.[2] When Ashbourne Hall and its parkland were for sale in 1846, to attract the 'Gentleman of private fortune' the agent extolled the virtues of its position near the parish church and the romantic scenery of Dove Dale. Then more prosaically he moved to attract the 'eminent merchant', noting the proximity of the railway station and that part of land could be adapted for the erection of a manufactory, 'or any premises of magnitude without obstructing the delightful views from the mansion'.[3]

The open and often wild hilly terrain of much of Derbyshire produced the obvious response of terraced gardens within protective walls. Indeed the walled garden hardly went out of fashion in the county. A ready supply of local stone, combined with terracing meant that the Italian style garden was at home here. There was no rush to demolish garden walls in the mid-eighteenth century, although fashionable open lawns crept up to larger country houses such as Chatsworth and Kedleston. When, two generations later, terraces and

FIGURE I. Holme Hall,
Bakewell, terraces
summer house and walls
1670s.

COURTESY J. STANSFIELD

flowerbeds became popular once again nationally, effectively they had never gone out of fashion in Derbyshire. Later the Arts and Crafts gardens, with their walls, terracing and pergolas, meant that many of its smaller gardens were easily very up-to-date. Derbyshire is fortunate in the survival and current restoration of several of these fine walled gardens, although in other ways the twentieth century was not so kind. A number of county house gardens and parks survive as public parks, with or without their house. The result can be a somewhat bland and soul-less landscape, since the focal point, the house, has gone, as at Darley, Markeaton and Shipley. The stunted remains of the halls at Allestree, Alfreton and Ashbourne are hardly any better. Yet even this is preferable to the destruction of Osmaston Hall, Derby, replaced by an industrial estate or Drakelow Hall, demolished for a power station.

For many years Derbyshire was not easily accessible and visitors responded differently over the years, from John Taylor in 1639: 'most dangerous ways, stony, craggy, with inaccessible hills and mountains,' to Mrs Thrale in 1774: 'The Triumphs of Art and Nature are surely all exhibited in Derbyshire'.[4] In 1745 the Rev. Nixon was 'agreeably surprised' to find that the Peak District had 'exceeding good roads', pure air, rich valleys and polite inhabitants.[5] Yet in 1747 Lady Sophia Newdigate, travelling towards Buxton, was unenthusiastic:

> Through the most uninhabited hill Bleak Country yt can be Conceived for many miles without ye sight of a Tree or even a shrub not a house or anything appeared to convince us we were not the first of all living things that ever ventur'd there.[6]

In 1755 Resta Patching took four hours to cover the six miles (9.6 km) between Chesterfield and Chatsworth, and his chaise had to be repaired three times on his Derbyshire travels because of the poor condition of the roads.[7] Yet tourists were undeterred and even local gentry enjoyed the scenery as when Sir Robert Burdett of Foremark Hall made 'a jaunt into ye Peake' in July 1759.[8] Visitors

were amazed at the wild countryside even before the Picturesque Movement gained momentum, as shown in the 1740s engravings by T. Smith of Derby, where well-dressed viewers admire the wild scenery. Mrs Thrale's report on her visit to Reynard's Cave Dovedale (1774) shows that the *frissons* usually associated with the wild and picturesque scenery of the Wye Valley and the Lakes were just as applicable to Derbyshire:

> We were shown another precipe the sight of which so frightened somebody that she fainted at the view, and must have fallen headlong had not a gentleman present caught hold of her suddenly and saved her life.[9]

By then Derbyshire was on the tourist route for its wild romantic scenery and fearsome, awesome caves. When Arthur Young published his Tour (1771) he enthused about the wooded precipes of a valley down to the river. His descriptions include 'gloomy', 'picturesque', 'beautiful', 'striking landscape', 'The roar of the falls in the river is fine'.[10] A hundred years later travel writers were still extolling the charms of Dovedale with 'its picturesque beauties ... gorgeous woods, its magnificent rocks, its beautiful river, and the wondrous variety of its scenery.'[11]

By the late seventeenth century the 'genteel' visitor had access to certain of the larger private pleasure grounds, as when the indomitable Celia Fiennes visited Bretby and Chatsworth in the late 1690s, providing full descriptions of their elaborate gardens. This was not open access to all: as Charles Cotton wrote in 1681, Chatsworth's entrance tower 'From the Peake-rabble does securely shut'.[12] Later, many who had come to admire the picturesque scenes of the Peak District went on to visit Chatsworth, Haddon, Hardwick and Kedleston.[13]

Many travellers went to Buxton and Matlock Spas for their medicinal water cures, leading to the development of private and public gardens there. The advent of the railway in the 1840s led to a new phenomenon: The Excursionist (day-tripper), looking for a short holiday break, change of scenery and a day's entertainment. A public holiday, such as Good Friday in 1873, was carefully prepared for in advance by traders, railway staff (and police) at Matlock Bath. Even so food ran out when 15,000 visitors descended on what was essentially a small town.[14] Its visitor attractions, such as the privately owned Heights of Abraham and the Lovers Walks, both with attractive hillside walks, were important to occupy the time of visitors. There were also tea and coffee rooms, hotels and spa shops to help pass the time. Matlock Pavilion and Gardens (1883), with a programme of indoor entertainments at a very modest cost, were vital if it rained. Their flower gardens were especially popular.[15] Derby Arboretum was another popular venue and special attractions were put on, such as the July 1857 musical band and balloon ascent and August 1861 brass band contest. On both occasions excursionists were admitted for 6d (2½p), or half price on production of their railway card.[16]

By the 1830s some smaller country house gardens were open for charitable events. A delightful account of one such an event, at Melbourne Hall, featured in the *Derby Mercury* 21 August 1839. About 500 people came, 'a numerous and respectable company, on the occasion of a public tea-drinking for the benefit of the national and infant schools'. It was a typically wet English summer day but doggedly the company had their tea and walked round the gardens with dancing, a band and 'also a party of glee singers'. A generation later there was a very different, rather supercilious, report in the *Mercury* 30 August 1871, after the railways had opened up this garden to the dreadful 'excursionists' who

> …gazed upon the elaborate leaden vase which Queen ANNE presented to the famous COKE who once owned the place, and wondered what it was worth for old metal; they flung stones into the ornamental waters; cut their initials on the trees, and strewed the glade with paper… They behaved, in short, in just such way as may be witnessed almost any day at Alton Towers…

Elvaston Castle grounds had been inaccessible, so there was great excitement when the fifth Earl Harrington inherited in 1851 and opened the gardens as an early example of trying to generate income to support their upkeep. There was some apprehension when the gardens were opened to the 'Working Classes' on Whit Monday 31 May 1852, through the good offices of the Derby Temperance Society. It was hoped 'that as a point of honour no one will be found to infringe upon the regulations printed upon the tickets, or in any way to break the good faith his Lordship has in the working Classes'. There was a 'first rate band', a refreshment tent and 'different companies of glee singers … to enliven the scene'. As an extra attraction several 'Popular Advocates of Temperance are expected to deliver Addresses on the great and important subject of Total Abstinence'. Special trains, 'all covered carriages', ran from Derby for 6d (2½p). The admission price was 1 shilling (5p) which in this case went towards building a new Temperance Hall in Derby. The day was cold, but the trains were full, people walked from the station and the roads were crowded. Guides were positioned to direct visitors and prevent access to private areas. To the great relief of all, there was no damage and over five thousand people enjoyed the treat.[17] It sounds like the equivalent of an early pop festival.

Other popular tourist attractions were Haddon Hall (Duke of Rutland) and Hardwick Hall (Duke of Devonshire), which as second homes opened their gardens when the family was away. Some smaller private gardens opened for special groups, as when in 1857 the Clarkes at Masson House, Matlock Bath, opened their spectacular new hillside garden to the Temperance Society.[18] Such events were mentioned in the local newspapers, which no doubt gave as much gratification to the owners as to the visitors. However excursionists could be regarded with suspicion and had a bad press. By 1890 the park at Lea Hurst was rented by a Mr Yeomans, who 'only requires a polite request to allow free access,' but soon with regret he had to restrict access because of 'the extraordinary depredations, and the shameful license taken by visitors'.[19]

By the later eighteenth century the main social and political rivals in the county were the wealthy Cavendish Dukes of Devonshire of Chatsworth and the Curzon Earls Scarsdale at Kedleston. Both hosted archery competitions.

> To the Members of the Derbyshire Archery, Greeting!
> All you who appear
> In army every year,
> Toxophilites hearty and steady,
> On Kedleston Plain,
> And the ducal Domain
> Of Chatsworth – to arms – and make ready...[20]

These were important events in the social summer calendar, attended by the great and the good of the locality, ladies and gentlemen competing. From the 1790s competitions were held in Kedleston Park with 'the attraction of Kedleston as a scene of beautiful country, and of the archery as an elegant pastime'.[21] By 1823 a special temporary pavilion was erected for use of those attending, with food and dancing in the evening.[22] The Duke of Devonshire probably scored a greater hit with a large painting 'the Great Picture of the Derbyshire Archery held at Chatsworth August 28th 1823', depicting over 100 people, which was exhibited for several weeks in Derby in 1824.[23]

Chatsworth House and gardens were open regularly and became more accessible with a railway station at Rowsley, from where local transport would bring the visitors. Numbers could be large, as with 4000 members of a temperance group from Sheffield in July 1849.[24] Marquees were erected on the lawn to cope with such special groups. By the end of the century political opponents were denigrating these popular openings as a mere vote catcher, which was denied in an editorial of 1892:

> Thousands of folk who live in the Midlands know that Chatsworth is an open house. Six days each week in the summer the beauties of the Palace of the Peak are enjoyed by excursionists and tourists in their tens of thousands... Few, if any of the grand homes of England are free like Chatsworth.[25]

In comparison, in 1884 a local paper bemoaned the now total lack of accessibility of Kedleston. 'The name of Lord Scarsdale is not one which appeals to the heart of the community', with park fenced off, hall inaccessible and the inn converted into a private residence. The Inn had 'offered rest and refreshment to the Derby toiler who walked thither and was at liberty to stroll amid the green glades of that glorious park, or drink from the healing springs … [now] peremptorily closed to the tourist'. There followed the telling comment: 'The liberal Duke of Devonshire shows the Conservative Lord Scarsdale a laudable example in this direction'.[26] However Lord Scarsdale was presumably anxious to be accorded positive newspaper space, so, in 1886, 1500 excursionists from Lancashire and Yorkshire were entertained with games of cricket, football and quoits and permitted to explore the park. These were largely middle and working class Conservative supporters who returned home enthusiastically supporting Conservatives and Curzons.[27] From 1896 the park was open to cyclists on Saturday afternoons between April and October.[28]

An Englishman's home was quite definitely his castle, and that extended to his pleasure grounds. Therefore any damage or theft therein was viewed with indignation and punished by the law accordingly. It was a problem affecting both the small town garden and the large estate, ranging from petty theft to malicious damage, despite heavy penalties for those convicted. Some reports of petty theft sound quite modern: in 1821 thieves forcibly broke into 'garden houses' in Derby and stole rakes, forks, spades *etc.*, causing an irritated owner to offer five guineas reward. There followed the rather obvious afterthought that

> As the Persons who committed the above Robberies must have had a great bulk to carry of the Articles stolen, either in a sack bag, or loose, if any suspicious characters were seen on Saturday night, information is requested to be given to H. Newton, Police Officer…[29]

Theft from gardens in Derby became such a nuisance in 1800 that professional gardeners there formed an Association to prosecute offenders jointly and offer a reward to those providing information.[30] This was one of several such Associations in the county around this period. Others took a different step, as in 1781 when the Earl of Rutland's steward offered a reward of five guineas for the conviction of thieves who regularly stole fruit from the gardens at Haddon Hall. He announced that 'Several Steel traps and Spring Guns are now placed in the Garden'.[31] This somewhat drastic action is not one would associate with the current idyllic gardens at Haddon. A lesser punishment for would-be thieves was recommended by the *Derby Mercury* 1 September 1841 following a spate of garden robberies at Wirksworth:

> To prevent garden and orchard robberies, we would recommend the placing of small barrels of coal tar secretly in various parts of the ground and lightly covered over with a few sticks and a little earth. This method has been practised with complete success by a gentleman in this neighbourhood.

Punitive acts of parliament in 1789 and 1825 allowed harsh penalties for theft and vandalism at nurseries or gardens, ranging from a fine to imprisonment or transportation, although there does not appear to be any standard pattern of severity of sentence. Theft of fruit, sometimes little more than the youthful scrumping of apples, was still regarded as an assault on private property. In 1830 two 14-year-old lads robbed a garden, and the Mayor and Magistrates decided to make an example of them because of the prevalence of this problem. They were sentenced to six months' imprisonment with hard labour, mitigated to two months' with hard labour. When in 1847 two men were given three months' hard labour for stealing from Mr Adams' orchard at Matlock, Adams, a surgeon, noted that in the last 17 years his orchard had been robbed on an average of 20 times a year.[32]

Fishponds were another target. The large sum of ten guineas was offered as a reward for the capture of a gang who stole fish from Melbourne Hall in 1754 and ten guineas also for the successful conviction of those who stole fish from the stews at Foremark Hall in 1770.[33] Even William Emes, the noted landscape gardener, did not escape. In 1781 ornamental Chinese carp were stolen from garden ponds at his Bowbridge Fields home.[34]

Vandalism was not uncommon at country estates, as when the canal in the garden at Foston Hall was wilfully emptied in 1754.[35] At Kedleston, Sir Nathaniel Curzon announced in 1760 that he would prosecute those responsible for uprooting young trees in one of his plantations. He reminded them that destroying trees planted for ornament was a felony under *The Black Act* of 1724. This did not prevent a repetition in 1773 when nearly 200 trees were destroyed and the huge sum of 100 guineas was offered as reward.[36]

Smaller properties also could be subject to vandalism and malicious damage. Certain 'atrocious villain or villains' destroyed fir trees in a garden in Wardwick, Derby in 1774 and the enraged owner offered 50 guineas as a reward for the conviction of the offenders.[37] Thomas Gisborne, clergyman at Darley Grove, offered five guineas as a reward for information about those responsible for the deliberate damage of young trees and box hedges in 1786.[38] In 1827 'some dastardly villains … wantonly and maliciously' destroyed fruit trees in a garden at Heanor and overturned four beehives. They returned the next week to damage shrubs and fruit trees, and also the new garden gate which replaced one they had destroyed previously. In 1838 the *Mercury* reported, with some satisfaction, that would-be thieves, who scaled the garden walls at house in Derby and damaged plants, accidently overturned two beehives 'which no doubt caused them to make their exit sooner than they would have done'. At Littleover in 1848 a gang went on the rampage, stole apples, pulled up railing and threw stones at windows. Apprehended, they received between six weeks' and 2 months' hard labour for their fun.[39] The list is endless.

Poaching was a time-honoured pastime, affecting fish, rabbits, hare, and deer, with large rewards offered by landowners for convictions. It was often accompanied by vandalism, as in 1769 at Sudbury when deer were stolen and a bridge over the river in the park destroyed. An enticing 50 guineas reward

FIGURE 3. Kedleston Church, copper engraving from *Gentleman's Magazine*, Feb. 1793.

AUTHOR'S COLLECTION

was offered for conviction.[40] Professionals poached in groups and could be very violent. At Bretby in 1817 and Alderwasley in 1818 they murdered the gamekeeper.[41] Well into the early twentieth century there were reports of particularly vicious confrontations between gamekeepers and armed gangs of poachers, with frequent cases at Kedleston and Locko Park.[42]

By no means confined to Derbyshire, the popularity of grottoes and rockwork featured at a number of properties, displaying wealth and culture and encouraged by the local availability of suitable materials. These have a chapter to themselves, but mention should be made of the incorporation of reclaimed material into gardens in the nineteenth century. Examples can be found in other counties, particularly using stones from demolished churches, but Derbyshire also has the controversial re-use of archaeological finds, of which the county had a ready supply. In 1781, when workmen digging the foundations of the Duke of Devonshire's new Crescent at Buxton discovered complete Roman Baths, the architect quickly ordered the workmen to fill in and build on top.[43] So perhaps one could feel relief at finding that some ancient and medieval stonework was rescued for gardens, including the early medieval 'Headless Cross', removed from Friar Gate, Derby, to the Arboretum.

Antiquarian enthusiasts used monastic stonework in the gardens at Breadsall Priory, Holt Hall and Newton Solney. Thomas Bateman of Lomberdale Hall became notorious for scattering round his garden numerous pre-historic and medieval articles he had excavated himself. More correctly in 1895 Sir William Fitzherbert of Tissington Hall returned part of an ancient cross acquired by an ancestor 'many years ago ... to help in the decoration of a grotto'.[44] Purchasing Derwent Hall in 1876 the Duke of Norfolk rescued its chapel font (1672) which had been used as 'a geranium pot in the Hall gardens.'[45] At Ogston tracery from a medieval church window enlivens the path to the kitchen garden. In 1928

FIGURE 4. Hathersage
Hall, eighteenth-century
summer house set in
garden wall.

Lord Curzon re-used heavily carved stone from the House of Lords to create impressive gate piers leading to the circuit walk at Kedleston.

Even when a country house was rebuilt and a village re-sited, there could be the deliberate retention of the old village church, from sense of family pride, for its picturesque antiquity or as an eye-catcher. At Kedleston Hall, after the removal of the village *c.*1760, the medieval church next to the house was retained for its ornamental value and reminder of ancient ancestry:

> Only an iron gate separates the ivy embowered and honeysuckle-clad house of God from the ancestral home of the family who came with the Conqueror.[46]

At Sudbury the village church, 'an ancient fabric, standing in the garden near the house; and being luxuriantly covered with ivy, becomes a picturesque object'.[47] When the wealthy industrialist Arkwrights built Willesley Castle, the ruins of a fifteenth-century chapel near the entrance gates were reclaimed from cottages, to suggest a link to the past. The sixteenth-century church close to Calke Abbey was rebuilt and enlarged with a tower in 1826–29, and then linked to the pleasure grounds by a lime avenue.

The summer house or gazebo was the most popular and useful garden building, with a wide range of size and style and is the feature most likely to have survived, such as the early eighteenth-century two-storey gazebo at Brampton Hall near Chesterfield, with its ogee roof with fish scale stone slates. In contrast with this sophistication the delightful mid-eighteenth-century summer house at Hathersage Hall is clearly designed by an amateur, (perhaps the owner), with its pyramidal roof, and a jolly little pediment terminating in small bucolic volutes. Such buildings could be tastefully furnished, as shown in an advertisement (1764) by Mr Campione. He came to Derby to sell his tasteful plaster casts and busts, modelled on Italian antiques, which would be 'the greatest Ornaments' for interior rooms and also for summer houses. Less robust was the 'portable summer house, in excellent condition' offered for sale in 1838.[48]

A feature found in many eighteenth-century country house gardens, the cold plunge bath, used for healthy cold dips, appears less frequently in Derbyshire, perhaps because of the popular Spas of Buxton, Bakewell and Matlock. Baths appear in advertisements in the *Derby Mercury,* such as a house in Derby (1767) for 'a Gentleman's family' which boasted a private cold bath in the walled garden. The ingenious Mr Dalby, also in Derby, (1813) had a small green house/summer house containing a 'hot or cold bath'.[49] In 1803 The Grove near Ashbourne, with 'tasteful pleasure grounds', offered shady walks, flourishing shrubs and a cold bath.[50] At Kedleston the Curzons had their own private bath house/fishing house designed by Robert Adam. Nearby, on the other side of the river, doubling as an eye-catcher, in 1759 they built a public bath in the classical style, which became a popular and lucrative attraction. Graffiti has been an issue from time immemorial, hence an admonition in a rather splendid poem about the public baths at Kedleston.

> *Kedleston Bath Guide: or, Monitions which might be of Use to several Persons who frequent that Place*
>
> PRAISE, highest Praise, for Streams like these we owe;
> To the great Source from whom all Blessing flow;
> …But SHAME, deserved Shame, on him abide,
> Whose impious Hand polutes the hallow'd Tide;
> Or, witless, as unmanly, sneaking scrawls,
> Indecent Ribbaldry along its Walls;
> And, with the Baseness of incendiary Stealth,
> Would injure Virtue, or diminish Health
> Kedleston Bath, June 25th, 1785[51]

While on the topic of poetry, some chapters include snippets of garden-related poems, of varying quality, by local poets: Charles Cotton and Aston Cockayne in the seventeenth century and Daniel Deakin, Nicholas Hardinge, and Francis Noel Clark Mundy in the eighteenth century. William Mugliston (1752–88), manufacturer of hosiery at Alfreton, wrote *Contemplative Walk with the Author's Wife and Children, in the Parke of George Morewood, Esq at Alfreton.* Unsurprisingly, given the quality of his verse (written in the spirit of Thompson), he failed to achieve advance subscriptions and so published at his own expense in 1782. It contains lines such as the children's little hearts 'will jump to see the sportive lambkin play'.[52] Was Mugliston responsible for another poem printed in the *Derby Mercury* 2 August 1787?

> *AN EPITAPH*
> On an honest, laborious, careful Gardener, who died a Bachelor, November 19, 1786
>
> BENEATH lie mould'ring into Dust,
>   A Gardener's Remains;
> A Man laborious, honest, just;
>   His character sustains;

In seventy-one revolving Years,
    He *sow'd* no *Seeds* of Strife;
With Pruning-Knife, Spade, Hoe and Shears,
    Employ'd his careful Life.
But Death who view's his peaceful Lot,
    His Tree of Life assail'd;
His Grave he *dug* upon this Spot,
    And his last *Branch* he nail'd.

Wirksworth, 14th Aug. 1787 [*sic*] AMICUS[53]

Notes

All quotations from newspapers are © The British Library Board. All rights reserved. With thanks to the British Newspaper Archive. (www.BritishNewspaperArchive.co.uk)

1. *DM*, 13 April 1764, 4
2. *DM*, 17 Jan. 1799, 3.
3. *DM*, 9 Dec. 1846, 2.
4. J. Chandler (ed.) *Travels Through Stuart Britain: The Adventures of John Taylor, the Water Poet* (1999), 163. He referred to the countryside near Wirksworth; M. Broadley (ed.) *Doctor Johnson and Mrs Thrale, including Mrs Thrale's Journal of a Welsh Tour made in 1774* (1910), 167.
5. HMC MSS of Rye and Hereford Corporations, 13th Report, App. IV, appendix E (1892), Rev. John Nixon to Miss Mary Bacon, 14 Sept. 1745, accessed on line December 2015. I am grateful to Sue Gregory and Randle Knight for this source.
6. WRO CR1841/7 Diary of Lady Sophia Newdigate, September 1747.
7. R. Patching, *Four Topographical Letters, written in July 1755, upon a journey thro Bedfordshire … Derbyshire* etc. (1757), 13, 23, 38, 49.
8. DRO: D5054/13/9 Personal Account Book of Sir Robert Burdett, entry 21 July 1759.
9. Broadley, *Doctor Johnson*, 171.
10. A. Young, *The Farmer's Tour Through the East of England* (1771), 205–207, 209.
11. L. Jewitt (ed.) *Black's 1872 Tourist's Guide to Derbyshire* (1999), 172.
12. C. Cotton, *The Wonders of the Peake* (1681).
13. A. Tinniswood, *The Polite Tourists. A History of Country House Visiting* (1998), 91.
14. *DM*, 16 April 1873, 2.
15. *E.g. DTCH,* 6 May 1871, 2; 10 June 1871, 8; 3 April 1875, 3; 27 April 1878; 4 July 1891, 2.
16. *DM*, 8 July 1857, 1; 7 August 1861, 4.
17. *DM*, May 26, June 2 1852, 3.
18. *DM*, 2 Sept. 1857, 5.
19. *DTCH*, 21 June 1890, 8; 5 July 1890, 6.
20. *DM*, 4 September 1822, 3.
21. *DM*, 8 August 1827. Events are reported 29 March, 16 Aug. 1792; 13 June; 3 Oct 1793; 24 April 1794 and in the 1820s. Like Chatsworth, Kedleston Hall was open to visitors by then.
22. *DM*, 2 July 1823, 3.
23. *DM*, 28 April 1824 *et al.*
24. *DM*, 4 July 1849, 3.
25. *DTCH*, 25 June 1892, 5.
26. *DTCH*, 29 March 1884, 8.

27. *DM*, 18 Aug. 1886, 2.
28. *DTCH*, 25 April 1896, 5; 10 April 1897, 5.
29. *DM*, 18 April 1821, 3.
30. *DM*, 20 Nov. 1800, 4.
31. *DM*, 16 Aug. 1781, 4.
32. *DM*, 21 July 1830, 3; 9 Jan. 1847, 3.
33. *DM*, 30 Aug. 1754, 4; 20 June 1755, 4; 14 Sept.; 5 Oct. 1770, 4.
34. *DM*, 16 Aug. 1781, 4.
35. *DM*, 26 July 26 1754, 4.
36. *DM*, 25 April 1760, 4; 10 Sept. 1773, 4.
37. *DM*, 25 Feb. 1774.
38. *DM*, 30 March 1786, 4.
39. *DM*, 24 Oct. 1827, 3; 5 Sept. 1838, 3; 2 Aug. 1848, 1.
40. *DM*, 25 Aug and 13 Oct. 1769.
41. *DM*, 16 Jan. 1817, 3; *Manchester Mercury*, 3 Nov. 1818, 4.
42. *DTCH*, 22 Sept. 1866, 4; 18 Oct. 1873, 3; 5 July 1879, 6; 12 July 1879, 3.
     Nottinghamshire Evening Post, 3 Aug. 1900, 3; 4 July 1903, 5; 9 Aug. 1912, 5.
43. *DM*, 30 Aug. 1781, 4.
44. *Nottinghamshire Guardian*, 10 Aug. 1895, 2.
45. *DTCH*, 18 Oct. 1876, 3.
46. *DTCH*, 30 May 1891, 8.
47. J. Britton and E. Wedlake Brayley, *The Beauties of England and Wales*, vol. 3 (1802),
     408.
48. *DM*, 9 Nov. 1764, 4; 3 Jan. 1838, 2.
49. *DM*, 2 Oct. 1767, 1; 17 June 1813, 1.
50. *Manchester Mercury*, 19 April 1803, 2.
51. *DM*, 30 June 1785, 2.
52. Derby Local Studies Library reference 6303C.
53. Reprinted *DM*, 3 June 1790, 4. See also another poem in the *DM*, 15 Nov. 1781, 3:
     '*A Contrast to the celebrated YOUNG'S Character of FLORIO, addrest to Mr Michael
     Bramley, jun. a noted Florist at Pentridge, near Alfreton.*' Alfreton 15 Nov. 1781.

CHAPTER TWO

The Enclosed Garden 1580–1700

....

The Garden in every landscape speaks of seclusion.

By the early seventeenth century gardens were usually a series of walled enclosures, providing privacy and shelter, well suited to Derbyshire where gardens need protection from the winds in open, hilly countryside. The classic layout had a house at the centre of an enclosed complex, with stables and outbuildings to one side, a garden or kitchen garden on the other side, walled pleasure garden behind and walled entrance forecourt in front.

Such was the layout at **Barlborough Hall**, built for Francis Rodes, a successful and wealthy self-made lawyer, who set himself up as a gentleman, buying lands and building a country house in 1583/4. His patron was the Earl of Shrewsbury, for whom the architect Robert Smythson designed Worksop Manor. Smythson was then commissioned to design Barlborough, a status symbol with high, many windowed turrets and large chimney stacks (now removed) above the battlemented roofline.[1] From the turret rooms and the flat roof Rodes' impressive gardens and extensive estate could be viewed and admired: especially important after he was appointed Justice of the Common Pleas in 1585 and Barlborough would be used for social entertaining.

FIGURE 5. Barlborough Hall, 1583–85. There were fine views of the gardens and estate from its flat roof.

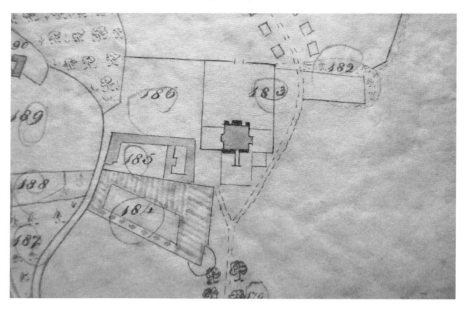

FIGURE 6. Barlborough Hall, detail of 1839 tithe map. The basic layout survives with walled enclosures round the house. The summer house is shown on the left (185), overlooking orchard and formal pond (184).

DRO: D2360/3/133

The first surviving estate map dates from 1723, but many details seem unchanged from 100 years before. The tall house presides over the enclosed forecourt and gardens, whose walls survive today, although reduced in height. The avenue leading to the house and then beyond, and also the gates to the forecourt and gardens are probably late seventeenth century. The main garden is divided into four simple plats, surrounded by grass walks, no doubt replacing original complex knot gardens. As was usual at this period orchards were part of the pleasure grounds.[2]

Surviving today is what appears to be a rare survival of an Elizabethan banqueting house, attached to the far end of the service wings. The upper floor room has a carved fireplace with the coat of arms of Francis Rodes, while several niches in the walls may have held candles or lamps. Providing views out over the former 'Old Orchard' is a superb bay window which has similarities with Smythson's semi-circular bay windows at Burton Agnes and Worksop Manor.[3] Such an extravagant use of expensive glass was a status symbol and novelty at this period. However some caution is needed, for although the fireplace and exterior stone panel (dated 1582/5), are original, the window bay is clearly an afterthought as it is not keyed into the wall. Was this added later to an existing building? Certainly the result looks authentic.

Only the service wing survives of **Swarkeston Old Hall**, now a farmhouse. However the fortuitous survival of extensive, although ruinous, garden walls recall its original grandeur. Swarkeston was one of several properties purchased by Richard Harpur (1515–77), a very wealthy man from a well-established merchant family at Chester. By 1567 he had built his large new house, taxed on 28 hearths in 1662.[4] Today you still approach via the large walled outer court, although its gatehouse has long gone. Even larger walled enclosures to the west side of the house were once 200 ft (*c.*61 m) square gardens, and also orchards and kitchen gardens. The sheer size of these now empty enclosures hints at the original great expenditure. Even the parish church was an integral part of this ensemble, with its tower close to, and appearing over, the garden walls.

In front of the house forecourt and its lost gatehouse is a walled enclosure with a compact pavilion, known as **Swarkeston Stand**. This may have been built in 1631/2 to celebrate the marriage of Sir John Harpur (1612–79), 'the richest man of his times in the county of Derby', to Catherine Howard, grand-daughter of the Duke of Suffolk and step-daughter of the Marquis of Newcastle.[5;6] Influenced by the style of John Smythson, the purpose of the Stand has been much discussed over the years. In 1892 it was described as:

> …the Banqueting house to the Hall … in the centre of the further side of a square walled in enclosure, measuring 76 paces by 61, which was once a garden. The building consists of two square towers with a colonnade in three bays between, open on the ground floor; above this was the banqueting room … covered in by a lead flat with a stone parapet on both sides.[7]

FIGURE 7. Barlborough Hall Banqueting House *c.*1585 attached to service wing.

A banqueting house for informal meals, music, card games, *etc.* is just one interpretation. Foster and Heath note that a local mason, Richard Shepperd, was paid £111 12s 4d in 1630–32 for the 'Bowle Alley house', and that the Harpur accounts name a Mr Wooldridge as Bowl Alley surveyor. They argue that the towers were an afterthought, as their lower storey is not bonded into the central core.[8] Interestingly at nearby Melbourne Hall 'a bowl alley' was made in 1631.[9] Paula Henderson suggests that the Stand was connected with sporting activity such as bear-baiting or tilting.[10] There is no evidence that the enclosed space in front of the Stand was ever a garden and some sort of sporting complex seems most likely, whether violent hunt or peaceful bowls, to be viewed from the Stand's richly decorated comfort. It survived the demolition of Swarkestone house in 1746–48, after the inheritance went to the Calke Abbey branch of the Harpur family, who had no use for such a large second home. Now it has been beautifully restored by the Landmark Trust.

FIGURE 10. Repton Park, the ruined remains of the Stand, early 1630s.

The **Stand** at **Repton Park Lodge** is close to Swarkeston and again may be the work of John Smythson. When Sir Henry Harpur purchased the Calke estate in 1622, it included the Repton estate, which he decided to use for hunting and recreation. Here in the early 1630s he built a substantial stone hunting lodge in the centre of a shallow quarry in hilly woods. Noted with just five hearths in 1662 Hearth Tax Assessment, the lodge's original appearance is unknown because it was greatly enlarged and gothicised in 1810–12, and then deliberately destroyed in 1896 following a family squabble.[11] Nearby, on a tree lined approach to this lost lodge, is an intriguing small stone building, built into the hillside and contemporary with the lodge. It has been called stables, lodge and gazebo, but extensive alterations over the years have disguised its original function.[12]

Now ruined, what survives is a three-bay ground floor with an arched entrance and two mullioned windows either side. Stepping inside there is the surprise of a stone barrel-vaulted ceiling, which once supported an upper floor, accessed via outside steps. From the window of this lost floor, and perhaps also from a roof platform, there would have been views out. Was it once a Hunting Stand, an important part of the ceremony of the Chase, used by ladies and guests as a raised space from which to view the excitement of the hunt? These could serve also as a summer house, retreat and eye-catcher in the park or near the house. Whatever its original use, the 'Stand' sits in a rather magical wood, with ancient trees, lost paths, animal burrows, pond and stream and in the centre hollow – the unexpected sight of stone foundations of the lost Lodge.

Built on a hill overlooking the river Wye, **Haddon Hall** looks almost too delightfully picturesque to be real. Approached through a stone gate-house, to

FIGURE 11. Haddon Hall, early seventeenth-century steps and balustrade. Lithograph by S. Rayner (1859).

the left there is a glimpse of the seventeenth-century dove-cote doubling as an eye-catcher, then a walk across the old stone bridge over the river, and sight of the irregular crenellations of the old hall above. Then comes the charming little gardener's cottage, (former lodge) with its eccentric huge nineteenth-century yew topiary, shaped as a Bear and a Peacock, the family crests.[13]

No doubt the original medieval hall had a small pleasure garden, but the present gardens date from the late sixteenth century. Early fascination with the gardens came from the romantic legend of Dorothy Vernon. In 1563, on the night of her sister's marriage, she is said to have escaped through the gardens to join her suitor, Sir John Manners, who had been rejected by her father. The couple married and four years later they inherited the Haddon estate and the legend of Dorothy's flight became inextricably linked to the steps leading down from the house to the gardens. Actually these date from 1649 but, not to ruin a good story, there must have been steps here previously.

Above the east side of the hall the sixteenth-century gardens had a long raised walk (later named 'Dorothy Vernon's Walk'), overlooking a wide bowling green terrace. The green was removed in 1645 and at some time replaced with three formal compartments, planted with clipped yew and holly. With the creation of the splendid long gallery on the south façade of the house in late sixteenth–early seventeenth century, there was a need for a formal garden below, to be viewed from the gallery. This was then linked to the former bowling green terrace, 10 ft (3 m) above it, by a flight of wide steps flanked by balusters, given further emphasis by long balustrades either side, along the retaining wall. Thereafter these balustrades were the inspiration for many a Victorian terrace, representing 'Olde England'.

Sir John Manners (1604–79), grandson of Sir John Manners and Dorothy Vernon, inherited Haddon in 1623. His unexpected acquisition of an

FIGURE 12. Haddon Hall,
terraced gardens, early
1900s aerial photograph.

COURTESY OF JUDY NOBLE AND
WWW.PICTURETHEPAST.ORG.UK

earldom (as seventh Earl of Rutland) in 1641 encouraged him to upgrade
the lower gardens with massive supporting stone walls, their size and rough
surface consciously matching the old house. Their buttresses are particularly
impressive seen from the lowest garden, which may date from the mid-
sixteenth century. The stone walls are functional but, since they are about
waist height at terrace level within, they permit views over and out, unlike
enclosed medieval gardens.

By the late seventeenth century fashionable clipped yews decorated the
terraces, but the gardens cannot have been elaborate since they were dismissed
by Celia Fiennes, in the late 1690s, as 'good Gardens but nothing very curious
[complex] as the mode now is'.[14] A plan (1817) has an aviary overlooking the
lower garden, which might date from this period, as there were contemporary
aviaries at nearby Chatsworth.[15] The family made Belvoir Castle their main
residence when John Manners (1638–1711), ninth Earl of Rutland, was created
first Duke of Rutland in 1703. Thereafter, Haddon was used occasionally and
the gardens slumbered, maintained but with the unclipped yews growing larger
and larger. James Reading, a somewhat unsophisticated Derby lad, visited in
April 1729 and wrote:

> very fine long gallery and very Plesant Look in into ye gardens wich is verry neate
> and pleasant with Rises and falls of steps verry plesant ye water running boy [by]
> itt down steps into ye garden.'

If this was a cascade it has long vanished without documentary evidence. He
described the new bowling green, which had replaced the original on the upper
terrace,

> we went to ye Bowling green up in ye Parke wich is a fine place[.] first you mounted
> up severall steps and in at a pare a[of] gates and into ye green and it is all walled

round and treas groing and nicely cut by ye wall … at ye upper Ende a fine sais [sized] Bantquiting house and a Chamber over itt and very plesant [.] went up steps with Rails an Banisters to ye top and it was a fine prospect on top [.] we markt our feett upon ye Led [flat roof]...[16]

Regrettably spelling and punctuation were not James' strong points. This fashionable new Bowling Green House had been built by the ninth Earl of Rutland in 1696. Its modernity suggests that, had not he not acquired Belvoir Castle in 1703, possibly he might have modernised or enlarged Haddon Hall itself, imitating nearby Elizabethan Chatsworth, which was being rebuilt in the 1690s.

The present gardens date largely from the 1920s and 1930s when the ninth duke began an exemplary restoration of the house, which had slept for over 200 years, while the duchess restored and replanted the gardens sympathetically in a romantic Arts and Crafts style. The attractive stone summer house in the corner of the higher terrace must date from this period. Today the gardens continue to develop under the guidance of Lord and Lady Edward Manners, with more modern planting to appeal to the thousands of visitors each year.

The story of 'Bess of Hardwick' (Elizabeth, Countess of Hardwick), and **Hardwick Hall** is well known but a brief summary may help to put the gardens into context. Her fourth marriage in 1567 to George Talbot, sixth Earl of Shrewsbury, has been compared to a modern business merger, also involving marriage between certain of their children, with great estates at stake. Certainly it was not a marriage made in heaven, and following the earl's reluctant guardianship of Mary, Queen of Scots, after 1569 the marriage inexorably collapsed in mutual acrimony. In 1584 Bess decided to return to her modest childhood home at Hardwick, leaving her husband in control of Chatsworth. She re-built the 'Old Hall' in a piecemeal fashion between 1585 and 1591, but after the death of her husband in 1590 decided not to move back to Chatsworth, now under the control of her eldest son Henry, who had supported his step-father, the Earl of Shrewsbury, against her. Instead, using the architect Robert Smythson, she built an aggressively modern house at Hardwick, to be left to her second, and favourite, son William. It also served as a secure home for her grand-daughter Arbella Stuart, with her dangerous claim to the throne. Thus the two Hardwick Halls reflect a heady mix of immense wealth, pride and ambition.

Bess of Hardwick is known as an indefatigable builder but there is little evidence that she had much interest in gardens, other than as a setting for her magnificent houses and the provision of herbs and flowers for medicine, cooking and to perfume rooms. From the leads of the roofs of both Halls she, and her awed guests, would look down across the park and admire the simple formal and productive gardens below. An estate map by William Senior (1609) shows the New Hall with its walled entrance forecourt on the west, orchard to the north and large garden area to the south. As with Robert Smythson's plan for Wollaton Hall at Nottingham, here is a grid pattern with the house in the centre of an 11-acre (*c.*4.5 ha) walled rectangle.[17]

The New Hall is approached through an elaborate entrance archway, flanked on each side by a triangular porter's lodge. On either side a high stone wall is decorated with large strap work arches/merlons terminating in obelisks. This, combined with elaborate strap work cresting on top of the lodges and gateway, is a tour de force, over which the roof line of the house can be glimpsed, with its huge ES monograms and sparkling windows. The entrance courtyard there would have been a practical working area, probably cobbled, not the present garden.[18]

In the south garden there is a banqueting house/gazebo at an angle in the south-east corner walls, whose impact is enhanced by parapets decorated with strap work arches and obelisks to echo the forecourt walls (Pl. 1). The household accounts for 1596–97 include substantial bills for glazing 'tenne pannes glase for fyv windows for the gathouse the tow [two] corner turrets in the court wall and the turret in the north orchard in measure four score foots at 5d the foot.'[19] The latter was another (matching?) summer house in the walled orchard, a reminder that orchards were an integral part of the pleasure gardens. Like the banqueting house on the hall roof, these were part of the ritual of entertainment and display, showing that money was no object, given the expense of glass at that time. Nothing in the county could compare or compete with this totally integrated design of house, garden and garden buildings.

Just two miles (1.6 km) from Hardwick, Bess of Hardwick built **Oldcotes** (or **Owlcotes**) between 1593 and 1596, also on behalf of her favourite son,

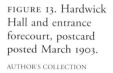

FIGURE 13. Hardwick Hall and entrance forecourt, postcard posted March 1903.

William Cavendish (1552–1626).[20] The only known depiction of house and garden is that on a map of 1659.[21] A contract to build the house, dated March 1593, specifies two turrets to rise above the roof.[22] These could have been prospect towers, from which to view the gardens and surrounding countryside. William Cavendish lived mainly at Hardwick until his marriage in 1604 and after the death of his mother in 1608. Following his purchase of Chatsworth from his elder brother Henry in 1610 William, created first Earl of Devonshire in 1618, had four large houses to maintain. It seems unlikely that much attention would have been given to Oldcotes, particularly given his notorious parsimoniousness.

William's son, the second earl, died with enormous debts in 1628 and the Oldcotes estate was sold to Robert Pierrepont, first Earl of Kingston in 1639. However, within 100 years, Oldcotes was again a second home and by the late 1840s had 'gone to decay, and its name is almost unknown': a dismal end to a once splendid house.[23] Basic information about the gardens can be gleamed from an estate map surveyed in 1659 and revised in 1688 (Pl. 2). It has a vignette of the house and outline of the gardens, where probably little alteration had occurred since the 1590s. The impressively tall and many windowed house was approached via an entrance lodge into a walled forecourt or garden, where on either side of a central path are triangular outlines which might represent fountains. There is an orchard on one side of the courtyard and paddocks on the other. Behind the house is the walled 'great garden' flanked by the two-acre (0.9 ha) 'Old bowleing green', next to the orchard.[24] The chance survival of part of a garden wall with shell niche seat suggests that these long lost gardens were once sophisticated and elaborate.[25]

Today, like both Hardwick Halls, **Bolsover Castle**, 'The Windsor Castle of Derbyshire', can be seen powerfully silhouetted on the escarpment alongside the M1 motorway.[26] Partly ruined, the castle complex is an evocative survivor of the lost world of Jacobean chivalry.[27] Like his mother Bess of Hardwick, Sir Charles Cavendish was an enthusiastic and inventive builder. In 1612, with the architect Robert Smythson, he began the transformation of the earthworks and remains of the medieval Bolsover Castle into a Jacobean conceit of a chivalric castle, a romantic escapist retreat never intended to be a main family home. After Sir Charles' death in 1617 his son, Sir William Cavendish, continued and developed the buildings, with Robert Smythson's son John.

The **Little Castle** (Keep) juts into the northern corner of a roughly oval enclosure, the original inner bailey, which became an enclosed garden, seen only from the Little Castle or from a raised parapet walk on top of the garden's thick enclosing walls. A secret space, separate from the main buildings of the castle, this was equivalent to pulling up a draw-bridge against an outside world. Early drawings show a garden empty except for the central Venus fountain, though there may have been espaliered fruit trees against the walls.[28] It was here that Ben Jonson's masque, *Love's Welcome to Bolsover*, was performed before King Charles I, Queen Henrietta Maria and their Court on 30 July 1634, with its theme of

FIGURE 14. Bolsover
Castle, Little Castle
enclosed garden with
Venus fountain.

mutual love, perfected in the example of the King and Queen.[29] A more robust interpretation of this Garden of Love was suggested by Timothy Mowl (1993), who delighted in drawing attention to the link between the painted decoration of Sir William Cavendish's private closet (Elysium Room) and the garden seen below:

> Here the ceiling is alive with the sensual loves of the classical gods… Through the window … lie the further sensual pleasures of the Venus Fountain Garden.[30]

Subsequent writers and the recent exemplary restorations by English Heritage agree that this garden was for pleasure and indulgence.[31] Its centrepiece and focal point is Smythson's fountain whose deep octagonal basin, topped by 'battlements', continues the castle theme and reflects the crenellations of the parapet walk. The sheer size and expense of this fountain, its water supplied from a nearby hill, can be compared with the Earl of Leicester's fountain in the garden at Kenilworth Castle, created for a visit by Queen Elizabeth in 1575.[32] At Bolsover the fountain:

> stands in an octagon reservoir six feet deep, which received the water from the images and heads placed in the angles and sides… In the centre is a square rusticated pedestal, with ornaments projecting from the angles. Towards the middle, is a cistern which was to receive the water from the masks on the sides of the pedestal, through which pipes are conveyed: the sides of this cistern are ornamented with good sculpture; … on the top of the pedestal is a statue of Venus in alabaster; she has wet drapery in her hand, with one foot on a kind of step, in the act of getting out of a bath.[33]

The inclusion of an earl's coronet on the fountain dates it post-1628, when William Cavendish was created Earl of Newcastle. The decidedly Rubenesque figure of Venus, said to be based on an original by Giambologna in Rome, provides a fittingly solid centre-piece for the heavy stone rustication of the base.[34] Local carvers obviously felt that the image from which they had to work was too under-nourished and, rather endearingly, made their statue more robust (Pl. 3).

Set within the thick medieval walls enclosing the garden are three alcoves, each with a stone seat. Three rusticated doorways give access to rooms created within the spaces of former medieval towers within the thick bailey wall.[35] Two are single rooms with a niche in one wall and fireplace opposite (Pl. 4). The third has a suite of three rooms more elaborately decorated. Its central room has a groined vault with pendant boss and hooded fireplace while the other two have segmental barrel vaults, one with a corner fireplace and wall recesses. Although now dark, damp and rather depressing, originally, when decorated and warm, these would have been rustic versions of the castle rooms and very welcoming. Their use is not documented, but they also have views out to the Venus fountain. This is certainly not a 'mainstream' garden and Bess of Hardwick would not have approved.

Staveley Hall, home to the Frecheville family since the fourteenth century, was a very large, imposing house with a subsequent depressing history of alteration and demolition, until little remains today. Peter Frescheville (1575–1634) was knighted in 1604 and celebrated by either remodelling an existing house or with a new build. It was probably in the 1630s that Sir John Frescheville (1607–82) remodelled the garden facade in the fashionable Artisan Mannerist style. Despite Civil War damage the house was assessed with thirty hearths in 1670. After the death of Sir John, the last Freschville, the estate was sold to the

FIGURE 15. Staveley Hall, remains of massive seventeenth-sentury retaining wall taken outside the garden.

Dukes of Devonshire, who demolished the East front in 1756. The house was then rented out, further reduced and much altered in the nineteenth century. Staveley District Council have offices there and are currently (2016) restoring and developing the site.[36]

Massive seventeenth-century stone walls and retaining walls survive from the lost terraced formal gardens, although clearing and further archaeological work is needed to reveal exactly was there. Fortunately the council and local history society are very active and more information about the gardens should come to light as their work progresses. The garden was created when the site was drastically altered with the levelling of the hill top for Peter Frescheville's new house. Surplus soil was used on slopes to the north and west to create a flat garden area, with steps down steep slopes to the area below, perhaps once a kitchen garden and orchard. The new 1630s garden façade was no doubt accompanied by a formal garden and later a bowling green. The medieval village church forms part of the garden's south boundary, although regrettably Gilbert Scott's enlargements have made it rather too dominant. On the north side massive stone walls support and enclose the garden, a reminder of a fine lost and undocumented garden. There are still fine views over the countryside.[37]

On the other hand, **Snitterton Hall** and its walled gardens appear unchanged after 400 years, although the current pristine appearance of the handsome 1630s stone house is the result of recent exemplary restorations. John Milward (1599–1670) purchased the Snitterton estate in 1631 and almost immediately enlarged and re-fronted the existing house to reflect his social ambitions.[38] He became High Sheriff of the county in 1635 and was a royalist colonel in the Civil War. After the Restoration he represented the county of Derby in parliament, usually supporting the court as a staunch Anglican. Milward appears to have had a special interest in gardening, shown by his inclusion of four plants carved on the stone over the entrance door: olive, oak, rose and mulberry copied from the *Great Herbal* (1533) and symbolising peace, strength, fidelity and prosperity.[39] Other stylised plants decorate the capitals of the classical Ionic columns either side of the door.

The house is surrounded by a series of walled enclosures which provide protection against the elements in a high, exposed position, exclude deer from the park, yet also allow views out to the countryside and hills.[40] The house and walled entrance forecourt (always a garden) are on a man-made plateau. An arched gateway in the stone wall leads into the forecourt, which had, set into two corners, stone pavilions with pyramidal stone roofs topped by a finial.[41] The surviving pavilion/banqueting house has mullion and transom windows, providing views over the courtyard garden and also out over the surrounding countryside at first floor level, which is reached by a raised terrace (Pl. 5). The terrace is accessed by steps from the forecourt gardens and from a side entrance in a crenellated wall along the (higher) west side of the house. The builder, and perhaps architect, was Richard Shepherd/Shepperd, a stone mason who had worked at Swarkstone Stand and Bolsover Castle.[42]

FIGURE 16. Snitterton Hall, walled alcove at end of garden terrace.

COURTESY K. ALCOCK AND S. HASLAM

On the east side of the house there are walled formal gardens which were probably four knot gardens or parterres. These might date from the earlier house but could have been re-vamped by Milward, copying the 'formes' or knots illustrated in William Lawson's *The Country House-Wives Garden*, incorporated into his *New Orchard and Garden* (1618, reprinted 1631). Lawson's were square and 'bordered about with Fruit, Raisons, Fea-berries, Roses, Thorne, Rosemary, Bee-flowers, Isop, Sage or such like'. His designs included 'Cinkfoyle [Cinquefoil], Flower deluce [fleur-de-lys], Trefoyle, Fret, Lozenges, Cross-bow, Diamond, Oval' and illustrate the mixture of utile and recreation in contemporary gardens.[43] To the north, at one end of a walled terrace, there is a recessed semi-circular alcove with seat for rest and contemplation, while the other end is a raised viewing platform.

On the far side a flight of stone steps led down to another long terrace and former orchard within a large triangular walled enclosure. Orchards were an important part of the pleasure gardens, with walks, mounts and seats from where the trees (apples, pears, cherries, plums, damsons, *etc.*) could be admired and the owner could contemplate in peace and quiet. Perhaps Milward followed Lawson's suggestion of a Bowling Alley or Archery Butt, utilising the terrace:

> To have occasion to exercise within your Orchard, it shall be a pleasure to have a Bowling Alley, or rather (which is more manly and more healthfull) a pair of Butts, to stretch your armes.[44]

Lawson recommended hedges or moats around orchards to keep out thieves, deer, sheep and wind, so the enclosing stone walls again fitted his practical advice.

Just outside the walled gardens, in former parkland, at the bottom of a shallow valley, are the remains of what was of what was once a large, wide 'V'

shaped fish pond created from a little brook. In its angle there are remnants of a small stone fishing pavilion. Milward was related to two famous fishermen of the period, Izaac Walton, author of *The Compleat Angler*, and Charles Cotton, whose iconic 1674 fishing pavilion survives at Beresford Dale.[45] Colonel Milward would have worked on his gardens in the 1630s, and during his enforced retirement from public affairs during the Protectorate in the 1650s. He was fully occupied in London as an MP in the 1660s, so if his pavilion was built in the 1630s, or even 1650s, it would pre-date the Beresford pavilion and might have influenced its design.

Ponds were not only for fishing, but as Lawson again enthused:

> Moates, Fish-ponds, and (especially at one side of a River) within and without your fence, will afford you fish, fence, and moystyre to your trees, and pleasure also, if they be so great and deep that you may have Swans, and other water birds, good for devouring of vermine, and boat for many good uses.[46]

Henry Milward inherited in 1670 and seems to have continued the family interest in gardens, as suggested in an elegy on his death in 1681 by the Derbyshire poet Leonard Wheatcroft:

> Wilt thou go hence, leave Snitterton this day?
> 'Tis pity! House with gardens bright and fair
> Should now grow wild, because thou'st left no heire[47]

Thereafter the estate went through various hands, becoming a farm house. There was some planting of yew trees in the early twentieth century and the house was for sale in 1932 with 'charming old world Gardens quite inexpensive in upkeep'. Photographs of the entrance forecourt show the walls and summer house smothered in climbing roses and creepers, with two plain lawns surrounded

FIGURE 18. Holme Hall and walled terraces with archway entrance next to house on two levels.

COURTESY JOHN STANSFIELD

by low hedging and a riot of flowers and roses in narrow flower beds.[48] However vicissitudes followed and finally drastic restoration and re-planting was undertaken, by Mr and Mrs Caplan from 1997–98 and Kate Alcock and Simon Haslam, the current owners.

Nestling against the escarpment overlooking the town of Bakewell, **Holme Hall** is another romantic early Carolean stone manor house. Built *c*.1626–8 by Bernard Wells (1573–1653), a wealthy Gloucestershire lead merchant, it incorporated an existing house.[49] Wells was establishing himself as a member of the gentry with his fine house and terraced gardens, which can be seen and admired far beyond their stone boundary walls. Clearly influenced by nearby Haddon Hall, the compact three storey house, with its full height porch and castellated parapet roofline still sits within walled, enclosed gardens, again apparently unaltered since built. The steep slope behind the house provided the garden with two terraces, to be admired from the original flat roof of the hall.

Anne Wells, heiress to Holme, married Robert Eyre of Highlow Hall, who enlarged the house with new wings and a chapel with direct access onto a garden terrace. The Eyres' architectural preference veered towards the Artisan Mannerism style popular mid-century, seen in the large stone arch with *oeil de boeuf* openings each side, which also gives access to the first terrace attached to the new wing. This terrace is supported by massive retaining walls. An impressive flight of steps to the middle of the 50 m long terrace has gone, but the eye is still led past their site up to the stone archway and the upper terrace. Directly above, now lined by newly planted clipped yews, is the classical belvedere or viewing platform, complete with a balustrade, and overlooking the gardens. This is a single bay version of de Caux's grotto portico (*c*.1645) at Wilton House, which could have been known to Eyre through Rowlett's contemporary published prints of Wilton.[50] Remarkably, two small busts survive from the top circular

niches, presiding over the gardens. Recently restored, one appears to be Thomas Hobbes, while the other, with a wreath, could be John Milton.[51]

The walls and terraces probably date from the late 1650s–early 1660s and the fortuitous survival of late seventeenth-century plans reveal that the gardens survive in outline, while recent restoration has been careful to remain faithful to the original plan.[52] The long lower terrace was noted as gravelled, and a narrow rill of water, fed by a spring at the top of the hill, crossed the gardens and provided a ready supply of water. There was no attempt to convert this into an ornamental feature such as a canal, cascade or fountain. Another area was plain grass with a sundial. To one side a little summer house, overlooking a small walled kitchen garden and melon ground, was placed to admire the productiveness of the ground below, while giving views out to the river nearby and the pleasant sound of its water (Figure 1).

At Holme the emphasis was on utility, with productive orchards (including cherry trees) and the orderliness typical of gentry who retired to the country during the Commonwealth. A poem by William Eyre (1642–1706) celebrates Holme as a rustic idyll far 'from London's noise and sulphurous influences', where a wealth 'of trees, of fruits, of herbs and starting springs' flourish, 'modest in unaffected beautys drest'. 'Art has a pleasant scene of gardens made/And many acres order does include'.[53] This is just as true today, for although Holme has changed hands several times, it has been sensitively restored. Currently John Stansfield continues this tradition, enhancing with careful replanting.

Practical husbandry was also seen at **Ashbourne Hall**. Anne Cockayne (1592–64), a daughter of Sir John Stanhope of Elvaston, ran the estate from 1639 until her death. She appears to have been an accomplished housewife in charge of the kitchen garden, as shown in a poem by her son Sir Aston, a minor poet and playwright. Among his poems published in 1658 is this one, addressed to his mother:

Let none our Ashbourn discommend henceforth;
Your gardens shew it is a place of worth.
What delicate sparagus you have growing there,
And in how great abundance every year?
What gallant apricots and peaches, brave,
And what delicious nectarins you have?
What melons that grow ripe without those glasses
That are laid over them in other places?
What grapes you there have growing? And what wine
Pleasant to taste you made last vintage time?
Plant vines, and when of grapes you have got store,
Make wine enough, and I will ask no more…[54]

Sir Aston Cokayne (1608–84), was an interesting, if clearly exasperating man, a friend of Donne, Fletcher and Drayton, who travelled round Europe for 12 years. Ultimately his extravagant life style led to the enforced sale of Ashbourne Hall in 1671.

Sometimes there is just a hint left of what could have been an interesting garden. **The Hallowes**, a stone gabled mid-seventeenth-century manor on the outskirts of Dronfield, is now a club-house for a golf club. What remains of the parkland is now the golf course and the gardens have long since gone. The present lawn in front of the house no doubt replaces a former entrance courtyard, originally at a lower level. At the side is a contemporary stone summer house or gazebo, somewhat rustic but rather attractive with a pyramidal slated roof. It is entered via five stone steps up to the door. Perhaps it was once on a raised terrace like Snitterton, and was there once a matching gazebo?

Another gazebo survives at **Eyam Hall**, which still sits snugly on the main street of the 'Plague Village' of Eyam. It appears seemingly little changed since its rebuilding by John Wright in the early 1670s, following its purchase by his

FIGURE 20. The Hallowes, Dronfield with mid seventeenth-century gazebo to side of former entrance court.

FIGURE 21. Eyam Hall, garden summer house with views over the village street.

father after the Civil War. The walled entrance forecourt still has its central iron gate, which allows a glimpse of the attractive main façade:

> A small terrace with a low wall raised eight steps above the fore court runs in front of the house out to a door in the right-hand wall, by which access is given to the garden down a flight of five semi-circular steps.[55]

Because of its village location the garden has retained its original surrounding stone walls, and against the street wall there is a much altered seventeenth-century garden-house. Its first floor windows provided views over the garden and also the village street, to enjoy the bustle of village life below. The walled garden below it is formed of three terraces: the top being a walk and the lower two, much wider, still divided into the original four compartments. To walk around the garden today is to experience a delightful mix of a seventeenth-century setting, including some original yews, now very large, with sympathetic modern interpretation and planting: formal and informal.

By the late seventeenth century gardens were becoming less enclosed, although still formal, with elaborate parterres near the house and often with water as formal canals. Clipped box and yew would be cut into mathematical or fantastical shapes such as birds and figures. Very occasionally examples from these topiary gardens survived as late as the nineteenth century, by which time the wheel had come full circle and they were back in fashion (vide Elvaston). In the 1840s William Bagshaw noted with some astonishment at Kilburn/e Hall:

> The garden, in the ancient style, is adorned with a splendid collection of yews, supposed to be about 300 years old. These trees are cut in a variety of figures, which the present owner is anxious they should retain and to the curious, present a sight perhaps not equalled in the kingdom.[56]

FIGURE 22. Risley Hall, garden terrace with statues and obelisks. 1865 woodcut by Joseph Barlow Robinson, copied from a now lost painting.

COURTESY OF WWW. PICTURETHEPAST.ORG.UK

Even in 1868 the yews were still clipped into the shape of birds and they were 'quaintly clipped in the Dutch style' as late as 1891.[57] Some overgrown yews survive overhanging the hall's boundary walls.

Topiary once featured in the sophisticated gardens at **Risley Hall**, an early Tudor building modernised following the marriage of the heiress Anne Willoughby (1614–88) to Hon. Anchitel Gray (1624–1702). Like Longford Hall (*qv*) it had massive projecting chimney stacks on the south façade and was taxed on the large number of 33 hearths in 1670.[58] The couple were probably responsible for the formal garden which included the long canal edged with balusters, which survives today. The pleasure grounds were renowned for their splendour, partly revealed in an old oil painting showing the house and the canal terrace decorated with obelisks and statues.[59] Unfortunately there is a dearth of estate papers, but a surviving account book for 1681–83 includes the payment of 10s 4d (52p: about 14 days' work for one man) for 'grubbing in ye Motts and the new intake', presumably maintenance work on the canals.[60]

This 'large and antient seat' was for sale in 1742 with 268 acres (*c.*108.5 ha) of parkland, and 'three Orchards, two Gardens, two very fine large Walks, and very fine Mote [moat], all very good, large and convenient to said Hall, fit for a Nobleman or Gentleman's Seat'.[61] When the house failed to sell, it was demolished in 1757 and the materials sold.[62] New owners rebuilt the house in the late eighteenth century and again in the late nineteenth century, when Ernest Terah Hooley (1859–1947), a rather colourful self-made millionaire, social climber, and later a notorious bankrupt, brought in the firm of Wm Barron and Son to work on the gardens in 1897. Following Hooley's enforced sale in the 1920s, the house became a community home and is now a hotel, with much of the original garden allocated to housing and a residential home.

FIGURE 23. Risley Hall mid/later seventeenth-century entrance 'gateway' and balustrade terrace.

COURTESY N. PARKIN, RISLEY HALL HOTEL

FIGURE 24. Risely Hall, stepped bridge over the canal (rear view of no. 23).

COURTESY N. PARKIN, RISLEY HALL HOTEL

The survival of part of the seventeenth-century formal garden at Risley was appreciated by Reginald Blomfield in his *The Formal Garden in England* (1892):

The terrace … is at some distance from the house, and runs along one side of the garden and beyond it. The terrace is separated from the garden by a long narrow piece of water, which was probably dug out to form the terrace. The terrace rises some nine feet above this water, with a retaining wall of masonry and a heavy stone balustrade above it. It is reached from the garden by a flight of seven steps rising over the bridge, with a rather elaborate stone gateway. The terrace is 289 paces long and is in two levels. That next to the balustrade is fourteen feet wide and gravelled.

Above this is a grass walk, 25 feet wide, with box hedges, and a ha-ha on the side of the park.

This balustrade had flat stone balusters with obelisks on the piers: 'a feature commoner in wood than stone', and indeed the balusters do look as if they are copied from wooden staircase balusters.[63] Originally and extravagantly, the balustrade ran the full length of the canal. The bridge gateway is a mixture of Artisan Mannerist and Gothic-survival style typical of the 1640s or '50s, with its rather heavy classical niches and crow-stepped gable with corner finials. The stepped bridge over the canal is unusual and would adapt to entertainments. The gardens were divided by walks, clipped yews and hedges. Blomfield noted 'a charming instance of cut yew – two doves about seven feet long billing each other, form an archway in a yew hedge'.[64] Classical statues added further interest. Tantalisingly little is known about this garden, which given the social standing of its owners and what still remains, would have been formal, elaborate and impressive.

When the young George Vernon (1635–1702) inherited the **Sudbury** estate in 1659, he built the present brick house with a viewing platform on the hipped roof, from which to view the surrounding countryside and to look down on his new walled gardens. These are celebrated in an oil painting by Jan Griffier, still at the hall (Pl. 6). Accessed by a short flight of steps from a terrace, the garden was divided into six sections by wide gravel paths, the long axial path divided by two ponds. The path terminated with a *claire voyée* between high stone pillars, from which steps led down to formal ponds outside the walled garden. Here stood the Neptune fountain, whose trident cascaded water, a popular choice at that period. It formed an eye-catcher in a pond in a row of formal ponds separated by grass walks planted with trees.

The four upper plats were simply grass, and at the centre of each was a copy of a well-known classical statue. These were probably lead painted white to resemble marble or stone, perhaps supplied from a London workshop, such as that of Van Ost/Nost, which Vernon could have visited whilst in London. The two end plats were newly planted with young fir trees, perhaps for a Wilderness. Espaliered fruit trees were trained against the brick walls, under planted with specimen flowers exhibited in narrow beds. So although still walled and enclosed, in the post-Restoration fashion the garden had no walled sub-divisions, while formal openings in the side walls allowed exit and views out. The layout was simple but expensive with its statues, urns and fountains. Beyond, a smaller garden had simple grass plats and trees clipped to pom-pom shapes, with yet more espaliered fruit against the brick walls.

The gardens may have been designed by George London and Henry Wise of the Brompton Park Nursery, London. Their efficient sales techniques are shown in a letter of August 1701 to George Vernon, who is reminded that he said that he needed 'a Considerable parcel of Pyramid Yews':

and now ye season offering itself for taking them up into Basketts I tooke ye freedome to intimate ye same to your Honor; for in takeing them up now into their baskets with putting good earth next ye rootes and setting them in ye shade and well watering them we find they soon strike fresh Roots and in a fortnight or 3 weeks time is prepared for transportation…

…Mr London designes to be at Mrs Cookes at Melbourne some time ye next month. Soe yt if he can be serviceable to your Honr in any of your designes and you please to let me know it, I'll let him know as much, if you would have him waite on your Honr and for what plants etc your Honor may have occasion for that Brompton Park affords you may assure yourself you shall buy noe where cheaper, nor better plants…[65]

The social and political importance of the immensely wealthy Cavendishes at **Chatsworth** was reflected in their gardens.[66] The estate with its deer park was purchased by the newly wealthy Sir William Cavendish (1505–57) in 1549, after his second wife, Bess of Hardwick, persuaded him to move from Suffolk. Here, at the bottom of a valley, next to the river Derwent, they built a large new courtyard house. Today it is difficult to imagine just how isolated and difficult of access Chatsworth was. Charles Cotton's poem *The Wonders of the Peake* (1681) bemoaned its setting in 'Nature's shames and ills, black heaths, wild rock, bleak crags, and naked hills' and concluded that the house and garden were 'what art could, in spite of nature, do'.

Two special buildings survive from this period. The sophisticated three-storey Hunting Tower or Stand on the hill overlooking Chatsworth house dates from the 1570s, perhaps to a Robert Smythson design, with banqueting towers on the third floor. From the roof it was said that ladies could watch the hunt and look over house, gardens and parkland.[67] Inside decorative plaster ceilings and expensive glass in the large mullion and transom windows were status symbols.[68] 'Queen Mary's Bower', is an open square structure, with a raised garden or platform surrounded by a parapet and balustrade, reached by a wide flight of steps. Originally it was sited in one of the oblong fish ponds of a water garden, replaced by the present quatrefoil moat in the early nineteenth century when Wyatville restored and 'improved' what had become an overgrown ruin.[69] By then the 'Bower' had become linked inextricably with Mary Queen of Scots, who was detained at Chatsworth in the 1570s and in 1581. Tourists loved to associate buildings with this romantic figure, so in 1802 it had become: 'the *Bower of Mary, Queen of Scots*, from a garden which occupied its summit, wherein that princess spent many of the tedious hours of her confinement'.[70] It made a good story and legend is far more romantic than mere fact.

The first accurate estate map was drawn by William Senior in 1617 and depicts the house on the east side of the Derwent in extensive parkland. A large walled garden encloses the south and east sides of the house, with fashionable banqueting houses each end of the terrace below the east front. Within this 'gardin' is a pair of obelisks, an elaborate turreted banqueting house and a mount. Above this, to the north, is an oblong fish pond in the walled 'ould orchard', apparently down to grass by then. To the north-west of the house is a twenty-acre walled ornamental water garden where grass walks separate seven large fish ponds, (one with Queen Mary's Bower).[71] These are mentioned in

FIGURE 25. Chatsworth
Hunting Tower, *c.*1582.
Woodcut *c.*1825.

COURTESY OF MISS FRANCES WEBB
AND WWW.PICTURETHEPAST.
ORG.UK

Thomas Hobbes' Latin poem of 1636, translated as *Concerning the Wonders of the Peak*:

> The River turning off a little pace,
> Part of a Garden's seen that fronts the Place.
> Two Rows of Crystal Ponds here Shine and dance
> Which trembling wave the Sun-beams as they glance,
> In which vast Shoals of Fishes wanton float,
> Not conscious of the Prison where they're shut...[72]

The 1601 inventory of Chatsworth mentions a turret at the bridge end, which crossed two of the fish ponds fronting the house entrance. There was also a 'turret in the mount' in the garden and both were 'fayre wainscotted'. This turret and an arbour were furnished with an alabaster table. Both would have been expensively furnished banqueting houses in addition to the two on the terrace.[73]

Naturally, Thomas Hobbes states that this 'palace' and its gardens were the work of the Countess of Shrewsbury herself, although she was totally occupied with work at Hardwick from the 1580s.[74] No doubt her son William Cavendish (1552–1625), first Earl of Devonshire, who bought Chatsworth in 1610 and lived there until his death, had some involvement. The third earl (1617–84), who inherited as a minor in 1628 and came of age in 1638, undertook considerable alteration in the Chatsworth gardens as revealed in Cotton's poem *The Wonders of the Peake*. The gardens are strictly private: 'A tower of antick model [turret-supra] the bridge-foot /From the Peake-rabble does securely shut'.

> Into the sweetest walks the world can shew.
> There wood and water, sun and shade, contend,
> Which shall the most delight, and most befriend;
> There grass and gravel in one path you meet,
> For ladies tend'rer, and men's harder feet.
> Here into open lakes the sun may pry,[fish ponds]
> A privilege the close groves deny;

The poem stresses the extent of water and grove and the varying heights between the different areas approached by steps, suggesting that the late sixteenth-century gardens have been modernised: 'The Gardens too i' th' reformation share'. Cotton appears to attribute the changes to the wife of the third earl, Lady Elizabeth Cecil (1619–89), whose family home was Hatfield, with its outstanding Jacobean gardens. This is an interesting suggestion, for the famous John Tradescant, noted for his introduction of new exotic plants, was head gardener at Hatfield until 1623 and his work could have had a considerable influence on Elizabeth Cecil. Since the Civil War was disastrous financially, with the third earl in exile, a date of the 1660s–70s for the changes would seem appropriate, once the family had returned from exile and recouped some of their financial losses.

Cotton supposes that there were once original flower gardens in 'a stately plat' (knot garden) which has been replaced by a huge parterre, having at its centre a fountain which throws water 20 ft (6.1 m) high. This is shown in Richard Wilson's copy of a lost seventeenth-century painting of Chatsworth at Chatsworth House. Cotton adds that nearby there are classical statues: 'Romans in statue'. Most telling of all for the additions to the Tudor garden is Cotton's description of what has replaced rocks and a cherry grove at the beginning of the hillside:

> 'Tis now adorn'd with fountains and cascades,
> Terrass on terrass, with their stair-cases,
> Of brave, and great contrivance, and to these
> Statues, walks, grass plats, and a grove indeed…
> And tho' all things were, for that age, before
> In truth so great, that nothing could be more;
> Yet now they with much greater lustre stand,
> Touch'd up, and finish'd by a better hand.

FIGURE 26. Chatsworth, Queen Mary's Bower after early nineteenth-century restorations. Print 1853.

AUTHOR'S COLLECTION

So Cotton reveals, without specific detail, that by 1681 the gardens at Chatsworth had been considerably altered and were sophisticated, ornate and classical in inspiration. This is supported by the comments of Leonard Wheatcroft who visited in February 1685 noting 'those admirable gardens and platforms [terraces], and those new invented waterworks.'[75]

The ambitious and restless William Cavendish, fourth Earl of Devonshire (1640–1707) inherited in 1684. Falling out of favour with King James II, he turned his attentions to Derbyshire, with an ambitious programme for house and garden. This became more grandiose after King William created him first Duke of Devonshire in 1694 for his leading part in the 'Glorious Revolution' of 1688. The duke did not hesitate to take inspiration from the French style of gardening, which dominated all Europe, although linked with the absolutist government of King Louis XIV. However the gardens as they developed owed more to baroque Italian gardens, with their hillside sites. As Charles Cotton's poem (1681) declared, the 'scorn'd Peak, rivals proud Italy'.

With vague grand ideas rather than an overall plan, the earl began his architectural changes with a new south (garden) front, designed by William Talman 1687–89, followed by his new east façade 1691–96. These magnificent baroque facades needed equally splendid gardens around them. Work began in 1688 with a small but elaborate south parterre with central apsidal pool with fountains. Beyond this a Bowling Green was given an elegant classical Bowling Green House in 1693 (later re-sited to its present position and named the Temple of Flora). Then London and Wise's 1694 complex design for the great south parterre replaced the mid-seventeenth-century parterre, whose large fountain was replaced by the exciting Triton and Sea Horse fountain complex by Caius Gabriel Cibber. Inevitably the Brompton Nursery supplied a huge number of plants and trees, many of which were clipped for double avenues, along parterre walls and in bosquets.

The 'chequer-board' layout of the larger gardens shown in a 1699 engraving, reproduced in Kip and Knyff's *Britannia Illustrata* (1707), fails to convey the steepness of the site with its layered terracing. Taking full advantage of the steep hillside to the east, the duke created an enclosed, inward-looking Italian water garden with cascade, fountains, terraces, flights of steps to existing inter-connected gardens, balustrading and classical statues. There was water everywhere, as formal pools and canals, small and large fountains, and the cascade. As you walked around the gardens the sound of water playing could be heard, some of which 'frothes like snow'.[76] Part of the Tudor fishpond complex was converted into another fashionable long canal with double avenues each side. In 1697, also to the north of the house, the old orchard's large rectangular pool was enlarged and supplied with a fountain. This was overlooked by a new fashionable greenhouse/orangery, whose scale was comparable with Talman's grand Orangery at Dyrham Park, for William Blathwayt, Secretary at War for William III.

Visiting in 1697 Celia Fiennes admired the famous Weeping Willow Tree

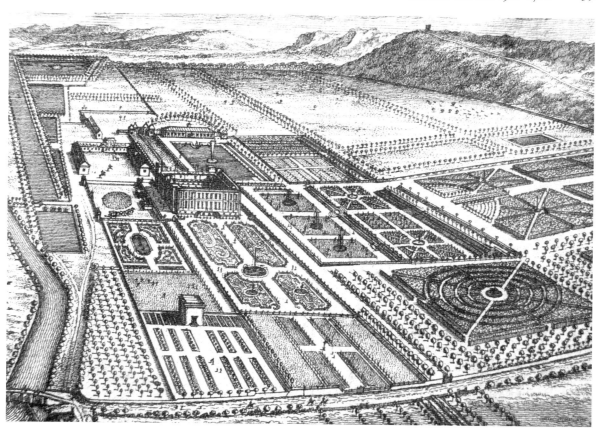

FIGURE 27. Chatsworth House and gardens *c.*1700. Engraving (*c.*1727) based on original by L. Kip and J. Knyff, *Britannia Illustrata* (1707), pl. 17.

Fountain, one of many features. This Italian inspired *giochi d'acqua*, (water trick) was placed at the centre of a formal grove:

> a fine Willow tree, the leaves barke and all looks very naturall, the roote is full of rubbish or great stones to appearance, and all on a sudden by turning a sluce it raines from each leafe and the branches like a shower, it being made of brass and pipes to each leafe but in appearance is exactly like a Willow.[77]

A dramatic addition to the gardens in 1694 was the cascade, some 120 yards (*c.*111 m) long with 30 steps. Inspired by Louis XIV's cascade at Marly, this was designed by Grillet, a French water engineer, and had over-arching water spouts along its length. Among other features, statues of River Nymphs, with pots under their arms, poured water into the cascade.[78] Soon, however, the duke wanted something even more dramatic and the cascade steps were extended up the steep hillside, culminating in the sophisticated Baroque Cascade House, completed in 1712 by Thomas Archer, one of a few contemporary architects who had actually studied in Italy. No less impressive was the still water of a new long canal, over 300 yards (*c.*274 m) long, sited beyond the Great Parterre and the moving waters of the Sea Horse fountain. The duke simply removed a hill to open the vista and level the land. As Defoe admiringly noted, the duke

FIGURE 28. Rowtor
Rocks, steel engraving by
T. Allom, 1837.

AUTHOR'S COLLECTION

'removed, and perfectly carried a great mountain that stood in the way, and which interrupted the prospect.'[79]

In short the new gardens were magnificent, reflecting the wealth, status and importance of the first Duke of Devonshire, who had set out to rival the gardens at Bretby (*qv*). The labour needed to create the terrace walks, the purchase of numerous statues, extensive drainage and piping of water, was prodigious in scale and expense.[80] No one designer is known for the gardens, which grew piecemeal over decades. Probably the first duke used much of the existing layout as a basis, aided by London and Wise at first. William Talman and Thomas Archer, both working on the house at this period, are known to have designed gardens and garden buildings, and the Chatsworth gardens had exceptionally well designed buildings such as the Bowling Green House (1693–95), Greenhouse (1697) and Cascade House (1702–08).

Although Chatsworth was sometimes known as the 'Versailles of the North' because of its size and magnificence, as already noted its gardens owed more to those in Italy than in France. John Macky's comments in the early 1720s reveal how contemporaries appreciated the achievements of the first duke who

> …in the middle of inaccessible Mountains, so frightful, that I thought myself among the Apenines in Italy, built a Palace fit for any Prince in Europe; and I must say, that the pain of getting to it, adds to the Pleasure of the Place.[81]

However not everyone at that time feared the Derbyshire countryside as 'wild rock, bleak crags, and naked hills' (*supra*). The Rev. Thomas Eyre (1628–1717) deliberately celebrated the wild views from his garden at **Rowtor**, where he embellished the huge rock formation, known as Rowtor Rocks, at the top of a steep slope which towered above his house. He cut narrow stone steps up to this pile of enormous gritstone rocks piled in a crazy, precipitous heap above. Over 240 ft (73 m) long and 50 ft (15.2 m) high, the rock formation is a natural phenomenon, with fissures, passages and open spaces within. Here Eyre created two open caves and carved 'chairs' and 'benches' from which to view the countryside stretched out below (Pl. 7). Steep flights of steps were cut into the rocks to provide access round all sides. It was said that Eyre had a study here in which to write his sermons and entertain friends.[82]

John Byng was fascinated by 'this curious spot' in 1790, and by the mid-nineteenth century it had become a tourist attraction with an inn.[83] When a group from the British Association visited in 1866, they saw an 'enigma puzzling alike to the geologist and antiquary ... [leaving] one greatly in doubt as to how much of the whole is natural and how much artificial.'[84] Inevitably the mystery of the site led to an association with Druids, hence the current *Druids Inn*. The late seventeenth century is not a period known for an appreciation of huge and threatening blocks of rock in a wild and empty countryside – one would more readily think of the frissons of awe and fear linked to the later Picturesque and Romantic Movement, but this is Derbyshire after all.

Notes

1. M. Girouard, *Robert Smythson and the Elizabethan Country House* (1983), 120–24.
2. DRO: D505/72/8 'A Map of the Land belonging to Sir John Rodes Bart in his MANNOR of BARLBOROUGH ... surveyed by Joseph Dickinson Anno 1723'.
3. Girouard, *Smythson*, 111–14, 185–86. My sincere thanks to the Headmaster, Mr N. Boys, for allowing access.
4. B. Foster and P. Heath, 'Swarkeston Old Hall': hand-out by South Derbyshire District Council for Heritage Open Days (rev. Sept. 2011).
5. Girouard, *Smythson*, 77, 277, 317.
6. Sir John Harpur was a Royalist who compounded for the huge sum of £4583 in 1645. S. C. Newton, 'The gentry of Derbyshire in the seventeenth century', *Derbyshire Archaeological Journal* 86 (1966), 24.
7. R. Blomfield and F. Inigo Thomas, *The Formal Garden in England* (1892), 192.
8. Foster and Heath, Swarkeston Old Hall.
9. G. Ward to Sir J. Coke, 27 January 1631, W. D. Fane (ed.), 'The Coke Papers at Melbourne Hall', *Derbyshire History and Natural History Society* 11 (1889), 62.
10. P. Henderson, *The Tudor House and Garden* (2005), 169.
11. Craven and Stanley, II, 183–85; P. Heath, Heritage Officer for South Derbyshire District Council, articles in *Heritage News*, no. 28 (Autumn 2008), no. 30 (Sept. 2009) and his typed notes for the Heritage Day Opening of the Park in Sept. 2011.
12. E.g. EH listing no. 82767:1967 as 'Ruins of Old House' – 'probably built as a folly'; Craven and Stanley, II, 183 – 'lodge and stable block'.
13. L. Jewitt, *Illustrated Guide to Haddon Hall* (1871), 13. An original copy at DRO: D5238/4/10.
14. C. Morris (ed.), *The Journeys of Celia Fiennes* (1947), 102.
15. D. and S. Lysons, *Magna Britannia* (1817), plan xxviii. David Trutt's transcription of

S. Rayner, *The History and Antiquities of Haddon Hall illustrated by 32 highly finished drawings with an account of the hall in its present state* (1836). Accessed via www.haddon-hall.com. Rayner also provides an interesting description of the gardens.

16. William Salt Library 2/411/42 Journal of James Reading, folio 71a.
17. Illustrated in colour P. Riden and D. Fowkes, *Hardwick a Great House and its Estate* (2009), 40; black and white in M. Girouard, *Hardwick Hall* (1996), 83; Girouard, *Smythson*, 85, 93.
18. Girouard, *Hardwick Hall* (1976), 52; Henderson, *Tudor House*, 56, 160, 169, 213, 226.
19. D. Durant and P. Riden (eds), *The Building of Hardwick Hall, part 2: The New Hall, 1591–98* (1984), 241.
20. Girouard, *Smythson*, 175–76; P. Kettle, *Oldcotes, The Last Mansion Built by Bess of Hardwick* (2000).
21. Kettle, *Oldcotes*, 14, 46–55, 58–59 citing an inventory of 1666.
22. *Ibid.*, 14.
23. *Ibid.*, 77–79; *Sheffield Independent*, 2 Sept. 1848, 6.
24. University of Nottingham, Manuscripts and Special Collections, Manvers Collection. Ma 2 P.238 'Old coats in the County of Derby … first drawn by Edmund Browne 1659 … ponds and park were made and replenished in ye yeare 1688. Fra Bainbridge'.
25. Illustrated Kettle, *Oldcotes*, 82; English Heritage Building ID 7952.
26. So named by Torrington in 1789: C. Bruyn Andrews (ed.) *The Torrington Diaries*, vol. 2 (1935), 34.
27. Girouard, *Smythson*, chap. 6; T. Mowl, *Elizabethan Taste, Jacobean Style* (1993), chap. 5.
28. M. Girouard, 'Early drawings of Bolsover Castle', *Architectural History* 27 (1984), 510–18, pl. 3b. This 1630s drawing is also reproduced in recent English Heritage Guidebooks for the castle.
29. R. Strong, *The Renaissance Garden in England* (1979), 199–200.
30. Mowl, *Elizabethan Taste*, 120–21. This interpretation is followed in English Heritage Guidebooks.
31. Henderson, *Tudor House*, 192–93, 207–208; L. Worsley, *Cavalier* (2007) interprets the castle, its rooms and garden.
32. See A. Keay and J. Watkins, *The Elizabethan Garden at Kenilworth Castle* (2013).
33. S. Glover and T. Noble, *The History, Gazeteer and Directory of the County of Derby*, vol. 2 (1829), 120.
34. L. Worsley, *Bolsover Castle* (2001), 28; Henderson, *Tudor House*, 208 suggests the figure may represent Bathsheba.
35. P. A. Faulkner, *Bolsover Castle* (1972), 63. P. Drury, *Bolsover Castle* (2014), 30–31: an exemplary account of the Castle. L. Worsley, 'Bolsover Castle in the Eighteenth Century', *Georgian Group Journal* 11 (2001), 169–84.
36. Craven and Stanley, II, 206–207; www.staveleytowncouncil.gov/uk
37. This account is based on the thoughtful www.staveleytowncouncil.gov.uk-Icosse Draft Report (2009); Chesterfield Borough Council, Staveley Conservation Area Appraisal, Nov. 2010 (accessed on line)
38. Craven and Stanley, II, 198–99.
39. T. Mowl and B. Earnshaw, *Architecture without Kings* (1995), 221; T. Mowl, *Gentlemen and Players: Gardeners of the English Landscape* (2000), 21.
40. M. Wiltshire and S. Woore, *Medieval Parks of Derbyshire* (2009), 214. They quote Leonard Wheatcroft's poem, (1672), which mentions hunting at Snitterton.
41. The matching pavilion had gone by the time of 1849 tithe map: DRO: D2360/3/119a.
42. Craven and Stanley, II, 199; Mowl and Earnshaw, *Architecture*, 221.
43. W. Lawson, *A New Orchard and Garden* (1631), 79–84; see J. Francis, '"My Little

Gardine at Dassett Paled" Sir Thomas Temple and his garden at Burton Dassett in Warwickshire, *c.*1630', *Garden History* 41 (1) (2013), 21–30, for an account of the creation of a contemporary garden.

44. Lawson, *A New Orchard*, 72.

45. Mowl, *Gentlemen and Players*, 22.

46. *Ibid.*, 16.

47. Quoted C. Kerry, 'Leonard Wheatcroft of Ashover', *Journal of Derbyshire Archaeology and Natural History Society* 18 (1896), 74.

48. DRO: D504/149/2/13 Sale brochure for Snitterton 1932. My sincere thanks to Kate Alcock and Simon Haslam for showing me around Snitterton gardens.

49. Craven and Stanley, I, 120–21 for a full description of phases of building.

50. R. Strong, *The Artist and the Garden* (2000), 183–93.

51. Mark Eaton, who restored these stone busts, noted the resemblance of one to Thomas Hobbes.

52. DRO: D7676 Bag/C779/23 n/d.

53. DRO: D7676/Bag C/314. Poem addressed to Holme and Bakewell, late seventeenth century. My sincere thanks to John Stansfield for showing me round Holme.

54. Cibber-Shiels, *Lives of the Poets of Great Britain and Ireland,* vol. 2 (1753), 450.

55. R. Blomfield and F. Inigo Thomas, *The Formal Garden in England* (1892), 97, 186.

56. W. Bagshaw, *Directory of Derbyshire* (1846), 185, quoted Craven and Stanley, II, 284; J. Farey, *General View of the Agriculture and Minerals of Derbyshire*, vol. 2 (1815), 138.

57. *National Gazetteer of Great Britain and Ireland, 1868; Kelly's Directory of the Counties of Derby, Notts, Leicester and Rutland* (1891), 243.

58. Quoted Craven and Stanley, II, 187–89; www.picturethepast.org.uk ref PTPD001133 Drawing of Risley Hall, 1865.

59. Craven and Stanley, II, 187–89.

60. DRO: D5780 Thomas Sawson's accounts for Hon. Anchitel Grey 1681–83. Entry 23 Nov. 1681. DRO: D393/1: an attractive estate map of 1722 shows the house but not the gardens.

61. *DM,* 20 Jan. 1742; part quoted Craven and Stanley, II, 188.

62. *DM,* 26 Aug.1757, 4.

63. Blomfield and Thomas, *Formal Garden,* 112–13, 177, 185.

64. *Ibid.*, 72.

65. DRO: D410M/Box25/1387 26 Aug. [1701] Wm Smith of Brompton Park Nurseries, to Vernon at Sudbury.

66. J. Barnatt and T. Williamson, *Chatsworth, A Landscape History* (2005); T. Brighton, 'Chatsworth's C16 House and Gardens', *Garden History* 23(1) (1995), 29–55; Chatsworth's own excellent guidebook, S. Seligman (ed.), *Explore the Garden at Chatsworth* (2008) uses their archives.

67. Britton and E. Wedlake Brayley, *The Beauties of England and Wales,* vol. III (1802), 492–93; Glover and Noble, *History, Gazeteer* pt. 2, 23–29.

68. Henderson, *The Tudor House,* 169; Girouard, *Smythson,* 119.

69. Brighton, 45–46.

70. Britton and Wedlake Brayley, *Beauties of England,* III, 493; repeated Glover and Noble, 228.

71. see Henderson, *Tudor House,* 6–9 for a short illustrated account of the Tudor garden.

72. T. Hobbes, *The Moral and Political Works of Thomas Hobbes of Malmesbury* (1750), 676 with English translation. accessed via www.openlibrary.org, March 2014.

73. National Trust, *Of Household Stuff: The 1601 inventories of Bess of Hardwick* (2001), 29–30; Girouard, *Smythson,* 311, for note on the plasterwork.

74. Hobbes, *Political Works,* 677.

75. Kerry, 'Leonard Wheatcroft'.

76. C. Morris (ed.) *The Illustrated Journeys of Celia Fiennes 1685–c.1712* (1982), 105.

77. *Ibid.*, 105.

78. *Ibid.*, 105; H. Kirke, 'The Peak in the days of Queen Anne', *Journal of Derbyshire Archaeological and Natural History Society* 26 (1904), 209: (Journal of an unknown traveller, 1709).

79. D. Defoe, *A Tour Through the Whole Island of Great Britain* (1724) eds P. N. Furbank *et al.* (1991), 250.

80. W. H. Hart, 'Proceedings in the Court of Exchequer respecting the Chatsworth Building Accounts', *Journal of the Derbyshire Archaeological and Natural History Society* 3 (1881), 40–52; Barnatt and Williamson, *Chatsworth, A Landscape History*, 56–75 for an excellent account.

81. J. Macky, *A Journey Through England*, vol. 2 (1724), 175.

82. Glover and Noble, *History, Gazeteer*, I, 280; I, II, 108; W. Adam, *Gem of the Peak* (1851), 275–76.

83. *Torrington Diaries*, vol. 2, 194.

84. *DM*, 5 Sept. 1866, 2.

CHAPTER THREE

Early Eighteenth Century:
From formal garden to *ferme ornée*

....

In every garden there should be some element of surprise or wonder.

George London and Henry Wise ran a highly successful nursery, with a landscape advisory business, at Brompton Park Nursery, Kensington. While Wise supervised the nursery, London made annual circuits round the country, advising landowners about planting and garden layout – naturally using stock from Brompton. Stephen Switzer asserted that London often rode 50–60 miles (*c*.80–96 km) a day:

> most times visiting all the Country Seats, conversing with Gentlemen, and forwarding the business of Gardn'ing in such a degree as it is almost impossible to describe [he] … actually saw and gave directions once or twice a year in most of the Noblemens and Gentlemens Gardens in England[1]

In Derbyshire the firm was involved at Chatsworth from 1688, Sudbury and Bretby from the 1690s, Melbourne in 1696 and Calke 1701–04.

An undated letter from George London to Thomas Coke of Melbourne shows how his networking operated. London, 'being in the company of the Earl of Northampton and my Lord Bishop of London', heard that they were going to Melbourne, where he asked to meet Coke. He would be in the area 'to see gardens and plantations, as my Lord Chesterfield's, [Bretby] Lord Ferrer's, [Staunton Harold] Duke of Devonshire's *etc*.'[2] This careful name-dropping nicely demonstrates the business acumen and energy of George London. Not surprisingly, given the number of gardens involved, the quality of a London design could be variable, which, as his admirer Stephen Switzer excused, 'might be attributed to the Haste he was generally in'.[3]

The largest gardens at this time were inspired by those of Andre Le Nôtre at Versailles, with elaborate parterres near the house, a wide central axial walk with balancing, but not necessarily identical, parterres, with bosquets or water features. The effect was 'tunnel vision' from the house at the centre of the design to the distance; formal, disciplined and contained within set boundaries. The gardens were punctuated by statues, urns, water and fountains. Avenues might radiate out into the countryside, like rays of the sun, emanating from the local source of power and influence. However by the 1720s gardens were becoming less elaborate and formal, and therefore less expensive to maintain. Through his writings Switzer, who had worked for George London, was influential in promoting these changes. He cannot be linked definitely with any Derbyshire landscape, although he is known to have visited Radburne Hall and Kedleston in 1733.[4]

Although this chapter looks at complex pleasure gardens, we must remember that integral to such gardens were fruit trees, which were not confined to the kitchen garden or orchard. They appear trained against walls, grown as standards, half-standards and miniatures within flower beds and walks. Many owners took a keen interest in their cultivation, developing and exchanging new varieties. For example the Earl of Chesterfield's active interest is shown in his correspondence with Thomas Coke of Melbourne, both of whom were noted for their elaborate French style gardens:

> [The north-east winds blasted] many of my young bearing peach trees, which I believe is almost as great a disappointment to me, who do only pretend to be a gardener, as the missing of a place at Court is to the Lord F…
>
> the cries of peas, cherries and strawberries do tell me that it is time for me to be at Bretby.[5]

Indeed the Earl was an authority on the care of tender plants, with summer and winter greenhouses at Bretby, in which he grew a large variety of lemons and oranges.[6]

A letter to Thomas Coke from his sister Elizabeth, who looked after Melbourne during his frequent absences, illustrates the social cachet of certain fruit. With a surplus of peaches and nectarines in August 1706, Elizabeth reported with satisfaction that she had 'disposed of some of them to those of your neighbours that have no walls of their own… Some of the peaches are from Brompton Park and very good'.[7]

A less common garden feature was ornamental decorative wrought ironwork, but this was well represented in Derbyshire. Decorative iron gates, often with elaborate overthrows, permitted views in and out, as *Claire Voyées*. Wrought ironwork had become increasingly elaborate under the influence of the brilliant French Huguenot refugee craftsman, Jean Tijou (fl. 1689–1710), whose complex Baroque garden screens at Hampton Court still dazzle today. Tijou probably trained Robert Bakewell (1682–1752) from Uttoxeter, who produced ironwork for Melbourne Hall gardens, 1706–11, with a workshop there and then moved to Derby. Over the next 40 years Bakewell produced high quality decorative ironwork for churches, house interiors and gardens in Derbyshire and neighbouring counties, although sadly much has been lost.

The iron trellis arbour 'birdcage' at Melbourne was a feature new to England and Elizabeth Coke's remark that its ironwork is 'very fine, and a great curiosity to see the manner of their doing it', reminds us how excitingly new this technique was at the time.[8] It established Bakewell's reputation and soon led to other commissions. His work at Bretby Hall has been lost, but happily his entrance gates and railing from Etwall Hall (demolished in 1955), were rescued, restored and re-erected in front of Sir John Port's alms houses at Etwall in 1985. His ironwork still

embellishes gardens at the halls of Barton Blount, Longford, Okeover, Radburne and Tissington. Bakewell's successor was his apprentice, Benjamin Yates, who set up his own business in Derby, advertising in 1752 'Iron Gates, Pallisadoes etc for Gentlemens Seats and other Publick Buildings...', by which time however wrought ironwork in gardens was seen as rather old fashioned.[9]

Among the most magnificent of the houses and gardens illustrated in Knyff and Kip's *Britannia Illustrata* (1707) was **Bretby**. In 1670 the French royal architect Louis Le Vau enlarged the original 1630s house for the second Earl of Chesterfield (1633–1713), to which William Talman added an imposing baroque chapel in 1696. By 1670 this grand house was assessed at 68 hearths and had magnificent interior decoration, with a garden developed in scale and complexity to match.[10] In 1683 the Marquis of Halifax hoped Chesterfield could come to London later in winter, when 'there is no more green left at Bretby, and that the joys of your garden are frozen for months'.[11] This may refer to the canal, pools and fountains, perhaps by Grillet, the hydraulics engineer, who was to be employed on comparable work at Chatsworth between 1684 and 1702.[12]

The Earl inherited in 1656 aged 23, spent time in the Tower for duelling and after the Restoration in 1660 held positions at Court, rising to become a Privy Councillor in 1681. However, as a staunch Stuart supporter his court career ended with the exile of James II in 1688 and his refusal to work for William III. The resulting enforced political retirement eventually suited the earl, allowing time to concentrate on further embellishing his gardens, no doubt as a riposte to the Whig Earl of Devonshire at Chatsworth, now in the ascendant with the accession of King William III. Chesterfield triumphantly recalled in 1705

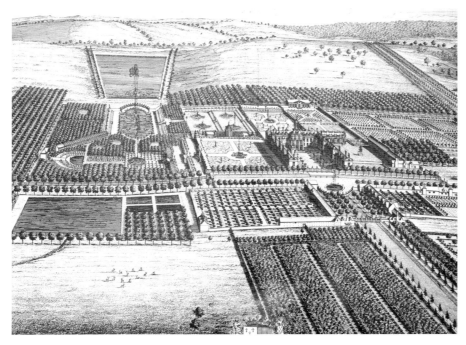

FIGURE 30. Bretby Hall, pl. 26 in L. Kip and J. Knyff *Britannia Illustrata* (1707).

AUTHOR'S COLLECTION

> I went and stayd at Bretby in the summer, where I mayd many water works in my garden ... I invited the French general Mansieur de Tallard, who was kept prisoner at Nottingham, to come to Bretby, where he seemed to be extreamly pleased with the gardens and his entertainment, and sayd, in a compliment, that, setting the King of France's gardens aside, there was not finer gardens in France.[13]

By 1705 London or Wise, 'sildome faill coming to my Lord Chesterfields or Mr Cookes of Melbourne every summer'.[14] London advised on the planting and layout, with elaborate parterres in the French taste decorated with statues, ponds and fountains. Water gardens down a valley were accessed from these parterres and decorated with a long row of greenhouses and serried rows of clipped trees. Change of levels with architectural features, large and small, created variety, shelter and incident around the elaborate gardens, while formal avenues stretched out over the park.

The gardens were considered exceptional, as shown by admiring descriptions, which also provide details not apparent in the only known visual representation of the gardens. In 1712 William Woolley enthused about:

> the gardens, fountains, labyrinths, grooves, [groves] green houses, grottoes, aviaries, but more especially the carpet walk and situation of the orange trees, waterworks before the summer house, which is built in marble...[15]

The redoubtable and well-travelled Celia Fiennes hardly knew where to start with her breathless detailed and admiring description of the park, house and gardens in 1698:

But that which is most admired … by all persons and excite their curiosity to come and see is the Gardens and Waterworks; out of the billiard roome the first was with gravell walks and a large fountaine in the middle with flower potts and greens set round the brimm of the fountaines that are paved with stone … in one garden there are 3 fountaines wherein stands great statues, each side on their pedistalls is a Dial, one for the sun, the other a Clock which by the water worke is moved and strikes the hours and chimes the quarters, and when they please play Lilibolaro on the Chyme … there is a great aviary of birds which stands like a sumer house open there is also many close averys; … there is some of the fountains that have figures in them that throws up water a great height, a cascade of water.[16]

The elaborate aviary must be the French *treillage* (trellis) enclosed arbour with a central octagonal 'tower' shown left of the house in Figure 30. Cassandra Willoughby's description (June 1710) reveals more of the subtlety and complexity of the waterworks:

From the Great Fountain at Lord Chesterfields to a Summer House floored and sided with Marble is a Walk set on each side with Orange Trees and between every Tree a Bason which throws up an Arch of water, which you walk dry under to another Fountain at the foot of the Summer House, on each side of which you ascend under a Bower of Water which play'd from the side of the fountain and the green bank on the other side of the walk you goe up. All that water is encompass with a fine Wood which affords a very pleasant Shade…[17]

A hundred years later visitors were fascinated still by the now lost garden. The fifth earl's steward, John Burton, supplies more information.

The water works were begun to be constructed in the year 1684, and finished in 1702, most probably by the same artist who constructed those at Chatsworth. They consisted of numerous jets d'eau, one of which, from a dragon's mouth, was thrown to the height of 50 ft (15.25 m). On the east side of the house was an oblong piece of water; in the centre of which was a lofty pedestal, supporting a statue of Perseus: from the sides of the pedestal issued numerous jets d'eau forming arches round its base. In this water were dolphins, swans and other animals, all throwing up jets d'eaux. The orangery was very extensive, its large and lofty trees all growing in the natural soil, the conservatory having a lofty roof, and the sides of glass, removable in the summer.[18]

Looking at the sophisticated perfection of the gardens illustrated by Kip and Kynff, there comes a salutary reminder that maintenance was a constant problem. In 1706, Chesterfield, now a melancholy and depressed old man after the death of his daughter, who had married Thomas Coke of Melbourne, wrote to Coke:

now my daughter is gone from me I am become a perfect hermit, for nobody can live a more solitary life. And since you are pleased to mention my gardens, I will tell you that I was never less pleased with them, for my orange trees are almost spoiled, as having neither fruit nor blossoms, nor hardly any leaves; and the ponds of water I made for my waterworks have lost all their water.[19]

The following year the opposite problem was noted at Melbourne, where 'the Great Pool stands very high of water, but the weeds are increased for it is almost entirely green over.'[20]

Bretby house and gardens had a sudden and sad end. The young fifth Earl of Chesterfield was persuaded that the house, which was by then rarely used, was decayed and it was demolished. 'These gardens appear to have been preserved complete, with the water-works, until 1780, when they were destroyed with the house.'[21] Items from the gardens offered for sale included

> Lead Images [statues] Flower-Pots, Urns etc. a large quantity of Pipe and Sheet Lead; also Stone Steps, Coping, Busts, Fruit Baskets and Variety of other curious Ornaments &. in the House and Pleasure Grounds.[22]

One wonders what happened to these. Shortly afterwards a new Gothic castle was built round a surviving office wing, now converted into apartments. A lone cedar from the chapel courtyard, planted in 1677, survived until 1953, but now there are just hilly field and traces of terracing and ponds, but no sense of a once magnificent scene.

In 1892 Reginald Blomfield, enthusiast of formal gardens, pronounced 'The gardens of **Melbourne Hall** are a perfect instance of the French manner in England on a moderate scale'.[23] Even today Melbourne is enjoyed as a rare surviving early eighteenth-century formal garden, whose owner set out to reflect some of the details he had admired when visiting French gardens on the Grand Tour. Although it has to be admitted that he might be rather surprised to see his tightly clipped formal yew hedges in their present huge, but charming, 'cloud' formations.

FIGURE 31. Melbourne Hall. Robert Bakewell's 1706–11 Arbour facing the garden façade of 1742 and overlooking the formal pool and former garden terraces.

When Thomas Coke (1675–1727) inherited at the age of 21, like so many young new owners he was keen to update an old fashioned house and garden, encouraged by his marriage to Lady Mary Stanhope, daughter of the Earl of Chesterfield. However Coke was frequently away in London serving as MP for the county between 1698 and 1710, and from 1707 at Court as Vice-Chamberlain to Queen Anne and George I.[24] His designs for a grander house proceeded piecemeal and modestly, which meant that his new gardens lacked a house of matching size and gravitas. As early as 1706 a rather blunt correspondent remarked: 'when your gardens are to your mind, [completed] you will not long endure the eyesore of your old house'.[25] There is still a feeling that the house is too modest for its formal gardens, although a later 1740s five-bay garden façade has an elegance of proportion.

A major challenge when creating the formal garden lay with the enclosed site. The house is still an integral part of the village, with the huge Norman church on the west side and the village street along the north side. So, perforce, the garden improved by Thomas Coke's father lay on the east side of the house, with a walled flower garden, then steps down to a formal kitchen garden and beyond this, two square 'moats' enclosing islands planted with trees, perhaps moated orchards. On the north side of the flower garden, between it and the village lane, was 'dove coat garden'.[26]

In the late 1690s Thomas Coke began ordering trees, shrubs and bulbs from the Brompton Nursery, which continued to supply plants and advise on design for several years. Coke himself took a very active part in the design as shown when George London wrote in August 1701 offering to meet while on one of his Northern 'circuits': 'so that if you take your draughts [plans] with you, we may come to some conclusion there'.[27] By 1702 the Earl of Chesterfield noted that 'Mr Wilkins is about casting a hundred yards of lead pipes to bring water to your garden'.[28] The noted hydraulic engineer, George Sorocold of Derby, worked on the water supply work for the pool in 1703. Work forged ahead from 1704 once Coke finally managed to obtain the freehold for the property, which had been leased since 1629.

Although off centre to the house, the existing axis was retained because of the proposed widening of the garden façade. The old flower garden was converted into two mirror-image French *parterres de broderie*, defined by low box hedges and pyramid yews. On each side double rows of yews were planted as a long arbour for shady walks. The wall separating the kitchen garden was removed and the central axis then continued down to a lawn which replaced the kitchen garden. This had rows of clipped yews and a row of statues each side. Two old moats became a single formal pond, 70 × 65 yards (64 × 59 m), with its far side extended as a wide apse. Crisp, clipped yews reflected the outlines of the garden and pool. An octagonal dovecote in the 'dovecoat gardens' next to the parterre became an early muniment room.

Wise said Coke chose a plan 'to suit with Versailles'.[29] However, the new layout was more like a simplified smaller version of the central section of the

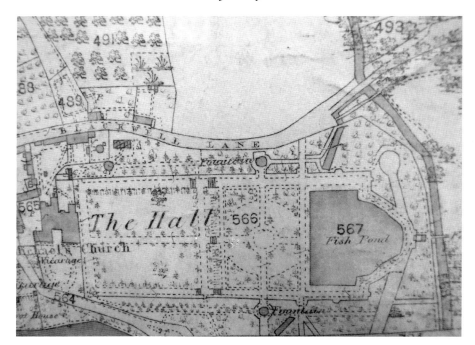

FIGURE 32. Melbourne Hall, formal garden near the house with pond and arbour (far right), hardly changed after 160 years. Detail from OS map 1881/2 at DRO.

gardens at Vaux-le-Vicomte (1656–61), also designed by André le Nôtre, which Thomas Coke had seen and admired. At Vaux the strong central axis led down to a large grotto with a formal pond in front. Here a statue of Neptune, with trident, stood on a square of elaborate rockwork with a triton at each corner, from whose conch water poured. This clearly made a great impression on Coke, since he suggested for the centre of his new formal pond:

> In ye midst of ye great piece of water a Venus coming out of the Sea, standing on a piece of rockwork and four nymphs at ye corners of ye rock. Ye rockwork to be like that under Neptune at Vaux le Vicomte.[30]

Coke would have known other examples of a large statue standing on rocks with side fountains, including his father-in law's Perseus fountain at Bretby and Cibber's Sea Horse Fountain at Chatsworth (still *in situ*). Then Coke changed his mind, abandoning the idea of the Venus fountain. Perhaps someone (his sister Elizabeth?) had a quiet word and pointed out the impropriety of a nude Venus as the main focal point of the new garden, even if Venus was also goddess of gardens. Instead of a fountain the view down the gardens terminated with Robert Bakewell's wrought-iron trellis arbour, another French feature.

Set behind the pool, against a brick garden wall, this master-piece was the young ironworker's first major commission, erected 1706–08 at a cost of £120. Originally painted green, it has *repoussé* work panels, (once painted or gilded), while certain motifs, such as the sun-mask and lambrequins, are French pattern book.[31] A wrought iron dome with lantern was added in 1711, providing wonderful patterns of ironwork foliage against the sky, still much admired and photographed today. It is interesting to note that when the ever practical Cassandra Willoughby visited in 1710, she admired this most 'extraordinary thing', but argued that it 'needs being covered with Wood to be shady'.[32]

Seats, statuary and urns were carefully placed to create incidents of interest and surprise on the circuit round the gardens. The John Nost (Van Ost) groups of delightfully playful lead cherubs were ordered in 1699–1700 before work started on the gardens. These were an unusual choice and perhaps due to Lady Mary Stanhope, who died in 1704. Costing £42 these '4 pr of Boyce cast in metall': the young Castor snatching a bunch of flowers from his brother Pollux; the young Castor hiding the flowers behind his back; the subsequent fight of the brothers and the final patching up of the quarrel.[33] Another Cherub is attacked by hornets, one falls off a tree and another shapes his bow. Painted to look like stone or marble they stood-out against the dark yew background. They provide a very informal and playful aspect to the garden, for whereas the cherub figures at Versailles are sophisticated and assured, those at Melbourne are wonderfully naïve and spontaneous.

FIGURE 33. Melbourne Hall, Van Ost's Blackamoor with Cherub group in background.

COURTESY LORD RALPH KERR. PHOTOGRAPH: THEA RANDALL.

Any French inspired garden needed copies of classical statues. In 1706 Coke bought three such copies in lead from the Nost workshop: Perseus (£25), Andromeda (£20) and Giambologna's famous winged Mercury (£50). Below the house both parterres had a fashionable kneeling statue by Nost: a Blackamoor (Africa) and an Indian (Asia), each costing £30 and painted to look life-like. In a thought provoking article (2011) Patrick Eyres argues that these versions of examples at Hampton Court Palace are part of an iconography in the Melbourne gardens, celebrating victory and trade under Queen Anne, following Coke's appointment as a Commissioner for Plantations and as Privy Councillor in 1706. The statues kneel facing the house 'and offer up their plenty to Britain', indicated by the decorated urns symbolising tropical bounty, which they carry on their heads. Furthermore Eyres argues that Perseus (=the warrior Duke of Marlborough) and Andomeda (=Europe) slaying the monster Medusa (=Louis XIV), re-enact the myth of Perseus as a parallel between the ancient world of the warrior-hero and the English victory in the War of Spanish Succession. It is a persuasive argument which would make sense of the otherwise seemingly random choice of statuary.[34]

Thomas Coke trebled the size of his garden by demolishing dog kennels on the south side of the former kitchen garden and extending his garden beyond. Ten acres (*c.*4 ha) with *allées* (rides or walks), lined with lime and hornbeam cut through newly planted *bosquet* (woodland or wilderness), providing both light and shade. The ground slopes up gently to a *rond-point* where the straight woodland *allées* converge. Here a 7 ft (2.1 m) high urn, Nost's magnificent and ornate lead 'Vase of the Seasons', acts an eye-catcher at the highest point of the gardens (Pl. 8). A cross axial *allée* is cut by three small ponds of different formal shapes, each with a fountain, while at each end there is a covered seat of painted wood and brick in which to sit in the shade, listen to the sounds of the fountains and appreciate the vista across the pools. Again the irregular shape of the area is concealed by rigid lines of trees and changes of levels. Its plan (1704) by William Cooke, the contractor on site, was approved by Henry Wise, and continues Thomas Coke's overall plan for a Le Nôtre inspired garden. By 1705 Elizabeth, Coke's sister, reported:

> All the dust and noisy work of your garden is finished, the gravel walks being done. I believe you will be pleased with them, and these late rains have refreshed the turfs and the trees, [so] that you will find it in great beauty … the little fountains are done with stone, and they have begun to level the ground in the larger grove.[35]

Coke was the guiding spirit throughout, as shown in another letter from Elizabeth in 1706 who noted that 'Cooke, the Gardener, is now here, and wishes much for your orders in several things, that would give the finishing strokes to the garden'.[36] At about the same time the Earl of Chesterfield was urging Coke to return from London 'for there is great want of your directions at Melborne'.[37]

Elizabeth Coke supervised work during her brother's absences in London, reporting both progress and problems, as in 1710 when she wrote:

> You will find a very great change in the beauty of your greens in the Parterre by last year, and this also. About six weeks ago they began to promise recovery in a great measure, but the same cold winds that have taken away the fruit have strangely took the Phyllereas that was left alive: and the laurels some of them are quite killed. The yews and the round hollies are well, but the spire hollies, some of them, look but ill.[38]

After Thomas Coke's death in 1727 the hall passed to daughters who lived elsewhere, so the gardens slumbered. When John Byng visited in 1789 he noted: 'such an old fashion'd garden of yew hedges, fountains and alleys, as now becomes a curiosity, and to be admired for that shade so much wanted in modern shrubberies'.[39] A hundred years later the gardens were admired for their French formality, now tempered by an English informality, the best of both worlds:

> The long yew walk, its width inside 12 feet … has grown into an impenetrable vault of branches overhead, so that it is proof against an ordinary shower of rain… Lead statues very easily lose their centre of gravity, and when once they begin to move over they become exceedingly comic. The flying Mercury … is slowly taking a header into the grass in front of his pedestal.[40]

By then painting lead statues was not approved and Blomfield regretted that originally they were 'painted and some covered with stone-dust to imitate stone, a gratuitous insult to lead, which will turn to a delicate silvery gray, if left to its own devices', a view largely current today.

London and Wise were also involved at **Calke Abbey**, a former Augustinian Priory, given the fashionable title of Abbey in 1808. The priory estate was purchased by a wealthy local landowner Sir Henry Harpur in 1622, the year he purchased his baronetcy. Sir John Harpur (1680–1741), fourth baronet, inherited in 1681 and careful management of the estates during his long minority meant that in 1701 he had access to the accumulated sum of £40,000 together with an annual income of over £3000 with 34,000 acres (13,767 ha) in Derbyshire, Leicestershire and Staffordshire. This, with his marriage to the wealthy Catherine Crewe in 1702, inevitably encouraged the young Sir John to rebuild the old fashioned house and to furnish it richly.[41] Because the new Baroque house simply encased part of the earlier building, the result, though modern and expensive, was disappointing, as Cassandra Willoughby remarked in 1710:

> Tho the outside is all new, the body of the House is only altered, which had made many faults … and they tell you this has cost as much as an entire new building would have done. Sir John Harper is going to make a Garden but the situation will not allow of its being very fine.[42]

In 1702 George London was paid £2 3s 0d for 'his garden draughts', plus £28 6s 0d, probably for plants from the Brompton Nursery. The same year £100 was spent on garden walling, presumably to enclose the new garden, although Cassandra Willoughby noted work was still in the planning stage in 1710. The new formal parterres on the east front, (the later 'best garden') may have been designed by William Cooke, involved at nearby Melbourne, as £5 7s 6d was paid in 1710 to 'Mr Coke ye Gardainer for his Draughts'.[43] Currently just lawn, this area would have had elaborate parterres terminated by three bastion semi-circles overlooking formal ponds in the wooded area beyond. Later the larger central semi-circle may have had Bakewell's wrought ironwork screens, perhaps with steps leading down to the land beyond, while the smaller ones either side were covered over and plastered, perhaps as seats.[44] In 1711 Henry Wise's bill for 'Box and Yews etc' came to £2 14s 0d and in 1713 London charged £14 for '5500 Hornbeame Setts that was sent to Caulk'.[45] This, with £70 for Robert Bakewell's ornamental balustrade for 'steps in the garden' in 1719, suggests a fine new formal garden, some 20 years in the making. Although Charles Bridgeman, (working at Kedleston), was paid three guineas in 1721 'for a draft for the alteration of the Ground before the house', there is no evidence that his ideas were used.[46] Sir John does not appear to have been decisive or in a hurry.

On the south side of this garden was a larger square wilderness attached to a walled orchard. As was usual at the time there was little attempt to landscape the gardens in sympathy with the rolling countryside of the park; formality was simply imposed. The outlines are clearly shown on an estate plan of 1761, with formal avenues radiating from the house, across the park and fields, some for grand effect rather than access.[47]

Sir Henry Harpur (1708–48), fifth baronet, inherited in 1741. He married Lady Caroline Manners (d. 1769), daughter of the Duke of Rutland and she was probably responsible for the up-to- date changes to the pleasure gardens from 1741 to 1760, when her son inherited. On visits to friends and relatives she saw new garden fashions and her purchase of Philip Miller's *Dictionary* in 1745 suggests an interest in plants.[48] The old fashioned parterres were converted to plain

FIGURE 34. Calke Abbey, sheep knuckle bone floor of lost summer house – probably mid-eighteenth century.

BY KIND PERMISSION OF THE NATIONAL TRUST

lawn and she introduced new features, one of which might have been a circular summer house or Hermitage, not far from the kitchen garden. All that remains is its mosaic floor, made of sheep knuckle bones. Certainly this has affinities with contemporary work at Lady Curzon's Ireton Gardens (*qv*).

Lady Caroline made a series of pools a focal point in the pleasure gardens (see Fig. 85). Running north of the house is a narrow valley whose little stream had been utilised by the Priory to create fish ponds, one of which had been enlarged in 1724.[49] 'Betty's Pond' was created in 1741 ('Betty' has still to be identified), and then the narrow 'Thatched House Pond', referred to as 'the new pool' in 1752. On its north side, on top of a mound, was 'Lady Catherine's Bower', a polygonal building, of which only the foundations, about 15 ft (4.6 m) diameter, survive and the steps up to it.[50] Castle Pool became 'Chinese House Pond' when Lady Caroline erected a very fashionable Chinese summer house on its island in 1746–47.[51] Chinese summer houses and pavilions became fashionable in the early 1740s, with Horace Walpole denouncing those at Wroxton Abbey, Oxfordshire (1739–40) as having 'the merit or demerit of being the progenitors of a very numerous race all over the kingdom'.[52] The fashion spread rapidly and Lady Caroline was responsible for the first example in Derbyshire. These little buildings were placed by water, preferably on an island accessed by boat, as with the rare surviving example at Shugborough, Staffordshire (1748) which had its own Chinese rowing boat.[53]

Lady Caroline specified that this Chinese House (probably painted wood and canvass), must be painted white with blue details as 'is more Chinese Taste and [the] blew should be dark.' She also mentions 'Chinese rails', perhaps for a boat, which might have been sheltered in a tunnel which survives in the dam to the pond. Her little building was decorated with dragons by the studio of Lewis Goupy and surmounted by Bakewell's wrought-iron weather vane.[54] Work continued on and off and in 1753 she wrote that the wood must be preserved 'by repeated paintings till my son comes of age to compleat it to his own Taste'.[55] Inside it was furnished with eight chairs and a mahogany table, presumably in the Chinese-style.[56] It must have been a delight to show to admiring neighbours and friends.

In contrast, close by on the north bank of Chinese House Pond, was a grotto which survives, albeit in a rather sorry state. It is made of a mixture of red brick and coursed rubble sandstone from the estate. The arched entrance has Gibbsian stone voussoirs and on each side rectangular opening as windows. Each end has a projecting single bay with a smaller classical arch. The unnecessary addition of a small stone niche over the entrance is a later conceit (Pl. 9). The interior is a semi-circular apse with some of the original plasterwork clinging the brickwork. This very private space provided views over the pond and Chinese House and later to the 1809 grotto. As we shall see, more drastic changes were to follow in the 1760s.

Enough survives of the early eighteenth-century gardens at **Longford Hall** to appreciate the original concept. Purchased by the Coke family in 1622, the brick early Tudor house was noted with 24 hearths in 1664, but was much reduced in size following a fire in 1942.[57] The gardens were laid out by Sir Edward Coke third baronet (1648–1727), and admired by William Woolley, with his usual vagueness, in 1713:

> [Coke] ... has a very large ancient seat which he has very much improved, particularly by gardens and water courses, which has made it one of the pleasantest and most commodious seats in the country [county].[58]

An 800 ft (244 m) terrace runs the length of the long south garden wing of the house, and below this, on a wider terrace, would have been the usual formal parterres. Below these a stream was dammed to create two long narrow fish ponds as a formal canal, whose herringbone patterned brick base was discovered when the water was dredged in 1985.[59] Attractively, the garden façade of the house still reflects in this water. The landscape beyond was accessed by a narrow raised walk between the canals. Unfortunately little is known about these lost gardens which must have been known and admired locally, for in 1724 Sir John Curzon took guests staying at Kedleston 'in Coach and Six to see Langford [*sic*] gardens'.[60] Perhaps they were embellished with statues, with various water courses converted into water features, long gone.

In 1733 the estate came to Robert Coke (1704–1754), nephew of Sir Thomas Coke of Holkham, Norfolk. In 1737 he commissioned Robert Bakewell to supply wrought iron gates, to be painted 'the same dark colour' as the palisading into which they were set 'For I like that colour much better than white for our works'.[61] Longford was then inherited by Robert's nephew, Wenham Roberts, who succeeded to the Holkham estates in 1759. Although Longford became a second home, Joseph Pickford was commissioned in 1761 to modernise the house. The gardens were probably replaced by lawn but the canals retained their formal straight edges until the mid-nineteenth century (Pl. 10).[62] The waterfall on the nearby trout stream could date to this period. The present division of the terrace into three parterres dates from the 1850s, when 'the grounds which have recently been enlarged and improved are laid out with great taste'.[63] Photographs (1865) show a small central fountain, further simplified in the 1920s, by which time there was an 'Italian garden'.[64] The estate was sold by the Coke family in 1920 and has changed hands several times since.

Wigwell Grange, near Wirksworth, must have had a fine early eighteenth-century landscape, known only through tantalising contemporary descriptions. A former moated monastic grange of Darley Abbey, the estate was acquired by Sir John Statham through his marriage to the heiress Bridget Wigley. Sir John (1676–1759), a staunch Tory, was proud, litigious and most unlikeable. Trained as a lawyer, he had political ambitions but failed to find nomination for MP for the Derby seat in 1708. He managed to be elected MP for Mitchell, Cornwall, in 1713–15 but then failed to win the Lichfield seat in the 1727 election. Knighted in 1714 for his service as Envoy to Turin 1713–14, he became a gentleman of the privy chamber 1714–27.

His vituperative turn of phrase is illustrated in a letter (1757):

> No person in the county has suffer'd more by vile Calumnies, than <u>Sir John Statham</u>, who for many years has been the Mark, at which the Faction [Whigs] have shot their envenom'd Arrows, and bent their whole Efforts. His neglecting, despising and contemning them, gave them too much encouragement to continue their reproaches. What Wrongs, Injustice and Oppression, have they not charg'd him with? And what mortgages, Judgements and other Securities, have they not loaded his Estates with? [65]

One feels that Sir John protests too much. His quarrelsome nature seems to have been inherited by his eldest son, Wigley Statham (1701–31), who killed a man following a drunken brawl in a tavern.[66] Unsurprisingly Sir John quarrelled with his only surviving son, John (1707–70), who later sold the estate.[67] One wonders if it was local dislike of Sir John's pride and personality that led to the theft of his deer and constant poaching and vandalism of his fish ponds and rabbit warrens in the 1750s?[68]

It is not known what changes he made to the Jacobean house, which William Woolley wrote that he had 'much improved'.[69] Sir John was very proud of his gardens, which were admired by James Reading in 1726, when he noted gravel and grass walks, fine trees and fish ponds.[70] Writing to Charles Stanhope of Elvaston, probably in the 1740s, Sir John described his garden, enthusing about his house and park with 'Venison, a Warren for Rabbits, Fish, Fowl, in the uttermost perfection', dovecotes, canals and well stocked fish ponds.

> a good bowling green and many long walks … Park, with delicious nut wood, full of singing birds, turtles [turtle doves] and Guinea hens, a delicate Eccho, where musick sounds charmingly. In it are labarinths, statues, arbors, springs, grottos and mossy banks, in the middle a large clear fish Pond with a draw bridge and Close Arbor…[71]

This was an elaborate woodland pleasure garden, as described and recommended in Stephen Switzer's *Ichnographica Rustica* (1718). Sir John was trying to persuade Stanhope to visit, anxious to show that his garden was as interesting as that at Elvaston, and also that he was a cultivated man of letters and science. As late as the end of the nineteenth century there was still a canal and a 'prettily timbered undulating park of about forty-six acres', with a 'charming Wilderness walk through shubberies'.[72]

Established in Derbyshire since the late twelfth century, the Curzons of **Kedleston** became the leading Tory family in Derbyshire, the social and political rivals of the Whig Cavendishes at Chatsworth. This was to be reflected in their increasingly ambitious plans for the house and grounds at Kedleston.

About 1700 Francis Smith built a new baroque house for Sir Nathaniel Curzon (1635–1719), shown in a contemporary oil painting still at the hall. It had small walled gardens at the rear, probably retained from the original house, and substantial outbuildings, stables, dovecote and barns to one side and village church on the other (see Fig. 3) A public road ran directly in front of the house with a scattered village close by. When Sir John Curzon, third baronet (1674–1727), inherited in 1719, he recalled Francis Smith of Warwick to make improvements inside the house, which continued on and off until 1734.[73] The old fashioned garden walls were demolished and the royal gardener Charles Bridgeman was commissioned to create a large baroque garden.

Bridgeman utilised the slope of the grounds for his trade mark abrupt change of levels combined with sharp angles. By the house were large parterres, probably fairly simple in design, and above these were long axial

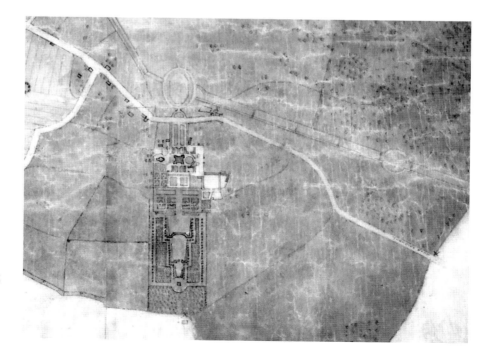

FIGURE 35. Kedleston, detail of survey map of estate (pre-1758) showing Bridgeman's formal garden and canal with oval pool.

lawns, cut into the slope and surrounded on either side by a row of clipped trees, with a small building or statue terminating the central vista. The entrance forecourt also had shaped lawns and gravel paths down to the public road, on the other side of which Bridgeman created another of his favourite features: a canal with cascades. Directly opposite the entrance front of the house was a large octagonal pool from which ran the long 60 ft (18.3 m) wide canal with four cascades, each having a fall of 3 ft (0.9 m). This canal, converted from a brook fed by the mill stream, continued roughly parallel to the road for the first half of its length. The last cascade fell into a circular pool and the canal

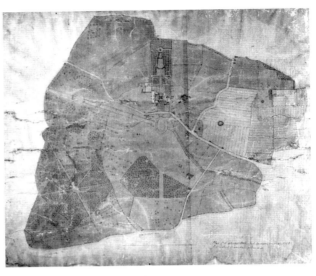

FIGURE 36. Kedleston, survey map of the estate (pre-1758), with formal features including gardens canal and walks cut through wood.

© NATIONAL TRUST IMAGES

then continued. The whole length was 3000 ft (914 m), of which the canal was 200 ft (610 m). Both canal and circular pool were edged by a row of trees.[74]

James Reading, whose uncle was steward at Kedleston, visited in 1724 and noted that you go 'down from ye dining Room a great many steps wer there is Balls of stone and banesters to a fine long terras walk'. James mentions a gravel garden with fish ponds and he rode in the park by the 'Bason of watter', which suggests that at least one of Bridgeman's pools was in place by 1724. Water was clearly a feature to impress as he notes that visitors were taken to 'se Sr Johns water works'.[75]

Sir John had ambitious plans for the park, although the public road running past the house was not removed until later in the century. Woolley (1712) had drawn attention to Kedleston's 'large and well-wooded and well stocked park'.[76] Another contemporary spoke of a 'thick Grove of Oaks, which are as great an Ornament to that fine Park, as any (as far as I know) that are to be seen in England'.[77] By the 1750s these woods had formal walks or rides cut through them, the larger having a central a *rond point* where six avenues met. A wide drive was cut through another area of woodland opposite the house entrance, forming a vista of octagonal pond, open park land and then this wide avenue and woodland.

It was for here that in 1726 James Gibbs designed pavilions for each side of the proposed ride, which was to terminate in an obelisk on a hill above.[78] Like Gibbs's design for a fashionable Palladian entrance front to the house, these were unexecuted when Sir John Curzon died in 1727.[79] Gibbs must have been bitterly disappointed that none of his building plans was taken up by Sir John's brother, Sir Nathaniel Curzon (1676–1758). Although as MP for the county 1727–54, Sir Nathaniel used the house for entertaining and he continued to implement his brother's ambitious planting in the park and woods.

In 1716 Sir Nathaniel married Mary Assheton (1695–1776), a keen and inventive gardener who passed on her enthusiasm to her sons, Nathaniel

FIGURE 37. Kedleston Estate map by Ingram (1764); detail of Ireton gardens.

© NATIONAL TRUST IMAGES

(1726–1804) at Kedleston and Assheton, first Viscount Curzon (1729–1820) at Hagley Hall, Staffordshire. She became well known for her own garden at Kedleston, the 1730/40's **Ireton Gardens**, created on the adjoining Little Ireton estate, acquired in 1721.[80] This was a period when several titled ladies took a great interest in the design and ornamentation of their own informal gardens, as for example Lady Luxborough at Barrells in Warwickshire, who had the advice of the poet William Shenstone. Her garden included a hermitage and shell grotto, which she decorated herself.

The Ireton Gardens have gone, but contemporary descriptions reveal their variety and charm and show that Lady Curzon had created her own *ferme ornée*. When Lady Sophia Newdigate visited in September 1747, she was fascinated by the buildings rather than by the setting:

Just without the Park is Lady Curson's Farm called Ireton about 30 acres of Land laid out in a Wilderness with a serpentine water 18ft wide running through it. There is a Bowling Green with two pavilions on each side, consisting each of one Room one 18ft by 24, the other 24ft cube. Behind these lyes the poultry Yard [.] on another side the Green is an Octagon Building made entirely within and without wt the knot of Crabs [crab-apples], wch exceeded my expectations tho' I had heard much of it[.] on ye outside under ye Cornice are Festoons in the same material extreamly well expressed. The Floor is made up of ye Knots of ye oak polish'd and suits prettily with ye whole, in another part of the Garden there is a Gothick Building composed of Sheeps bones, … tis extreamly curious and yt Taste so exactly followed yt I never saw anything prettier [.] Everything in this place is perfectly new, there is a seat made of pebbles wch I cant say answers so well as the rest, several of them are polish'd and ye whole is a meer bauble, an Alcove by ye water side coverd wth pieces of Bark painted makes an extream good rustic stone building and such a one as wd deceive many. In ye Laying out ye ground here there is not so much Ingenuity shewn as in ye Buildings, for wch it seems they should have a great deal of wood, as well as a great deal of mutton.[81]

Lady Newdigate's companion Mary Conyers also described the gardens, stating that Lady Curzon 'alone has had the laying out of [the Garden]'. She writes of 'two Pavilions, not very richly fitted up, the [one] is intended to Dine, the other to drink Tea in'; the Octagon a 'little Rotond Room' has 'the floor and seats are inlaid in squares of the bark of rough oaks, polished and a black wood which I cannot tell the name of'. She also mentions that the Gothick building is made from sheep bones and says that the Alcove has:

2 Rustic Pillars, the Rustick Part is the rough bark of trees, nailed and painted, which looks extreme well, there is also a seat in the form of an Escallop shell made of Pebbles some of which are [so] finely Polished so that people have thought it worth their while to pick them out and carry them off.[82]

No wonder they admired this version of the *Ferme Ornée*, with its poultry yard, a suitable hobby for a lady, and rustic garden with two pavilions (for dining and taking tea), opening into a bowling green for recreation. The gothick building and shell shaped seat must have consumed an enormous number of very small bones and pebbles.

When the Rev. John Nixon visited in 1745 he remarked that Ireton 'affords sufficient scope for Lady Curzon to display her fine genius in gardening and architecture, the whole being planned and executed by her ladyship's sole direction.'[83] He noted that one of the summer houses 'has the panels of the doors withoutside, as well the floors, seats, and windows within, all inlaid with woods of divers sorts and colours in a pretty manner.' Not surprisingly the gothic building amazed him:

> the most whimsical fabric I ever saw… The materials that compose it would tempt one to call it the temple or triumphal arch of Death, while its colour and appearance challenge the name of the ivory gate described by Virgil… In short, it is a kind of little Gothic fort or lodge, of three arches in front, made altogether of bones in their proper colour. The walls within are all wainscoted with the round ends of sheeps' trotters, as those without exhibit nothing but the smooth protuberances of marrow bones of large cattle. The other members of the building are finished with a variety of bones in a very natural and beautiful manner; particularly I observed her ladyship had been greatly obliged to the vertebrae of joints of the backbone of a cow or horse for principal part of the Gothic ornaments which enriched the arches, windows, and battlements of this romantic structure.

A delightful watercolour *c.*1745 (private collection) shows the gardens seen from pastureland where sheep and cattle graze, while a milkmaid milks a cow to provide cups of milk for some beautifully attired gentlemen. A picket gate in a hedge gives access to the gardens, where a serpentine canal has a fisherman on a boat conversing with two beautifully dressed ladies and a gentleman. Behind them is the wilderness with its pollarded trees in clumps and rows. The alcove seat is visible among the trees and at the top of the sloping ground the rotondo peaks out – a labour-intensive pastoral scene of sophistication and charm, yet with the latest *avant garde* styles.

The use of bones to ornament garden buildings was unusual but by no means unique. The octagonal rustic 'Moss House' at Heythrop, Oxfordshire (home of the Duke of Shrewsbury), had a floor made of animals' teeth.[84] Black marble and horses' teeth made a complicated pattern on the floor of the exotic shell grotto at Goodwood house, Sussex, decorated by the Duchess of Richmond and her daughters. Lady Curzon may have had advice from the noted grotto builder, Mrs Mary Delaney, who visited Kedleston and made sketches of the parkland.[85] Mrs Delaney described (1746) Lord Cornbury's park in Oxfordshire, where there was a former stone quarry;

> now improved into the wildest prettiest place you can imagine – winding walks, mounts covered with all sorts of trees and flowering shrubs, rocks covered with moss, hollows filled with bushes intermixed with rocks, rural seats and sheds; and in the valley beneath a river winds.[86]

This has many similarities with Ireton, where a grotto was cut into the side of in a small quarry. In 1744 *The Gentleman's Magazine* felt that Ireton gardens were sufficiently noteworthy to include a poem:

> Written in the Grotto, in Lady Curzon's Garden, at Ireton, near Derby
> Peculiar grace, *Curzona's* hand,
> And matchless worth bestows,
> How all around me, as I stand,
> With radiant lustre glows:
> The *Phrygian* king[Midas], so fable sings,
> At pleasure might lay hold,
> And turn at once the meanest things
> To all-alluring gold:
> But she, her charming art is such,
> Surpassing *Midas* far,
> Exalts, with more enobling touch,
> Each pebble to a star[87]

To confuse matters the Rev. Nixon refers to this as a 'hermitage or tea-room, in a kind of stone quarry, in the front of which a cascade is destined to fall down over the rude shelves of rock.' Later Robert Adam suggested ambitious plans (unexecuted) to transform and decorate this 'rockroom in ye Pit near the Garden.'[88]

The *Derby Mercury*, 12 September 1760, reported the theft of flowers from the Ireton garden. This flower garden was inside a walled garden whose interior south facing wall had ten segmental alcoves for maximum shelter. Sadly the fantastic but ephemeral garden buildings have all gone and even in 1872 it was reported that 'the gothic Temple, erected as a summer-house, ... [is] in ruins.'[89] More research is needed on Lady Curzon and her literary circle.

FIGURE 38. Ireton Gardens, the site of the lost grotto/hermitage in a small quarry.

COURTESY HON. R. F. N. CURZON

Knowle Hill, Ticknall is a problematic garden. Early in the eighteenth century William Woolley wrote:

> Mr Walter Burdet, an elderly bachelor of the ancient family has made a very agreeable habitation, ... where two Knowles or hills covered with woods and two pleasant valleys on each side, [meet] with two murmuring rivulets running along them, to which natural disposition he has added a great deal of art which renders it a most delightful place...[90]

FIGURE 39. Ireton Gardens, view down to serpentine walls of Lady Curzon's kitchen/flower garden.

COURTESY HON. R. F. N. CURZON

The vague 'a great deal of art' is especially frustrating as this is the only contemporary description of an exciting and enigmatic site. Depending on interpretation, the gardens could be a very unusual early eighteenth-century landscape or simply an interesting mid-eighteenth-century picturesque garden.

Walter Burdett (1646–1732) was the third son of Sir Francis Burdett (d. 1696) of Foremark Hall, about two miles (3.2 km) distant. A practising barrister in London, he wanted a small country retreat, and in 1686 he rented Knowle Hills, 45 acres (10.2 ha) of fields and wood, adding a further three acres (1.2 ha) in 1688. The owners were the Coke family of Melbourne, with whom the Burdett family had very close and friendly links. After the death of his father in 1696 Walter spent more time in Derbyshire. He helped look after Foremark, where his mother and family lived, while his eldest brother Robert spent most of his time at his Warwickshire estate.[91] Then Walter built his own small country house at Knowle on the edge of a deep valley, with superb views down the valley with its stream and the countryside beyond.

Little is known about Walter Burdett, other than his interest in horse breeding and fox hunting. He appears to have been humorous, sociable and enjoyed company, as when Elizabeth Coke reported that 'My cousin Walter was there you may be sure, and danced with the ladies till late at night.[92] A bachelor, Walter Burdett entertained at Knowle Hill. In one letter he thanked Thomas Coke for the gift of trout 'to entertain my good friends Sir Nathaniel Curzon [and family] and brother John at Knowle Hills'.[93] Coke was a close friend who, following the death of his wife in 1704, frequently escaped to Knowle Hill for peace and quiet.[94] For both men Knowle exemplified the classical idea of rural retirement from the cares of the business or state. It may be significant that Walter Burdett's circle included the Chesterfields from Bretby, Harpurs from Calke and Coke from Melbourne – all of whom who had made, or were making, elaborate and fashionable formal gardens at this period.

Walter created a long platform on which to build his house. On the south side a long narrow terrace was separated from the countryside beyond by a stone wall incorporating at least one stone seat. Below this terrace was a wider terrace on the same level as the house. Here a seat in an alcove faced the house and looked down to the countryside beyond. At the top of the valley a formal pool was created with a raised walk around. Originally there was a small building here. From the pool a cascade continued downhill gently into a small stream, passing below the house and terracing. Stone revetting along the stream created a narrow rill, with small steps making the occasional mini cascade. The rill continued to another formal pond and more cascades.

Below the site of the (now lost) house, on a steep drop, are the confusing remains of a complex of brick walls and arches built into the hillside (Pl. 11). One theory is that these are remnants of cellars and rooms of the lost house, or perhaps later work dating from the 1760s.[95] This idea may be traced to an interpretation in 1802 of what were even then derelict features: 'a singular but pleasant house, climbing irregularly from the bottom of the dell to the summit

FIGURE 40. Knowle Hill, brick alcove with steps up to viewing platform above on the top terrace.

of its western bank'.[96] It seems an expensive and rather bizarre idea to build down and into a hillside when there was plenty of space along the top. A more interesting theory is that this mass of ruined brick walls once supported Italianate terrace gardens. This concept was supported by Christopher Currie who undertook archaeological work (1993) for the Landmark Trust, the current owners.[97] Certainly the top terrace here has a series of classical niches, which once may have contained statues or busts, and there is also an elliptical stone wall below the ramp leading back up to the house level.[98]

At a lower level a tunnel with recesses on each side (for lights?) in the sandstone walls leads into in two roughly circular small chambers, each with classical niches.[99] This is clearly a classical garden feature, not a domestic cellar. It has been suggested that originally the opening might have been framed by rock-work as part of the terracing.[100]

Such Italianate terracing can be seen at Powis Castle, which may have included an orangery or summer house. Dating from the 1680s complex brick terracing at Albury House, Surrey, has similarities, and includes a bath house and pool.[101] Given the sophistication of surviving features on the top terrace, a possible architect or designer could be Thomas Archer, whose work at Heythrop Park, Oxfordshire, has similar features, and who was working at Chatsworth from 1702.[102]

Shortly after Burdett's death in 1732, the little estate was purchased by Nicholas Hardeing (1699–1758) who owned land in Derbyshire and whose successful government career included Clerk to the House of Commons 1731–51. A classical scholar and poet, Hardeing was soon writing enthusiastically about Knowle as a rustic idyll, to retire from the cares of office and state: very much the standard eighteenth-century emulation of Virgil and Horace. Unfortunately his poetic descriptions are deliberately vague, stylised and evocative, concentrating on the woodland and water. His poem 'Knoll Hills written in 1735' begins:

> Where lurks my cave's recess, my lov'd abode,
> Near Trenta's playful stream, her bank, the road.
> Beyond that rising dale with harvest crown'd
> Impending woods the secret nook surround.

FIGURE 41 *(left)*. Knowle Hill, early eighteenth-century classical niches in terrace wall below site of house.

COURTESY THE LANDMARK TRUST

FIGURE 42 *(right)*. Knowle Hill, interior of tunnel leading to the first space with its classical niches and seating – early eighteenth century?

PHOTOGRAPH: JACKI MOSELEY. COURTESY THE LANDMARK TRUST

> Lead me, ye Muses, to the lov'd retreat,
> Lead to *Nolillula's* [a nymph] inviting seat,
> Where, by a fountain's gentle source supplied,
> Down the soft bank still ebbs the silver tide…[103]

By now well into his stride, Hardinge wrote a second poem the same year, with the same theme, and predictable references to Virgil, Horace and Milton. Clearly Knowle Hill was inspiring the man:

> What cliff's projected brow, what caves retreat,
> What bower shall hide me from the summer's heat?
> My indolence the shelter'd vale approves,
> The tuneful streams, the deep-embosom'd groves.
> Beneath cool steeps, in loftiest wood array'd,
> Place and protect me with extended shade.
> This was *my* wish – Fate's pleasing gift – a farm
> Not undorn'd in rural beauty's charm;
> A garden, clean, though guiltless of parterre,
> A sylvan shade o'erspread – a fountain near,
> Whence fresh-distilled perpetual water glides,
> Whose glist'ring path its verdant slope divides;[104]

FIGURE 43. Knowle Hill, Sir Robert Burdett's gothick 1769 summer house replacing original house, looking over the valley (garden wall is modern).

COURTESY THE LANDMARK TRUST

Was this a reference to the grotto/cave in the hillside? There is no mention of the formal niches and terracing – is this because they were not there or are omitted simply as not fitting into his rustic idyll? Tantalisingly in a poem of 1748 Dr Sneyd Davies praises Knowle and its 'grotto's waving slopes,' 'thy cave's recess'.[105] Oh for an accurate and down to earth prose description!

After Hardinge's death in 1758, Sir Robert Burdett of Foremark rented Knowle while Foremark Hall was being rebuilt between 1759 and 1763 and then purchased it as a small retreat. He demolished Walter Burdett's house and replaced it with a smaller one, adding a charming gothick summerhouse or prospect tower on the edge of the terrace in 1769. Thereafter Knowle was used for picnic parties from Foremark Hall: a form of entertainment much enjoyed by Sir Robert (*vide* Anchor church). One argument is that the cave and classical niches were made at this time, but Sir Robert does seem to have preferred the romance of gothick with his crenellated summer house.

Knowle Hill became increasingly dilapidated and overgrown, with the house tenanted as a cottage. By the mid-twentieth century much of the land and woodland had been alienated, and the cottage and summer house ruinous. The Landmark Trust acquired it in 1989, restored derelict buildings and started the daunting task of clearing the gardens and valley of undergrowth and Forestry Commission conifers. This is a wonderfully atmospheric place, with much yet to be explained.

Notes

1.   S. Switzer, *Ichnographia Rustica*, vol. 1 (1718), 81.
2.   George London to Thomas Coke at Hampton Court n.d. HMC, 12th Report, Appendix. Pt. III, *MSS of the Earl Cowper, preserved at Melbourne House*, vol. 3 (1889), 179.
3.   Switzer, *Ichnographia*, 82.
4.   Francis Webb wrote to Switzer from Radburne Hall in 1733, and it is clear Switzer had visited Kedleston that year. Switzer was paid £15 in 1732 by Chas Chandos Pole-though this may just be for seeds and plants. W. A. Brogden, Stephen Switzer, *Garden Design in Britain in the Early Eighteenth Eentury* (PhD thesis, University of Edinburgh, 1973), 302, 325. Accessed online.
5.   Earl of Chesterfield to Thomas Coke, 21 May 1702, *MSS of the Earl Cowper*, vol. 3, 9; Earl of Chesterfield to Thomas Coke, 3 June 1701, *MSS of Earl Cowper*, vol. 2 (1888), 427.
6.   M. Woods and A. Warren, *Glass Houses: A History of Greenhouses, Orangeries and Conservatories* (1988), 32–33.
7.   *MSS of the Earl Cowper*, vol. 3, 73.
8.   Lady Elizabeth Coke to Thomas Coke, 2 Aug. 1707, *MSS of the Earl Cowper*, vol. 3, 77–78; 8 April 1711, 173.
9.   *DM*, 1 Dec. 1752, 4.
10. Craven and Stanley, I, 53.
11. Marquis of Halifax to Earl of Chesterfield, 23 Aug. 1683, *Letters of Philip, 2nd Earl of Chesterfield to Several Celebrated Individuals* (1835), 247.
12. J. Harris, *William Talman* (1982), 44.
13. *Letters of Philip, 2nd Earl of Chesterfield*, 63. This letter is from his memoirs.
14. Sir Edward Bagot, Blithfield Hall, Staffs to Sir Roger Newdigate, Arbury Hall, Warks, 30 May 1705: WRO Newdigate papers CR136/ B1419.
15. C. Glover and P. Riden (eds), W. Woolley, *History of Derbyshire* (1712), Derbyshire Record Society 6 (1981), 149.
16. C. Morris (ed.) *The Illustrated Journeys of Celia Fiennes 1685–c.1712* (1982), 153–54.

17. E. Hagglund, 'Cassandra Willoughby's Visits to Country Houses', *Georgian Journal* 11 (2001), 196.

18. D. and S. Lysons, *Magna Britannia, Being a Concise Topographical Account of the Several Counties of Great Britain*, vol. 5 (1817), 241. A few traces of various levels of part of the garden are said to survive hidden in undergrowth: see South Derbyshire District Council, 'Bretby Conservation Area Character Statement' (2010), 10–11, accessed on line.

19. Chesterfield at Bretby to Coke at St James Palace, 22 June 1706, *MSS of the Earl Cowper*, vol. 3, 72–73.

20. Elizabeth Coke to Tho. Coke, 2 August 1707, *ibid.*, 77–78.

21. Lysons, *Universal British Directory* (1793) Staffordshire with Ashbourne and Birmingham, 422.

22. *DM*, 16 & 23 June 1780, 3; 2 July 1779, 1. Over 30–40 tons of large lead pipes were for sale, some of which must have been from the garden waterworks.

23. R. Blomfield and F. Inigo Thomas, *The Formal Garden in England* (1892), 65.

24. H. Colvin, *A Biographical Dictionary of British Architects 1600–1830* (1995), 264–65.

25. W. Stratford to Thomas Coke, 27 May 1706, *MSS of the Earl Cowper*, vol. 3, 71.

26. C. Hussey, *English Gardens and Landscapes 1700–1750* (Country Life 1967), 57–58; map of 1690. Reproduced P. Kerr, 'Melbourne Hall, Derbyshire', *CL* 7 April 1928, 498.

27. London to Coke, 20 Aug. 1701, *MSS of Earl Cowper*, vol. 2, 43.

28. Earl of Chesterfield to Tho. Coke, 21 May 1702, *MSS of Earl Cowper*, vol. 3, 9.

29. Hussey, *English Gardens*, 59 n/d.

30. Quoted Hussey, *English Gardens*, 61. Hussey's chapter has formed the basis for much of the writing on Melbourne since, including this piece. Craven and Stanley, II, 150–51.

31. *Melbourne Hall Gardens*: Guidebook (1984), 4.

32. Hagglund, Cassandra Willoughby's Visits, 197.

33. Hussey, *English Gardens*, 61; Bill of 7 August 1706 displayed at Melbourne Hall's exhibition 'Up the Garden Path.' Problems with moulds delayed delivery so the bill was not submitted until August 1706.

34. P. Eyres (ed.) 'The Blackamoor and the Georgian Garden', *New Arcadian Journal* 69/70 (2011), 52–62.

35. Elizabeth Coke to Tho. Coke, 30 July 1705, *MSS of the Earl Cowper*, vol. 3, 165.

36. Elizabeth Coke to Thomas Coke 19 Oct. 1706, *ibid.*, 167.

37. Chesterfield at Bretby to Coke at St James Palace, 22 June 1706, *ibid.*, 72–73.

38. Elizabeth Coke to Tho. Coke, 8 May 1710, *MSS of the Earl Cowper*, vol. 3, 170.

39. C. Bruyn Andrews (ed.), *The Torrington Diaries*, vol. 2 (1935), 73–74.

40. Blomfield and Inigo Thomas, *The Formal Garden*, 154, 222.

41. National Trust, *Calke Abbey* (1996), 8–12, 22–23, 83.

42. Hagglund, Cassandra Willoughby's Visits, 194.

43. G. Jackson Stops, 'Restoring the Garden at Calke,' *CL*, 18 May 1989, based on research by Philip Heath.

44. *Calke Guidebook*, 81–82.

45. See also H. Colvin, *Calke Abbey, A Hidden House Revealed* (1985), 123.

46. *Ibid.*; H. Colvin, 'Calke Abbey, Derbyshire I', *CL*. 20 October 1983, 1065.

47. DRO: D2375M/296/2, estate map 1761.

48. DRO: D2375M/264/11 folio 19 April 1745; D2375M//76/122 – Lady Caroline's Expenses, 1750.

49. DRO: D6430/2/8 Howard Colvin's working papers, letter 8 August 1724 'R. S.' to T. C. [Thomas Coke] (X94 Lothian Box 219).

50. My thanks to Bert Cove for his guidance on-site; Colvin, *Calke Abbey*, 125–26.

51. *Calke Guidebook*, 76. Shown on the 1761 estate map by four dots, it might have been a kiosk or gazebo with canvas sides.

52. Quoted P. Edwards, 'The Gardens at Wroxton Abbey, Oxfordshire,' *Garden History* Spring 1986, 55.

53. T. Mowl and D. Barre, *The Historic Gardens of England: Staffordshire* (2009), 107–109.

54. DRO: D6430/2/8 Lady Harpur in Bath to Mr Cheetham at Calke, 5 September 1746. Copy letter in Howard Colvin's working papers. Lady Caroline's State Bed at Calke Abbey (c.1734) with its Chinese silk hangings has a dark blue background.

55. *Ibid.*, Lady Harpur to Mr. Cheetham, 10 March 1753.

56. Colvin, *Calke Abbey*, 125.

57. Craven and Stanley, I, 141–43.

58. Woolley, *History of Derbyshire*, 125.

59. Information from Mrs S. M. Barnes of Longford Hall in May 2000.

60. WSL/2/42/42 Journal of James Reading Folio 49, August 1724.

61. Quoted Craven and Stanley, I, 141.

62. DRO: D3249/3 – Map of 1834; D804/A/P1 48a tithe map 1840. The canals had been joined and widened on the 1890 OS map.

63. *A History, Gazetteer and Directory of the County of Derby* (1857), 213.

64. Craven and Stanley, I, 141; OS map 1890; DRO: D302/ES9 Sale particulars for Longford estate, 1920, which also mention an old bowling green. *DTCH* 28 Aug. 1920, 3. *CL*, 6 May 1905, 630–36.

65. DRO: D3287/21/8/4 19 March 1757; address unknown; also quoted in full: J. Sleigh, 'Sir John Statham of Wigwell', *Journal of the Derbyshire Archaeological and Natural History Society* 4 (1882), 38–39.

66. Journal of James Reading, entry 28 March 1724. However he still became Sheriff of the county 1725–26.

67. D. Hayton *et al.* (eds), *The History of Parliament: The House of Commons* 1690–1715 (2002), 557; www.wirksworth.org.uk/PR087.htm accessed May 2013 for Statham birth dates.

68. *DM*, 26 Jan. 1759, 4.

69. Craven and Stanley, II, 319–20; Woolley, *History of Derbyshire*, 199. A Regency house replaced it.

70. Journal of James Reading, April 1726.

71. Sleigh, 'Sir John Statham', 39–40. reproduced in J. Pendleton, *A History of Derbyshire* (1886), 51.

72. DRO:D7107/4/1, Sale of Wigwell Grange, 1892. 1882 OS map.

73. A. Gomme, *Smith of Warwick* (2000), 47, 116–17, 219.

74. L. Harris, *Robert Adam and Kedleston* (1987), illus. 52 and 53. The estate map (pre-1758) is on display in Kedleston Hall. Bridgeman's design for the cascade matches the canal with cascades shown on this map.

75. Journal of James Reading, ff. 45–48, May–August 1724.

76. Woolley, *History of Derbyshire*, 96.

77. F. Webb to S. Switzer, 20 Sept. 1733 quoted Brogden, Stephen Switzer, p. 302.

78. P. Willis, *Charles Bridgeman and the English Landscape Garden* (2002), p. 87. Illustrated in J. Gibbs, *Book of Architecture, containing designs of buildings and ornaments* (1728), plate LXX. In Sept. 1726 Gibbs received ten pounds, probably for the design of the temple.

79. Illustrated in National Trust, *Kedleston Hall Guidebook* (Swindon, 2010 edn), pp. 32–33.

80. Keldeston Archives: George Ingram's map of the estate (1764) has a plan of these gardens. I thank Simon McCormack of the National Trust for supplying a copy.

81. WRO: CR 1841/7 Lady Sophia Newdigate's Travel Journal, 5 Sept. 1747.

82. WRO: CR136/B/2668a Mary Conyers' Travel Journey, Sept. 1747.

83. HMC MSS of Rye and Hereford Corporations, 13th Report, appx IV, appendix E (1892), Rev. John Nixon to Miss Mary Bacon, 14 Sept. 1745, accessed on line December 2015. I am grateful to Sue Gregory and Randle Knight for this source.

84. T. Mowl, *The Historic Gardens of England Series: Oxfordshire* (2007), 58–59.

85. See S. Bennett, *Five Centuries of Women and Gardeners* (2000), 62–67.

86. S. Chauncy Woolsey, *The Autobiography and Correspondence of Mrs Delany* (revised from Lady Llanover's edition), vol. 1 (1879), 336. She sketched the quarry in 1746: National Gallery of Ireland, Mrs Delany's sketchbook, no. 41.

87. *The Gentleman's Magazine* 14 (1744), 44; printed in the *DM* 18 Nov. 1743. A portrait of Lady Curzon at Keldeston depicts her as a fashionable shepherdess with what might be the Ireton gardens behind. The Kedleston archives have further details of Lady Curzon, her literary circle and her garden which the author hopes to access in due course.

88. L. Harris, *Robert Adam and Kedleston* (1987), 84–85.

89. E. Jewitt (ed.) *Black's 1872 Tourist's Guide to Derbyshire* (1999), 228.

90. Woolley, *History of Derbyshire*, 142.

91. The background information for this account is from H. Usher, *Knowle Hill Ticknall, and the Burdetts* (2006) and Charlotte Haslam's unpublished notes on the history and restoration of Knowle for the Landmark Trust. I am grateful to the Landmark Trust for permission to visit Knowle.

92. Elizabeth Coke to Tho. Coke in London, 6 April 1698. *MSS of the Earl Cowper* vol. 2, 372–73.

93. Walter Burdett to Tho. Coke, 28 July 1700. *ibid.*, 402.

94. Earl of Chesterfield to Tho. Coke, 18 April 1704. *ibid.*, 34.

95. H. Usher, *Knowle Hill*, 14, 18

96. Britton and Wedlake Brayley, *The Beauties of England and Wales*, vol. 3 (1802), 402.

97. C. Haslam, *Knowle Hill, Notes on its History and Restoration* (Typescript, Landmark Trust, n.d.).

98. Burdett may have known Thomas Langley, another London barrister, who created a garden with two steep terraces supported by massive brick walls at Golding Hall, Cound, near Shrewsbury in the later seventeenth century. Originally the levels were linked to the house by interior corridors. I thank Mr Hartley for his guided tour and history of these gardens.

99. D.Bickerstaffe, 'The Chamber at Knowle Hill', *The Grampian Speleogical Group Bulletin*, 4 ser. 5 (1), Oct. 2011, 13–14 gives the overall length as 40 ft (12.2 m), including the two chambers 8 ft 6in and 6 ft 4in (*c.*2.6 × 1.9 m) long.

100. Haslam, *Knowle Hill*, 10–11.

101. V. Rolf, *Bathing Houses and Plunge Pools* (1988), 11–14.

102. Helen Lawrence, an authority on Thomas Archer's garden work, answered an enquiry from the author. She wrote that there was a mention of another Burdett family member in Archer's notebooks, but nothing else. Also she noted that Archer probably created cascades on the circuit walk at Heythrop. Archer worked (1706) at Cliveden House, Buckinghamshire which had a terrace with an arcade of blank niches underneath (by William Winde).

103. N. Hardinge, 'Knoll Hills, written in 1735', in *Poems, Latin, Greek and English: to which is added an historical Enquiry and Essay* (1818), 129, 131. (google ebook).

104. *Ibid.*, 132–33, 135.

105. Haslam, *Knowle Hill*, 22.

CHAPTER FOUR

Capability Brown and William Emes

… the park swept over the garden.

Geometric formality in garden and landscape-park had been slowly, but surely, falling out of fashion by the 1730s with a talented generation of designers and writers popularising the concept of a more natural landscape with a degree of informality: Charles Bridgeman (1690–1738), Alexander Pope (1688–1744), Stephen Switzer (1682–1745), William Kent (1684–1748) and Batty Langley (1691–1751). Sometimes an individual landowner created a landscape which was sufficiently different to attract admiration and exert influence, such as Philip Southcote (1698–1758) with his *ferme ornée* at Woburn Farm (Surrey) in the late 1730s and the poet William Shenstone (1714–63) at the pastoral Leasowes (Worcestershire) in the 1740s. From the 1750s Lancelot 'Capability' Brown (1716–83) supplied and popularised a formula for landscapes which could be applied nationally, appealing to a new generation ready for a revolution in style. Influenced by Brown, but working independently, William Emes (1729–1803), Derbyshire's own landscaper, was consulted by a wide range of wealthy clients from the 1760s.

A reminder of just how complex a design could be is shown by proposals on an estate map *c.*1737, for **Foremark**. Sir Robert Burdett, third baronet (1640–1716) inherited in 1696 and his accounts books show expenditure on his formal gardens with their waterworks, yew arbour, 'Grass Plots and Walks'.[1] Woolley noted a 'well wooded park and coney [rabbit] warren adjoining'.[2] When Sir Robert, fourth baronet (1716–97) came of age in 1737, he apparently considered an ambitious remodelling of the park, as detailed on a large (60 × 80 in/150 × 200 cm) and remarkable map.[3] The proposals are aristocratic in scale, sophisticated and hugely expensive, despite utilising existing pools, woodland and park avenues.

Ponds and cascades are clearly influenced by Charles Bridgeman who had worked at Kedleston in the 1720s. Wide areas of open lawn or grassland have formal circular clumps of trees and most spectacular of all – an extraordinary huge bastion, whose outline resembles a fortification. Twelve points radiate from a circle, at whose centre is a raised area with a baroque 'basilica' shaped 'lodge or stand in ye highest Point of view in ye Park'. This may be influenced by Switzer's plan for an octagonal kitchen garden (*Practical Kitchen Gardener* (1727), pl. 13). It would have been a massive undertaking, with wide avenues radiating from it, presumably through existing woodland. More informal (and modern) is a grove plentifully supplied with springs and brooks, where curving paths meander and link formal open spaces, the largest of which has a large cold bath or plunge pool with an octagonal conduit to supply it and the house.[4] There are four 'little fountains or Batheing Places', each a different shape, while little squares could indicate statues, making a truly sophisticated, magical private area, with the sound of water everywhere.

With its water gardens and martial themes, buildings such as a Rotondo, 'An Open Circular Temple', Alcove Seats and statues and a Menagerie near the house its concept and scale would rival nearby Bretby and even Chatsworth. Who was the designer? Switzer had been at Radburne and Kedleston in 1733.[5] His concept of the Forest Garden with informal walks, features in groves, the bastion fortification, all figure here. Recently Charles Bridgeman had designed the canal and cascades complex at Kedleston, and the cascade rills shown are a typical Bridgeman feature. The sophistication of the plunge bath area, military precision of the avenues, clumps and circles, combined with the buildings (baroque in outline plan), suggest that this could possibly be a James Gibbs/ Bridgeman landscape design: the two worked together at Kedleston in 1725. Whoever designed it, such a scheme was the last gasp of the formal baroque park, which stylistically was already outdated. Unsurprisingly the proposals were not implemented.

By the 1730/40s there was a mixed reaction to the formal gardens at **Chatsworth**. In 1735 John Loveday still felt that 'The waterworks here are esteemed the best in England… Nothing in short can be more grand and elegant'.[6] However carping criticism came from visitors who wished to show that their taste reflected fashionable new trends. In 1747 Lady Sophia Newdigate pronounced that 'The waterworks are very fine in the old fashioned Taste'.[7] Once the third Duke of Devonshire (1698–1755) inherited in 1729, simplification of the elaborate gardens began. A painting by Thomas Smith of Derby *c.*1743 (at Chatsworth) shows much simplified walled gardens, with lawns replacing the upper terraced parterres east of the house, leading up to the bosquets, now also more informal, on the hill above. The result was still rather formal, rigid and inward looking to the south, but outward looking, simple and informal above to the east. As part of these changes the Greenhouse and Bowling Green House were moved to their present position in the late 1740s. In spite of the great expense of maintaining pipes and sluices, many famous water features were retained.

In the late 1730s William Kent produced some delightful drawings with fairy tale, extravagant ideas for huge Palladian garden buildings in an informal wooded landscape at Chatsworth, suitable for the duke to discuss with friends at convivial gatherings rather than actually build.[8] It is however quite possible that it was Kent who suggested creating the expanses of lawn and informal planting beyond the walled gardens.[9]

Dramatic changes came once the fourth duke inherited in 1755 at the age of 35, although he died just nine years later. He wanted a more coherent overall plan, so between 1759 and 1767 'Capability' Brown continued the simplification,

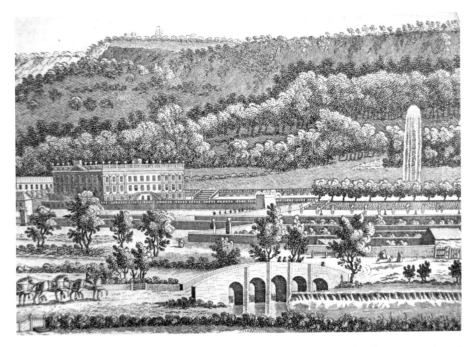

FIGURE 44. Chatsworth from the south-west, after Thomas Smith of Derby (*c.*1743).

AUTHOR'S COLLECTION

completely transforming the landscape. Garden walls were finally removed and replaced by ha-has and serpentine paths replaced old formal walks within the remaining gardens and shubberies. A new landscape park was created with the removal of roads and old hedges, planting new clumps of trees, re-contouring and forming pastureland. In accordance with new fashions the Kitchen Garden was moved further away from the house.

The result was revolutionary for Chatsworth. The house now dominated parkland down to the widened river below, which was given a new importance after the levelling of ground around it. The Tudor fish ponds and canals were filled in and the clutter of old stables, barns etc, to the north of the house were removed. The fashionable architect James Paine designed a huge new classical stable block (1763) and a new bridge (1762) for access over the river to the north wing, now the principal entrance of the house. The bridge was then embellished with statues removed from the gardens. Paine's classical Corn Mill of 1761–62 became, as it is still, an attractive eye-catcher in the park.

Chatsworth is one of Brown's most attractive, confident and successful landscapes, which, although hugely prestigious, was to be his only commission in Derbyshire. A large range of new trees and shrubs were added to the pleasure grounds, including new varieties from America, which added colour later in the year. Happily, some links with the past were retained with Queen Mary's Bower and the Hunting Tower and the celebrated water features of The Cascade, Willow Tree, Canal Pool and Sea Horse fountain. Yet their retention drew criticism for years to come. When Arthur Young visited in 1771, in the true spirit of the age, he praised the woods and the river, but

as to the waterworks, which have given it the title of Versailles in miniature, they might be great exertions in the last age; but ... such fine things as these are now beheld with the utmost indifference.[10]

In 1778 William Bray was irritated that while 'The conceits in the water-works might be deemed wonderful when they were made, it is high time they should be destroyed'.[11] The poetess Anna Seward naturally disapproved of the 'forced and formal cascade', believing that the water should 'strike the eye with transient sublimity and roar adown the mountain...'[12]

More important than Brown in Derbyshire was William Emes, Head Gardener at Kedleston, who inaugurated changes in the landscape there between 1756 and 1760, before leaving with the ascendancy of Robert Adam. From his new home at Bowbridge House near Derby Emes then set up a successful practice as a landscape designer, producing beautifully drawn plans which he would oversee if required. The hallmarks of an Emes plan are a narrow irregular or serpentine lake or linked pools, clumps of trees in fairly open parkland, curving paths in long walks in shrubberies and thin woodland, a few carefully placed garden buildings and the re-siting of flower gardens near the house.

In Derbyshire, besides Kedleston, Emes can be connected with some confidence with work at Foremark (1763); Calke Abbey (1776); Markeaton and Shipley (1770s); Wingerworth (1777); Darley Park (1778); Alderswasley (1784); Osmaston (1789); Radburne (17900; and Locko Park (1792). Unfortunately many landscapes have suffered badly in Derbyshire, making it difficult to appreciate them fully and there are doubtless others undocumented. In 1789 Emes moved away from the county after the death of his wife, and the sale of his house contents indicate his prosperity, with items such a 'handsome Four-Post Bed… A Collection of Capital Prints, drawings and pictures; A handsome fine-toned Organ made by Green, cost 50 Guineas'.[13]

Leaving Kedleston for later consideration, an early commission was **Foremark Hall**, where it seems that actually Sir Robert Burdett, fourth baronet, did little on the estate until his marriage to Catherine, widow of Sir Henry Harpur of Calke in 1753. The Hall was rebuilt as a large Palladian house in 1759 and then Emes, recently moved from Kedleston, was commissioned to create new pleasure grounds and parkland, for which no plans survive.[14] We know that roses and flowering shrubs were purchased between 1761–65, probably for shrubberies.[15] There was extensive tree planting, with Arthur Young noting in 1771 that some of the distant plantations on the hills were young and that the pleasure grounds were not yet completed. Young praised the picturesque woody walk to the river Trent, with the sudden surprise of the cliffs down to it, with their precipitous walks 'one of the greatest curiosities in this country [county]'.[16] Fashionably, two existing pools were formed into a lake, which received lukewarm praise:

> were the dimensions of this pellucid sheet somewhat more enlarged it would become a very interesting feature in the scenery, but it is at present too diminutive; and, except from the walk in the grove, where its boundaries are not visible, conveys an idea of insignificance rather than grandeur.[17]

At **Calke Abbey,** once Sir Henry Harpur (1739–89) sixth baronet came of age, he commissioned Samuel Wyatt to survey the estate. The survey showed that, other than a lawn replacing old fashioned parterres, the gardens had retained their formal outline, while formal avenues stretched across the park. In 1764–65 William Emes was called in to simplify the gardens and bring them up-to-date. Unfortunately his 'Plans and Estimates for Gardens and Pleasure Ground at Caulk' have not survived and he was not paid until 1776.[18] It is uncertain to what extent Emes' plans were executed and it seems that Sir Henry himself preferred to direct the innovations. Certainly any remaining formal garden went and a new large four-acre (1.7 ha) walled garden was created in 1773, well away from the house. This was the traditional mix of productive and ornamental, with a heated five-bay classical conservatory (1777), to which a dome was added in 1836. There was a physic garden and flower garden while its brick walls were screened from the house by trees and shrubs. Most of the formal avenues in the park were removed and the park itself increased to 500 acres during the 1770s.[19] As Glover enthused in 1829:

> It is a noble mansion, standing in the centre of an extensive park, of which the verdant and well wooded elevations rise on all sides from the Abbey. These elevations afford rich and interesting prospects, and the valleys which intersect them are adorned with venerable oaks and other ancient forest trees. Few spots exceed this in variety, and wood intermixed with sheets of water is met with amid this charming diversity of hill and dale.[20]

There is a gap before Emes' next known Derbyshire commission, in 1772, at **Shipley**, which had come to a cadet branch of the Mundy family of Markeaton, with the marriage of Edward Mundy (d. 1767) to the Shipley heiress, Hester Miller. The couple built a new house in 1749–50 within existing, fairly simple, formal pleasure grounds with intersecting paths, wilderness and pool. Their son Edward Miller Mundy (1750–1822) inherited in 1767, with his sister Hester running the estate between 1767 and 1772. Once Mundy achieved his majority he called in Emes to improve the parkland. Emes' bill of estimates for December 1772 survives, but unfortunately not the accompanying plan. The total came to £171 9s 3½d, which was to prepare the ground around the house, including much levelling, filling in a ha-ha and 'the hollow road' (old village street), and also preparing the ground for 604 yards (552 m) of walks, seven ft (2.1 m) wide, and cutting and laying turf, 72 yards (66 m) wide, either side.[21] The planting of ornamental hollies may date from this period, as they were noted as 'immense' 100 years later.[22] This is simply part of a wider scheme, which included the removal of the old formal gardens when Miller Mundy rebuilt or remodelled the house 1778–79. The three irregular long lakes shown on an early nineteenth-century estate map are very much in Emes' style.[23]

Emes' 1772 estimates rather unexpectedly mention 'leaving the inside of the Menagery to be finished at leisure.' When Lady Hester Miller (now Lady Newdigate) visited her former home in 1781 she wrote that 'I have been to the Menagery, seen 12 fine young Pheasants, and I have taken upon me to order some Alterations for their Security from Ratts'.[24] More often a 'Menagerie' was an Aviary, an exotic place to entertain visitors and would have proved useful as such when Miller Munday became MP for Derbyshire from 1783 to 1822. At this period the village was moved away to its present site, facilitating the family's mining ventures from the mid-1760s. However, by the 1820s collieries encircled the hall and park, proving fatal to both.[25]

The twentieth century was not kind to **Markeaton Hall** and park. In 1929 Derby Borough Council was given the Hall for use as an art gallery or museum, but, following 30 years of neglect, it was demolished in 1963. Joseph Pickford's Orangery survives but is defaced with anti-vandal window covering. Now a public park, the Derby bypass (A38) has sliced Emes' long lake, and Derby University's tower block looms over the area, making it rather difficult to appreciate a once picturesque landscape.

The timber framed Tudor house was rebuilt in 1755, when its old fashioned gardens walls were presumably demolished at the same time. This new house was then remodelled following the inheritance and marriage in 1770 of Noel Clarke Mundy (1739–1815) to Elizabeth Burdett of Foremark Hall. The couple belonged to Derbyshire's intellectual circles and entertained widely. Their new nine-bay Palladian orangery was used for entertaining, its east pavilion fitted as a kitchen with formal planting in front and classical urns (Pl. 12).[26] Although altered, appropriately it serves as tea-rooms today. Ironically, their new Tuscan portico to the house, erected in the 1790s, was thought old fashioned by

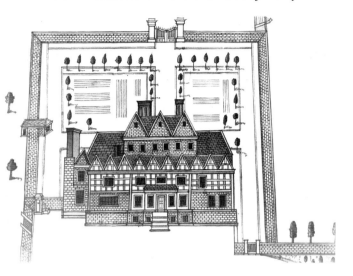

1904, and removed to the far end of the west walk as an eye-catcher. There it survives today, partly concealed behind shrubs, while generations of locals have enthusiastically carved their initials on its stonework.

The Mundys, with their fashionable appreciation of natural landscape, wanted to improve their own landscape, which was flat but plentifully supplied with streams. So they called in William Emes, living at nearby Bowbridge Fields. Soon fashionable lawns came up to the house, the village was moved, while a picturesque mill and cascade were incorporated into the scene. Emes created shelter belts of trees and plantations with walks and his trade-mark long, narrow, serpentine lake from a brook in 1776.[27] The result was pleasant but somewhat uninspiring.

Mundy was a romantic at heart and (of course) a poet. He rented Eland Lodge, in Needwood Forest, as a hunting box and inspiration for his muse and 'inspired with the thousand natural charms around him penned the beautiful poem *Needwood Forest*.[28] Written in 1776, this was much admired at the time and shows Mundy's regard for William Emes, who said that he took his best ideas from the scenery at Needwood:

> Emes, who yon desart wild explor'd,
> And to its name the scene restor'd;
> Whose art is Nature's law maintain'd,
> Whose order negligence restrain'd,
> Here, fir'd by native beaut , trac'd
> The foot-steps of the Goddess, Taste.
> Won from her coy retreats she came,
> And led him up these paths to fame.

Sadly both house and park at **Wingerworth**, near Chesterfield, were lost in the 1920s, but fortunately Emes' plan of 1777 survives and is one of his more imaginative and confident. The Hunlokes, who owned the Wingerworth estate

FIGURE 46 *(left)*. Markeaton Hall, Derby, drawing 1753. Detail of Sir John Mundy's Tudor house shortly before demolition.

FIGURE 47 *(right)*. Markeaton Hall (1755), with fashionable lawns up to the house. Late eighteenth-century print.

from the late sixteenth century, were Catholics and thus excluded from public office until 1829. Fortuitously their taste for lavish expenditure was supported by rents from their extensive lands and by various industrial activities on the estate, which by the mid-nineteenth century included iron works and collieries.[29]

Francis Smith of Warwick designed a splendid Baroque house for Sir Thomas Windsor Hunloke (1684–1752), third baronet, who inherited in 1715. Much influenced by nearby Chatsworth, it had grand interiors and furniture.[30] When Henry Hunloke, fourth baronet (1724–1804), inherited in 1752 he approached William Baker of Audlem to re-plan the 107 acre (43 ha) park.[31] According to a surviving estate map of 1758 formal gardens near the hall had been replaced by lawns but wide formal avenues survived on two sides of the house.[32] Also intact were three fish ponds at the front of the hall, and two more, much larger, in the park, one with an island (Pl. 13).

With more money coming in from a new venture of coalmining on the estate, William Emes was approached in 1777 to extend and redesign the park.[33] He suggested that the three fish ponds before the house be enlarged to create a single 'reservoir'. In the parkland, the large pond with an island should be enlarged to form a small lake, with the typical Emes 'tadpole tail'. The formal avenues were to be reduced to form fashionable clumps, with selected trees from former hedgerows left as single specimens. The house, next to the church, stables and extensive outbuildings would be set in a much extended woodland with a perimeter walk and views out. Although the standard perimeter belt of trees encircles the park, the emphasis is on the new rides and drives which meander around the interior.

Just south of the house an 'Exotic House' (greenhouse), with views over the park, would be glimpsed as you drove along the approach to the house. The only park building, this was an important element in the landscape and circuit and was 'Guarded from the Deer', as was the house, not by a ha-ha but 'Post and Single rail to keep the Cattle from the Windows'. The kitchen garden was some considerable distance from the house, in the new Brownian fashion of the period, and approached by a gravel walk from the house. It is not clear how much of his plan was effected, but a map of 1819 shows the kitchen garden as drawn and formal avenues swept away more robustly than Emes had proposed.[34]

The Hurts, another established county family owned **Alderwasley** from 1690, and developed lucrative industrial interests based on iron and lead on their land, with a forge erected in 1764 near the river Derwent (carefully screened from the estate by a thick belt of trees). A modern iron smelting furnace near Heage followed in 1780. These industrial interests were furthered by the marriage of Francis Hurt (1753–1801) to Elizabeth Shuttleworth in 1778 and the marriage of his brother Charles to Susanna Arkwright, of neighbouring Willersley, in 1780. Francis' son was to marry another Arkwright in 1802, by which time extra purchases of land bought the estate to over 3000 acres (c.1215 ha).

On inheriting the estate in 1783 Francis Hurt enlarged and modernised the house and then commissioned William Emes to bring the parkland up-to-date.

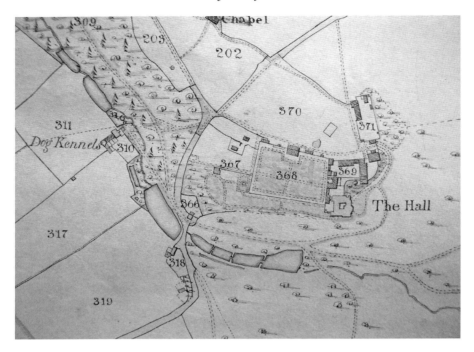

FIGURE 48. Alderwasley, tithe map 1841 DRO, showing Emes' kitchen garden; linked fishpond below.

Emes' 1784 proposals show a well-wooded estate with an area of open parkland balanced by areas for sheep pasture and meadows – the Hurts were after all down to earth entrepreneurs as well as owners of a country estate. Two typical Emes' features are shown: a long narrow, partly walled, kitchen garden near the house with a small flower garden next to it. A single walk winds its way through the thick woods, with just one open temple or alcove indicated along the way, completely surrounded by trees, and with no view out. Another walk, through an elliptical belt of trees which encircles a sheep pasture, does have a few vistas across.[35] The 1841 tithe map suggests that the kitchen garden was made, although to a different shape, and the string of fishponds have not been replaced by Emes's suggestion of just two.[36] The whole plan is oddly unsatisfactory. One would have expected Emes to create a more impressive lake from the ponds, but perhaps Francis Hurt was not prepared for the expense. Certainly his son appears to have regarded trees above all as a source of income:

> The hall is a handsome and substantial built stone mansion, situate on rising ground on the west bank of the river Derwent, surrounded by hanging woods that crown the neighbouring hill. A deer park and rich lawn, adorned with venerable oaks, spreads before the mansion and affords many beautiful landscapes... The timber on this estate is considered equal to any in the kingdom; and trees of great magnitude have been felled. For many years past Mr Hurt has regularly cut down timber producing upwards of £2000 per annum.[37]

The Hurts sold the estate in 1920 and Alderwasley is now a special school.

By 1790 Emes had been designing landscapes for nearly 30 years, he was firmly established and his style had become more fluid and confident, as seen at **Radburne**. A map of the estate (1711) has a stylised drawing of a gabled house next to the church, with ten acres of 'orchards, yards and gardens' to one side and the 32-acre (13 ha) 'cuningrey' (rabbit warren) on the other.[38] There was a substantial kitchen garden with a hothouse for melons and at least one fish pond.[39] The present Palladian house, 'most perfect of all the Georgian houses in Derbyshire', was built nearby between 1739 and 1745, for the Jacobite, German Pole (d. 1765).[40] He was succeeded by his nephew, Colonel Edward Sacheverel Pole (1718–80), a military hero who had been seriously wounded in the Seven Years War. In 1769, at the age of 51, the Colonel married the 21-year-old Elizabeth Collier, half-sister to Lady Curzon of Kedleston. In retirement he settled down to farming, breeding cattle and growing wheat, much to the approval of Arthur Young:

> Colonel Pole is an honourable instance of a change from war to agriculture; he has long trod the field of *Mars* with sprit: I have little doubt but he will now sacrifice to *Ceres* with equal ardour.[41]

Elizabeth Pole was keenly interested in her garden at Radburne, and appears to have been rather charming, lively and likeable and also an excellent mother.[42] Certainly she charmed Dr Erasmus Darwin when he treated her children in the 1770s. Darwin, then in his 40s, developed an unrequited passion for Mrs Pole and against the odds she agreed to marry him in 1781, after the death of Colonel Pole. The marriage turned out to be very happy, the couple both having

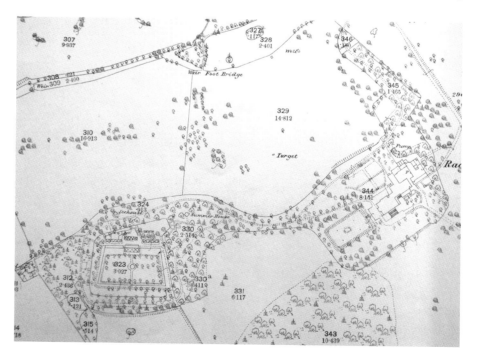

FIGURE 49. Radburne Hall, 1886 OS map shows implementation of Emes' plan with linked ponds (top), oval shrubbery, with new kitchen garden (left). Map at DRO.

a passion for nature, gardening and for their children. Elizabeth produced a further seven children with Darwin, in a household which had her three other children plus assorted illegitimate children of both husbands – not exactly the conventional home. They only lived at Radburne for two years, after which when they moved to Derby.[43]

Sacheverel Pole (1769–1813) came of age in 1790 and once he inherited the Radburne estate, perhaps as a gesture of independence from his loved, but somewhat dominant mother and step-father, he almost immediately married a much younger woman.[44] William Emes was approached to redesign the landscape. He suggested damming a nearby stream to create a series of long, gently sinuous and narrow pools, which gave the appearance a river from a distance.[45] These had small wooded islands, and the largest had a fishing house and boat house. From the house a path led to a large oval shrubbery, where an open lawn in the centre had a 'greenhouse' conservatory and 'Mrs Pole's seat', positioned to look over the lawn viewed between trees and shrubs. There was the standard perimeter walk, separated from the surrounding sheep pasture and fields by a ha-ha.

For once Emes did not include a flower garden. The area around the house was also open lawn, which may have been Pole's reaction against what could have been extensive flower gardens of his mother. As Emes moved to Hampshire in 1790 John Webb, his former foreman, implemented much of the plan.

Approaching **Locko Park** today by the main entrance, with its late eighteenth-century classical lodges, the drive swerves round Emes' long lake of 1792 and then the 1720s' Baroque (original entrance) facade is seen briefly across parkland. In 1747 John Lowe (1704–71) purchased the Locko estate,

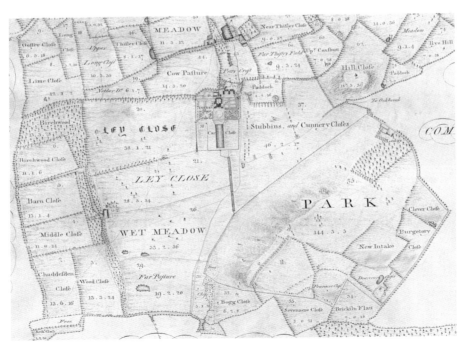

FIGURE 50. Locko Park, map 1763, surveyed by Beighton. The formal gardens survive.

MANUSCRIPTS AND SPECIAL COLLECTIONS, UNIVERSITY OF NOTTINGHAM, DRURY-LOWE DR4 P2

with its newly built house by Francis Smith of Warwick. An estate map of 1763 shows a very old fashioned layout of the gardens, which could even pre-date the Baroque house.[46] Formal areas surround the house, with wildernesses either side of the entrance-court. On the east side of the house a formal garden has a canal or moat on two sides. On the west side two lawns or bowling greens have a terrace walk and the kitchen gardens above them. To the rear of the house, are the stables and a series of spring fed fish ponds. These springs fed the moat and the large rectangular canal shown before the entrance forecourt. This area is empaled to separate it from pasture lands and the water supply then continues from the canal in a narrow straight ditch into the park.

When William Drury (1753–1827) inherited the estate in 1785, he took the name Drury Lowe and shortly afterwards, in 1792, approached William Emes for a plan to remove the old fashioned gardens and extend the park over the pasture land, doubling its size. Emes proposed a large new lake at its centre as the focal point.[47] He left the kitchen gardens near the house, with a large greenhouse overlooking quarters of neat planting. They would be doubled in size and given protective walls, concealed behind trees, as part of the pleasure grounds, to be included on a new walk. The walk wound round the wooded perimeter of the new park, utilising existing boundary trees and woodland including 'Birchwood', with several views over the new park. All of this could be achieved with a minimum of expense by utilising existing mature trees.

On the other hand the removal of the large formal canal, and its replacement by a new amoeba- shaped lake, a few hundred metres to the south, would have been a major effort. Its water supply came from the diverted long thin pond or ditch, noted by Emes as 'An open ditch to carry the flood waters into the lake'. The approach drive from Spondon was given entrance lodges with their own gardens and it then wound around the lake and curved up to the entrance of the house. What appears to be Emes's first proposal for the lake survives as an undated and unsigned plan.[48] Here the existing canal is retained and joined as an 'arm' to a new lake which is an irregular curved quadrant. The main approach road crosses this lake via a wooded island, and becomes a bridge over a thin stretch of water, before joining the Ockbrook approach drive to the house. This would certainly have given a dramatic approach to the house, but it was not a very practical scheme and was dropped.

Work was in hand by January 1793 when labourers were needed: '20 or 30 men to make Fish Ponds, and level Ground. Good hands will be employed for 12 or 18 Months certain'.[49] By 1800 much of Emes' plan had been put into effect, under the supervision of John Webb, who was also involved with work on the house, although the lake was given a somewhat different outline. Woodland strips with walks were in place, but two fields yet to be included in the enlarged park. More remained to be done as criticised in *The Beauties of England and Wales* (1802):

> [Locko] consists of agreeable slopes, and pleasant inequalities of ground, enlivened by a good artificial lake. The style of planting of the last century is however too apparent. The rows of trees in some places forming right angled triangles, and the clumps appearing tasteless and formal.[50]

The criticism was repeated by J. C. Loudon in 1822: 'the plantations ... made when the geometric taste was in fashion, do not accord well with the variations of the surface'.[51] This suggests that the park and land had more formal planting of avenues and clumps of trees than shown on the 1763 map, and that much still survived. In 1826 a public footpath and public bridleway were diverted from the park but the transformation of the gardens had to wait another 30 years.[52]

Emes was doubtless responsible for other undocumented landscapes in Derbyshire and his influence must have been considerable, as for example at The Pastures, Littleover, Derby (now Rykneld Hall). This compact, elegant and fashionable gentleman's villa was built by Josias Cockshutt in the 1780s with a small agricultural estate of 88 acres (35.6 ha), of which 14 were pleasure grounds. Plans from the 1841 and 1878 sales show a large open lawn with two pools, one the typical Emes 'tadpole' shape with an island, an informal walk round the pools and perimeter, and kitchen garden near the house.[53]

At **Kedleston** considerable changes came with Sir Nathaniel Curzon (1726–1804), created first Baron Scarsdale in 1761. In 1756 he took over the running of the estate from his elderly father (who died in 1758), and with his enthusiasm for classical architecture lost no time in commissioning Matthew Brettingham to design a new Palladian house. Soon James Paine was also involved, but in 1759 Robert Adam persuaded Sir Nathaniel that he was the man to create the required masterpiece and by 1760 Adam had sole charge. For over a decade the family lived in the attached pavilion wing during building work. Eventually, with the magnificent state rooms furnished with expensive furniture, silver, paintings and sculpture, Sir Nathaniel had achieved the desired result of showing his wealth, good taste, culture and artistic sophistication. He could compete with Chatsworth:

> *Kedleston*, the seat of Lord Scarsdale, which may properly be called the glory of Derbyshire, eclipsing *Chatsworth*, the ancient boast of the county… It is the ancient set of the *Curzons*, a family of great antiquity, wealth, and interest in this county.[54]

The young William Emes was appointed head gardener in 1756 and immediately began major landscape improvements. The scattered houses of the old village were removed to the western edge of the park and the public road was re-routed well away from the front of the house. Part of Bridgeman's old fashioned canal was broadened and the octagon pond made into the irregular upper lake with an island in the centre.[55] At some stage Bridgeman's formal terraces were removed to form a sloping lawn. Although Michael Henry Sprang's design for a three arched classical bridge in 1758 was not built, an elegant classical bath-house by Jason Harris was erected in 1759 and a delightful Gothic Temple 1758–60 was added on the edge of the Ireton Gardens.[56]

Emes was clearly a practical, imaginative and competent landscaper, but then came the surprising appointment of Robert Adam. As early as December 1758, after his first meeting with Curzon, Adam triumphantly wrote to his brother James, that he had:

> got the intire management of his [Curzon's] Grounds put into my hands with <u>full powers</u> as to Temples Bridges Seats and Cascades. So that as it only is Seven miles round you many guess the play of Genius and Scope for Invention. A noble piece of water, a man resolved to spare no Expense, with 10,000 a Year, Good Temper'd and having taste himself for the Arts and little for Game.[57]

FIGURE 52. Kedleston, gothic summer house 1758–60, near Ireton Gardens.

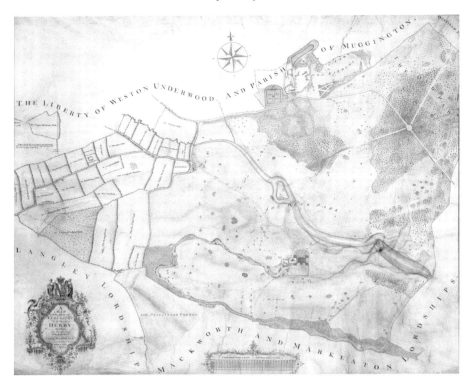

FIGURE 53. Kedleston Estate, Ingham's map 1764 with the conversion of the formal canal into informal lakes.

© NATIONAL TRUST IMAGES

Adam now had the opportunity to put forward ideas for expensive garden and park buildings, naturally to his designs, to a receptive young and wealthy client. He may even have thought he could have a useful secondary career in garden design, reflecting on the prestige and patronage being achieved by the equally ambitious and talented Capability Brown. It would certainly have opened up opportunities to extend his architectural practice. One can only imagine the chagrin of poor Emes, a local man, beginning to transform the landscape just as the wily cosmopolitan Adam, with his beautiful plans and drawings, persuaded Curzon that he was the best man for the job.

Adam's reference to a 'noble piece of water' confirms that Emes had begun to create the lake from the canal pool by late 1758.[58] Sensibly, William Emes promptly left Kedleston in April 1760, to develop his own successful landscaping career, leaving Robert Adam to put forward his own ideas for embellishing the landscape. These were numerous, inventive and often with ludicrously excessive architectural bravura. He started by offering a large classical domed Pheasant House with porticos, a classical pedimented greenhouse, a tall stone Milestone column and a classical four storey Viewing Tower 84 ft high and 50 ft wide (25.6 × 15.2 m) (to rival the old Elizabethan hunting tower at Chatsworth?).[59] Fortunately Lord Scarsdale (as Sir Nathaniel became in 1761), either because of the expense, or using common sense, selected just a few of the most attractive and sensible of the extravagant proposals.

With Capability Brown's perimeter walks and paths in mind, Adam's first design sketches 1759–60 for a new landscape park suggested a wooded perimeter walk around an area roughly the shape of a comma (site of the former village and agricultural strips), with a large open space within, divided by a central wooded path, all irregular in shape. One area was a park for red deer and the other for highland cattle and sheep to graze. On the perimeter circuit he suggested putting three temple eye-catchers/seats including a Pantheon, no doubt to rival Flitcroft's famous example (1753) at Stourhead, Wiltshire.[60] By the time of George Ingman's 1764 map this had evolved into the present 3 mile (4.8 km) 'Long Walk' or circuit. This starts west of the house and was extremely expensive and labour intensive in its execution, involving a huge amount of earth moving to raise the walk for the first mile, with a wide ha-ha on both sides. It weaves its way round as an irregular, roughly oval walk within a tree belt, with views over the pastoral landscape and park. Half-way along this walk there is a view across to the south façade of the house, where the house itself, with Adam's magnificent 'Triumphal Arch' centre and 'Pantheon' dome, seen across open lawns becomes an eye-catcher to be admired, no doubt from a suitable seat.

The first section of the walk was planted with flowering and scented shrubs, many purchased from a nursery at Ashbourne, run by the brother of the John Sandys, the new Kedleston gardener from 1760.[61] The only one of Adam's garden building actually erected seems to have been the Hermitage, 1761–62, encountered about half a mile (0.8 km) from the house. Presently ruined, this small circular sandstone building, originally thatched, had a large rough stone entrance arch and was much influenced by the designs of Thomas Wright.[62] No other buildings suggested by Adam in his initial plan appear to have been built, although no doubt there were rustic seats along the route.

It is open to debate exactly how much of the Long Walk, which was not completed until 1776, was actually the design of Robert Adam. Certainly it bears little resemblance to the shape of Adam's only surviving plan of 1760, and it is only through the absence of any other designer's name that it is attributed to Adam.[63] Indeed it is the only known garden plan in Robert Adam's own hand. He may possibly have reworked a suggestion by Emes, but so far there is no evidence for this. There is however another possible designer – Lady Caroline Curzon (1733–1812). Certainly Arthur Young attributed the walk to her in 1771:

> From the garden front Lady Scarsdale has traced with great taste a pleasure ground; a winding lawn decorated with tree, shrubs, and knots of wood, and a gravel walk through it … parted from the park on each side by a sunk fence; and as the scattered trees and clumps are prettily varied, they let in, as the walk rises on the hill, very picturesque views of the lake, and the adjoining woods. It rises to the summit and there commands a very noble prospect of all the adjacent country. You look down into the park vale, with a large river winding through it, accompanied with spreading lawns; and bounded by very noble woods of oak… The walk from hence, with its attendant decorations, is to be carried through many plantations quite around the fourth part of the park... It is then to lead through other woods down to the water, and follow its shore to the garden…[64]

FIGURE 54. Kedleston, Robert Adam's south front seen as an eye-catcher from the far side of the perimeter walk.

BY KIND PERMISSION OF THE NATIONAL TRUST.

Arguably the most exciting developments were to the north of the entrance front, to be admired by visitors on their approach to the house and also to be viewed from the house. The removal of the old road meant that a new approach was needed. Adam's brilliant North Lodge of 1760–62, based on the Arch of Octavia in Rome, gave a hint to visitors of the taste and aspirations of Lord Scarsdale. As always, an eye was kept on what was happening at Chatsworth where Capability Brown was naturalising the landscape and bringing the new approach road across a bridge (1762) over the river. Arthur Young's 1771 description of Kedleston again sets the scene with the on-going developments

> The approach from Derby is through one of these woods, and the road leaving it, you gain an oblique view of the house: by entering another very fine wood it is lost; but on coming out of the dark grove, you break at once on the house backed with spreading plantations, which when they all get up, will have a noble effect. The water winds before it through the vale in the most agreeable manner; you command both the reaches that form the island; and move up to the house over a fine bridge of three large arches.[65]

By now the Upper Lake had been in existence for over ten years, with Bridgeman's canals transformed into the Middle and Lower Lakes in the 1770s, which were linked by a cascade, crossed by Robert Adam's bridge. This was both the principal route to the house and also a splendid eye-catcher from the state-rooms of the house. Adam's first designs (1759–61) were for a single arched bridge over a cascade.[66] Naturally, once the Duke of Devonshire at Chatsworth had erected a three arched bridge designed by James Paine, Lord Scarsdale patently needed to compete with an even more impressive bridge. So Adam produced a revised design for a three arched bridge which was not erected until 1770/1.

Adam was almost certainly responsible for completing the landscaping of the lakes and cascades, although their concept was by Emes.[67] At the edge of the Upper Lake Adam's outstanding eye-catcher building, combining Fishing Pavilion, Cold Bath and Boat House, is a *tour de force*, erected about the same time as the bridge. It is designed to be viewed from the bridge itself, with a plainer façade at the rear, (the single storey fishing pavilion), facing the park (Pl. 14). Originally it was surrounded by flowering shrubs which would have helped to conceal the strictly functional, rather ugly, side walls. At lake level there are three heavily rusticated round arches. The outer two are boat houses topped by shallow pediments, while the centre one covers an enclosed semi-circular cold bath. Above the bath house is the elegant fishing room with a large Venetian window, chimney piece, niches and stucco panels with a maritime theme. A highly sophisticated room, this was used for light refreshments and entertainment.[68]

The cold bath was fed with fresh water via Bentley's Well, a charming little feature designed by Adam in 1763, set in the lawn close to the approach road just beyond the bridge, and which most modern visitors fail to notice. It is a small rustic sand-stone arch covered by a low stone gabled roof, with a lion's mouth spouting water from a spring into a tiny semi-circular pool. Adam's design sketch of 1763 gives it far more prominence than it has today, by providing it with a weeping willow close by, so it is both functional and serves as an 'incident' while walking.[69]

For the Ireton Gardens Adam designed a richly decorated classical grotto, top-lit by a cupola, which appears as a small rotondo temple sited on a rock eminence. Like his large and *avant garde* garden 'Hut' for Miss Curzon, the design remained on paper. Would Robert Adam have been satisfied with his final commissions, having submitted so many designs for expensive follies without success? In the end he had to be content with his Bridge, Fishing Pavilion and Well. The Hexagon Temple (1775), now *ex situ*, is not an Adam design and it was not until 1799 that an orangery was built by Richardson. In 1767 Samuel Wyatt designed a quite extraordinary deercote in a Moorish style complete with Minaret, which suffered the fate of Adam's more outlandish designs. By the

FIGURE 55. Kedleston Hall and Robert Adam's bridge (1770). Early nineteenth-century print.

late 1760s Adam must have realised that Lord Curzon appreciated eye-catching designs but that his real enthusiasm was centred on the house and its collections. Ultimately Robert Adam's forte was architecture not landscape gardening.[70] One has to wonder what Emes might have achieved had he stayed.

One can only speculate what Lord Scarsdale and Robert Adam would have thought of the rather unusual use for their splendid new bridge in 1805. During the Napoleonic war the new Lord Scarsdale provided facilities for manœuvres by 1700 men of the Derbyshire Volunteers:

> A sham fight and skirmish then took place, between the light infantry companies, and the supposed enemy, who procured the bridge of the fine sheet of water in the front of Kedleston house, which was then passed by the remainder of the brigade in close column, who after forming in line fired a most excellent volley and charged.[71]

Also in the park was the Sulphur Bath-house (1759–62), built over a sulphur spring on the north side of the lower lake. This classical building was constructed by Jason Harris, a London carpenter working for Matthew Brettingham at Kedleston. It had two plunge baths, in pedimented pavilions, one each side of a central portico with paired columns.[72] Now rather derelict and isolated in the middle of a golf course, originally it served as an eye-catcher from the house and from strategic view-points when walking in the park. The spring water was both for drinking and for bathing in, as described somewhat graphically in an 1829 gazetteer:

> Kedleston water is principally valued for its anti-scorbutic qualities, When taken inwardly it acts as a diuretic, and has given relief to persons affected with the gravel. It has also been found efficacious, from external application, in various cutaneous diseases, but more especially in ulcerous complaints.[73]

No less important was its commercial use. To accommodate the large number of visitors to these baths, in 1762 Lord Scarsdale built the handsome Kedleston Inn to Adam's design, on the new turnpike road which by-passed Kedleston Hall. From it a footbridge led to the baths. This superior Inn had its own bowling green.[74] The nearby chalybeate spring at Quarndon, which had attracted visitors since at least the early eighteenth century, helped to draw visitors to the area and so the inn proved lucrative for the Curzons.[75]

Notes

All quotations from newspapers are © The British Library Board. All rights reserved. With thanks to the British Newspaper Archive (www.BritishNewspaperArchive.co.uk).

1. DRO: 5054/13/5/1 Burdett Accounts Book 1695–1708 by Thomas_Shipton, entries March and June 1696; Sept. 1699; Aug. 1702; pool – June 1702; March 1704; 1707.
2. C. Glover and P. Riden (eds), *William Woolley's History of Derbyshire* (1981), 143.
3. DRO: D5054/26/1. Under restrictive copyright regulations this map cannot be illustrated here but a visit to view it at Derbyshire Record Office is strongly recommended for anyone interested in Baroque landscape.
4. See T. Mowl and D. Barre, *The Historic Gardens of England: Staffordshire* (2008), 65

for a plan for part of Trentham gardens *c.*1731, which has similar baroque shapes cut into woodland.

5. S. Switzer, *Ichnographia Rustica*, vol. II (1718), 174–77 for bastions, and 201, 205 for features in groves. W. A. Brogden, *Stephen Switzer, Garden Design in Britain in the Early C18* (1973), letter no. 25 Francis Webb at Radburne to Switzer at Westminster, 20 Sept. 1733; see also G. Jackson Stops, *An English Arcadia 1660–1900* (1992), 46–48.

6. S. Markham, *John Loveday of Caversham 1711–1789: The Life and Times of an C18 Onlooker* (1984), 193.

7. WRO: CR1841/7 Travel diary of Lady Sophia Newdigate, 1747.

8. Illustrated J. Dixon Hunt, *William Kent, Landscape Garden Designer* (1987), 117–19, 122.

9. J. Barnatt and T. Williamson, *Chatsworth: A Landscape History* (2005), chap. 4, an academic but accessible account of the changing landscape. This account is based on their work.

10. A. Young, *The Farmer's Tour Through the East of England*, vol. I (1771), 212. He also warned against staying at the Inn at Edensor, where the traveller 'will find nothing but dirt and impertinence'.

11. W. Bray, *A Sketch of a Tour into Derbyshire and Yorkshire* (1778), 96–97.

12. *Letters of Anna Seward Written Between the Years 1784 and 1807*, vol. 2 (1811), 371–72, letter XCI, Anna Seward to Humphry Repton, 17 Feb. 1790.

13. *DM*, 9 April 1789, 4; 17 Sept. 1789, 3.

14. DRO: D5054/13/9 Account book of Sir Robert Burdett, entry 20 October 1764 'Mr Emes on the settling his accounts for the Pleasure Ground by agreement made for £93.16.0'. It noted that Emes had paid out £137 7s and a further £20 was allowed. Other details are missing.

15. DRO: D5054/13/9 entries for payment for 200 rose trees 11 Feb. 1761, three flowering shrubs 1 July 1762 and 10 June 1765.

16. Young, *Farmer's Tour*, 178–82.

17. Britton and Brayley, *Beauties of England and Wales*, 400.

18. G. Jackson-Stops, 'Restoring the Garden at Calke', *CL*, 18 May 1989. Emes asked for 14 guineas but was given ten.

19. National Trust, *Calke Guidebook* (1996), 25, 73–74; *A Short Guide to Calke Abbey Garden* (2007).

20. T. Noble (ed.) and S. Glover, *The History, Gazetteer, and Directory of the County of Derby*, pt 2 (1829), 183.

21. DRO: D517 Box A-7 11 December 1772 'Calculations for laying out in the neatest manner the Ground immediately around the house at Shipley' He was not paid until 1782.

22. *The Gardeners' Chronicle*, 18 Aug. 1883, 211–12. Close to the site of the former graveyard, a dense grove of old variegated hollies and yews behind the long curved stone ha-ha wall might be from Emes' period. A seat placed here would have given 180° views out into the countryside.

23. DRO: D6272/66/1 Plan of part of the Estate at Shipley n.d.

24. WRO: CR136/B2717, Lady Hester to Sir Roger Newdigate (n.d. but 1780/1).

25. Craven and Stanley, II, 192–95.

26. Craven and Stanley, I, 148–49.

27. J. Farey, *General View of the Agriculture and Minerals of Derbyshire*, vol. 2 (1815), 175 notes that *c.*1791 'Mr John Sands (late Gardener of Kedleston Hall)' pruned newly planted belts and ornamental Plantations at Markeaton. Craven and Stanley, I, 147–49; *DM*, 9 Aug. 1776 advertised for labourers to cut a sheet of water at Markeaton.

28. Stebbing Shaw, *History and Antiquities of Staffordshire*, vol. I (1798), 68.

29. D. G. Edwards, *The Hunlokes of Wingerworth Hall* (1976), 27. This provides details of the Hunloke finances and this account owes much to his research and from the website http://lh.matthewbeckett.com/houses/lh_derbyshire_wingerworthhall.html

30. Craven and Stanley, II, 239–41; G. Worsley, *England's Lost Houses from the Archives of Country Life* (2002), 35–36 has photographs.

31. Craven and Stanley, II, 240. The plan is lost.

32. DRO: D1306 A/PP1 Estate Map of property of Sir Henry Hunloke at Wingerworth, 1758.

33. Chesterfield Library map A387; William Emes' plan of Wingerworth. This is encased in heat-sealed clear plastic for conservation, so it was not possible to photograph at a reasonable standard.

34. See T. Warner, '"Combined Utility and Magnificence": Humphry Repton's commission for Wingerworth Hall in Derbyshire: the anatomy of a missing Red Book', *Journal of Garden History* 7.3 (1987), 280.

35. DRO: 2535/M/19/1 A Plan of the Park and part of the Demesne Lands at Alderwasley … with some Alterations by Wm Emes 1784.

36. DRO: D2360/3/369 Alderwasley Tithe Map 1841.

37. Noble (ed.), Glover, *History … of the County of Derby*, pt 2, 6. I have not managed to see the restored deercote shown on the tithe map, but is not shown on the Emes map.

38. DRO: D5557/9/1 'This map done in the year 1711 by Thomas Hand'.

39. Radburne Accounts, December 1697 in *DM* I.I (1956), 103; A list of seeds purchased in 1697–98, *DM* 2.7 (1961/2), 350–52.

40. Craven and Stanley, II, 178–80.

41. A. Young, *The Farmer's Tour*, 170–72.

42. D. King Hele, *Erasmus Darwin* (1999), 139, 174.

43. *Ibid.*, 125–28, 136, 174, 189–90.

44. *Ibid.*, 250, 253.

45. DRO: 5557/9/2 'A Plan of the Desmense Lands at Radbourn, the Seat of Sacheverall Pole Esq. with some Alterations by Wm Emes 1790'.

46. The University of Nottingham, Manuscripts and Special Collections, Drury-Lowe Dr 4 P1/2. A Map of the Manor of upper and nether Lockoe … the Estate of John Lowe Esq, surveyed in the year 1763 by Beighton.

47. Drury-Lowe Dr P 72. 'A Plan of the intended Park etc at Locko, The Seat of Wm Drury Lowe Esq, with some alterations by Wm Emes 1792'.

48. Drury-Lowe Dr P 73.

49. *DM*, 31 Jan. 1793, 4.

50. Britton and Brayley, *The Beauties of England and Wales*, vol. 3, 385.

51. J. Loudon, *Encyclopaedia of Gardening* (1822), item. 7574.

52. *DM*, 20 Dec. 1826, 1.

53. DRO: D6104/59 Plan of the The Pastures estate (1841). Craven and Stanley, II, 304–305 suggest that the Rev. Christopher Alderson may have designed the grounds.

54. Bray, *A Sketch of a Tour into Derbyshire* (1778), 66.

55. *Ibid.*; L. Harris and G. Jackson-Stops, 'When Adam Delved: Robert Adam and the Kedleston Landscape', *CL* 5 March 1987, 99.

56. It is now a holiday let. The Vassali stuccowork inside has been removed. There is design drawing with the Adam Drawings at the Sir John Soane Museum SM 40/45, which does not ascribe the design to Adam.

57. Quoted L. Harris (ed.), *Robert Adam and Kedleston* (1987), 74; Harris and Jackson-Stops, 'When Adam Delved', 99.

58. In 1762 Emes offered to complete the unfinished Upper Lake for Lord Scarsdale. I thank the late Dr Keith Goodway for this information. I have not had access to Emes' account books or other papers in the Kedleston Archives.

59. Harris, *Robert Adam*, 75–76; R. White (ed.), *Georgian Arcadia: Architecture for the Park and Garden* (catalogue to exhibition 1987), no. 366, designs for ornamental ruins; G. Jackson-Stops, *An English Arcadia, 1600–1990* (1992), 98–99. See Sir John Soane's Museum website: Robert Adam drawings.

60. Harris and Jackson Stops, 'When Adam Delved'; Harris, *Robert Adam,* 75.

61. *Ibid.*, p. 100; M. Laird, *The Flowering of the Landscape Garden* (1999), 299–303.

62. illustrated Harris, *Robert Adam*, 86. However this design by Adam, although it is given the title of Hermitage, looks more like a deer shelter than a hermit's habitation. Description in English Heritage list entry 1109088 (1986).

63. Jackson-Stops, *English Arcadia*, 98; M. Laird, *Flowering of the Landscape Garden*, 303.

64. Young, *The Farmer's Tour*, 203–204.

65. *Ibid.*, 202–203.

66. Harris, *Robert Adam*, 78–79 Soane Museum, Drawings from the Office of Robert and James Adam.

67. Craven and Stanley, I, 127–30, who note that John Whitehurst may have provided the expertise for the hydraulic works needed by Adam to make the cascades operate successfully.

68. E. Harris and A. Laing, 'No Fishy tale: a true account of the Fishing Room at Kedleston', *Apollo* 1 April
 (2006); Harris, *Robert Adam,* illustrations pp. 80–83.

69. Harris and Jackson-Stops, 'When Adam Delved', 98–101; Harris, *Robert Adam*, 71.

70. See R. White, 'Robert Adam's Rustic Designs', *Georgian Group Journal* 23 (2015), 167–78 for a discussion of Adam's highly inventive, but apparently unexecuted, designs for rustic garden buildings, including two extraordinary pavilions for Kedleston, which would not look out of place at Marie-Antoinette's, slightly later, hameau at Versailles.

71. *DM*, 30 May 1805, 3.

72. White (ed.) *Georgian Arcadia* (catalogue item no. 25).

73. Noble (ed.), Glover, *History of the County of Derby*, pt 1, 31.

74. *DM*, 28 Aug. 1767, 4.

75. J. Pilkington, *A View of the Present State of Derbyshire*, vol. 1 (1789), 238.

CHAPTER FIVE

Late Eighteenth Century 1760–1800

…the utmost extreme to which artificiality can go is the mock-natural.

Meanwhile, independent of, although no doubt influenced by, the formulaic designs of Capability Brown and William Emes, many Derbyshire landowners went their own way. A new generation of head gardeners was clearly able to advise owners, as shown by Emes himself when he started as head gardener at Kedleston, while landowners travelled widely and absorbed new fashions. There was less emphasis on garden follies, although here it must be noted that while garden history books can give the impression that many eighteenth-century parks had a profusion of follies, eye-catchers and buildings – *vide* Hagley, Stowe, Stourhead, Painshill, this was not the case. More usual were a few practical, yet attractive features such as Elvaston's modest wooden 'seat round ye tree' (1742) and wooden boat house which could double an ornamental feature.[1] At Eggington in 1782/3, when Sir Edward Every landscaped his park in a picturesque style, he added just an arbour, temple and a wooden Chinese bridge for the cascade over the new lake.[2] Most gardens and parks would have

FIGURE 56. Shardlow Hall, early nineteenth-century garden seat in alcove.

COURTESY S. FRAWLEY

a summerhouse and an alcove or covered seat, as with Shardlow Hall's early nineteenth-century garden seat, sited at the end of the house terrace. A mixture of ashlar stone and pebble work, its central niche has a Dutch gable with blank arches either side; a design influenced by William Kent.

Not everyone followed Capability Brown's lead in removing flowers from the immediate vicinity of the house as seen at **Osmaston Hall Derby**, home of the Wilmot family from the early seventeenth century. In 1696 the house was rebuilt by Robert Wilmot MP, who created 'most curious gardens and other plantations'.[3] His son Robert (1708–72), who inherited in 1738, was private secretary to the Duke of Devonshire from 1734 and, after the Duke became Viceroy of Ireland, became his Resident Secretary in England from 1740 to 1772. He was created a baronet just before his death. Although Wilmot spent most of his time away from Osmaston, leaving a caretaker in charge, he could not resist improving the house and grounds.

Wilmot's correspondence reveals an attention to detail and his practical horticultural knowledge. When his new 'Study or Flower garden' was created in 1770 Wilmot sent detailed lists of flowers and shrubs to be planted in the flower beds, which ran in four chevrons, centred on the study steps down into the garden, with an eight-foot wide gravel path around three edges. Precise instructions were sent to Thomas Cave, caretaker, jobbing gardener and handyman, who looked after Osmaston Hall with his wife. Cave replied to one letter:

> I perfectly understand your model or plan for the Study or Flower Garden and will make it according to your order.
>
> I should be glad to know what sort of Flowers you would have the Borders decorated with [.]I have by me the following sorts: Carnation a few; Brumton Stock; annual stock; rockets; Polyanthes; Mezerien-shrubs a few; Hepaticas; Pionies; Chine-atray; african and French mary-gold; Lark-heels; Lupines; Sweet scented pease; Narcissus; Crocus… I shall soon be ready for seeds.[4]

Wilmot's reply gave precise instructions about what to plant in the modern style of denser planting of flowers. He added scented honeysuckles, damask roses, moss roses and jasmines.

> each sort of seed should be sewn separate in small Patches and pretty thick in shallow drills two or three inches asunder. The larger seed should be covered About halfe an inch the smaller about one Quarter of an Inch deep.
>
> They must all be well watered out of the sprinkling noze of the watering pot both before and after the Plants appear and after they have been up about a Fortnight, thin em when too Thick clearing away the weaker and leaving the strongest plants to flower.[5]

Cave soon reported back:

> The study stepts and Garden according to your model and Dyrections is compleaded and looks very Beautiful, and is a fine prospect from the Study Door … I shall begin this week to lay down the Terrice walk and the Gravil walks on the North side.[6]

In what seems to have been a repeated pattern, Wilmot opted for the cheapest option after Thomas Cave enquired:

> I could be glad to know what sort of a Fence you would have betwixt the new wall and the Yew Hedge. I think a little China palisade-work would look very well[,] for hedges are apt to harbour vermin which are offensive, and destroys young plants.

Wilmot opted for a cheaper plain fence, having a deep rooted reluctance to spend too much on a place he rarely inhabited.[7] However he did think it was time to add interest to his wider landscape and in 1769 he approached his nephew John Wilmot, who clearly had some architectural knowledge:

> I write to you as the representation of Inigo Jones – I want a model for an Obelisk, Pillar or Column, to put at the top of the hill opposite the South Door [of] Osmaston when there are a few trees planted[.] you will consider whether a Round (I don't mean a fluted) Column or a square Pillar will be best; a square would be least expence and most easily erected[8]

His nephew replied with some unsolicited ambitious ideas:

> We [he and his father] thought at first of an open Druid Temple or some ruins interlaced with ivy, but we have waved that thought as not consonant to the architecture of the house, but if ever you think of establishing a Dairy Farm in the Fields we are clearly of the opinion that if water can be found there you might mix the *utile dulce* by adorning the Front next the house in the Grecian, Roman or Gothic taste…
>
> We sometimes think of an elegant windmill. It is too far off the House and too near a wood for a Dovecote, but if it must be either a pillar, obelisk or Pyramid, we prefer the former but are not yet quite clear concerning the dimensions. We consider that the ground in respect of the House is very high, and as we guess it to be nearer two thirds of a mile to the top of the hill where the Pillar is to be placed, we apprehend that the general rule is to be departed from, and that we must not have too taper and gracile a Pillar, but must rather lean to strength and breadth which the eye will not lose in its progress to it, and we think a guilt Ball at the top as upon Trajan's Pillar, would give a solemn majestick and Imperial air, But it should be big enough to hold the ashes of three or four generations.[9]

Needless to say nothing happened and far less exciting was the landscaping by William Emes in 1789 for Robert Wilmot (1752–1834), who inherited in 1772. The result appears to have been competent rather than inspired:

> The grounds of Osmaston were laid out by Emes, and though not of any remarkable beauty, are still pleasant; as their situation, being somewhat more elevated than the adjacent country, gives them a greater command of prospect than the neighbourhood could be supposed to afford. The estate is tolerably wooded; and the vicinity of the house improved by an ornamental fish-pond, and pleasure ground: the latter, with the kitchen garden, includes about five acres.[10]

The family lived at Catton Hall after 1806 and Osmaston Hall was let, until sold in 1888 to the Midland Railway Company for use as offices. Acquired in 1938 by Derbyshire County Borough, the house was demolished and its remaining land became an industrial estate.

FIGURE 57. Osmaston Hall and lake, from Britton and Brayley (1802).

Four miles (6.4 km) north of Chatsworth the river Derwent winds along one side of a wide and deep valley. Above one deep curve is a platform on which sits **Stoke Hall**, whose dramatic site looks across to the hillside of Curbar Edge with its skyline of ragged rocks. The Rev. John Simpson (1699–1784) may have decided to build his new house to mark the marriage in 1755 of his daughter and heiress, Elizabeth (1735–1806), to Henry Bridgeman (1725–1800), MP for Ludlow and heir apparent to Weston Park, Staffs. His architect was almost certainly James Paine who was working at nearby Chatsworth. The estate quarry provided the building stone for the new house, whose plain Palladian exterior contrasts with elaborate interiors. The Rev. Simpson preferred plain lawns round the house and used woodland along the valley just north of the house to add winding walks, with picturesque views down to the river Derwent below and across to the escarpment.

Henry and Elizabeth Bridgeman lived at Weston Park but their eldest son Orlando (1762–1825) and his wife Lucy lived at Stoke Hall for a while. A few delightful letters (1798), written to Orlando by his nine-year-old son George Augustus, show the family actively involved in practical gardening. The children planted seeds and flowers and created a tiny nursery of seedling trees:

> April 27 John says the scarlet Beans should not be watered till they come up and Mamma not knowing this has watered then every day. Do you not think we had better sow some more…[11]

George's letters provide a date for the new cold plunge bath in the woodland and show that it had a changing room with chimney attached. He wrote on 9 May 1798 that 'Fletcher has finished the outside of the Bath and in the bank just under the Chimney I have found a Wren's nest'. Approached by a winding

FIGURE 58. Stoke Hall, plunge bath (1798) and remains of cascade in the woods.

COURTESY S. DRURY

path down from the house, this L-shaped Bath House was built from local stone and supplied with water from one of the many little streams down the hillside, which then runs out into a narrow rocky cascade down to the river. Part of the picturesque scenery, the Bath's barrel vaulted stone roof may have been turfed originally, while a large open window space (now much altered) gave views over the cascade, down to the river and the hills opposite. Nearby is another cascade, while above huge rocks create a seating area and yet another viewing point.

In April 1798 George wrote that 'we are going to go to Flora this evening to look for Birds Nests'. This was Flora Plantation, just beyond the far end of the main woods, a short walk or ride from the hall.[12] Still known as 'Flora Wood', from a statue of Flora placed there at some time in the later eighteenth century, it is the subsequent subject of many lurid legends. Now restored after vandalism, the statue stands in a clearing, gazing over the countryside to Stoke Hall (Pl. 15). It may be that the statue, reputedly a gift from Chatsworth, was protected within an open temple, as a map in the 1839 sale brochure, notes a 'Temple', approached on a circular walk.

Stoke was for sale in 1835 and 1839.[13] The auctioneer was the brilliant and eccentric George Robins of London (1778–1847), a poet *manqué* who lost no opportunity to burst into purple prose and hyperbole. His enthusiastic descriptions mention the cascade and cold bath, the river Derwent which encircles the estate, set within 'stupendous hills, which form an amphitheatre of prodigious extent'. A long riverside walk takes full advantage of the trees, rocks along the banks and in the river, providing a 'Claude-like picture' resembling 'THE GARDEN OF EDEN'.

By now house and pleasure grounds were somewhat neglected for:

The imaginative powers of a man of taste (or lady if it be preferred) may be successfully employed in renovating and embellishing this hospitable Mansion. THE EXTENSIVE LAWN AND PLEASURE GROUNDS are fully adequate, and, by a little tact and cleverness, may soon be restored to their pristine state.

The final selling point was that within 12 months the railway would 'bring Stoke Hall within an eight hours' trip to the metropolis'. Since then Stoke has changed hands several times, eventually rescued and restored by Richard Jowitt in 1982 and more recently by the Drurys, who are also carefully restoring the nearly lost woodland landscape.

George Venables Vernon (1709–80) inherited **Sudbury Hall** in 1719 and, once he reached his majority in 1730, swept away the formal gardens to create open lawns and shrubberies. The canal ponds were naturalised into an irregular long lake: one of many examples of the removal of formality in pleasure gardens before Capability Brown's influence. For a visitor in 1745 the scene was pastoral:

On the garden side was a large area sloping down to a serpentine river and encompassed with an amphitheatre of greens, which scene, being at that time enriched by a set of haymakers actually at work afforded, what the French call *une beau paisage*.[14]

When Bishop Pococke visited in June 1751 he too thought that the lake was a 'serpentine river [which] runs through the lawn behind the house'. Two months later the Duchess of Beaufort reported:

On the garden side is a fine gentle Slope before the house, at ye bottom of which runs a piece of water of 20 Acres and an open Grove on either end of it. The Schrubbery and Garden very pretty.[15]

The bowling green, noted in a report of theft from the house in *Derby Mercury* 2 September 1784, may date from this period. In 1763 Philip Yorke appreciated the lake 'round which a very pleasant gravel path is carried, and a prospect of the country up to the hills is very agreeable'.[16] He went on to note that 'Lord Vernon is building a Gothic dairy at the end of his terrace, and intends to extend the extremities of his lake'. The dairy, which would be appropriate for a *ferme ornée,* must be the square building shown in a 1770 view of Sudbury Hall. It shows a crocketed gable-end facing the terrace and an open three arched arcade on the side.[17] Vernon appears to have favoured the fashionable gothic/gothick style of architecture for his garden buildings, perhaps as a cheaper option to remodelling the expensive interiors of his Carolean house.

He made no attempt to divert the road which still runs directly in front of the house, but erected a gothic deer shelter, which doubled as striking eye-catcher, in the parkland opposite. Some writers date it as early as 1723, which, if true, would make it one of the earliest eighteenth-century gothic park buildings in the country.[18] However Vernon was still a minor then. It is more probably the work of the talented local mason-architect, Richard Trubshaw (1689–1745), who recorded unspecified work in 1734 'done for Master Vernon-Sudbury'.[19] This large square enclosure, with low castellated enclosing walls and corner towers, was an exercise in romanticised medieval gothic, popular by the mid-eighteenth century. Its present appearance owes much to Sanderson Miller, gentleman architect and landscaper who specialised in gothick, and who had just designed a gothic tower for Lord Chetwynd at Ingestre, Staffordshire in 1749–50. In August 1750 he noted in his diary that he was drawing a design for 'Mr Vernon of Sidbury'.[20]

Miller further gothicised the building and to make it more prominent added a central 'gate-house'. In 1751 Bishop Pococke admired 'a square arcade, with a turret at each corner, and trees being planted about it.'[21] A contemporary painting at Sudbury Hall shows four white castellated towers peering above the surrounding belt of trees, looking like an old castle. Afterwards Sanderson Miller was probably asked to landscape the surrounding area in the deer park, utilising a stream to create long narrow pools near to the dove-cote.[22] A later writer (1824) declared that oak trees in a belt on the south-east of the park were sown 'about 1764', suggesting ongoing improvements to existing rather

FIGURE 59. Sudbury Hall, 1798. A lawn stretches down to a lake after the removal of the walled gardens.

FIGURE 60. Sudbury Hall, gothic dovecote seen as an eye-catcher from the house.

FIGURE 61. Tutbury ruined tower, 'improved' by Lord Vernon in the early 1770s.

haphazard landscaping following Vernon's elevation to the peerage in 1762 as first Baron Vernon.[23]

Of course a genuine medieval castle is even better. The ruins of Tutbury Castle served as a distant eye-catcher, shown in a mid-eighteenth-century oil painting (at Sudbury Hall). From the mid-seventeenth century the Vernons had leased the ruined castle from the Duchy of Lancaster, using it for occasional entertaining, enjoying its romantic associations with Mary Queen of Scots (a prisoner there), and King Charles I. When Bishop Pococke visited in June 1751 his description of deliberate demolition work there makes grim reading. He noted of the Mary Queen of Scots apartments, that 'this building is now taking down and there are great heaps of white plaster floors of the rooms'.[24] No doubt the ruins were in a precarious state, but this still seems rather drastic, not least because the Vernons and their guests put great store on the castle's evocative associations with the tragic Queen.

By 1777 George Vernon had decided to add his own contribution to the castle, enhancing the silhouette of the ruins with a new, but deliberately ruinous, tower on the motte, created from local stone and salvaged stone on site.[25] In 1791 lightning split this 'great tower', while part of the castle, recently repaired by Lord Vernon and 'occupied as a dwelling house, and occasionally used as a ball-room, was also much damaged'.[26] From its gaping apertures the surrounding countryside is shown in a truly picturesque fashion, making Tutbury Castle a genuine folly.

The next Vernon felt the need for professional advice for the pleasure grounds near the house and used John Webb (1754–1828), a local man who lived at Lichfield, who had worked with William Emes and then had his own successful landscaping practice.[27] The lawns to the lake were left untouched but by 1794 woods and shrubberies between the kitchen gardens and lake had fashionable gently meandering paths, with a simple summerhouse near the boat house at the far end.[28] By now flowering shrubs were much in evidence in fashionable pleasure grounds

The Leake family had lived at **Sutton Scarsdale** since the fifteenth century, and in the 1720s Nicholas Leake (1680–1736), fourth and last Earl of Scarsdale, decided to replace his Elizabethan house with a baroque house by Smith of Warwick. A riposte to the Cavendish family's Bolsover Castle and Hardwick Hall, both clearly visible across the valley, the new house was magnificent inside and out, with terracing, formal gardens and landscaping with a 'great pond' created in 1728.[29] However the earl's extravagances caused the enforced sale of the estate following his death. The house and part of the estate were purchased by Godfrey Clarke of Somersall Hall, Chesterfield, who added the spectacular bastion-shaped four-acre (1.6 ha) kitchen garden, an unusual octagon with 14 ft (4.3 m) high walls, in 1745.[30] The formal gardens were separated from the deer park by iron fences. A 1770s map shows traditional formal avenues, circular clumps of trees, oblong plantations and two series of fish ponds in the park.[31] There was a deer house surrounded by a belt of trees and possibly the menagerie complex near the house, noted in 1808.[32]

After the death of Clarke's son in 1774 the estate was rented out to the Kynnersley family until 1815, when it reverted to Lady Ormonde, Clarke's niece, who died in 1817. Her husband, the first Marquis of Ormonde, then undertook a protracted and complicated lawsuit against the Kynnersley heir for illegal felling of timber while his family were tenants. Kynnersley was accused of cutting down trees planted for ornament and shelter, also saplings and young trees in other parts of the estate, which diminished the value and beauty of the estate.[33] In defence of his late uncle, Thomas Sneyd Kinnersley argued that trees had been removed from the approach avenue 'to open a vista through' to Hardwick Hall. One tree was felled 'for the express purpose of affording from the Terrace at the South Western part of the said Mansion House another view of Hardwick House'. To the north and east, many trees had already gone or were in a decayed state before the Kynnersleys arrived, so the careful removal of 'straggling remains' of a belt gave:

> the remaining trees the appearance (as far as it could be effected) of small groups and of letting in various views of the Sutton estate and of different Clumps of trees growing in various parts thereof and varied views of the seats of Hardwick Hall, Hucknall woods, Bolsover Castle, Staveley Church, Renishaw and other places.[34]

In short, Kynnersley was updating the old fashioned park, yet contemporary maps still show formal avenues and clumps, with ponds and pools not converted into a fashionable lake.[35] History repeated itself and in 1824 the Marquis had to sell the estate to cover huge debts of £450,000. The auctioneer George Robins astutely summed up the material benefits of acquiring a prestigious estate of 5500 acres (2227 ha), rich in coal and iron, with the social cachet of owning 'a seat that fairly competes with Chatsworth and Hardwicke' [*sic*]. The park was impressive, 'diversified by avenues of fine old elm trees, beautifully feathering

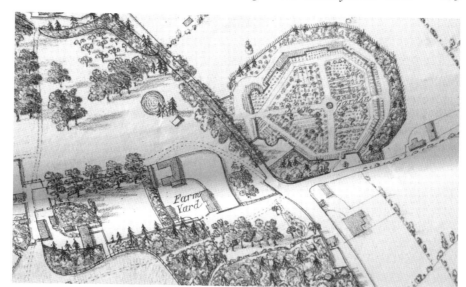

FIGURE 62. Sutton Scarsdale *c.*1820, walled kitchen garden (1745) on right, menagerie to left of farm yard.

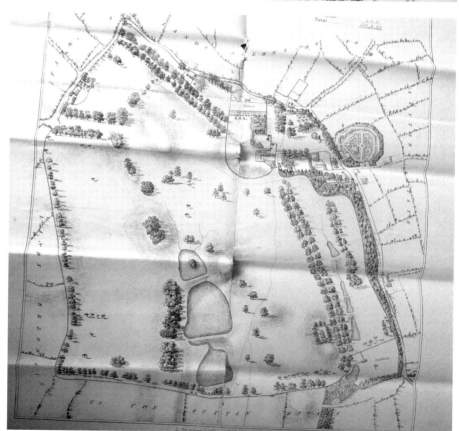

FIGURE 63. Sutton Scarsdale *c.*1820 estate map showing surviving old formal avenues and fish ponds.

to the ground, and wide spreading chestnuts, relieved occasionally by pieces of water of some extent'.[36] There was rumour that this highly desirable estate was to be purchased by the Duke of Devonshire who 'has sold the town of Wetherby, in order to become the purchaser of the noble domain of the Marquis of Ormonde, in Derbyshire'.[37] However, in a successful coup at auction, it was purchased by the hugely wealthy businessman Richard Arkwright junior (of Willersley Castle) for £216,000, continuing the heady social rise of that Derbyshire industrialist family.[38]

In the mid-sixteenth century Thomas Gresley built **Drakelow Hall** near Burton-on Trent, then an attractive town.[39] The views across the river bend below the hall were admired by the Duchess of Beaufort in 1751:

> There is a fine Terrace which commands a very fine view of the Trent running at the bottom of it, bounded on the other side by a hill is Ld Uxbridges Park [Sinai] cover'd with a fine wood: Burton upon Trent makes a fine point of view from this Terrace.[40]

The Trent provided good fishing while some fish ponds on the estate appear to have become formal canals by this time. A patron of James Brindley, Sir Nicholas Bowyer Gresley (d. 1808) seventh baronet, who inherited in 1787, was an enterprising man, although unfortunately his own attempt as *entrepreneur* – the porcelain factory he established at Gresley Hall in 1795 – was an expensive failure.[41] In 1793 Sir Nigel commissioned Paul Sandby to decorate the dining room in the house with remarkable *trompe l'œil* paintings. A quite overpowering decorative scheme, it appeared as if you were actually within a landscape, with the ceiling decorated as the sky. Anna Seward described this early example of what was to become a Regency period enthusiasm for bringing the garden inside:

> one side painted with forest scenery, whose majestic trees arch over the coved ceiling. Through them we see glades, tufted banks and ascending walks in perspective. The opposite side of the room exhibits a Peak valley, the front shows a prospect of more distant country, vieing with the beauties of the real one, admitted opposite through a crystal wall of window. Its chimney-piece, formed of spars and ores and shells, represents a grotto. Real pales, painted green and breast high, are placed a few inches from the walls and increase the power of the deception. In these are little wicket gates that half open, tempt the visitor to ascend the forest banks.[42]

Outside the house any remaining formality was removed, with a simple lawn sloping down to the river, enclosed on each side by mature trees.[43] To the north and east of the house, was 'The Wilderness', a thick protective belt of trees with walks, which skirted the large walled kitchen garden. Nearby, just within the Wilderness, and in total contrast and surprise, was a formal circular flower garden, whose shape, a large 'cartwheel' with eight 'spokes', had the hallmark of a Repton 'Rosary' (see Fig. 134). Repton argued that a flower garden should be 'of a character totally different from the rest of the scenery, and its decorations should be as much those of art as of nature.'[44] Indeed Repton may have been asked to advise Sir Nigel in 1793, although there is no known Red Book.[45] So Drakelow has two surprise 'garden rooms' – inside the house and outside. As we shall see, all was to be transformed in the 1890s.

Repton would have approved of **Sealwood Cottage**, a small *cottage orné*, hidden in the countryside near Swadlincote. One of the most unusual and early examples of the picturesque style, recently this has been lovingly restored (Pl. 16). The Rev. Thomas Gresley of Netherseal Hall was a country parson whose family had owned much of the village since the early seventeenth century. He planted out the grounds between 1756–59 and then *c.*1774 created this delightful little retreat at on the edge of his woodlands, 1½ miles (2.4 km) from the hall. The cottage was self-consciously rustic, with a thatched pyramidal roof over rough timber-framed walls with brick infill, extending to a semi-pyramidal lean-to on each side. There was crude large circular chimney stack towering above the thatch, simple Gothic pointed doors and small pretty leaded windows. The interior was similarly charmingly simple, rustic and ingeniously planned with great attention to detail. The first floor room doubled as a bedroom and prospect room, with views over the countryside. A (tiny) wine cellar shows that it was used for picnics or alfresco meals and entertaining small parties.

Philip Heath's research shows that the cottage was built to a (lost) sketch by William Combe (1741–1823), later famous for his *The Tour of Dr Syntax in Search of the Picturesque* (1812).[46] In a letter to Gresley (1773) Combe discussed the importance of placing garden or park buildings in an appropriate situation, arguing that a

FIGURE 65. Sealwood Cottage probably as built.

WINE BOTTLE IMAGE COURTESY OF ELIZABETH AND JOHN GOODALL AND P. HEATH

FIGURE 66. Spondon
Hall Lodge, Derby
(demolished 1929). Early
nineteenth-century
thatched rustic lodge.

COURTESY OF DERBY CITY COUNCIL
AND WWW.PICTURETHEPAST.
ORG.UK

cottage is more natural than a costly classical temple on an English lawn.[47] For
the cottage he recommended 'Irregularity in the Outline', while 'The 'Wood
Front' should be smothered in ivy and the front 'toward the open country'
should be painted white.[48] Smoke rose from the tall chimney in the manner
much approved by Humphrey Repton, advocate of the picturesque view. In his
Red Book for Blaise Castle (1795–96), Repton argued that 'the occasional smoke
from the chimney' of his proposed woodsman's cottage, sited on a bend of his
carriage route, would produce 'that kind of vapoury repose over the opposite
wood which painters attempt to describe'.[49] Although extended and altered,
with tiles replacing thatch, Sealwood Cottage still charms.

Another use for the *cottage orné* was as an entrance lodge to an estate: a
picturesque introduction to the grounds. There was a delightful example at
Regency Spondon Hall, near Derby, demolished in 1929 and replaced by a
housing site. With a gothic coach house it contrasted with plain villa built
by Roger Cox, a local lead entrepreneur, who was surely demonstrating his
modernity with contrasting, but up-to date architectural styles.[50]

The late eighteenth-century Picturesque movement delighted in wild, rugged
landscapes as a reaction to the bland, manicured and predictable landscapes of
Capability Brown and his followers. Dramatic scenery in Derbyshire invoked
the desired feelings of awe, and even *frissons* of fear, from the visitor. The river
near Matlock, hemmed in by cliffs and with its bed strewn with fallen rocks
was seen as particularly awesome:

> a bed so broken and disjointed, that the foaming waters roar over the obstructing
> masses with restless rapidity, and considerable noise. After sudden and heavy rains,
> the impetuosity of the current is greatly increased, and the sublimity of the view
> proportionably augmented.[51]

This was the setting for Sir Richard Arkwright's **Willesley Castle** at Cromford,
where in the 1770s Arkwright (1732–93) used the river to power his highly

FIGURE 67. Willersley Castle, from Britton and Brayley (1802).

AUTHOR'S COLLECTION

FIGURE 68. Willersley Castle, hillside walk with rock face on right side.

COURTESY A. ALLAWAY, WILLESLEY CASTLE HOTEL

successful cotton-spinning mills, the first in the world to be worked by water power. Like many eighteenth-century industrialists he preferred to live close to his factory to keep an eye on things, so he purchased land at Willesley in 1788 on which to build a house reflecting his wealth and social position following his knighthood in 1786. For pure drama of site Willersley Castle is difficult to match. Built on a man-made platform, nestling high against the steep hillside of Wild Cat Tor, looking down the green slopes of a deep valley with the river Derwent below, it faces a sheer rock cliff. There is a clear view down to Cromford Mills, the source of Arkwright's wealth, while wooded walks along the hillside give views down to Masson, his other mill (1783) on the bend of the river. John Byng, viewing in 1789, sneered:

> It is the house of an overseer surveying the works, not of a gentleman wishing for
> retirement and quiet. But light come, light go, Sir Rd has honourably made his great
> fortune; and so let him still live in a great cotton mill![52]

Willersley Castle was built in 1789–91, but immediately gutted by fire. Arkwright
began rebuilding but died soon after and so never lived there. It is a large Neo-
classical house, yet with its oddly battlemented facades and semi-circular turrets
on the wings, is neither fully classical nor gothic.[53] Built against the hillside 'its
castellated appearance, judicious proportions, exact symmetry, and beautiful
surrounding scenery, forming a *coup d'œil* that is seldom witnessed.'[54] Given
that Arkwright senior, a ruthlessly ambitious and driven man, died reputedly
worth half a million pounds, his son Richard (1755–1848) had less to prove, but
had the money to continue to develop the picturesque landscape using John
Webb, former assistant to William Emes.

In front of the house there are simple lawns. To one side, a little distance
away, a path divides. The lower path bends round and down the wooded hill,
with seats in the occasional deep hollow carved into the rock giving views down
to the river Derwent below and also Masson Mill across the river. The upper
path is wider and more dramatic, with fallen rock apparently randomly littering
the slopes, covered with moss and often with trees growing out. Beech and yews
cling desperately to the slope throwing out wide roots to keep a foothold. At
times there is sheer rock cliff behind and glimpses of the river below, doubtless
once viewed from strategically placed rustic seats. Other paths higher up also
wind along the steep slopes.

> In the midst of the wood are several romantic rocks, round which, and on the
> declivity of the hill, the principal walk winds in a circuit of nearly a mile. The walk
> leading from the castle on the west gradually turns to the north, taking a direction
> parallel to the course of the river, and passes under some perpendicular rocks, though
> yet elevated to a great height above the stream. The rocks are in some parts of bare
> vegetation, but are occasionally fringed to their tops with trees, particularly the
> yew and ash, the roots of which insinuate themselves into the clefts and fissures in
> a singular manner. The walks were laid out under the direction of Mr Webb, and
> are kept with the greatest neatness. The number of trees planted by Mr Arkwright
> [junior], on the average of the last seven years, has been 50,000 annually.[55]

Originally the walks contrasted with pleasure gardens to the rear of the castle:

> Standing on the brink of a precipice, the visitor may on the one hand look down
> with feelings of awe and contemplate the scene beneath, whilst on the other hand
> may be seen the most splendid collection of choice and beautiful plants and flowers,
> forming a scene altogether the very reverse of the other.[56]

Richard Arkwright junior allowed the public access on set days each week.[57]

Even the approach to the castle and grounds was picturesque with an
attractive medieval bridge and a ruined chapel, freestanding once cleared of a
clutter of farm buildings. Next to it was a classical fishing pavilion based on
Isaac Walton's at Beresford Dale. The group makes a consciously appealing
ensemble prior to the sharp turn into the castle drive with its attractive little

gothic lodge. Nearby, a small classical chapel and canal warehouse with a battlemented tower acted as distant eye-catchers within the landscape.

In total contrast were the house and grounds created by another wealthy manufacturer, the hosier, John Baker (d. 1783), who utilised the power of the river Wye for his stocking factory at **Litton**, near Cressbrook, a still isolated area to the north of Buxton. Nearby he took advantage of the picturesque river valley to build 'Rock House' against a towering limestone cliff. After 1763 Baker acquired the wooded Litton Frith, where he transformed the steep slopes of the valley as a commercial venture. He created watercress beds in the brook, lavender and peppermint beds and herb garden on the lower slopes, and fruit trees and bushes (apple, plum and damson) among the rocks on the higher part of the slopes. To help pay for this ambitious project Baker agreed to lease land to Sir Richard Arkwright on which to build a new cotton spinning mill. Arkwright then bought the estate after Baker died in debt.[58] Litton Frith was advertised for sale in 1786:

> ALSO, that beautiful Piece of Garden-ground, called Bee Stones [now Water-cum Jolly], adjoining the said River Wye, containing between two and three acres, well planted with a variety of the best Fruit and Filbert Trees in full bearing, the Produce of which, is remarkable for its extraordinary early Ripeness and fine Flavor, owing the high surrounding Rocks, the Tops whereof are beautifully planted with a variety of forest trees, possessing near Four Acres of Land, capable of great improvement by way of Pleasure Ground… At one end of the Garden is [Rock] House three Stories high, built under a beautiful high concave Rock, forming a compleat Roof, which adds greatly to the romantick Scene.[59]

Even for Derbyshire this was extreme gardening.

A topic in its own right is the clerical horticulturalist-botanist, of whom there were several in Derbyshire, raising plants, patrons of local horticultural shows, serving on committees and exhibiting. The Rev. Christopher Alderson (1738–1814) probably designed several landscapes in Derbyshire. From 1763 he lived at Aston in South Yorkshire as curate to the influential poet-gardener Rev. William Mason (1724–97), author of the celebrated poem, *The English Garden* (1772–82). Mason designed the much admired flower garden at Nuneham for Earl Harcourt in 1776, which 'excels every flower-garden which ever existed either in history or romance [with] Bowers, statues, inscriptions, busts, temples'.[60]

Doubtless it was Mason who recommended Alderson as designer for Queen Charlotte's garden at her new home at Frogmore, Windsor in 1792. The resulting landscape was admired for its walks, woods and lake. On Mason's death Alderson was presented to the living at Aston. However he was also rector of **Eckington** from 1784 to 1814, where he enlarged the rectory and redesigned the gardens, known to us through the enthusiastic response of *The Gentleman's Magazine*, October 1795 (p. 826). He was praised for his tasteful and 'elegant improvements' at the rectory:

> Mr Alderson is very happy in disposing pleasure grounds, and has been, I am told, employed at Frogmore. Some specimens that I have seen deserve much praise,

particularly at Ford House, Derbyshire. He has made as much as he could of the confined limits at Eckington… Facing the house there is a pretty piece of water, across which he has thrown a handsome bridge, and at one end placed a rustic temple.

The accompanying illustration shows the elegant new neo-classical garden façade of the house, a small classical temple, a lawn with just two small flower beds and lined with shrubbery, as approved by Mason who advocated the use of laurel and flowering shrubs, next to paths.[61] The house façade has similarities with Joseph Badger's 1795 stables at Renishaw, which would tie in with Sir George Sitwell's belief that Alderson was responsible for the removal of the old formal gardens at Renishaw and their replacement with open lawns.[62] 'Ford House' is presumably **Ford House**, Stretton built 1766 for Thomas Holland, a malster, whose son Thomas was a close friend and pupil of Joseph Wright of Derby.[63] Future research will doubtless discover other garden designs by Alderson.[64]

The Rev. D'Ewes Coke (1747–1811) of **Brookhill Hall**, Pinxton, on the Derbyshire-Nottinghamshire border, was rector of Pinxton and South Normanton and also owner of a local colliery. Coke, with his new wife Hannah, moved to Brookhill in 1771, the year that he was ordained. Improvements were soon made to the Jacobean house, probably by the fashionable Joseph Pickford of Derby.[65] A painting by Joseph Wright, (at Derby Museum), shows Hannah, D'Ewes Coke and his cousin Daniel Parker Coke MP, carefully posed beneath a tree in an open landscape. They are shown considering a piece of paper held by Parker Coke, perhaps a plan for the landscape they are all earnestly viewing. The painting dates from the early 1780s, when the park at Brookhill was being landscaped, probably to designs by D'Ewes Coke, with advice and encouragement from his wife and cousin.

A memorandum book (1771–86) of D'Ewes Coke reveals a delightful man, with a passion for planting and for nature.[66] It is very detailed for the period 1771–73, with Coke recording his planting of seeds, vegetables, salad, fruit trees and forest trees. He recorded happily in 1771: 'the Filbert in full flower together with snowdrops and winter aconite' (26 February); 'Syringas, Laburn[um], Guelder rose beginning to bud' (15 March) and 'the bulbous violet has been in flower about a week' (4 May). A 'hands-on' gardener he 'planted', 'transplanted', 'sowed', 'made a hotbed', 'put moss under melons, fresh earth to hand glasses', collected seeds and took cuttings. He clearly loved flowers noting: '[I] transplanted Sweet Williams, stock, gilliflowers, hollyhocks and Canterbury bells, double Columbines'.

An entry for 22 March 1772 when he 'went a hunting with the Duke of Portland til 8 at night, went afterwards to Welbeck', is a reminder that the rector was also a well-connected member of a wealthy gentry family.[67] Unfortunately the detailed entries in the memorandum book finish in 1773, with just a summary until 1786. However this does suggest that Coke himself designed the landscape at Brookhill in 1783, creating the lake and stocking it with '70 Brace of trench and 60 brace of Trout'. This large, narrow, crescent- shaped lake could be viewed from the house and was the main feature in a well-wooded landscape.[68] (Pl. 17).

In 1785 he planted 'a Plantation at the bottom of Nether Lake' and in 1786 'made a road through the grounds to the Mansfield Turnpike'. These would be the final touches to the extensive tree planting undertaken since 1771, with 756 trees purchased 1781–82.[69] Coke's youngest son John (1776–1841) joined with William Billingsley, an expert flower painter at Derby Porcelain factory, to start a commercial venture in 1796. This was a new China manufactory based at Pinxton, which produced beautiful china, including ware with images of Brookhill Hall, but it closed in 1813.[70]

By the 1770s **Ashbourne** was a small thriving market town, with several coaching inns, a bookseller, wine-merchant, tea warehouse and Assemblies held at the Blackamoor's Head.[71] A least one public house had gardens and a 'neat' bowling green.[72] Members of the gentry and successful commercial and professional men owned fashionable new houses on Church Street, with their large walled gardens, stocked with fruit trees and flowers, no doubt supplied by the local Sandys family nursery (*qv*). When Thomas Dawson moved house in 1767 he advertised for sale his collection of 'auriculas, polianthos and carnations'.[73] Summer houses and alcove seats featured in several gardens, such as the alcove with rusticated pilasters (*c*.1740) at Oswald House, Church Street.[74]

An additional attraction, at the bottom of gardens on the south side of this street, was the river Henmore, which ran roughly parallel and was specifically mentioned in advertisements.[75] When a property opposite the Grammar School was offered for sale in 1843, like a small country house it had ten bedrooms,

FIGURE 69. Ashbourne, Oswald House, Church Street. Alcove seat *c*.1740 in garden.

PHOTO: PAUL WINFIELD

coach house, stables etc. 'extensive Gardens with Greenhouse, Pleasure Grounds, large Paddock, with Fishponds etc.'[76] Extra land was often available beyond the walled gardens, as when 15 Church Street was let in 1810 with five acres (2 ha) of land 'contiguous to the Garden' if required.[77] These could be turned into paddocks or even parkland to enhance views from a house and as a status symbol.

Two very different gentlemen lived at Ashbourne in the eighteenth century: Dr John Taylor, worldly *bon viveur* friend of Dr Johnson, and Sir Brooke Boothy, poetic dreamer and admirer of Rousseau.

The Rev. Dr John Taylor (1711–88) was a native of Ashbourne, a lawyer and then a pluralist cleric, becoming chaplain to the Duke of Devonshire for several years and also holding several lucrative benefices outside Derbyshire. A strong Whig and a JP, Taylor settled back in Ashbourne, where in the 1760s, as a wealthy man, he proceeded to rebuild the Mansion House in the Palladian style, creating the most impressive house in the town. The street façade had a Diocletian window over a Venetian window, for maximum impact for all to admire. A life-long friend of Dr Johnson, the 'King of Ashbourne' was an influential and well-known figure, who lived the life of a gentleman surrounded by his collection of silver, pictures and china displayed in his elegant new house.

When Mrs Thrale visited in July 1774 she admired Taylor's gentlemanly life-style:

> We went to the Church, where Dr. Taylor has a magnificent seat; indeed everything around him is both elegant and splendid. He has … a waterfall murmuring at the foot of his garden, deer in his paddock, pheasants in his menagerie, the finest coach horses in the County, the largest horned cattle, I believe, in England, particularly a Bull of an enormous size, his table liberally spread, his wines all excellent in their kinds…[78]

Onto the back of his house Taylor added a delightful octagonal music room, from which you entered the garden via a little Doric portico.[79] Little remains of the once extensive garden and its small park, but we know some details via the redoubtable Dr Johnson, who visited his friend several times in 1737, 1740 and between 1767 and 1779. In the 1770s Dr Johnson brought Boswell and Mrs Thrale for visits, but found Ashbourne society lacking in intellectual stimulation and his old friend somewhat tedious company. One of Dr Taylor's many interests was his garden and Johnson reported, somewhat condescendingly in 1775, that:

> Dr Taylor wants to be gardening. He means to buy a piece of ground in the neighbourhood, and surround it with a wall, and build a gardener's house upon it, and have fruit, and be happy.[80]

Earlier Johnson had written; 'Dr Taylor's is a very pleasant house with a Lawn and a Lake, and twenty deer and five fawns on the Lawn [paddock]'.[81]

This small deer-park was given a battlemented deer-barn and the whole effect must have been rather charming, with the garden leading to a small lake,

FIGURE 70. Ashbourne, The Mansion; Dr Taylor's classical summer house, 1760s.

created by diverting and damming the Henmore, with the paddock beyond. On another visit in 1777 Dr Johnson noted that Taylor had just:

> emptied his pond of the mud, and laid it upon the ground behind him. He thinks he now has six feet of water… The walk in the garden is covered with new gravel which will be continued to the waterfall, which now roars tolerably well.[82]

Johnson was sufficiently enthusiastic about the waterfall to join Boswell, when they were walking around one evening, to unclog the water, which must have made a rather amusing picture. The gravel walk referred to may also have led to the classical summerhouse on the terrace below the house. Built against the side boundary wall, it has a Roman Doric 'temple' façade with three round arches under a pediment and reinforces the concept of a miniature country estate attached to a villa, reflecting Dr Taylor's sophisticated tastes among his country neighbours.

When Miss Parker's 'highly respectable Boarding School for Young Ladies' was offered for sale in 1815, a selling point was the walled garden and 'an admirable View of Sir Brooke Boothby's Park and beautiful environs'.[83] This is **Ashbourne Hall** at the other end of the town and had belonged to the Boothby family since 1671, when purchased by Sir William Boothby from the impecunious Sir Aston Cockayne. William Woolley noted the 'pretty paddock stocked with deer, and good fishponds adjoining,' which were to form the basis of the eighteenth-century park.[84]

In 1772 the house was to let with a kitchen and flower garden, meadow and pasture land nearby, with several fish ponds, amounting to 50 acres (20.2 ha) in all. The park was separate and covered 40 acres (16.2 ha) not including wood and water.[85] In 1784 Brooke Boothby (1744–1826) inherited. His main interests were philosophical and artistic, and he belonged to the literary circle of Lichfield, with Erasmus Darwin and Anna Seward. Also interested in botany, he purchased rare plants and was a founder member of the Botanical Society of Lichfield with Dr Darwin in 1778. However it has to be said that the Society never grew beyond its three founder members and there is no evidence that Boothby actually contributed much.[86]

After his marriage in 1784 Sir Brooke used his wife's dowry and his own fortune, to remodel his park and house and to purchase works of art, including works by Joseph Wright of Derby, to whom he was patron. In 1781 Wright had painted Sir Brooke in the well-known painting (at the Tate Gallery) where Sir Brooke is shown lounging negligently in a romantic pose in an idealised glade. Sir Brooke's reflective, contemplative mood reflects this would-be philosopher who wrote poetry and entertained Jean Jacques Rousseau when he was staying at nearby Wootton Hall. The two became friends and Sir Brooke went on to translate and publish, at his own expense, Rousseau's autobiographical *Dialogues* in 1780.

Today the house has been much altered and the park is just a public open space with much lost to development, so it is difficult to imagine what it would have been like in its prime. Contemporaries were guarded in their comments:

> The mansion is not possessed externally of any architectural beauties; but within, every part is disposed with taste and elegance… The situation of the house is low, in a narrow valley on the bank of the river Henmore; but the park and gardens have been laid out in a style of beauty and gracefulness which compensate for the want of more picturesque scenery.[87]

FIGURE 71. Ashbourne Hall, with attached conservatory and trellis work on house. Detail from a lithograph 1839.

The public road, which ran directly in front of the house, dividing it from its parkland was diverted behind the hall, and concealed by a belt of trees. The hall then stood at the edge of flat parkland and the front was given a fashionable new conservatory, trellising and a rose garden, as popularised by Humphry Repton. It was probably at this time that the kitchen garden was moved away into the park. The large serpentine pools in the park were formed from the existing fishponds, fed by the Henmore, 'one of the finest trout streams in the county'.[88] They were joined by a cascade, and the smaller had a wooded island in the middle. Yet it does not appear that the pretty park was ever enlivened with follies, which is surprising given Sir Brooke's interest in architecture and his romantic outlook. One might have expected a rustic hermitage or grotto at the least, or even a gothic ruin, as befitted a friend and patron of Henry Fuseli.[89]

The devastating loss in 1791 of Sir Brooke's only child Penelope, at the age of five, closely followed by the breakdown of his marriage, caused him to lease the hall to stave off his creditors. This was followed by restless and sad travelling in England and then abroad, until his death in Paris as a practically penniless exile. Ironically history was repeating itself with poetic owners at Ashbourne Hall, when both Sir Aston Cokayne and Sir Brooke overspent hopelessly. The estate was sold not long after Sir Brooke's death, and split up.

Notes

All quotations from newspapers are © The British Library Board. All rights reserved. With thanks to the British Newspaper Archive (www.BritishNewspaperArchive.co.uk).

1. DRO: D518M/F150 Elvaston Account Book, 3 July 1742.
2. Egginton Hall was demolished in 1955, but in 1994 it was replaced with a smaller classical house. Craven and Stanley, I, 91–92. The bridge was replaced by an iron bridge from Coalbrookdale in 1812.
3. C. Glover and P. Riden (eds) 'William Woolley's History of Derbyshire', *Derbyshire Record Society* 6 (1981), 137.
4. DRO: D3155 WH1779 Thomas Cave to Robert Wilmot, 25 March 1770.
5. D3155: WH1779 Robert Wilmot to Thomas Cave, St James , 4 April 1770.
6. D3155: WH1779 Cave to Wilmot, 20 May 1770.
7. D3155: WH 1779 Cave to Wilmot 10 April 1770; Wilmot replied 2 May.
8. D3155: WH1780 Draft to nephew John [Wilmot] at Bedford, July 1769; Wilmot owned a stone quarry at Weston.
9. D3155: WH1780 John Wilmot to Robert Wilmot at Huntingdon, 10 July 1769. He enclosed a rough sketch.
10. J. Britton and E. Wedlake Brayley, *The Beauties of England and Wales*, vol. III (1802), 395.
11. SRO: D1287/18/10 (P/831) letters from George Augustus Bridgeman to his father Orlando Bridgeman in London, April–May 1789. I am grateful to Thea Randall for bringing these to my attention and Rebecca Jackson for her help,
12. DRO: 5430/12/6/1-3; the auction was to be 27 June 1839.
13. *DM*, 22 July 1835, p. 1; 15 May–16 June 1839.
14. Rev. J. Nixon [*sic*: Dixon] to Miss M. Bacon in 1745 – quoted in *Staffordshire Advertiser*, 12 May 1894, 3. My thanks to Sue Gregory for this reference. There were *Fermes Ornées* not far away at Sugnall and Shugborough, Staffordshire.

15. J. Cartwright (ed,), *The Travels Through England of Dr Richard Pococke during 1750, 1751 and later years* (1888), 218–19; J. Harris, 'The Duchess of Beaufort's Observations on Places', *Georgian Group Journal* 10 (2000), 38: 30 August 1751.

16. M. Charlesworth, *The English Garden, Literary Sources and Documents*, vol. II (1993), 136.

17. Illustrated in G. Jackson Stops, *An English Arcadia 1600–1990* (1991), 102.

18. B. Jones, *Follies and Grottoes* (1979 ed.), 217; J. Meir, *Sanderson Miller and his Landscapes*, (2006), 170.

19. S. Trubshaw, *Trubshaw Family Records 1285–1876* (Stafford, 1876), p. 39.

20. Meir, *Miller*, 168–71.

21. Pococke, *Travels*, 219.

22. Meir, *Miller*, 168–71; DRO: D5903/1 Map of Vernon estates 1794; D2360/3/260a Tithe map 1845.

23. J. Farey, *General View of the Agriculture and Minerals of Derbyshire*, vol. 2 (1815), 166. DRO: 5903/1 A Plan of the estate of … Lord Vernon 1794 by Saml. Botham.

24. Cartwright, *Travels of Dr Pococke*, 218–20. June 1751.

25. See a drawing, August 1777 by S. Bentley: www.staffspasttrack.org.uk; SV-Xi.83a. A watercolour by Paul Sandy, British Museum no 1904, 0819.49 shows the picturesque ruins inside the castle dominated by new folly tower as a rural idyll (1793).

26. *DM*, 3 Feb. 1791, 4.

27. SRO: D1788 parcel 57 John Wedge to brother Francis at Aqualate, 30 June 1804. 'Gentlemen for whom [John Webb] is now, or has been employed … Mr Webb is reported to be a man of skill and of credit…' In Derbyshire : Joseph Walker Esq., Aston Hall; E. M. Mundy Esq., Shipley; Arkwright, Matlock [Willersley 1792]; Pool Esq. Radburn; Mr Drury Low, Esq. Derby [Locko, 1792–93]; Lord Vernon, Sudbury.

28. DRO: D5903/1 (1794); DRO: D5903/2 (1823).

29. Craven and Stanley, II, 216–18. An English Heritage display board on the site (2016) shows the results of a geophysical survey, which revealed formal seventeenth-century parterres on the sloping grounds facing Bolsover Castle.

30. SRO: D(W)1733/C/3/143. It can be dated to 1745 through a brick inscribed 'Godfrey Clark Esq 1745', and shows the influence of the bastion kitchen garden in the Switzer's *Practical Kitchen Gardener* (1727) opp. p. 369. Images of England no. 79387; *DM*, 25 Aug. 1824, 1.

31. Sale details *DM*, 5 May 1775, p. 4; SRO: D(W)1733/C/3/137 'Plan of Sutton Park as when it became the Property of Mr Kynnersley' (1775). *DM*, 13 Oct. 1824, 1.

32. SRO: D(W)1733/C/3/131 Plan which notes 'the Menagery' west end of the House 1808.

33. SRO: D(W)C/3/280; D(W)1733/C/3/303 Proceedings of the court case Clarke v. Kynnersley.

34. SRO: D(W)1733/C/3/190 (N/D-1832) Chancery Case Ormonde *v* Kynnersley; affidavits of Thomas Hollowes *et al*. This was supported by no less a witness than the young Joseph Paxton when the case rumbled on into the 1830s: D(W)1773/C/3/290-1.

35. SRO: D(W)1733/C/3/148 (1815); D(W)1733/C/3/129 (1817); D(W)1733/C/3/137 (1820), D(W)1733/C/3/144 (1824).

36. *DM*, 25 Aug., 22 Sept., 13 Oct., 24 Nov. 1824.

37. *Manchester Mercury*, 26 Oct. 1824, 3; 7 Dec. 1824, 2.

38. *DM*, 24 Nov. 1824, p. 3 has an amusing account of the brilliant bidding tactics of George Robins and Richard Arkwright.

39. Craven and Stanley, I, 84–86. It was taxed on 23 hearths in 1662.

40. Harris, 'The Duchess of Beaufort's Observations', 37. She visited 22 August 1751.

41. J. Wain, *The Story of Drakelow* (1966), 10. Wain provides a useful account of the family.

42. Craven and Stanley, I, 84–85; K. Bradley Hole, *Lost Gardens of England from the Archives of Country Life* (2004), 139. Illustrated in G. Worsley, *England's Lost Houses from the Archives of Country Life* (2002), 88–89. Part of the room was rescued and is in store at the Victoria and Albert Museum – V&A no. P12.1934. *The Letters of Anna Seward written between the Years 1784–1807*, vol. III, 380–81(Edinburgh, 1811).

43. The Georgian Group, Pardoe Collection DERBO 17. A sketch by Penelope, wife of Sir William Nigel Gresley, 1855.

44. J. C. Loudon (ed), *The Landscape Gardening and Landscape Architecture of the Late Humphrey Repton* (1840), 215. The circle is shown on the 1882 and 1901 OS maps.

45. Craven and Stanley, I, 85, citing Peacocke's *Polite Repository or Pocket Companion, June 1793*, which has a drawing of the hall with its terrace.

46. P. Heath, 'Sealwood Cottage Derbyshire: An Early Cottage Orné by 'Dr Syntax.' *Georgian Group Journal* 18 (2010), 105–14; P. Heath, 'Notes for Heritage Open Day, September 2011'. This section is based on Heath's information.

47. Heath, 'Sealwood Cottage', 112.

48. *Ibid.*, 109. The approach then was from the opposite direction to the present approach.

49. Quoted T. Mowl, *Historic Gardens of Gloucestershire* (2002), 111.

50. Craven and Stanley, II, 308.

51. Britton and Brayley, *Beauties of England*, III, 509.

52. C. Bruyn Andrews (ed.) *The Torrington Diarie*s, vol. 2 (1935), 40.

53. M. Craven, 'Willersley: An Adam Castle in Derbyshire', *The Georgian Group Journal* 22 (2014), 109–22.

54. Britton and Brayley, *Beauties of England*, III, 517.

55. *Ibid.*, 521–2.

56. *DM*, 20 Aug. 1834, 3.

57. *DM*, 20 Aug. 1834, 3; W. Adam, *Gem of the Peak* (1851), 672; E. Jewitt (ed.), *Black's 1872 Tourist's Guide to Derbyshire* (1999) 131, provides full and enthusiastic descriptions.

58. www.aboutderbyshire.co.uk/cms/places/cressbrook.shtml; Tom Bates-Cressbrook. www.cressbrookclub.org.yk/village.html accessed February 2015.

59. *DM*, 17 Aug. 1786, 3. 'Rock House' and the rock face, now called the Rubican Wall, is much loved by climbers. See also J. Pilkington, *A View of the Present State of Derbyshire*, vol. I (1789), 16.

60. Lady Llanover (ed.), *The Autobiography and Correspondence of Mary Granville, Mrs Delaney*, 2nd ser., vol. III (1862), 101. F. Montague to Mrs Delaney, 5 August 1782.

61. W. Burgh (ed.),W. Mason, *The English Garden A Poem in Four Books* (1786). Book 3, lines 234–39.

62. D. Kesteven, *Renishaw Hall Gardens* (2010).

63. DRO: D37/M/H13 estate map of Ford House *c*.1780, shows a rather empty agricultural landscape enclosed by a meandering stream, and next to it an open classical temple as an eye-catcher from the house.

64. Craven and Stanley, II, 189 suggest Alderson was responsible for the pleasure grounds at Romiley Hall (1785) and also (vol. I, 162–63) that he was involved with the park at Norton Hall, Sheffield.

65. Craven and Stanley, I, 59–60. DRO: D1881/BoxD/13(papers of Coke of Brookhill) item in memorandum book: 1780 16 December 'Pickford came'.

66. DRO: D1881/BoxD/1.

67. See P. Armstrong, *The English Parson – Naturalist: A Companionship between Science and Religion* (2000), 17.

68. Shown on the Brookhill Hall Teapot at Derby Museum..

69. DRO: D1881/BoxD – a loose sheet. The total came to £19.19.7 which matches the bill from Joseph Outram, paid in March 1783.

70. See N. D. Gent, *The Patterns and Shapes of the Pinxton China Factory, 1796–1813* (1996).

71. Ashbourne Local History Group, *A Georgian Country Town Ashbourne, 1725–1825*. Vol. 2, *Architecture*: an excellent, well researched book.

72. *DM*, 9 Feb. 1776, 4; 14 Feb. 1777, 1 'The Sign of the Prince of Brunswick'.

73. *DM*, 3 April 1767, 4.

74. See Images of England IoE 79863, 79865 Dove House; 79804, 79944 7, Church Street; 79945, 49, Church Street.

75. *DM*, 23 Dec. 1813, 3 (28, Church Street); 17 May 1820, 1 and 5 Dec. 1821, 1.

76. *Aris' Birmingham Gazette*, 6 Nov. 1843, 4.

77. *DM*, 10 May 1810, 2.

78. T. Taylor, *A Life of John Taylor, LLD of Ashbourne* (1910); M. Broadley (ed.), *Doctor Johnson and Mrs Thrale, including Mrs Thrale's unpublished Journal of the Welsh Tour made in 1774* (1910), 164.

79. Craven and Stanley, I. 28–29; E. Saunders, *Joseph Pickford of Derby, a Georgian Architect* (1993), 71–74. I am most grateful to Mr J. Cartland for permission to visit the Mansion House and for his advice on this and other Ashbourne properties.

80. R. W. Chapman (ed.), S. Johnson, *The Letters of Samuel Johnson*, vol. 2 (1952) no. 417, Dr Johnson to Mrs Thrale, 11 July 1775.

81. Chapman, *Letters*, vol. 1, no. 236. Dr Johnson to Mrs Thrale, 20 July 1770.

82. Chapman, *Letters*, vol. 2, no. 541 Dr Johnson to Mrs Thrale, 4 September 1777.

83. *DM*, 21 Sept. 1815, 2.

84. *W. Woolley's History of Derbyshire*, 212.

85. *DM*, 22 May, 21 Oct. 1772, 4; M. Wiltshire and S. Woore, *Medieval Parks of Derbyshire*, (2009), 22–23; Ashbourne Conservation Area Appraisal: 5. Setting the Conservation Area: www.derbyshiredales.gov.uk.

86. D. King Hele, *Erasmus Darwin, a Life of Unequalled Achievement* (1999), 51, 179, 191.

87. Britton and Brayley, *The Beauties of England and Wales, or, Delineations, Topographical, Historical, and Descriptive, of each County*, vol. 3 (1802), 423.

88. *DM*, 26 Aug., 9 Dec. 1846, 2 – sale details for the Ashborne Hall Estate. Hall, pleasure grounds and park totalled 91 acres (36.4 ha).

89. Boothby owned Fuseli's painting *The Nightmare*, now in the Detroit Institute of Art. Fuseli also painted a powerful picture of Penelope Boothby being taken to heaven: *The Apotheosis of Penelope Boothby*, 1792 now at Wolverhampton Art Gallery.

CHAPTER SIX

Caves, Hermitages and Grottos

....

…a grotto encrusted with sea-shells or fantastic pebble-work.

In October 1752 the *Universal Magazine of Knowledge and Pleasure* included a picture of the Grotto of Antiparos, in the south Aegean, where tourists stand awestruck in the huge cavern with its stalagmites and stalactites. Yet there were equally awe-inspiring caverns for the tourist in Derbyshire. In the late seventeenth century Celia Fiennes described Poole's Hole Cavern, whose strange shapes included the Queen of Scots' Pillar, 'which is a large white stone and the top hangs over your head like a canopy, all great white stones and in spires of large iceickles, and glistering'.[1] In 1755 Resta Patching plucked up courage to explore some Derbyshire Caverns and was amazed by the 'Devil's Arse' near Castleton, whose high arch he felt was 'in the Gothick Taste'. Its 'Chancel' or Cavern was lit by dozens of candles by locals, for the benefit of the tourists who were expected to give tips afterwards.[2]

Bagshawe's Cavern, two miles (3.2 km) from Castleton, was discovered by lead miners in 1806 and soon opened to the public commercially. Advertised in 1808, with the 'exquisite beauty of its various sparry crystallized incrustations', there seems to have been no sense of irony in advertising its desecration:

> to be Sold at this place, Incrusted Stones and Icicles [stalactites] of various colours, forms and sizes, all specimens of this inimitable Wonder, and calculated in the highest degree to enrich and adorn the first collections.

The self-righteous assertion that 'This surprising Wonder is not shewn on a Sabbath Day' hardly compensates for this asset-stripping, some of which doubtless transferred to man-made garden grottoes.[3] When Rutland Cavern at Matlock Bath opened in 1817, it was admired for its 'rich treasure' of fossils and minerals 'forming the most splendid natural Grotto in the World … with Pillars, Arches and Bridges … Labyrinths, Arcades, Walls, Roofs, and Floors, embellished with the most glittering Crystals'.[4]

Raynard's Hall on the river Dove near Ashbourne was a privately owned natural cave, converted by a local family, the Fitzherberts, for their entertainment. It was also much visited by the tourist in search of the picturesque. In 1747 Lady Sophia Newdigate wrote:

> we climbed up to a place which makes me almost giddy to relate, called Renards Hall from ye Foxes of ye Country making it their Asylum, when persued. Tis a Cave in ye Rock to which ye owner of this place Mr Fitzherbert has made ye access more easy as he often uses it to dine or drink Tea in.[5]

FIGURE 72. Foremark,
Anchor Chapel.

Its fame and destination on an itinerary was assured when John Boydell included a print in his *Collections of One Hundred Views in England and Wales* (1749), reprinted in *The Lady's Magazine* October 1790 (see Fig. 2).

Two small caves in hilly outcrops in Derbyshire were reputed to have been home to hermits in the Middle Ages, and therefore were of special interest at a period when landowners were erecting 'hermitages' as a picturesque feature in the designed landscape (*vide* Kedleston). In contrast with sophisticated classical follies, such hermitages reminded visitors of the virtues of a simple life, secluded from human company, encouraging reflection. They were often made from tree roots, with a pebble or bone floor and with sparse rustic furniture, providing scope for moralising and contemplation. Ironically, these two genuine hermit's caves were used, not for contemplation, but for family picnics.

About half a mile from Foremark Hall, across fields and woods, on the south side of the river Trent, is a long limestone outcrop. Among its many fissures, small natural holes and caves, is a cave known as **Anchor Chapel,** reputedly once a cell and chapel for a solitary medieval hermit or anchorite. Within the cave crude columns form chambers with holes for windows and doors cut into the rock. As Woolley understated *c.*1715: 'an anchorite's cell, and it really is a most a most solitary, pleasant place'.[6] Pools below the cave were linked to the river and were fished for the Burdetts from the 1690s.[7] A delightful painting by Thomas Smith of Derby *c.*1745 shows the family enjoying a walk along the river bank, and fishing, the beautifully dressed adults and children mixing town elegance with rusticity, suggested by the pastoral cows on the river bank opposite. By then the cave had been enlarged into rooms accessed by outside steps and was used for entertaining (Pl. 18).

FIGURE 73. Dale Abbey Hermitage cut into the rock cliff overlooking the abbey remains.

Josiah Wedgwood included three views of Anchor among the 34 views of Derbyshire in his Frog Dinner Service for Catherine the Great of Russia 1773–74.[8] By 1790 the scene accorded perfectly with the enthusiasm for the picturesque – 'a more beauteous and romantic scene is not to be found'.[9] When John Byng visited 'this picturesque scenery of delight' that year, finding the caves locked, he felt that visitors should have better access with a guard on site, (in a little house) and a guide book. 'Here might the owner, then, store up his fishing tackle, some few books, with a snug corner of good wine; comfortable apartment'.[10]

Such a cosy concept was anathema to the picturesque movement, and by the end of the century the cave was allowed to become overgrown to make it look even more romantic:

> …The summit of the rock is crested by old oaks and firs, and irregularly broken by deep fissures and abrupt prominences, half covered with brush-wood and ivy, which mantling over the Gothic-like door and windows of the hermitage, give a very picturesque character to the whole mass'.[11]

The second hermitage was at **Dale Abbey**, thirteenth-century home of Premonstratensian Canons. Today all that remains are sections of the great East window, marooned in a field with a few stone village houses close by, clearly monastic in origin. However in 1716, when purchased by the Earl of Chesterfield, the abbey ruins were far more extensive, as shown in Buck's view of 1727. The Abbey is sited below a rocky escarpment in which is a Hermit's cave, cut out of the solid rock face, reputedly by a hermit in the 1130s. The story is that a Derby baker, Cornelius, had a vision of the Virgin Mary who told him to go to Depedale, (as the area was called then), to live the solitary life of a hermit. Thus inspired Cornelius went, cut out his cave in the sandstone ridge and from this modest start there soon followed a chapel and ultimately the abbey below.

The cave is quite large – about 20 ft long and nine ft (6.1 × 2.7 m) wide and high. The central entrance is a gothic arch with two suitably primitive 'doors' and 'windows'. Four joist holes above suggest that once there was once some form of protective covering, part of the enlargements perhaps made by a member of the Stanhope family from Elvaston, five miles (8 km) away. Reputedly it was used for scenic picnics, as at Anchor Chapel. Earl Stanhope, the owner, actually lived at Chevening, Kent, but his Elvaston relatives no doubt had his blessing to use the evocative site, with its romantic views down to the abbey remains, fields, stream and monastic fishponds.[12] Reynard's Cave, Anchor Church and Dale Abbey, although privately owned, were accessible to tourists.

Derbyshire was well supplied with materials to make and decorate grottoes, which must have encouraged the building of these fashionable follies. There was a ready supply of stone and also tufa, a soft, light porous stone, easier to transport, which was valued for the rustic, natural effect it provided both outside and inside grottoes. For interiors local minerals included 'Mock Amethyst, or what is vulgarly call'd Blue John', which sold at 2–5 guineas a ton in 1769.[13] Its prime use was for decorative items but scraps would find their way into grottoes. In 1780 there was advertised for sale at the Red Lion, Wirksworth, 'A Quantity of a very curious Sort of PETRIFICATIONS or WATER-ICEICLES'.[14] These ancient stalactites had been removed from local caves for use in man-made grottoes. There were also lime-stone crystals in hexagonal and pyramidal shapes of quartz crystal, which could be a rose colour ('Derbyshire diamonds'). Calcareous incrustations available from most caverns came in rose, blue, dark blue and varying shapes.[15] In short, Derbyshire was a grotto maker's Paradise.

Grottoes were retreats for retirement and contemplation, yet were also rather expensive statements of wealth and culture. In 1667 John Woolridge's *Systema Horti-Culturae or The Art of Gardening* recommended a grotto for a garden as:

> a place of repose, cold and fresh in the greatest heats. It may be Arched over with stone or brick, and you may give it what light or entrance you please. You may make secret rooms and passages within it and in the outer Room may you have all those before mentioned water-works, for your own or your friends divertisements…[16]

A century later a poem, by the local William Mugliston of Alfreton, included the inevitable platitude – 'Now tis within the weeping grotto's cell /Where solitude and contemplation dwell'…[17]

Traditionally grottoes were positioned near water, whether river, pool, fountain or cascade, and featured in books of architectural designs ranging in style from the rustic to classical. In the eighteenth century their often exotic decoration was seen as a suitable pastime for ladies, with material imported from the Indies, but also utilising more accessible minerals, spar and pebbles and even industrial waste such as slag. Alexander Pope's grotto in his garden at Twickenham set the pace in the 1720s with his use of shells and glass which reflected the moving light of the nearby river Thames. In 1747 the *Derby Mercury*

(18 December) devoted two full pages describing the gardens at Stowe, Bucks, where the grotto by the river was 'furnished with a great Number of Looking-Glasses in Frames of Plaister-work, set with Shells and broken Flints.'

Grottos were now fashionable, with expensive and exotic shells needed in huge quantities, often combined with petrifactions. As John Farey commented of Derbyshire in 1815:

> In several gardens, I saw Grottos, fitted up with the double view of affording a cool retreat in hot weather, or from a shower, and of preserving and showing to strangers, large specimens of the most noted Minerals of the district.[18]

He cited Calke, Chatsworth, Eyam and Newton Solney, but there were others at Alfreton, Kedleston, Bakewell and Matlock.

At **Eyam** William Longsdon's (1745–1811) interest in geology was reflected in his grotto, created as a romantic retreat not far from his home in the village. Utilising the dramatic lie of the land at Middleton, with its narrow valley and stream, by the late 1770s:

> [he] placed a seat on the summit, has planted some trees, and made a grotto with the spars. etc. found in the neighbourhood. One Benneson [a lead miner] earns a livelihood here by collecting them and has a number of specimens at his house.[19]

For the poetess, Anna Seward, who had been born at Eyam, musing on the 'savage magnificence of Eyam-Dale' (1804), this area was primitive and awe-inspiring:

> Mr Longston of Eyam, has adorned a part of this scene by a hanging garden and imitative fort [tower]. The steep winding paths of the garden are planted with wild shrubs, natives of sterile soil, and which root their fibres in the fissures of the rocks. The effect, in descending those paths from the cliffs above, is very striking. They command the stupendous depths of the vale below and a considerable portion of its curve.[20]

Yet by 1817 the grotto had been asset-striped, although the picturesque valley site was still enjoyed by visitors:

> The shelvings of the rock are covered with luxuriant trees and shrubs, wildly intermixed, and appearing to grow as planted by the hand of nature. Half way up the rock the late Mr. LONGSDEN, of Eyam, to whom the place was indebted for its embellishments, had constructed a grotto, where specimens of the choicest and most beautiful spars and fossils of the county, were tastefully displayed to the admiring spectator... But these are gone; and only enough is left to make the visitor regret the destruction of the remainder.

> On a ledge of rock below the grotto, is the entrance to Merlin's Cave… Higher up, and directly over the grotto, is a kind of Martello tower, and a little to the left, on the summit of the rock, are the remains of yet another building, where the wearied traveller may yet find a seat, and enjoy a prospect, varied, extensive and sublime.[21]

By then Merlin's Cave was the main attraction for visitors, with its 'beautiful Stalactites well preserved, by the care of the late William Longsdon Esq.'[22] A local poet enthused in 1836:

Where Merlin's cave beneath a hanging shade,
Deep wonders open'd to the winding glade;
Wild gardens flourish'd on the scanty soil,
And Flora bade the barren rocks to smile...
An ivied yew sprung out, above the cell,
At the shy entrance dripp'd a crystal well...
Spar, pebbles, crystal, glitter'd in the wave,
Whence dancing sunbeams play'd along the cave[23]

White Watson (1760–1835) is an important figure in the story of Derbyshire grottos. He was responsible for, and influenced, several grottos here in the late eighteenth–early nineteenth century. Watson was a noted polymath: geologist, sculptor, stonemason, marble worker, plants-man and published influential works on geology, fauna and flora. He took over his uncle's business at Bakewell in 1786 as a stonemason and carver, by which time he had started his impressive collection of Derbyshire minerals and fossils. He enjoyed the patronage of the Dukes of Devonshire and Rutland, advising the Duchess of Devonshire on the creation of a fossil room. In 1798 he created a grotto for her at Chatsworth, designed to look like a cave with tufa around the entrance, planted with ivy and rock plants. At a cost of £66 18s 9d the interior was carefully lined with specimens of Derbyshire fossils as found in their original geological stratas. Therefore this apparently frivolous garden feature was actually a quite serious geological showcase, reflecting the Cavendishs' enthusiasm for the subject. It was replaced by the present grotto in the 1830s, when the collection of fossils was replaced by specimens of copper ore.[24]

Watson created two grottoes at Bakewell, one of which was a rustic grotto over the water source adjoining the Bath and his house, in the new botanic gardens which he had designed for the Duke of Rutland. Again he seems to have used geological specimens and covered them with plants to fit in with the theme of the garden. In his 1811 book on Derbyshire geology Watson included a poetical description 'by a Gentleman of Bakewell' (the local poet Michael Williams):

By Watson grac'd the Fount is seen to rise;
From latent dark retreat, obscur'd from sight,
In stony limits bound there greets the light;
An Antique pile of stones adorns its head,
By Scient[ific] hand in rude disorder laid;
Here Stalactites, their spiral heads above
Shoot up and form a pyramidic grove,
And moss grown stones lie rudely at their base
Adding a cell-like semblance to the place:
While flow'ry tendrils, jutting from between
Give a wild grace and beauty to the Scene:[25]

A surviving grotto designed by White Watson at **The Manor, Stanton Woodhouse** lives up to expectations. The Tudor house was purchased in 1760 by the Duke of Rutland, from nearby Haddon Hall, as 'a shooting seat ... situated on a natural terrace overlooking this beautiful Dale'.[26] It stands in open hilly countryside with wide sweeping views over fields. The terraced garden is walled round in stone, the outline of which must surely date back to the seventeenth century, as must several ancient and huge yews which line the top terrace, at one end of which the grotto was erected. Originally the garden was less open, for White's *Directory of Derbyshire* (1857) notes the Elizabethan house 'situated on a fine elevation, surrounded with terraces, ancient yews, Spanish chestnut, walnut, elm, and other trees, commanding extensive prospects.'[27]

The fifth Duke of Rutland enlarged the hunting lodge and embellished the gardens in 1816 with the grotto by White Watson, assisted by a local mason, George Berrisford.[28] Its siting is little unexpected, for since grottos are traditionally associated with water, the obvious position would have been near the north wall of the garden, where there was a little stream. This still runs from a small cascade near the entrance front, although now diverted in a pipe through the garden. Instead the grotto was built to the south side of the house, at the end of the main terrace on which the house sits.

The grotto is on two levels, with the house terrace giving access to the upper level through a single arch, (the rear of a curved grotto), which then gives access under another arch to an open viewing platform, where the duke could entertain guests (Pl. 19). Underneath this a four-centred arch leads into a plain stone barrel-vaulted underground room, where one likes to think that bottles of wine were stored ready for drinking on the platform above. The main grotto is a curving passage with three tufa arches giving views out over the countryside. The grotto entrances have rusticated classical keystones and architraves, with a strong Italian Mannerist influence, including a rough niche inside. Today the floor is paved with small paving stones surrounded by pebbles, (the latter

FIGURE 74. Stanton Woodhouse, White Watson's grotto; lower chamber with three openings.

presumably the original flooring material). Walls are made from large tufa stones while the occasional surviving stalactite shows that much decoration has been lost. However much survives, in spite of some disturbance and partial collapse. It is intricate, sophisticated and elaborate and one wonders from where Watson took his inspiration- perhaps from a more overtly classical three-arched arbour illustrated in Book II of Thomas Wright's *Universal Architecture* (1758)?

Possibly Watson might be linked with a lost late eighteenth-century grotto at **Alfreton Hall**, where only the 1898 wing survives as a tea-room in what is now a nicely wooded public park. Rowland Morewood commissioned Francis Smith to build a Baroque House in the 1720s and later engaged Edmund and Joseph Outram of Alfreton to lay out the gardens.[29] Morewood was an enthusiastic planter of oak trees:

> which passion being inherited by his son he saw many thousands rise into shady groves and sturdy timber, which, added to rich veins of coals, increased a moderate fortune to a very considerable one.[30]

When George Morewood (1720–92) died his widow Ellen (1740–1823) inherited the estate and the following year she married the Rev. Henry Case. They sold the estate to Adam Palmer of Alfreton in 1798, who immediately enlarged the house.[31] An 1812 description of the park describes lost features, which suggest a sequence of follies in the upper woodland (Pond Wood):

> a piece of woodland, the upper part of which is intersected by two avenues: one of them which branches off to the other. [The one] on the right is terminated by a *Temple of Diana, and a bust*, and the other of them by an *obelisk*, above and below by a piece of water, the boundaries of which, not being seen from the farthest point of view, the imagination is left to form to itself the idea of unlimited expansion and transform a little fish pond into an extensive lake. Below are *several moss huts and a grotto* built of different mineral productions of all that diversity of form and colour exhibited by the mineral substances of the Peak. It is of an octagonal figure and painted within are several representations of scenes in Walton's 'Angler'.[32]

The straight avenues are shown on an 1822 map with the pond but unfortunately no buildings or other features are indicated.[33] The follies are probably post-1782 as William Mugliston, the aspiring local poet with a decidedly un-poetical name, failed to mention any park ornaments in his lengthy poem of 1782 'A Contemplative Walk with the Author's Wife and children in the Parks of George Morewood, Esq. at Alfreton'.[34] The grotto seems to have been a sophisticated building, and, since White Watson supplied specimens of inlaid marble to the house in 1796, it is possible that he was responsible for the grotto with its geological specimens.[35] Given the mention of painted walls or ceiling, it could be that the octagon had a grotto on the ground floor and painted chamber above. It would be helpful to have more than this single contemporary description, as it must have been known and admired locally.

The remains of another grotto, for which also there is little information, lie largely concealed in undergrowth, against a stone boundary wall, seemingly once part of the **Bowden** estate near Chapel-en-le-Frith. This rustic grotto was

FIGURE 75. Bowden, near Chapel-en-le Frith. Ruined, overgrown stone grotto and brick tower.

built from rough large stones and overlooks a nearby stream. It stands next to the shell of an eighteenth-century brick built tower, perhaps once a folly, set into the corner of the boundary walls. Are the two features contemporary and, if so, were they a picturesque retreat half a mile from the house? Information has proved elusive.

Eighteenth-century grottos at Calke and Kedleston are considered in other chapters, but mention should be made of an early nineteenth-century grotto at **Melbourne Hall**, discretely hidden away from the old baroque formal gardens. It is an open rustic grotto, decorated with spar, minerals, ore and shells, its pool fed by natural springs. At the rear is a classical niche with a small marble slab on which is carved a poem by George Lamb (1784–1834), brother of Lord Melbourne (although tradition naturally prefers the notorious Lady Caroline Lamb as author). It brings up-to-date the traditional idea of retreat, not from cares of state but now from industrial pollution:

> Rest weary stranger in this shady cave,
> And taste, if languid, of the mineral wave,
> There's virtue in the draught, for health that flies
> From crowded cities and their smoky skies
> Here lends her power to every grove and hill
> Strength to the breeze and medicine to the rill

A totally unexpected place to find an expensive and sophisticated grotto was in a garden of a spar manufactory and shop in King Street, **Derby**, owned by **Frances Spinks** (1762–1819?). An able businesswoman, she took over the business on the death of her husband in 1810 and immediately announced a special attraction for customers and visitors: 'An elegant Grotto', planned by her late husband and completed by her 'in the most appropriate style'. The charge to view was 1 shilling (5p) and children 6d (2½ p):

> The Building is of an octagonal form, with a pyramidal Roof, terminating in a glazed Dome; from whence the light is transmitted internally through polished circular Specimens of choice transparent Fluors, the various and beautiful hues of which are by this means shewn to great advantage. It receives light also from four Gothic Windows of transparent Paintings on Glass, representing the Four Seasons. The internal decorations of the Walls consist of fine Specimens of the Crystallizations of Minerals, Stalactites, etc. collected at a very considerable expence from various parts of the Kingdom, but particularly Derbyshire. Also a great diversity of Corals, Shells, and other marine Productions, from many different parts of the World. And opposite the Entrance, is a curious Chimney-piece supported by Columns of Alabaster cut in diamonds.

With its 'combination of natural and artificial Beauties' this grotto summer-house appeared to have been a success, as soon afterwards Mrs Spinks proudly announced that it 'has lately been enriched with several additional Curiosities'.[36] Since most people would not have had access to see a grotto in a private landscape, indeed this must have been a novelty to admire. However in 1818 Mrs Spinks decided to offer for sale this 'most beautiful and universally admired Grotto, situate in a Garden ... [and] allowed by competent and experienced Judges to be the finest specimen of its kind in Derbyshire'.

Someone purchased this masterpiece, for the following year 1819 Mrs Spinks announced that 'she has just completed the erection of an Entire New Grotto which is now ready for exhibition in her Flower Garden.' It seems to have been a close copy of the original but now the setting was enhanced, as now it was 'approached by a group of romantic rock work'.[37] Mrs Spinks retired (or died) soon afterwards, and under new ownership the grotto was for sale in 1822:

> That most beautifully and universally admired Grotto [with its] tasteful arrangement of numerous Shells, Corals, Spars , Fossils etc and of the most curious and beautiful kinds; the Roof terminating in a Dome of Stained Glass, through which the rays of the Sun are transmitted so as to produce the most pleasing effect.[38]

One would like to know more about Frances Spinks, business-woman, entrepreneur, and designer of grottos. Was she influenced by the Alfreton grotto? What happened to her grottos? Ironically it would appear that the most sophisticated example of a grotto in Derbyshire was actually behind a factory, even if in an attractive garden.[39]

Only occasionally were there such opportunities to buy a complete grotto. Sometimes materials for grottos could come from private sales, as at Bretton Hall, Yorkshire in 1832 with 'the entire fittings of a grotto in British Spa'.[40] The contents of the Museum of Natural History at Lichfield were sold in 1800, including a large variety of shells and 'many thousand specimens of Minerals, Spars, etc for collections, chymical experiments and grotto work'. Also for sale in 1800 was a natural history collection from Fisherwick Hall, near Lichfield,

PLATE 1. Hardwick Hall, south gazebo, 1590s, in corner of garden.

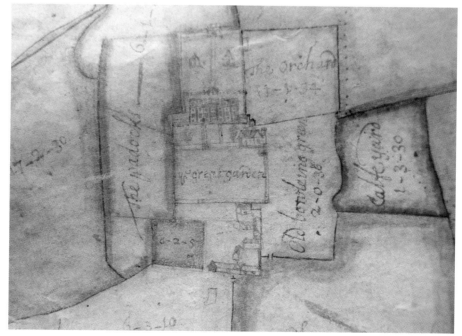

PLATE 2. Oldcotes 'first drawn by Edmund Browne 1659 … ponds and park were made and replenished in ye yeare 1688. Fra Bainbridge'.

PLATE 3. Bolsover Castle, Venus Fountain by Robert Smythson.

COURTESY OF ENGLISH HERITAGE

PLATE 4 *(left)*. Bolsover Castle, Little Castle garden, retreat room within the wide garden wall.

COURTESY OF ENGLISH HERITAGE

PLATE 5 *(below)*. Snitterton Hall, Corner Pavilion and terrace overlooking entrance courtyard garden.

COURTESY K. ALCOCK AND S. HASLAM

PLATE 6. Sudbury Hall
and gardens from the
South; painting by John
Griffier *c*.1690.

PLATE 7. Rowtor Rocks
with a seat alcove today.

PLATE 8. Melbourne Hall, Van Ost's lead *Urn of the Four Seasons* with *allée* to pool behind.

COURTESY LORD RALPH KERR

PLATE 9. Calke Abbey, remains of mid-eighteenth-century grotto.

BY KIND PERMISSION OF THE NATIONAL TRUST

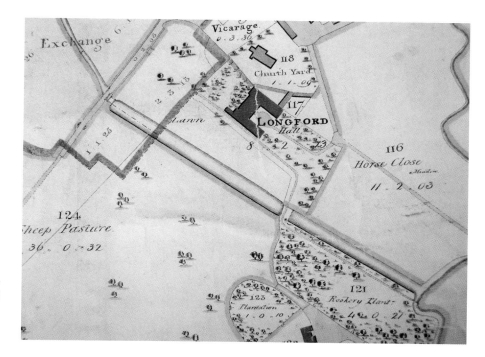

PLATE 10. Longford Hall, tithe map (1834) showing the long canal along the terrace.

PLATE 11. Knowle Hill, terracing below site of original house, with surviving eighteenth-century brickwork.

PLATE 12. Markeaton Hall, Joseph Pickford's Orangery, now a tea-room.

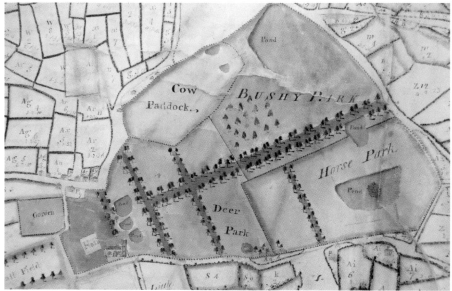

PLATE 13. Wingerworth, Estate Map of property of Sir Henry Hunloke, 1758. A long avenue leads to fish ponds and hall on left.

PLATE 14. Kedleston Hall, Robert Adam's Fishing Lodge and Bridge.

PLATE 15 *(left)*. Stoke Hall, Statue of Flora in nearby 'Flora Wood'.

COURTESY S. DRURY.

PLATE 16 *(above)*. Sealwood Cottage, mid-1770s as restored with tiles replacing original thatch.

COURTESY E. AND J. GOODALL

BROOK-HILL   HALL.

PLATE 17. Brook Hill Hall, Pinxton. Similar images decorated Pinxton porcelain *c.*1796–1813.

COURTESY OF G. LAYCOCK AND WWW.PICTURETHEPAST.ORG.UK

PLATE 18 *(above)*. 'Anchor church, Foremark', popular venue for tourists. 1823 engraving.

PLATE 19 *(left)*. Stanton Woodhouse, White Watson's grotto, upper entrance from house terrace.

PLATE 22 *(left)*. Elvaston Castle, rockwork and grotto along the side of the lake.

PLATE 23 *(below)*. Breadsall Priory, Mawson's rock garden 1910 with a modern fountain.

COURTESY J. GUTTRICH, MARRIOTT HOTELS

PLATE 26 *(above)*. Derby Arboretum, the central fountain today with even higher safety railings.

PLATE 27 *(left)*. Cressbrook Hall, Edward Kemp's colourful parterre garden with fuchsia, standard roses and four foot Irish yews at each corner.

PLATE 28. Ogston Hall,
Thomas Chambers Hine's
1860 Conservatory today.

Courtesy OF D. WAKEFIELD

PLATE 29. Locko Park,
Lioness, Lion and
Eagle from Val D'Osne
foundry (after 1892).

Courtesy MRS L. PALMER.

PLATE 30. Renishaw Hall,
Gothick conservatory
(1808) converted into an
Aviary by the 1840s and
now a garden feature.

Courtesy MRS A. HAYWOOD.

PLATE 33. The Green, Eckington, garden by C. E. Mallows and Edwin Lutyens; view of pergola from house terrace.

COURTESY OF D. AND J. NORTH

PLATE 34. Netherseal Old Hall, door to garden shed and greenhouse range, 1915.

COURTESY A. AND E. DEVEY SMITH

PLATE 35. Thornbridge Hall, terrace below house leading to the rock tunnel; early twentieth century with later planting.

COURTESY J. AND E. HARRISON

PLATE 36. Park Hall tea pavilion/summer house 1933.

COURTESY K. AND M. STANIFORTH

PLATE 37. Herbert Lodge, Interior of the Millennium Grotto (2002).

COURTESY O. AND N. GERRISH

with shells, pebbles, marbles, minerals etc. for collections and 'grotto work' with thousands of shells purchased for an unexecuted grotto.[41]

In the nineteenth century materials were more accessible. In 1824 a shop at Matlock Bath advertised tasteful ornaments in spar, and also 'spar'd tufa for rock work and grottos'.[42] In 1838 Mr George Twigg, of Butterton, near Leek, supplied 'Gentlemen with Fossils and Mineral Specimens for Grottos etc'.[43] A Manchester advert (1837) offered 'Beautifully Painted and Stained Glass, of the finest colours and exquisite workmanship … suitable for … conservatories, greenhouses … and grottos'. Its final item was intriguing – 'a very complete portable grotto, with twenty seven lights, finished in the ancient style'.[44] A reminder that not all grottoes were rustic was a sale in Birmingham (1847) advertising 'splendid plaster statues, groups, busts from the antique … embellishments for Halls, Vestibules, Grottoes, Niches, Pleasure Grounds'.[45]

To create a grotto a large quantity of building material was needed. Gypsum (plaster of Paris) was a useful base material and a ready supply was available from the Fauld mine on the Derbyshire/Staffordshire border. By the 1840s it was noted as having supplied much of the kingdom for Ornamental Grottos and Rockeries, 'and thousands of tons can be raised at comparatively trifling expense'.[46] Then artificial stone began to appear. In 1825 a nurseryman in Derby offered a 'Rockery or artificial rock, with appropriate alpine plants'.[47] In 1837 Austin's artificial stone was confidently advertised in the *Derby Mercury* as suitable for a remarkably imaginative and ambitious range of objects, requiring 'neither painting nor colouring, is impervious to water, and will not sustain injury from the severest winter'. Its use included 'fountains, flower pots, statues, cascades, artificial ruins, mausoleums and grottos'.[48]

In 1854 William Lonsdale of Nottingham, manufacturer of Roman cement, offered 'a very beautiful variegated Plaster rock for Grotto and Garden purposes'.[49] Then Pulham and Son invented 'Pulhamite', a hugely popular artificial stone which used a base of brick and clinker, over which Portland cement was added, treated to resemble a naturalistic looking rough stone. It was used extensively in Victorian gardens for grottos and rockwork. (*vide* Osmaston).

From the mid-nineteenth century the term 'grotto' could also mean a rockery or group of stones, as revealed in advertisements for houses to buy or rent in Derby. Included in their gardens were: an 'ornamental grotto arch' (1861), 'extensive grotto work' (1871 and 1876) and 'fern grottoes' (1897). These would be simple rockwork.[50] In 1873 a farm sale included a 'quantity of grotto' and an advert in 1891 offered a 'ton and a half GROTTO', i.e. rockery stones.[51] In the 1915 sale particulars for Parwich Hall, large rocks arranged to form seating areas were referred to as 'Grottoes', whereas they were really unroofed rock alcoves.[52]

However, traditional grottoes were still built, such as the one at Netherlea, now **Southwood House**, Belper, built in the late 1880s for the Bourne family of the Denby pottery company, Joseph Bourne and Sons. The firm was run by Sarah Bourne from 1869–98, who commissioned the grotto and also a rockery,

FIGURE 76. Southwood House (Netherlea). Interior of grotto, Pulham and Son, 1880s.

COURTESY J. SCHOLEFIELD, HOLBROOK SCHOOL.

FIGURE 77. Thornbridge hall, grotto alcove 1890s, probably Backhouse and Son, York.

COURTESY J. AND E. HARRISON

most probably by Pulham and Son.[53] Sited underneath the garden façade of the house, the grotto has two arched entrances leading to three small chambers, the centre one of which originally had a coloured glass ceiling to cast attractive colours over the plants. The grotto also provides views down over the garden. The garden at **Thornbridge Hall** (*qv*) with extensive rockwork by Backhouse and Son of York, has two grotto/alcoves dating from the late 1890s. Happily grottoes continue to appeal with their rough rock exteriors leading to cool dark interiors, as at Herbert Lodge Bonsall where there are two superb modern examples in a traditional idiom (*qv*).

Notes

All quotations from newspapers are © The British Library Board. All rights reserved. With thanks to the British Newspaper Archive (www.BritishNewspaperArchive.co.uk)

1. C. Morris (ed.) *The Illustrated Journeys of Celia Fiennes 1685–c.1712* (1982), 107.
2. R. Patching, *Four Topographical Letters, written in July 1755* (1757), 28, 33.
3. *DM*, 23 June 1808, 1.
4. *DM*, 24 July 1817, 2.
5. WRO: CR 1841/7 Lady Sophia Newdigate's travel journal, entry 4 Sept. 1747; WRO: CR 136/B/2668 Mary Conyer's Travel Diary (1747), 6.
6. *William Woolley's History of Derbyshire*, Derbyshire Record Society 6 (1981), 143; B. Jones, *Follies and Grottoes* (1979), 309.
7. DRO: 5054/13/5/1 Burdett Accounts Book 1695–1708. Thomas Shipton for Robert Burdett (1640–1716), '5th April 1697 Pd to the Fishermen for fishing ye Anchor church pools 6/-'; also April 1698 and April 1699.
8. M. Raeburn *et al.*, *The Green Frog Service* (1995), illustrated p. 264.
9. *The Topographer* 10, January 1790, 39–40.
10. C. Bruyn Andrews (ed.), *The Torrington Diaries*, vol. 2 (1935), 162–63.
11. Britton and Brayley, *The Beauties of England and Wales*, III (1802), 401. A door was fitted in 1845.
12. The Hermitage is an English Heritage listed monument (no. 315546) illustrated www.picturethepast.org.uk. B. Jones, *Follies and Grottoes* (1979), 309 says that it was Sir Robert Burdett who extended the cave and picnicked there, but she is confusing Dale Abbey with Anchor Church. This error has been followed.
13. *DM*, 17 Feb., 10 March 1769, 4.
14. *DM*, 24 March 1780, 4.
15. T. Noble (ed.), S. Glover, *The History, Gazetteer, and Directory of the County of Derby*, pt 1, (1829), 92, 100.
16. Quoted. J. Dixon Hunt and P. Willis (eds) *The Genius of the Place: The English Landscape Garden 1620–1820* (1988), 91.
17. Derby Local Studies Library 6303B. *Monody Written at Matlock Bath, and Dedicated with Great Respect to Thomas Hallet Hodge, Esq.*
18. J. Farey, *General View of the Agriculture and Minerals of Derbyshire* II (1811), 36–37.
19. W. Bray, *A Sketch of a Tour into Derbyshire and Yorkshire* (1778), 100.
20. P. K. Wilson *et al.*, *Anna Seward's Life of Erasmus Darwin* (2010), 108.
21. A. Jewitt (ed.) *The Northern Star, or Yorkshire Magazine*, vol. I (July 1817), 93.
22. Farey, *A General View*, I, 294.
23. R. Furness, *Medicus-Magus A Poem in Three Cantos* (1836). Another rock system is Cucklet Delf, Eyam which doubled as the open air village church in the 1665/6 plague.

24. T. Brighton, 'The Ashford Marble Works and Cavendish Patronage, 1748–1905', *Bulletin of the Peak District Mines Historical Society* 12(6) (Winter 1995), 64 (accessed on line).

25. White Watson, *A Delineation of the Strata of Derbyshire* (1811), 36; the poem is partly reproduced in *Derbyshire Times and Sheffield Herald*, 8 May 1897, 4.

26. Craven and Stanley. II, 205–206; *Journey Book of England: Derbyshire* (1841), 106.

27. F. White and Co., *History, Gazetteer and Directory of the County of Derby* (1857), 651. A roughly contemporary drawing shows the house surrounded by trees: DRO: D258/54/2 Lysons, *Magna Britannia* (1817), with illustrations added by Mrs I. Thornhill.

28. Craven and Stanley, II, 206.

29. Craven and Stanley, I, 2–5. Edmund is described as 'gardener' in his will 9 Oct. 1774 (DRO: D2189/1/3). He died in 1774.

30. Glover and Noble, *History of the County of Derby*, pt II, 13.

31. DRO: D8/B/T/31; Craven and Stanley, I, 24–25.

32. C. Bateman, *A Descriptive and Historical Account of Alfreton* (1812); other descriptions copy this, so in effect this is the only known contemporary description of the park ornaments.

33. DRO: D2554 estate map of Alfreton Park 1822.

34. Copy at Derby Local Studies Library, LSL 6303c.

35. Craven and Stanley, I, 25.

36. *DM*, 14 March, 25 July 1811, 3.

37. *DM*, 24 June 1819, 3.

38. *DM*, 30 Sept. 1819, 3; 3 July 1822, 3.

39. For a more detailed account of Mrs Spinks see D. Barre, 'Entertaining Women: shaping the business of gardening in the Midlands, 1780–1830', in M. Dick and E. Mitchells (eds), *Landscape and Green Spaces: Gardens and Garden History in the West Midlands* (2017).

40. *DM*, 1 Feb.1832, 1.

41. *DM*, 13 Feb. 1800, 1; 20 Feb. 1800, 4.

42. *DM*, 4 Aug.; 27 Sept. 1824, 3.

43. *Staffordshire Advertiser*, 27 Jan. 1838, 1.

44. *Manchester Courier and Lancashire General Advertiser*, 7 Oct. 1837, 2.

45. *Birmingham Gazette*, 29 March 1847, 2; also a similar sale Manchester in 1853 – *Manchester Courier and Lancashire General Advertiser*, 4 June 1853, 12.

46. *DM*, 25 April 1841, 2; 25 August 1845.

47. *DM,* 18 May 1825, 2.

48. *DM*, 22 March 1837, 3.

49. *Nottinghamshire Guardian*, 16 March 1854, 7.

50. *DM*, 9 Oct. 1861, 1; 5 June 1871, 1; 19 July 1876, 1; 16 June 1897, 1.

51. *DM*, 19 March 1873, 1; *DDT*, 19 Oct. 1891, 1.

52. DRO: D504/116/41 Sale particulars Parwich estate, 1915.

53. C. Hitching, *Rock Landscapes, the Pulham Legacy* (2012), 303; I am grateful to Lynne Protheroe, Holbrook Centre for Autism, Southwood for her kind help to visit the grotto.

CHAPTER SEVEN

Early Nineteenth Century: Regency to early Victorian gardens

....

The house requires a platform as a statue requires a pedestal.

Humphry Repton (1752–1818), the leading early nineteenth-century landscape gardener, helped to popularise the return of some formality near the house, with parterres of rather fussy small and colourful flower beds, ornamental shrubberies, conservatories or verandas, trellising, and balustrading or iron fences. The 'Picturesque' movement favoured by landowners now moved to J. C. Loudon's more compact 'Gardenesque', espoused by entrepreneurs wealthy from the Industrial Revolution and Napoleonic Wars.[1]

Repton's influence is seen at **Snelston Hall**, a 'spectacular piece of romantic Gothicism ... a miniature Alton Towers', largely demolished in 1951.[2] The 800 acre (324 ha) estate was acquired by a Derby lawyer John Harrison (1782–1871) in 1821, following an acrimonious and protracted legal battle. Harrison claimed the estate on behalf of his wife Elizabeth Bowyer, a relative of the last owner, William Bowyer. A man of considerable social ambition, Harrison commissioned a large new house in the gothic style in 1827. His architect was L. N. Cottingham, later famous for his gothic revival architecture.[3] Cottingham also designed the rich interiors with matching opulent and ornate gothic furniture.[4]

FIGURE 78. Snelston Hall, entrance front and gardens by L. N. Cottingham. print *c.*1830.

The house, on an incline overlooking a park, had prominent pinnacles and 'Tudor' pepper-pot turrets. The south façade of the house was linked to a large five bay gothic conservatory, with Cottingham's flower garden alongside, contained by a large retaining wall.

The gothic theme was repeated in his designs for garden furniture such as an octagonal fountain and tree seat.[5] The flower gardens had serpentine paths, cedars, agaves and roses.[6] The estate village at Snelston was also the work of Cottingham and probably the informal parkland, linking an existing series of fishponds to form a long irregular lake.[7]

FIGURE 79. Wingerworth Hall, Repton's drawing before 'improvement' in his *Red Book* (1809). Published in *Fragments on the Theory and Practice of Landscape Gardening* (1816, between pp. 64–50).

Although possibly involved at Drakelow (*qv*), Humphry Repton can be associated definitely with only one estate in Derbyshire, **Wingerworth**, for which his Red Book of 1809 survives.[8] When Sir Thomas Windsor Hunloke (1773–1816) inherited as fifth baronet in 1804, the estate was heavily mortgaged. However this did not prevent him from approaching Repton, who declared however that he would 'not advise the alteration of what has been so recently finished', that is the 1777 alterations by William Emes and planting of woodland to the south by Sir Henry Hunloke in the 1790s.

However Repton did recommend converting the east entrance front of the house into a garden façade and placing a balustraded terrace in front of it, both for effect and to exclude animals in the park, rather than creating a ha-ha. From this terrace would be views to a large new lake, formed by damming the river Rother, which would direct attention away from the 'smoke and flame of the [Hunloke] foundry' visible from the house in the mid-distance. A classical lodge should be erected at the beginning of a new approach to the house.[9] Needless to say few of Repton's expensive suggestions were followed up, although J. C. Loudon stated shortly afterwards (1822) that Repton 'enlarged the water, and planted some trees, and gave breadth to the lawn in front of the house'.[10]

Repton's most interesting proposal was for a Menagerie, although again it was not built. Sir Thomas was an enthusiastic collector of wild animals, which he housed in the main house itself and in the stables. Since this small collection included wolves, emus, bears and monkeys, besides a larger collection of exotic birds, this arrangement was hardly satisfactory.[11] The proposed Menagerie complex was to be placed in woodland on the eastern edge of the estate close to the new lake. There would be the usual Keeper's cottage in the centre, which could double as a summer house for family entertainment.[12] An exercise in rustic picturesque, this two storey building with first floor open balconies had

FIGURE 80. Wingerworth Hall, Repton's drawing of his suggested improvement with the removal of overlay (1816).

more than a passing resemblance to Marie Antoinette's Hameau at Versailles, created in the 1780s. Lady Hunloke would have specific use of one room, with windows looking out to a pool with birds, while another window looked out to cascades. Presumably the animals would be kept in secure enclosures. However Sir Thomas' exotic collection remained in its unsuitable accommodation, and was enlarged further by his son Henry (1812–56). In 1815, with mortgages of £54,000, Sir Thomas and family retreated to Paris, letting the hall and selling land. In 1816 the contents of the house were put up for sale, with 'a large collection of scarce Green House and Pine Plants, flowering Shrubs etc.'[13]

Then in 1856 the estate went a distant cousin Henrietta Hunloke, authoress of the evocatively named, three-volume, *Sadness and Gladness*.[14] Her sale of the menagerie collection in 1865 drew a large crowd of 2000 people from near and far. A pair of wolves sold for 19 guineas, while four bears (£61.19.0) were rather depressingly purchased by 'Mr Youdan of the Surrey Music Hall, Sheffield'. Sir Joseph Paxton purchased the emus 'very fine specimens of their kind [for] … the garden of the Crystal Palace, Sydenham.' Most of the lots were for exotic birds and Mr Youdan, with an eye to the future, also snapped up 'Cantelo's patent incubator, or egg hatching machine', a sound investment at £5 10s 0d.[15]

Henry Hunloke had rarely used the hall and sold the extensive coal beds on the estate.[16] Consequently coal pits soon approached the house, joining existing foundries. In 1920 when family debts finally led to the sale of the estate, there were just 260 acres (105.3 ha) left. Sale particulars mention formal gardens enclosed by yew hedges, ornamental trees, a rose garden with a central circular pond surrounded by rhododendrons, woodland walks, and a well-wooded park with seven lakes or ponds, 'one with a beautiful Wilderness Island'.[17] These attractions failed to compensate for the prominent unattractive industrial activity and in 1924 the house was largely demolished, with some parkland surviving, now enclosed by modern housing.

Of course not all landowners needed or sought the advice of professionals, as shown in a charming early nineteenth-century sketchbook by D'Ewes Coke (1774–1856), eldest son of the Rev D'Ewes Coke of Brookhill Hall, Pinxton (*qv*).[18] Showing the growing popularity of rustic and Gothic architecture it includes designs for garden features such as seats round trees and rustic bridges and hermitages. These may have sketched on visits to other estates but were probably been D'Ewes Coke's own ideas for possible use at Brookhill.

FIGURE 81. Hassop Hall with church as eye-catcher, printed view by Stephen Glover.

DRO: D258/54/1

By the Regency period flower beds near the house were back in fashion. Soon, even at Melbourne Hall, noted for its old fashioned formal walks and statuary, the parterres were given 'groups of lovely flowers apparently placed in elegant baskets…'[19] Popularised by Repton, such large circular or oval 'baskets' had open-work iron sides, looking like a huge version of a bread basket (as in the contemporary flower garden at Calke). Enthusiasm for exotic flowers, such as camellias, led to increased use of greenhouses, as at **Hassop Hall**. The Eyres purchased the estate in the fifteenth century and rebuilt the house *c.*1600 on a hillside. The family was Catholic, and in spite of the usual fiscal penalties, the lead-rich estate provided sufficient revenue for the family to thrive and to improve and extend the estate which amounted to 4875 acres (1974 ha) when sold in the early twentieth century. The fine new south façade *c.*1774, perhaps by Joseph Pickford, became the principal front, with views down a gentle slope to the landscape-park and fishponds below.[20] Rowland Eyre (d. *c.*1774) and his son Thomas (d. 1792) landscaped the park with woodland walks and pools, including 'Hermitage Pool' with a fashionable hermitage (now lost).[21]

In 1778 William Bray noted that 'Mr Eyre … has built a green-house and hot-house'.[22] Sited in a walled garden on the top terrace, on the steep south-facing slope overlooking the house, these were converted into a camellia house in the 1820s, when this exciting introduction became fashionable. Although demolished years ago, its size can be appreciated by a report of the jolly 21st birthday celebrations held for Thomas Eyre in 1811:

> upwards of 200 of the tenantry sat down to dinner in the Green House … the walls of which were decorated with appropriate paintings for the occasion… About 8 o'clock the tables having been removed, dancing commenced in the Green House, which being upwards of 120 feet in length, was well adapted for the amusement.[23]

This upper terrace probably had ornamental flower beds in front of the green houses, while the terrace below was a walled kitchen garden, (now a tennis Court). Both are wide and long, accessed by steep flights of steps.

In 1792 the estate passed to an uncle, Francis Eyre (1762–1827) of Warkworth Castle, who in 1814 claimed the title of sixth Earl of Newburgh through his wife's family. This rather debateable and controversial acquisition of a title encouraged more improvements at Hassop. At the top of the village entrance drive, about two hundred yards from the house, a Catholic chapel was built in 1816–17 on a truly impressive scale, as a Doric Temple with a tetrastyle portico, resembling Inigo Jones' Covent Garden church. Clearly visible from the gardens before they were walled off from the approach road, it doubled as a 'garden temple' eye-catcher.[24]

Thomas Eyre (1790–1833) inherited in 1827 as seventh Earl and further altered the house, moving the entrance from south to west. He built a large ballroom, separate from the house, near new stables and coach house, which were given a charming little gothic tower: a contrast to the severe classicism of the nearby chapel. Later a mock Tudor gatehouse (1853) doubled as a gazebo at the corner of the pleasure garden. Its roofline merlons match those on the original east façade of the house, while the lead lights of its mullion and transomed windows mimic those on the long gallery at nearby Haddon Hall (Pl. 20). Building styles at Hassop illustrate the changing enthusiasms of the nineteenth century which included Neo-classicism and Tudor re-revival. Following the purchase of the Hall in 1975 by Mr Thomas Chapman it became a hotel, with the garden on the south side given an elaborate parterre with a fine Victorian fountain while at its far end a new oak pergola enhances the 'Tudor' gazebo nearby.[25]

Holt House, **Two Dales**, is unusual in that its name appeared for a short time at the top of the banknotes issued by 'Dakeyne and Sons, Cotton Spinners and Bankers', based at their family home. Daniel Dakeyne (1733–1819) inherited a small 200 acre (81 ha) estate in 1777 and built this small, classical stone house 'in an elegant style of Architecture and well adapted for a small genteel Family', set in eight acres of lawn and shrubberies.[26] Dakeyne was an entrepreneur, building a flax mill on the estate in 1780, utilising the Sydnope brook which flowed through the grounds, but unfortunately another enterprise, the bank, failed in 1801. A high profile and lengthy bankruptcy followed, involving Dakeyne and three of his sons. The estate, flax spinning mill, cotton mill and Holt House were put on the market several times between 1802 and 1812, but failed to sell.[27] Daniel Dakeyne junior (1763–1806) combined his income-generating career of barrister with the money-losing activities of poet and antiquarian. The different gifts of the family were noted by Glover in 1829:

> The late Mr. Daniel Dakeyne, of Holt House, was a poet and an eminent antiquary …[who] collected considerable materials for the compilation of a Topographical and Genealogical History of his native county … Edward and James Dakeyne, his younger brothers, are eminent mechanics, and have obtained patents for their inventions and improvements of flax and spinning machinery and steam engine.[28]

Daniel became a well-known poet locally, causing one smitten lady to address him in 1783:

> From Darley's shady Groves benignly rise,
> And tuneful Sing, O favour'd of the Skies…
> For sure no bard sublime surpasses thee
> In depth of Sentiment and Harmony!…
> Rise-spread thy Name to Fame's eternal Gale,
> Thou flower and Honor of fair Darley Dale.[29]

His slim volume of poetry was published in 1790. In *The Vanity of Ambitious Expectations* Dakeyne's stylised sentiment contrasted the simple and pure affections of a young rustic before the 'siren' ambition seized him.

> Charmed with the soft delight that nature lends,
> A garden fair he form'd in rural taste;
> Besides its walks a winding water wends,
> Whose fragrant banks the fairest flowerets grac'd.
> Amid its groves, where ivies green embrac'd
> The arching trees and honey-suckles twin'd,
> The chair for sweet society he plac'd,
> Where Amarillis oft his musings join'd
> And trac'd with tender thought, the beauties of his mind.[30]

This may be an idealised version of his own garden and parkland, where he is said to have added a gothic folly *c.*1800 and to have re-erected a fine Saxon Cross shaft, found in a nearby field, (later removed to the churchyard at Bakewell). Even the new stable block had a date stone '1416' inserted as if to explain the amateurish early gothic design. Perhaps had he lived longer, Dakeyne would have been as enthusiastic a decorator of his grounds with ancient reclamation as Thomas Bateman and Sir Francis Sacheverell Darwin (*qv*).

There is a rather delightful apocryphal legend attached to the summer house/tower in the ornamental kitchen garden at **Hopton Hall**, Wirksworth. The estate had belonged to the Gell family since the fourteenth century, with the core of the present house dating from 1584–94. Sir Philip Gell (1723–95) enlarged the house and gardens, and while diverting the road near the house his workmen unearthed a Romano-British pot, reputed to have on it part of an inscription: I F C/GELL/PRAE III COH/VI BRIT LEG. Thus encouraged, Sir Phillip promptly claimed descent from a Roman soldier named Gellius.[31]

Sir Philip probably converted what may have been a south-facing formal terraced garden into an ornamental kitchen garden. About this time variants of 'crinkle-crankle' (serpentine) brick walls appear to have had a brief popularity in south Derbyshire. Only one brick thick they were cheap to build, retained the heat for espaliered fruit and were also a very attractive feature in an ornamental kitchen or flower garden. The earliest surviving example in Derbyshire is the mid-eighteenth-century wall, with its linked curves, at Ireton Gardens (see Fig. 39), while the 1760 accounts of Foremark Hall include: 'building the Serpentine

FIGURE 82. Hopton Hall, serpentine wall with central brick tower, taken from outside the garden.

Wall against the stables'.32 Variants at Langley Hall, Kirk Langley, Sudbury Hall former walled garden, Egginton Hall and Sutton Hall, Sutton-on-the-Hill are roughly contemporary with Hopton.

The Hopton wall has broad shallow curves and at its centre is a curious high and windowless brick tower, reputedly built *c*.1790, perhaps as a summer house or orangery, with storage space above. There is a story that Sir Philip Gell, in a hurry to set off for London, impatiently said to the builders, who were asking for instructions, 'Oh for God's sake go on building.' Consequently on his return, he found that this is exactly what the builders had done. They had built a 30 ft-high (9.1 m) windowless tower. Sir Philip then simply roofed his somewhat unusual garden feature.[33] The rather flat pyramidal roof is said to have had a cupola on top to light a pigeon loft, which would have helped to enliven its somewhat heavy appearance.

However, legend apart, if the tower is dated to his son Philip (1775–1842), it is possible that its design was directly influenced by an illustration in a book written by his brother, Sir William Gell (1777–1836). Sir William was a keen classicist, who published a large folio *The Topography of Troy and its Vicinity* in 1804. One plate illustrates a walled villa where two towers have flat pyramidal roofs, very similar to the Hopton tower. Having seen the illustrations Philip Gell may have decided to build his own version, also attached to a wall.[34] Today the tower looks over attractive modern rose gardens, and since the bottom (south wall) is at a lower height to maximise sunlight, there are views over the surrounding countryside.

The Romantic Revival, influenced by Sir Walter Scott's *Kenilworth* (1821) and *Peveril of the Peak* (1823), brought a fascination with unchanged, musty, historic mansions and their gardens. **Haddon Hall** was a prime example of the sentimental admiration of 'Old England', where ancient rooms 'carried the mind irresistibly back to the days of old; when men of hardy and fearless manners, fond of war and savage sports, lorded it over a world'.[35] Visitors revelled in the romantic decay of Haddon and its gardens. In 1829 the *Derby Mercury* devoted a long column to Mrs Hage, 'The Late Old Housekeeper at Haddon', who had shown the 'ancient baronial residence' to visitors for over half a century, repeating the stories of her predecessors. 'She never failed to point out a door into the garden, through which she said the Heiress of Haddon (a Vernon) had escaped to join her lover (a Manners)'. However, scrupulously, the editor felt obliged to note – 'This traditionary [*sic*] tale may have no other foundation than the union by marriage of two noble families'.[36]

The artist David Cox (1783–1859) often visited between 1831 and 1850, delighting in the old interiors and the run-down and evocative gardens.[37] Its balustrades were copied at other country houses including nearby Sydnope Hall, and Darley House, Darley Dale, with its 'fine Old Tudor balustrade'.[38] Tourists' enthusiasm continued over the decades:

> a flight of broken moss-covered steps, Dorothy Vernon's Walk, which is above the Upper Terrace, and bounded with splendid lime-trees. After exploring this once beautiful walk, we again descended the steps to the Terrace, and traced out its old parterres, among ancient yews, their branches reaching nearly to the ground.[39]

When *Country Life* photographed in 1901, the famous steps and balustrade were overwhelmed by huge trees hanging over, with massive yews underneath the balustrade along the top garden (Pl. 21).[40] In the 1920s–'30s the ninth Duchess of Rutland undertook the daunting task of sympathetic restoration of the gardens. Her luxuriant planting of climbing roses linked house and garden, with scented roses clambering over building, garden walls and balustrade, combined with superb herbaceous borders, continuing the romanticism of Haddon.

A huge draw for tourists was any connection with the romanticised story of Mary Queen of Scots, with the inevitable outburst of sentimental poetry, such as this 1783 poem on Chatsworth:

> Lo! Through the Shades, by the Moon's glimm'ring ray
> The pensive Spirit of a mournful Queen
> To yon forsaken Turret glides away*
> Where deep-ton'd Lyres are rung by hands unseen

> *a mounted Tower and Walk near the Bridge,[the Bower] said to have been the usual resort and walk of Mary Queen of Scots.[41]

This period also saw the encouragement of the spurious legend that Mary Queen of Scots had stayed at **Hardwick**. To reinforce the story, the sixth Duke of Devonshire brought over Sir Richard Westmacott's 1822 statue of the Queen, intended originally for her Bower at Chatsworth. There had been a period of benign neglect at Hardwick New Hall in the eighteenth century, once Chatsworth became the main family home.[42] The old hall was partly demolished between 1745 and 1757, but the south elevation was retained, probably for its ivy covered picturesque effect.[43] The current, much admired 'authentic' interiors of Hardwick New Hall are largely the work of the sixth Duke from the 1830s, who carefully brought in appropriate old tapestries and furnishings to re-create and

FIGURE 83. Hardwick Hall, entrance front and gardens. Lithograph, T. Allom, 1837.

AUTHOR'S COLLECTION

augment the 'olde England' atmosphere of the hall at its prime. At the same time his niece Blanche transformed the enclosed entrance court with a fussy and elaborate flower garden in 1833. Two flower beds, in the shape of an E and S, were surrounded by circular beds, scrolls and borders, which reflecting the stone letters for Elizabeth of Shrewsbury on the hall parapet. These survived until the twentieth century.[44] The crisp outlines of the hall were lost with creepers and large shrubs, which would have annoyed Bess of Hardwick greatly had she been able to see this.

Within a wider landscape there remained an enthusiasm for a looser interpretation of romantic landscaping with gently curving paths and irregularly shaped sheets of water. However, unlike Repton's recommendations, by now this was independent of the architectural style of the house, as illustrated in a design for the grounds of **Derwent House**, built in 1672 but now lost under Ladybower reservoir.[45] In 1831 John Read (1777–1862), a wealthy Sheffield businessman and philanthropist, purchased what had become a farmhouse. He then invited Joshua Major (1786–1866) to submit plans to improve the neglected gardens. Major, who ran a nursery at Knosthorpe, Leeds, advertised as 'Landscape-Gardener and Garden Architect' and was to become well known and involved in the design of several early public parks.[46]

Major pronounced that 'the kitchen garden ought never to be considered a portion of the pleasure ground ... with the constant presence of workmen ... decaying vegetables, manure etc.' Therefore his proposed (strictly utilitarian),

FIGURE 84. Calke Abbey,
engraving *c.*1852.

COURTESY OF DERBY CITY COUNCIL
AND WWW.PICTURETHEPAST.
ORG.UK

kitchen garden is placed well away from the house.[47] Believing that 'all formality should cease with the terrace-wall', and that shrubberies should replace clipped hedges, Major's plan for Derwent included the creation of a long 'rococo' swirling-edged pool or lake close to the house, probably enlarging existing ponds. Enclosed by the river on two sides, an area of gently curving paths would divide lawns interspersed with small irregular flower beds and shrubberies, illustrating Major's preference for:

> gentle and graceful sweeps, with natural, or irregular and varied, masses and groups of trees and shrubs, blending softly and gracefully with intricate glades of smooth lawn...[48]

The formal walled garden next to the house would be retained and given a central walk lined with flower beds, two greenhouses (glass house/conservatories) and what are probably urns at each corner, with statues at the centre of the lawns. His suggestions were partly implemented as plans, relating to the sale of the property in the 1840s, show an irregularly shaped lake and the formal gardens laid out, but without greenhouses.[49] In the late 1870s Robert Marnock (1800–89), a leading landscape gardener, provided plans to further extend the lake, but these were probably too expensive for what was now just a shooting box belonging to the Duke of Norfolk. So the old fashioned walled gardens remained until the house was demolished in the 1940s for Ladybower reservoir.

Sir Henry Harpur, seventh baronet (1763–1819), inherited **Calke** in 1789 and with him began the eccentricity and reclusive tendencies for which the family became well known. Immensely wealthy, Sir Henry lived at Calke with his mistress, a lady's maid, whom he married in 1792. His main interest, indeed obsession, was improving his house and grounds, uncannily foreshadowing the Earl of Harrington at Elvaston. However despite a retiring nature and his marital misalliance, Sir Henry had social aspirations, changing the family surname of Harpur to that of Crewe in 1808, in an unsuccessful attempt to revive a dormant barony.[50] The same year he gave the former priory of Calke the historically incorrect title of 'Abbey', which sounded more impressive (*vide* William Beckford's Fonthill Abbey and Alton Abbey, later Alton Towers). Fortunately there was no expensive attempt to gothicise the house itself and Sir Henry contented himself with the extensive remodelling of his hunting lodge at Repton Park (*qv*) into a romantic gothic castle, landscaping its woodland, creating tree-lined carriage drives and enlarging a pool into a small lake with islands.[51]

When Lord Torrington visited Calke in June 1789 he laconically noted that 'many men are employed in blowing up a long extent of hill, in front'.[52] This was no less than the removal of the hillside before the south front to open the views from the house, which was given a huge Greek revival portico in 1806–08. A stone balustrade was added to the roofline to make the building look more impressive in an extended and landscaped park with new plantations and approach road.

In the park valley Sir Henry added a new pond, Mere Pond (1800), linking Thatch House Pond to China House Pond in a long sweep, with a cascade where they joined. On the northern bank of Mere Pond, behind a now lost boat house, he created 'an ancient monk's cave', a small brick-lined alcove surrounded by old golden yews.[53] So now a walk along the northern banks of the pools led past Lady Catherine's Bower, boat house, cave and the grotto. Probably the Chinese House had gone by then. Somewhere along the pools, perhaps linking China

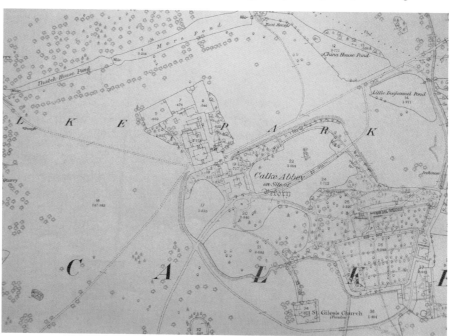

FIGURE 85. Calke Abbey, OS map 1881 showing the linked ponds, abbey, lawns and kitchen garden on lower right.

FIGURE 86. Calke,
Samuel Brown's grotto
(1809), restored 2015.

BY KIND PERMISSION OF THE
NATIONAL TRUST

House Pond with Dog Kennel Pond, an exciting addition to the landscape was erected in 1815. This was a huge single arch bridge:

> Sir Henry Crewe is at this time erecting an arch in his Park at Calke, partly for ornament and partly for use, under the direction of Mr. Samuel Brown his Architect, which spans 119 feet![54]

Brown was a local architect from Derby and his plans and estimate for drawing the bridge are dated 1810.[55] If ever completed, this ambitious project soon vanished. Sir Henry's other bridge, a three arched gothic bridge on a new carriage drive in the eastern part of the estate, was submerged under Staunton Harold reservoir in the early 1960s. It also flooded Dog Kennel Pond, the furthest of the ponds in the sweeping curve of eighteenth–nineteenth-century pools, with its island with trees and an unknown building on its north side.

Sir Henry also employed Samuel Brown to design a grotto in 1809, positioned at the end of the lawn which had long replaced the formal gardens, and was originally hidden behind an encircling belt of trees and shrubs.[56] Approached through a stone arch and rock-work passage and apsidal in shape, its walls were set with an array of Derbyshire minerals, including calcite, fluorite and iron oxide, mixed with artificial stalactites made of Coade stone – a unique example. Its tufa-lined arch is apparently 'supported' by tufa pillars, reminiscent of Buontalenti's famous grotto at Florence. Water flowed from the back into an irregular pool. Recent restoration has revealed the charm and originality of the grotto, but it needs more enclosing greenery to restore the original element of surprise, rather than presenting the present odd looking lump in the lawn.

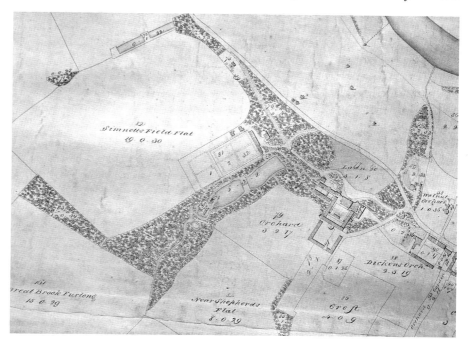

FIGURE 87. Newton Solney, detail of estate plan 1827, showing the steam, cascade and grotto: centre, above orchard.

Sir Henry's died unexpectedly following a carriage accident in 1819. His successor, Sir George Crewe (1795–1884), re-faced the Elizabethan church in 1827–29, adding a tall tower, to double as an eye-catcher near the house. The 1770s conservatory was given a central glass and iron dome, its shape typical of the 1830s. Near the walled garden a small flower garden was created, with an oval stone fountain in a pond encircled by 'Reptonian' basket-weave ironwork and the corner auricular 'theatre' *c*.1830. Later as 'Lady [Georgiana] Crewe's Garden' it was decorated with small ornamental beds in elaborate Victorian shapes cut into grass around the fountain, currently planted by the National Trust with appropriately colourful displays.

In 1836 the auctioneer George Robins enthused about the 'singularly eligible' estate of **Newton Park** at Newton Solney. Having stressed how healthful the village was with only two funerals in 1829 – both for very elderly persons – Mr Robins concluded 'East Indians [merchants] will do wisely to think seriously of such a purchase'.[57] The estate had been purchased in 1797 by Abraham Hoskins, a successful solicitor and businessman from nearby Burton-on-Trent. Philip Heath argues that Hoskins intended to build a new house on top of nearby Bladon Hill, to designs by Jeffry Wyatt, but then changed his mind and instead remodelled an existing farm house close by, retaining the farm buildings.[58] A house on Bladon Hill was indeed built, but as a castellated gothic folly (see below).

When Abraham Hoskins Jnr (1759–1842) inherited in 1805, the estate was in financial difficulties following his father's extravagant building programme and delusions of grandeur. To compound the problem, his own life style was expensive including huge sums spent on his breeding hounds and stud. Hoskins also spent extravagantly on his kitchen gardens, building an impressive hot-house '153 feet long, 17 wide in the centre, and 13 at the ends, of the most perfect construction, … stored with 16 sorts of Pines, [pineapples] and 24 sorts of Grapes, in full bearing'.[59] Close to the kitchen garden two pools led to a meandering stream with tufa-lined paths and ferns, 'rippling cascade, rockwork and rural bridge'.[60] There was a grotto at a large bend of the stream near one pool, which in turn has a little island on it.[61] With lawns and shrubberies, in the 1836 sale Mr Robins rather desperately termed the area a *ferme ornée* (implicitly picturesque) because of the working farm buildings around the new house.[62]

Overspending led to this sale, when Mr Robins stated that over £5,000 had been spent on house and garden and noted that:

> A Mr BROWN (*not* CAPABILITY BROWN, *but equally capable in every respect*) ONCE SOJOURNED AT NEWTON, and greatly contributed to the improvement of the Estate.63

Philip Heath suggests this is Samuel Brown who worked at Calke and Repton Park.[64] When the house contents were finally sold in 1838, items from the garden included citrus trees, '200 green-house plants in pots' and a 'patent garden engine' and 'patent mangle.'[65] Clearly Mr Hoskins enjoyed the newest gadgets.

Newton and Bladon Castle were purchased by a neighbour, the Earl of Chesterfield, who let Newton to the Burton-on-Trent brewer, William Worthington (d. 1871). He acquired various pieces of medieval salvage to ornament the park, including a medieval arch from a bridge and masonry from Burton Abbey, which were formed into a folly.[66] The house was rebuilt in 1880–82 and became a hotel in 1959, with much of the park and kitchen garden sold off for luxury housing.

Bladon Castle, erected on top of Bladon Hill, served as a commanding gothic eye-catcher for Newton Park. Built between 1792–5 as a crenelated wall, between 1801 and 1805 it was enlarged with two octagon towers and converted into living space to designs by Jeffrey Wyatt (Wyatville).[67] However Hoskins decided to live at Newton Park. The Castle was sold in 1836 when George Robins' extravagant hyperbole spoke of 'This Derbyshire Elysium', with its terrace walk and views equal to those at Windsor Castle no less (also by Wyatville):

> Nothing can exceed the beauty of the umbrageous drives and walks through the Plantations, ever and anon catching a glimpse of the Trent; the Lawns and Pleasure grounds are delight, and the Scenery everywhere luxuriant to a degree.[68]

So here was the somewhat unusual situation of a park eye-catcher commanding as much attention as the main house itself, and as carefully landscaped with its extensive woodland and shrubbery walks. Sadly today the Castle is completely concealed by trees.

Linking late Regency to Victorian gardens is **Elvaston Castle,** one of the most exciting, and indeed amazing, gardens of the nineteenth century. When Charles Stanhope, Viscount Peterham (1780–1851), Regency dandy and eccentric, inherited in 1829 as fourth Earl of Harrington, with typical insouciance he proceeded to

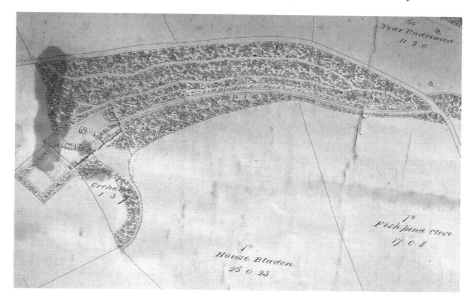

FIGURE 88. Bladon Castle, detail of estate plan 1827, showing the long narrow castellated castle (on left), with its woodland walks along the hill.

marry his mistress, Maria Foote (1797–1867). A beautiful but notorious actress, Maria was quite unacceptable in polite society, so the couple retired to Elvaston and proceeded to create a make-believe escapist Camelot, from which outsiders were excluded. The Jacobean house had been partly gothicised between 1815 and 1829 and this was enhanced in the later 1830s by Lewis Cottingham, fresh from Snelston. William Barron (1800–91), a brilliant up-and-coming Scottish gardener, was engaged in 1830 and created outstanding romantically themed gardens for the couple. Not surprisingly legends and myths were created (and encouraged) about the gardens, many of which are still in vogue.

By the 1840s it must have been extremely galling for the talented William Barron to watch the growing reputations of George Fleming at Trentham Hall and Joseph Paxton at Chatsworth, while his equally innovative and exciting schemes at Elvaston were hidden and unknown to all but a few. Barron had clearly intended to create a name for himself in horticulture circles, for the *Derby Mercury* (31 October 1832) reported the cultivation of impressive onions by 'Mr Baron [*sic*], the Earl of Harrington's scientific gardener (late of the Botanical Gardens, Edinburgh)'. Thereafter Barron vanishes from that newspaper. However once the earl died in 1851 Barron became an astute self-publicist. His book, *The British Winter Garden* (1852), a practical guide on the cultivation of evergreens and their transplanting (on which he was a famous expert), also glorified his work at Elvaston. Barron gave the impression that he found little of value on his arrival there, other than the avenues and typical early nineteenth-century flower beds. There was:

> A flower garden on the north side of the castle … a few large beds in the east avenue for roses and honeysuckles and a small flower garden on the site of a former gravel-pit; a kitchen-garden of two acres and a labyrinth which remains unaltered, constituted the whole of the gardens.[69]

In fact probably much remained from the Baroque gardens with their parterres, waterworks, canal and long avenues.[70] Very little is known about these formal gardens, but there are hints in surviving account books. In 1714 work at a fishpond came to £20 6s 10d and at Swan Pool £41 18s 3d, such large sums suggesting these were new creations.[71] In 1741/2 there is mention of an island, approached over a bridge, and a summer-house with a table, '3 seats and sideboard'; 5s 6d was paid 'for painting ye post and rails round ye Island House', which was probably a fishing lodge as 1s 6d was paid 'for painting ye fishing chaire'. There was also a boat house, so the river would have been used for the popular pastime of boating.[72] A rather poor copy of a lost plan *c.*1772 shows the survival of a formal gardens with wildernesses, parterres, woods and a long avenue, and much could have survived well into the nineteenth century.[73] As late as 1823 it was noted that the hall was approached via a mile long avenue and that 'The gardens are chiefly laid out in the ancient manner, with vases and statues, interspersed amid the foliage'.[74] Much of this must have been incorporated into Barron's new gardens with their statuary and urns.

Barron seems to have initiated the story that Capability Brown had turned down a commission at Elvaston for the second Earl of Harrington (1719–79). Barron declared ('I believe') that Brown suggested planting two avenues, but decided:

> that the place was so flat, and that there was such a want of capability in it, that he would not meddle with it, but at the same presenting to his Lordship six cedars of Lebanon, and proposing that they should be planted on the east side of the mansion, forming the commencement of an avenue…[75]

This rejection seems highly unlikely given that Brown was perfectly capable of landscaping flat ground, and the avenues were already established by 1772, but of course it would make Barron's subsequent transformations, including large scale drainage and formation of the lake, all the more telling. Although he admitted that the third Earl had planted trees extensively, Barron underplayed everything else: 'But besides the gardens which existed in 1831 … not anything had been done to ornament the grounds'.[76]

However Barron's work over 20 years at Elvaston is justly famous, with his creation of elaborate enclosed topiary gardens, new lake and rockwork, all on a grand scale. For contemporaries Barron's fame came through his monumental planting of hundreds of specimen trees, including moving and successfully transplanting mature trees, often over considerable distances, because the Earl, by then well in his 50s, was in a great hurry to complete the garden.[77] Such transplanting was nothing new – it had been done successfully by Capability Brown, while in the 1820s Sir Henry Steuart developed his own method of encouraging new root growth prior to removal. In 1818 at Teddesley Hall, Penkridge, Staffs, Lord Hatherton transplanted 'two large Holly trees which I had brought with a machine from Wolgarston … one of them was nearly … 200 years old'.[78] What Barron achieved was the transplanting of huge trees on a grand scale, with almost complete success each time, which he never failed to publicise. It became one of his trademark activities and after the 1860s he sent his skilled workmen round the country (and abroad) to work at public and private gardens, using his own transporting machines.[79]

Barron, a Wesleyan of deep moral and religious convictions and 'an ardent temperance advocate', appeared to have worked in close harmony with his employer, a very different man. No doubt an almost limitless budget and great freedom to interpret his ideas helped:

> every time … I had to make a new plan for his lordship's approval, and as soon as it was passed, he was like a child with a new toy, to see it finished.[80]

Although the earl and his wife occasionally resided in London in the 1830/40s, the death of their only son in 1836 at the age of five, further contributed to their self-imposed exile at Elvaston, where they shunned society.[81] Famously the Earl is reputed to have said 'If the Queen comes, Barron, show her round; but admit no one else'.82 Yet the Duke of Wellington and 'a select party of Nobility' stayed at the castle in January 1838.[83] Printed descriptions of the gardens by Loudon in 1839 and the *Gardeners' Chronicle* in 1849 suggest that the earl wished his achievements to be known and their exclusiveness regretted by the society he shunned.

When J. C. Loudon visited in 1839 the new gardens were unknown. He described the newly planted avenues of Irish yew and cedars and the large scale planting of evergreens and pines:

> a series of ancient flower gardens, surrounded by and intermixed with yew hedges, and containing yew trees of large size, brought from all parts of the country, many of which have been clipped into curious shapes.[84]

Newly designed gardens emphasised traditional late seventeenth-century formality, including:

> an Italian garden, richly furnished with vases, statues (many of which are of grotesque forms), richly gilt, basins, fountains and other works of art … There is a fourth flower-garden just commenced, with the flower beds arranged in architectural forms, bounded by masonry.

Early photographs show the amazing huge and beautifully clipped topiary of the enclosed gardens, of which only echoes survive today. Yet even these are remarkable.[85] The emphasis on evergreens of various shades made the gardens independent of the seasons, although flowers often featured. This eclectic mix included the *Alhambra Garden*, overlooked by its bizarre Moorish Temple, with its hint of Chinese and Gothic. This strange building was described (but not illustrated) in the *Gardeners' Chronicle* 1849, with its now lost exotic, almost decadent, surroundings:

> …the Alhambra summer-house, a building enriched in the most gorgeous oriental style, gilded and otherwise embellished in a manner peculiar to the age it represents. From this house an imposing view of the castle [house] is obtained through the Alhambra garden, where statuary and trees – both works of art – one of the chisel, the other of shears, rise in bold relief in the foreground to the massive building.

FIGURE 89. Elvaston Castle, Moorish Temple in the now lost Alhambra Garden.

The description also mentions walks paved with octagon tiles, yews perfectly shaped 'as if they were hewn out of stone or marble', circular beds with marble statues, and others with gilded statuary. The long, breathless description includes four seven-foot antique statues on stone plinths which 'produce a suitable effect amongst the fastigiated plants drawn out in military order in front of them'.[86]

Another elaborate garden, *Mon Plaisir* or bower garden, below the south façade of the house, featured a curving living green tunnel, eight ft (2.4 m) high and wide, with 'windows' cut into both sides, providing views on the inner side to the centre of the garden with its monkey puzzle tree, rare and expensive at that time. This stood in a star shaped bed surrounded by garlands of climbing roses, supported by poles with eight seats by each point of the star. On the terrace next to the castle two eight-foot high Irish yews were shaped as semi-circles, and in the concaves facing the castle 'are pedestals in gold, supporting richly carved figures in gold also'.[87] Like the seventeenth-century formal gardens which inspired it, this garden was also designed to be viewed from a terrace or from the house.

The garden of *Fairstar* had valuable antique statuary, marble busts on plinths with shrubs formed into columns (some terminating in crowns), pedestals and minarets. More typically Victorian were its extremely colourful scrolled flower beds:

> arranged and contrasted so as to work out the idea of a richly embroidered carpet; baskets about 6 feet across, gilded in gold, and filled with scarlet Pelargoniums are placed in the four divisions of this garden.[88]

House and gardens were approached from the original long avenue and through The Golden Gates:

FIGURE 90. Elvaston Castle, Mon Plaisir Garden, as illustrated by Adveno Brook (1858).

of the most elaborate and exquisite workmanship, exceedingly massive, and gilded in the most costly style. They were originally in the possession of Napoleon Bonaparte, and were obtained [1819] from the Petite Trianon by the father of the present Earl.[89]

They acted also as a *claire voyée*, excluding the viewer while allowing a glimpse of house at the end of an enclosed avenue.

By 1837 another garden was created between the north front of the house and Barron's new long lake, with 'caves, grottoes, bridges, mounts, statues and various other ornaments'.[90] The terraces are now bare but foundations of a grotto with its fountain survive on the lowest lawn. It was a rather eclectic mixture of formal Italianate pond with carved stone edges, fountain in the centre and, as a complete contrast, three rough stone arches behind. By the 1850s it was surrounded with elegantly shaped trees, cedars, pines and willow with piles of rocks artistically placed around it. The fountain of the Fountain Garden had jets of water 40 ft (12.2 m) high and there was a shell grotto with a gilded statue of Queen Eleanor in the its centre.[91]

Facing the gardens was Barron's new lake with its island, created by extensive draining operations, with the huge volume of excavated soil piled along the far bank, creating mounds and hills down to the water which Barron arranged to give 'a feather edge on both sides'.[92] More excess soil was used to form the garden terraces mentioned above, looking across the lake to what appeared to be ruins of an ancient castle 'the best balance I could think of for the fountain and grotto nearly opposite'.[93] The 'ruined castle' stood on a tall mound of spoil and was described in late 1860s:

rough, ragged rock to the water's edge, and in one case closely resembling a ruined castle, covered with moss and ivy, and the effect increased by broken mullioned window bars set against one of the openings.[94]

As the enthusiasm of Barron and the Earl grew with each improvement, rock work was extended out from the 'castle', winding paths were sunk within the new embankments and at the lake edges 'at intervals, all round, little bays, promontories, and creeks were formed'. Clever planting allowed view points and concealed points of interest on the way round the lake edge. Mature trees were planted to give instant venerability and a huge variety of trees, bushes and small plants added, and the whole was backed with a plantation. Massive rocks, promiscuously scattered along the lake side, were planted with variegated ivy and other plants to offset the dark Irish yew and cedars. The *Gardeners' Chronicle* admired this as:

> entirely a work of art, and consider[ing] the tens of thousands of tons of rocks all brought from a great distance, employed in its formation, we are left to conclude that it has not only no rival as a work of art, but there is nothing at all approaching it, in any garden in country.[95]

So much for Paxton's much vaunted work at Chatsworth!

Barron used a new technique of incorporating artificial stone within his genuine rockwork, which included tufa and large blocks of sand and grit-stone:

> to form foundations for masses of rock; and likewise long pieces should be raised and projected in oblique directions, and cased over with good specimens of tufa, the whole united by breaking all the joints with Roman Cement, mixed with a large portion of sand, dashed on as roughly as possible, in imitation of the rock.[96]

FIGURE 91. Elvaston Castle, engraving by W. L. Walton, 1850s. View over lake to fountain and rockwork, cedars with castle in background.

FIGURE 92. Elvaston Castle, remains of former Italianate fountain in pond shown in previous image.

FIGURE 93. Elvaston Castle, rock arch, part of the extensive rock work around the pool.

Holes were made in some rocks to take ferns and rock plants. Along the walk varied rock arches, sometimes circular in shape, were placed at strategic points, through which picturesque views were seen. Close to the ruined castle was a long grotto, composed of tufa and stone and a few lumps of lumps of marble, with various sized niches in some of which seats could be placed with views across the lake to the house (Pl. 22). Today, even in its eroded and over-grown state, the rockwork at Elvaston is evocative of its past splendours.

Such a garden was hugely expensive to create and maintain. When Leicester Stanhope inherited on the death of his brother in 1851, retrenchment followed quickly, with the number of gardeners reduced from over 80 to 11. The 80 acres (32.4 ha) of pleasure grounds were opened to the public at the not inconsiderable fee of 3 shillings (15p) a head. Yet visitors arrived by the thousand, keen to see this extraordinary but hitherto inaccessible garden. For a while William Barron continued as head gardener, but encouraged by the new Earl he took over the Elvaston tree nursery and then set up his own very successful nursery at nearby Barrowash, joined by his only son in 1867.[97] 'Barron and Son' became a prominent nursery and garden design business well into the twentieth century, with commissions throughout England, including several public parks nationally and in Derbyshire. After 1900 the firm specifically emphasised landscaping, advertising as 'Landscape and Artistic Gardeners' in 1915.[98]

Eventually Elvaston was sold in 1963 to meet death duties, and the empty house and 390 acres (158 ha) were purchased by Derbyshire County Council and Derby Corporation in 1969 to establish a country park. For once the house was not demolished, but both it and the landscape are at risk. This fairy-story really does deserve a happy ending.

Notes

All quotations from newspapers are © The British Library Board. All rights reserved. With thanks to the British Newspaper Archive (www.BritishNewspaperArchive.co.uk)

1. For a useful introduction see L. Mayer, *Humphry Repton* (2014), 47–60 and M. Batey, *Regency Gardens* (1995).
2. N. Pevsner, *The Buildings of England, Derbyshire* (1953), quoted S. Jarvis, 'Gothic rampant: designs by L. N. Cottingham for Snelston Hall', *The V&A Album* 3 (1984), 323.
3. Craven and Stanley, I, 196–98.
4. Some of Cottingham's drawings of furniture designs survive at the V&A and DRO.
5. DRO: D157MT/3037 'South east view of Snelston Hall ... by L. N. Cottingham January 7, 1827'. DRO: D157MT/3042 'A gothic seat designed for J. Harrison Esquire of Snelston Hall, Derbyshire'.
6. Jarvis, 'Gothic rampant', 326.
7. DRO: D157M/T4094 Plan of Snelston 1824, by Robert Bromley, Surveyor. F. R. Kowsky, *Country, Park and City: The Architecture and Life of Calvert Vaux* (2003), 16. I was not able to walk the site but from the road there is a tantalising glimpse of the remains of the house, retaining wall and archway, set in attractive, undulating parkland.
8. It is now in private hands. Information here is taken from an excellent account by Tim Warner: '"Combined Utility and Magnificence". Humphry Repton's commission for Wingerworth Hall in Derbyshire: the anatomy of a missing Red Book', *Journal of Garden History* 7.3, 271–301. My thanks to Charles Boot for providing access to this article. The scheme is partly reproduced in J. C. Loudon, *The Landscape Gardening and Landscape Architecture of the late Humphry Repton* (1840), 462–66. Part of the Red Book was included in Repton's *Fragments on the Theory and Practice of Landscape Gardening* (1816).

9. Warner, 'Repton's Commission', 291–92; S. Daniels, *Humphry Repton, Landscape Gardening and the Geography of Georgian England* (1999), 247.

10. J. C. Loudon, *Encylopaedia of Gardening* (1822), item 7574. The illustration closely resembles Repton's 'improved' view of hall and Park from the River Rother Valley, in his Red Book for Wingerworth, 1806.

11. Warner, 'Repton's Commission', 292–93; *Foll-e, The e-Bulletin of the Folly Fellowship*, issue 15, July 2008 accessed through www.Follies.org.uk.

12. Other examples include Thomas Wright's 1750s 'Menagerie, Horton, Northants, and the 1770s Menagerie at Combe Abbey, Warks': T. Mowl and C. Hickman, *The Historic Gardens of England Series: Northamptonshire* (2008), 93–95 and T. Mowl and D. James, *Warwickshire* (2011), 128–29.

13. *DM*, 26 Sept. 1816, 3. D. G. Edwards, *The Hunlokes of Wingerworth Hall* (Chesterfield, 1976).

14. *DM*, 19 March 1856, 4.

15. *DM*, 23 April 1856, 8.

16. *DM*, 13 June 1838, 3.

17. DRO: D593/2 Wingerworth Sale Brochure, 1920.

18. DRO: D1881 Box A, D'Ewes Coke's Sketchbook n.d. Possibly the sketch book may be his father's as the drawings could be late eighteenth or early nineteenth century, but Regency period seems most likely.

19. *DM*, 15 May 1839, 4.

20. Craven and Stanley, I, 115–16 for a full history of the complex rebuilding and changes of ownership. English Heritage (Images of England ref. 81717) argues that the south façade dates from the 1820s remodelling, whereas Craven argues for the 1770s.

21. DRO: D307/1/8/16-17 'Specification for making the proposed carriage road … near the Hermitage to Hassop Hall' (1829). DRO: D7676/Bag C/247 Map of Hassop estate 1831.

22. W. Bray, *A Sketch of a Tour into Derbyshire and Yorkshire* (1778), 93.

23. *DM*, 31 Oct. 1811, 3. These derelict buildings were demolished. Planning permission has been granted to rebuild and use as extra accommodation for the hotel: http://pam.peakdistrict.gov.uk/09070879,(2007).

24. See DRO: D258/5/1, lxii, copy of Stephen Glover's drawing of Hassop Hall.

25. I am grateful to Mr. Chapman for permission to visit and for answering queries.

26. *DM*, 13 Aug. 1812, 1, sale particulars.

27. *DM*, 8 July 1802; 18 Oct. 1804; 22 Sept. 1808; 16 Aug. 1810; 12 Aug. 1812.

28. T. Noble (ed.) and S. Glover, *History, Gazeteer and Directory of the County of Derby*, pt 2, 364. The antiquarian collections eventually came to his near neighbour, Sir Francis Sacheverell Darwin of Sydnope Hall, another keen antiquarian.

29. *DM*, 18 Sept. 1783, 4, 'Lines addressed to Mr D. D. Jun of Darley in the Dale'.

30. D. Deacon, *Poems by Daniel Deacon, jun* (2011), 117.

31. Craven and Stanley, I, 123–24. Sir Phillip built a four mile (6.4 km) road, the *Via Gellia*, along the valley bottom between Cromford and Grangemill, connecting the family lead mining interests around Wirksworth.

32. DRO: D5054/13/1 Burdett accounts, entry 22 Dec. 1760.

33. B. Jones, *Follies and Grottoes* (1979), 308. A tall square contemporary water tower at Bradley hall also has a pyramidal roof and incorporates a dovecote (www.imagesofengland.org.uk ref. 80294).) At Stainsby House, Smalley a contemporary pair of tall circular brick towers with conical roofs is also attached to kitchen garden walls, See Images of England no 78809; Picture the Past web site. ref DCHQ009721.

34. Illustrated in Sotherby's Catalogue for the *Hopton Hall Sale*, 5–6 September 1989, pl. 408, p. 56.

35. W. Adam, *Gem of the Peak* (1851), 177. The first edition was 1838.

36. *DM*, 18 Nov. 1829, 3.

37. Birmingham Museums and Art Gallery have six fine watercolours of Haddon by David Cox: Accession nos 1908 P30; 1919 P103; 1925 P291 and P316-7; 1953 P138.

38. DRO: D504/116/19 sale catalogue for Darley House, 1923. Also Smedley's Hydropathic establishment, Matlock.

39. Adam, *Gem of the Peak*, 180.

40. *CL* 9, 1 June 1901, 693; R. Blomfield and F. Inigo Thomas, *The Formal Garden in England* (1901), 114.

41. Derby Local Studies Library 6303E '*Chatsworth or the Genius of England's Prophecy* – A Poem by the Author of the Naval Triumph' (added underneath 'P. Cunningham Curate of Eyam, Derbyshire') printed Chesterfield 1783.

42. B. Cowell, 'Hardwick Hall in the Eighteenth Century', *Georgian Group Journal* 16 (2008), 43–58. William Salt Library, Stafford,: Staffordshire Views, J. Buckler's water colour of Hardwick New Hall (1813) with a plain lawn in courtyard, accessed on line through www.Staffordshire.gov.uk/gatewaytothepast.

43. M. Girouard, *Hardwick Hall* (1996), 83.

44. Girouard, *Hardwick Hall*, 44, 92; *CL*, 23, Oct. 1897, 434–35; 30 Oct. 1897, 464–65; 13 Oct. 1900, 464–70.

45. Craven and Stanley, I, 81–82.

46. See entries in B. Elliott, *Victorian Gardens* (1986). *Leeds Mercury*, 6 June 1829, 3; *Gardener's Magazine* 10 (1834), 21.

47. J. Major, *The Theory and Practice of Landscape Gardening* (1852), 21–22. He shows designs for various types of gardens, which include many of the features suggested for Derwent, 20 years previously. DRO: D7676/Bag C/261, Plan for laying out the grounds at Derwent Hall 1833 by Joshua Major, Knosthorp, Leeds.

48. Major, *Landscape Gardening*, 23, 75.

49. DRO: D7676 Bag C/307,309a, Sale plans 1841, 1851.

50. See NT Guide to *Calke Abbey* (1989) for a full history of the Abbey, park and family.

51. The castle was deliberately destroyed in 1896 following a family quarrel: see P. Heath's articles in *South Derbyshire Heritage News* 28 (Autumn 2008) and 30 (September 2009) and his typed notes for the Heritage Day Opening of the Park in September 2011. Convincingly Heath attributes the landscaping to Samuel Brown who was currently working at Calke.

52. C. Bruyn Andrews (ed.), *The Torrington Diaries* II (1970), 73.

53. P. Heath, *South Derbyshire Heritage News* 26 (February 2008) accessed online.

54. J. Farey, *General View*, 45.

55. DRO: D6430/2/8, Howard Colvin's working papers, photocopy of estimates dated 21 November 1810, which include a plan and model for a cascade and design for a 'Grotesque Rock' which appear to relate to Calke.

56. These are shown on an estate map of Calke dated 1857: DRO: D2375/296/4.

57. *DM*, 18 May 1836, 2; DRO: D2293/1/1 sale particulars for Newton Park estate, 21 July 1836.

58. P. Heath, *Heritage News* 21, Winter 2005–06, 9–10; Craven and Stanley, II, 195–96.

59. J. Farey, *General View,* 137.

60. *DM*, 18 May 1836, 2. Sale particulars.

61. Farey, *General View*, 37 mentions a grotto here; A sale of timber in 1841 includes timber lying 'from the Grotto to the Oat fields': *DM,* 21 April 1841, 2.

62. SRO: D3009/2 Plan of Newton Solney, 1827.

63. *DM*, 7 May 1836, 2. DRO: D2293/1/1-2 printed brochure of the sale particulars, 21 July 1836.

64. P. Heath (ed.), *South Derbyshire District Conservation Histories: Newton Solney* (2009). Accessed via www.south-derbys.gov.uk/Newton Solney Conservation History.

65. *DM*, 21 Feb. 1838, 2.

66. Images of England nos 82865, 82866. These are now on private ground and were not visited by the author. The folly image DCHQ10134, www.picturethepast.org.uk may be part of this folly group, placed outside the gardens.

67. Craven and Stanley, I, 42.

68. *DM*, 18 May 1836, 2.

69. W. Barron, *The British Winter Garden* (1852), 2.

70. Craven and Stanley, I, 92, 94. They note that a Stanhope cousin, the Earl of Chesterfield, created the huge gardens at nearby Bretby

71. DRO: D518M/E27 Elvaston Account Book, 1713–14.

72. DRO: D518M/F150. Francis Moore's accounts. Fish were stolen from the canal and fish ponds in 1775: *DM*, 2 June 1775, 4.

73. DRO: 4996/6/66 photocopy of 'A Map of the Parish of Elvaston in the County of Derby belonging to the Right Honorable William Earl of Harrington' by G. Grey. DRO: D518 M/F492, plan of parterre and canal *c.*1700, may relate to Elvaston.

74. J. P. Neale, *Views of the Seats of Noblemen and Gentlemen*, vol. 6 (1823).

75. Barron, *Winter Garden*, 2. The story is now repeated as fact – *e.g.* official guide to Elvaston Castle; similarly Humphry Repton is said to have rejected a commission on precisely the same grounds – again this is unlikely. Craven and Stanley, I, 94.

76. Barron, *Winter Garden*, 5.

77. See: Derbyshire County Council, *Elvaston Castle Country Park* (undated guidebook); B. Elliott, 'From Arboretum to the Woodland Garden', *Garden History* 35(2) (2007); P. Elliott *et al.* 'William Barron (1805–91) and nineteenth century British Arboriculture', *Garden History* 35 (2) (2007), 129–48, who argue that Barron saw Elvaston as one large pinetum artistically planted.

78. K. Lees (ed.), *Extracts from the Personal Diary Between the Years 1817–1862 of Edward Walhouse Littleton, Afterwards the first Lord Hatherton 1791–1863* (2003), Entry 23 Jan. 1818.

79. Elliott *et al.* 'William Barron'; *Staffordshire Sentinel and Commercial & General Advertiser*, 16 July 1881, 7. *Chester Chronicle*, 1 Jan. 1841, 4.

80. Barron's Obituary, *GC*, 25 April 1891, 523; *Derby Daily Telegraph*, 4 March 1927, 3.

81. The Harringtons stayed at their London house in the 1840s: *Morning Post*, 17 Oct. 1840, 3; 13 April 1843, 3; 29 Oct. 1845, 5; 6 Oct. 1848, 3; 20 March 1849, 5; *DM*, 13 and 20 April 1836. They had also a daughter Jane (1833–1907).

82. *GC*, 25 April 1891, 523; repeated in *Elvaston Castle Country Park*, 10.

83. *DM*, 3 Jan. 1838, 3.

84. J. C. Loudon, 'Recollections of a Tour made in May, 1839', *Gardener's Magazine* (1839), 458–60.

85. *JHCG*, 9 Sept. 1875, 229 (their first illustration of Elvaston); *GC,*25 April 1891, 523; *CL*, 14 Jan. 1899, 48–52, 21 Jan.1899, 80–83; E. Adveno Brooke, *The Gardens of England* (1857).

86. *GC*, 1849, 789 Articles by Robert Glendinning, 773, 789, 805, 820–21; 1850, 4, 21, 36–37.

87. *GC*, 1849, 805.

88. *GC*, 1849, 821.

89. *GC*, 1849, 773.

90. *GM*, May 1839, 460; Mrs J. Loudon, *Plain Instructions in Gardening* (1874), 274.

91. *GC*, 1850, 21.

92. Barron, *Winter Garden,* 71.

93. *Ibid.*, 73.
94. H. Winthrop Sargent, *Skeleton Tours Through England, Scotland and Ireland, Wales …
    With Some of the Principal Things to See, Especially Country Houses* (1871), 30.
95. *GC*, 1850, 37.
96. Barron, *Winter Garden*, 76.
97. See Barron's obituary *GC*, 25 April 1891, 522–25.
98. *DDT*, 13 March 1901, 4 and regular adverts thereafter; 24 Nov. 1915, 4.

CHAPTER EIGHT

The Early to Mid-Victorian Period: Reclamation, rockwork, conservatories

Planes of stubborn rocks lifting themselves in the sky.

'Re-cycling' or reclamation flourished with widespread restoration of medieval churches. Even York Minister was not spared when, following a fire in 1840, a sale offered ancient statuary, carvings, pinnacles *etc.*: 'the possessor of extensive pleasure-grounds may at this sale secure the most beautiful lots for the erection and adorning of temples, grottos or rockwork'.[1] In Derbyshire the earliest example of incorporating architectural salvage into pleasure grounds seems to have been at Breadsall Priory but the most notorious was slightly later at Lomberdale Hall.

The **Breadsall** estate had been purchased in 1799 by Erasmus Darwin, eldest son of Dr Erasmus Darwin of Lichfield. He committed suicide the following year, leaving the estate to his father who moved there in 1802, only to die very shortly afterwards. Rather poignantly his appreciation of Breadsall is shown in the last letter Dr Darwin ever wrote, in May 1802:

> We have a pleasant house, a good garden, ponds full of fish, and a pleasing valley somewhat like Shenstone's [The Leasowes] – deep, umbrageous and with a talkative stream running down it. Our house is near the top of the valley well screened by hills from the east and north and open to the south ...
> Four or more springs rise near the house, and have formed the valley.[2]

This plentiful supply of fresh water would have been an important factor when the Augustinian Canons chose the site to establish a small priory in the thirteenth century.

The widowed Elizabeth Darwin lived at Breadsall until her death in 1832, when her second son, Sir Francis Sacheverell Darwin (1786–1859) of Sydnope Hall, inherited. A keen antiquary, Sir Francis, with his gardener Joseph Heathcote, laid out a rockery (perhaps as folly ruins), incorporating pieces of gothic tracery and architectural fragments excavated from the medieval Breadsall priory. Three trefoil-headed arches and their shafts were re-erected against an outside wall of the house, while two seventeenth-century stone caryatids (now inside the house), probably from a Jacobean fireplace, were placed in the garden. There were also fragments of the crocketed pinnacles of All Saints, Derby, which was being restored in the 1830s.[3] Part of a late sixteenth-century church monument became another garden ornament, described disapprovingly in 1905:

FIGURE 94. Breadsall
Priory, pets cemetery
corner, 1850–1990.

COURTESY J. GUTTRICH, MARRIOTT
HOTELS

a headless and otherwise mutilated alabaster effigy of a man in armour kneeling on a pedestal. This was most improperly turned out Breadsall church, and placed here about 1840 ... it was then not a little broken and disarranged, for [a drawing] shows that the head and trunk had been turned round to face the feet.[4]

This was enthusiastic, if somewhat undiscriminating medieval reclamation. By the time Sir Francis died in 1859, his gardens contained assorted and scattered medieval fragments complementing two medieval priory fishponds near the house. The picturesque walk through the trees following the stream down the valley became 'The Wilderness' leading to a lake.[5] Sir Francis also began that typically Victorian feature, a pets' cemetery, which now has 15 little commemorative headstones dating from 1852–1990.[6]

In 1860 the estate was purchased by Francis Morley (1810–83), a Nottinghamshire hosier who promptly rebuilt and enlarged the compact Elizabethan house in a battlemented gothic style with an octagonal tower. He engaged William Barron and Son to landscape the grounds at a staggering cost of £4000.[7] This probably included the creation of two small islands on the park lake and planting around it. Morley continued to emphasis the picturesque nature of the gardens with more shrubberies and a flower garden. Darwin's 'talkative' picturesque little tree-lined stream and with its Wilderness Walk through trees and shrubs, with flowers on its banks, was given a summer house. There were informal paths round the extensive lawn with perimeter shrubberies and a circular summer house at the end of the terrace walk along the house.[8] The old priory fish pond nearest the house was transformed from a roughly oval shape into a large formal, stone-revetted Italian pool with a central fountain.[9]

Sometime between the sale of 1884 and resale of 1897 the sloping lawn was shaped into terraces with stone steps down to the formal pond. The top terrace

FIGURE 95. Breadsall Priory, nineteenth-century formal pond replacing medieval fishpond.

COURTESY J. GUTTRICH, MARRIOTT HOTELS

had 'exceedingly pretty Flower Parterres'. Winding paths led to 'a charming terraced rosary and rustic summer house. From the latter a delightful Wilderness walk leads through a Dell…'[10] In 1897 Sir Alfred Seale Haslam (1844–1927), an industrialist and former Mayor of Derby, bought the estate and further enlarged the house. In 1910 he employed the fashionable landscape gardener, Thomas Mawson, but it is difficult to quantify his work as so much has been changed. At the west end of the top terrace Mawson is said to have erected a rustic summer house with stained glass windows: a typical Mawson feature, but now lost.[11]

The rectangular sunken rose garden in the lower gardens (presently flower beds) was presumably Mawson's work, which regrettably entailed the loss of Darwin's rockery with its medieval stones.[12] There is another attractive rock garden below this area, intimate in scale, with stone paths meandering through and it probably contained a fernery (Pl. 23). Some of the stone here (and also forming the ha-ha) is dressed and cut, perhaps from the priory remains but also in plentiful supply from the estate quarry. This may be the work of Mawson. The rivulet (Darwin's 'talkative stream') has been embellished with stone edges and stepping stones to enhance the sound of running water, and although rather overgrown is still a most attractive feature. Breadsall Priory is now a hotel, with inevitable alterations and modern extensions. However the gardens are well maintained and the conversion of the park into a golf course has at least protected the lake and 'Wilderness Walk'.

However the best known, and indeed notorious, example of decorating a garden with ancient stonework was by Thomas Bateman at **Lomberdale Hall**, Youlgreave. For several hundred years exciting archaeological discoveries, from prehistoric to Roman times, have been made in Derbyshire. Among the first systematic archaeologists in the county were the wealthy William

Bateman (1787–1835) and his son Thomas (1821–61) of Middleton Hall. The latter's passion for discovering and unearthing the past led him to open hundreds of barrows/tumuli in Derbyshire and Yorkshire and to remove the contents.[13] After reaching his majority and inheriting his father's wealth, in 1844 Thomas Bateman built himself a new home, Lomberdale Hall, to his own designs. He proceeded to

FIGURE 96. Lomberdale Hall, The gardens aren't shown but reclaimed gargoyles can be seen on the walls. J.Bushfield 1848.

COURTESY OF MISS FRANCES WEBB AND WWW.PICTURETHEPAST. ORG.UK

embellish it, inside and out, with archaeological trophies from nearly 400 excavations, soon possessing 'the greatest number of specimens of British antiquities … of any gentleman in the county'.[14]

By the 1850s Bateman was well-known and often highly regarded for his work, which today would be viewed as unscientific and destructive, although he did publish accounts of many of the finds, and produced accurate drawings on site. *Black's Tourist's Guide* (1872) noted that of 75 ancient coffin lids found at Bakewell church during restoration, 18 were now at Lomberdale Hall.[15] The collection was sold to Sheffield Museum by his profligate son to help pay off his debts, at which time most of the fragments scattered about the garden must have been removed.[16] One can only surmise how the ancient pieces were displayed in the garden but the overall effect might have been similar to our modern presentation of neat ruins with tidy piles of stone surrounded by grass. This was Victorian antiquarianism not eighteenth-century picturesque.

Sir Francis Sacheverell Darwin was involved with a different sort of rockwork at **Sydnope Hall**, near Matlock. He purchased the Sydnope estate in 1826 and immediately enlarged the house in a Tudor style, adding balustrading at the front copied from that at Haddon Hall. By 1829 the gardens were 'tastefully laid out with fountains, grottos, harbours etc.'[17] If this refers to the rockwork gardens they would pre-date those at Elvaston and Chatsworth. Since Darwin inherited Breadsall Priory in 1832 (*supra*) and thereafter transferred much time and energy to that property, living there permanently after 1847 until his death in 1859, it may well be that the Sydnope rock gardens date from the late 1820s/early 1830s.[18]

Leading from the main formal gardens behind the house, these rock gardens along the hill-side have winding paths and little pools, lined with huge grit-stone rocks. Strange rock formations form outcrops; fissures have water dripping down; columns, recesses and a grotto (now collapsed) all create a magical world, now surrounded by huge rhododendrons, yew and mature conifers which hang over the rocks. The contrast between these and the manicured lawns and flower gardens by the house is as great now as it was then. It is said that Paxton was involved. Certainly the design of the rockwork is sophisticated in its apparent natural simplicity and a few of the rock formations resemble others at Chatsworth.[19]

Could Paxton have been inspired by Sydnope and copied on a grand scale at

FIGURE 97 *(left)*. Sydnope Hall, winding path with rockwork, ferns and water.

COURTESY P. JACKSON AND DIRECTORS OF SYDNOPE HALL APARTMENTS LTD

FIGURE 98 *(right)*. Sydnope Hall, stone bridge over cascade at end of rockwork walk.

COURTESY P. JACKSON AND DIRECTORS OF SYDNOPE HALL APARTMENTS LTD

Chatsworth? On the other hand, if the Sydnope rockwork was erected over several years, well into the 1830s, Paxton could have advised on extending its scope.

Equally exciting is the continuation of the rock garden path as a carriage drive, about 12 ft (3.7 m) wide, as a circuit along the wooded hillside. A little stream runs on the higher side with a stone ha-ha supporting wall on the lower edge. Strongly influenced by Repton's carriage drives of the 1790s–early 1800s it has views down across the valley (now obscured by later tree planting), including a now lost view to Sydnope Stand on the hill ridge, which was its destination.[20] Totally unexpected is the sound of water and the sudden glimpse of a terrific natural cascade, which has been embellished by massive rocks placed deliberately under, and each side of, the running water. There is a ten foot (3 m) wide bridge over the water for the carriage drive to continue. At this point the route has made a sharp turn to continue to Sydnope Stand, erected by Darwin as a hunting stand and eye-catcher from the house.[21] Also seen from the rockwork circuit was the Gardener's House, an octagonal castellated tower, 'a replica of one of the Lodges at Windsor Castle'.[22]

Whereas to the modern eye the rock gardens and waterfall look contrived, albeit very striking, in 1874 the author of an article on Sydnope had a different view:

> The stones are in great masses of several tons weight, and in their arrangement art is not painfully evident; on the contrary, the whole of this work has a natural and pleasing appearance, water trickling down here and there among the rocks, which afford nooks for many a Fern, besides holding soil enough in their crevices for the support of low-growing shrubs…
>
> [The waterfall] rushes down in a broken stream from a height of some 70 feet above the walk …In quarrying stone on the opposite side of the ravine masses of rock had fallen over and these constitute a bed over which water has been conducted, forming a grand waterfall, which owes more to nature than to art.[23]

FIGURE 99 Chatsworth, French garden with stone pillars from courtyard of house. photograph, *c.*1870.

Typically for that period the writer was just as interested in the thousands of rhododendrons in the valley: 'what a gorgeous display they must make when in flower' and approved of the garden bedding-out schemes based on that in London parks. A formal terrace, with elaborate flowers beds, was dominated by a five-tiered fountain. This was divided when Charles Boot of Thornbridge Hall (*qv*) purchased Sydnope and in 1939 rather unfortunately took three tiers of the fountain to Thornbridge, leaving just two at Sydnope.

At **Chatsworth**'s gardens a gigantic rockery was just one feature among many which evolved after the sixth Duke of Devonshire (1790–1858) inherited in 1811, by which time the gardens were seen as an unsatisfactory mix of baroque water display and picturesque landscape:

> the artificial waterworks … are curious and interesting as works of art, but, it must be confessed, that works of ingenuity of this class appear to be misplaced among the sublimities of nature which particularly characterize the surrounding scenery.[24]

However the duke resolutely retained favoured baroque features during nearly 50 years of extravagant innovation. In the 1820s a new long north wing of the house was designed by Wyatville, an Orangery was incorporated, and then, as an afterthought, the belvedere storey at the far end. The increased length of the house was balanced by the Broad Walk, a third of a mile (*c.*500 m) long, extending from Flora's Temple (the former Bowling Green House), past Wyatville's new North Wing and Talman's East façade, then continuing parallel to the Canal Pond of 1702. Some formality was added to the gardens by replacing lawns with fashionable Regency flower beds designed by Wyatville and Joseph Paxton. To the west front Wyatville added architectural terraces with eight stone 'baskets', 'elegantly sculptured for shrubs and flowers, 32 ft (9.75 m) square each'.[25] Classical statues were placed in the gardens, many purchased specially over several years by the sixth duke.

A parterre was created (1812) in front of the first duke's Greenhouse (moved in the eighteenth century to its current position). In 1828 this was embellished with stone columns removed from the inner court of the house and became known as the French Garden.[26] It was converted to a rose garden in 1939. Immensely proud of his gardens, the duke welcomed visitors, as J. C. Loudon noted approvingly in 1831:

> The humblest individual is not only shown the whole, but the duke has expressly ordered the waterworks to be played for everyone, without exception. This is acting in the true spirit of great wealth and enlightened liberality.[27]

The arrival of the young Joseph Paxton (1803–65) as head gardener in 1826 rapidly accelerated changes, but as his extraordinary career achievements have been thoroughly researched and published, here is simply an outline of some of his exciting work at Chatsworth.[28] The close partnership of Paxton and the sixth duke has been compared to that of Le Notre and Louis XIV, based on mutual respect and affection.[29] Both were very competitive and keen to impress with ambitious building, plant collecting and display, supported by the duke's huge revenues, which were ultimately stretched to the limit. The duke had what amounted to a mania for collecting, including rare plants and orchids and also garden statuary, while he expected, and obtained, miracles from his head gardener.

Paxton, like Barron, was an expert at moving and transplanting mature trees. In 1830 he master-minded the move of a 50-year-old, eight-ton weeping ash, from Wilson's Nursery, Derby (*qv*) to Chatsworth 28 miles (45 km) away, using 40 men and several horses. On arrival this was planted to the north-west of the entrance front on a newly-raised mound of earth, where 'it will add greatly to the picturesque and romantic effect of the scenery'.[30] This was an early example of the single-minded determination and disregard of expense on the part of Paxton and the duke to transform the pleasure gardens as speedily as possible, to universal amazement and admiration. Like so much else at Chatsworth, the ash thrives today.

Other early expensive and important additions included the Orangery (1827), an integral part of the new north wing, housing orange trees formerly part of Empress Josephine's collection at Malmaison, together with fine statues.[31] The Pinetum (1829) was stocked with new introductions; The Orchid House (*c*.1832–4) was erected specifically for the duke's expanding collection from all over the world. Trees in the new 40-acre (16.2 ha) Arboretum (1835) were scientifically labelled with their botanical classifications, with 'A two mile walk where all the plants are classed according to their botanical arrangement without interfering with the wildness and beauty of the walk'.[32]

One has to wonder if there was rivalry between Chatsworth and Elvaston? At both estates there was tree planting on a princely and imaginative scale, with Paxton's Pinetum at Chatsworth closely followed by Barron's at Elvaston. We have no proof that Paxton knew about developments at Elvaston Castle in the

1830s, but these were known amongst the aristocracy, *vide* Wellington's visit there in 1838 with 'a select party of the Nobility'.[33]

Implicitly, and perhaps deliberately, certain improvements at Chatsworth in the 1840s outshone Elvaston. In a small way Paxton's Luttrell's Seat (1839), an open summer house with two arches and in a disciplined Moorish style, was a *riposte* to the oddly eclectic Alhambra at Elvaston, where there were also new and significant collections of pines and firs, large transplanted trees, araucaria and rock work by 1839.[34] So at Chatsworth, the Broad Walk was then lined with the newly introduced monkey puzzle trees (*Araucaria Araucana*) in the 1840s.

Paxton's rock gardens of the early 1840s are quite different to Barron's equally extensive rocks at Elvaston. The ever resourceful Paxton invented steam-powered machinery to move hundreds of huge boulders into carefully arranged piles to appear as if they were natural formations, complete with narrow passages and outcrops seemingly precariously balanced. The duke happily noted: 'The confusion of Paxton's rock works look as if he and other giants had been storming heaven'.[35] It came as a complete surprise for the visitor to come across, and walk through, masses of these huge rocks.

Paxton's genius was shown again with the famous Conservatory (Great Stove) of 1836–41, the largest conservatory in the world, built to house the duke's magnificent plant collections from his own financed expeditions, plus acquisitions and gifts. This astonishing glass house was 227 ft (84 m) long, 123 ft (37.5 m) wide and 67 ft (20.4 m) high, made possible by Paxton's use of the ridge and furrow glass roof invented by Loudon in 1818, with internal cast-iron hollow supporting columns. Paxton worked with the architect Decimus Burton, who as the duke acknowledged 'designed the architecture part and by his knowledge secured the strength of the construction'.[36] Costing the enormous sum of £33,000 it needed eight boilers to heat it, fed by seven miles (11.3 km) of pipes. Coal came in via a concealed underground railway and the chimney flues also went underground to a stack hidden some distance away.[37] Greatly admired at the time, sadly it was too expensive to maintain and was demolished in 1920, to be replaced by a maze in 1962.

FIGURE 100 *(left)*. Chatsworth, Paxton's rockwork gardens 1840s; photograph *c.*1868.

COURTESY OF DERBYSHIRE LIBRARIES AND WWW. PICTURETHEPAST.ORG.UK

FIGURE 101 *(right)*. Chatsworth, Paxton's Great Stove, 1836–41, demolished 1920.

COURTESY OF DERBYSHIRE LIBRARIES AND WWW. PICTURETHEPAST.ORG.UK

FIGURE 102. Chatsworth, Paxton's Emperor Fountain (1843) in the Long Canal; mid-nineteenth-century lithograph from *Horto van Houtteano*.

AUTHOR'S COLLECTION.

Besides his engineering abilities utilised at Chatsworth's various greenhouses, hothouses and the Great Conservatory, the polymath Paxton also developed an expertise in hydrology. A huge undertaking was the Emperor Fountain (1843) in the long Canal Pond, created specifically for a possible visit by Czar Nicholas, a friend of the Duke. The highest fountain in England it was fed by gravity-powered water, piped from a new lake in the hills above the house. This in turn was fed by water channelled from the moors:[38]

This marvellous fountain throws up a thick jet of water no less than 267 ft [*c.*80 m] in height, which, spreading out as it falls, forms a liquid sheet of spray, on which, not unfrequently the sunlight produces an exquisite rainbow. The quantity of metal, we are told, required in the formation of the pipes, etc., for this gigantic work, amounted to nearly 220 tons... Near the 'Emperor' are other fountains of great beauty, and when all are playing the effect is beyond description.[39]

In 1849 the Duke of Newcastle thought it even better than Versailles, 'a most Extraordinary as well as really glorious sight – for the situation adds value and importance to this astonishing work of art'.[40] Paxton's many other works at Chatsworth, his published Journals, his work on public parks, business interests, work as an MP, his design and erection of the Crystal Palace, are all aspects of a workaholic Victorian genius, made possible by the unstinting support of the Duke of Devonshire (not to forget his long-suffering wife Sarah who looked after his work at Chatsworth during his frequent long absences).[41]

The Victorian enthusiasm for rock gardens was matched by one for the glass conservatory for exotics. These appear at aristocratic Chatsworth at their most inventive and expensive but Derbyshire has other examples of splendid conservatories, some of which enabled industrialists to demonstrate their wealth and fashionable interests.

Vestiges of a Paxton designed conservatory survive at **Burton Closes**, Bakewell, in what were once impressive gardens. The house was built for John Allcard (1779–1856), a wealthy Quaker banker and stockbroker, who purchased 73 acres (29.6 ha) of land from the Duke of Rutland of nearby Haddon Hall in 1845.[42] Here he built a compact Tudor/Gothic Revival house sited half way up a

FIGURE 103. Burton Closes, with Paxton's much altered conservatory (late 1840s) attached.

COURTESY C. J. D. FISHER, BURTON CLOSES HALL

hill, with views down a valley. House and grounds were designed by his friend Joseph Paxton as his first major domestic commission.[43] Allcard commissioned a dazzling list of designers and craftsmen which reads like a 'Who's Who' of Gothic Revival taste. A. W. N. Pugin and J. C. Crace were given a free hand for the interior with fine fireplaces, carved woodwork, painted ceilings, furniture and flock wallpapers. Tiles were from Minton and stained glass by John Hardman.

Allcard's son had a large family and therefore extended the house between 1856 and 1858 in a sympathetic matching style. The extension on the garden (south) façade included a perpendicular-style octagonal prospect tower, from which were views over the garden terraces and also the fine collection of specimen trees. Paxton had designed an attractive eight-bay conservatory as an integral part of the original south façade. Sixty-two feet (18.9 m) long, it housed Allcard's collection of rare exotic plants. Dismantled in 1856, this was re-assembled at the end of the enlarged south facade.[44] Regrettably now much altered, this light and airy building had the latest technological ideas, with a ridge and furrow roof, supported by elegant thin iron columns with gothic detailing.

The family fortunes were lost in the Stock Market crash of 1866, leading to the sale of the estate. The sale particulars in the *Derby Mercury* 15 June 1870 mention 'a very extensive ornamental rockery, filled with the most beautiful ferns and heath [heathers]'. This tufa stone rockery, also designed by Paxton, edged the carriage drive before it entered the courtyard of the house and remnants still survive, with a few ferns lingering on. Paxton used the eighteenth-century device of a long approach drive from his entrance lodge, which circuited the house along the south, providing views up to the house, seen through the trees. The drive then curved sharply and swept up to the courtyard entrance, past this hillside rockery.

On the south and east the house has an upper and lower terrace, with square corner bastions supported by stone walls and once filled with flowers. Just one of several decorative iron gates on the terraces survives (Pl. 24). This house and garden, on which so much expense, care and attention had been lavished, fell on hard times and the house was partially demolished. It became a care home although the gardens, woods and parkland are now largely covered by housing. The garden terraces survive and the area immediately surrounding the house is maintained and is still retrievable from encroaching undergrowth and self-set trees. Sadly the Paxton conservatory has lost its elegant glass roof to a heavy slate roof and its replacement wooden framed windows no longer relate to the architecture of the hall.

Richard Barrow was another wealthy businessman who amassed and enjoyed exotic plants. George Hodgkinson Barrow, his brother and business partner in the Staveley Iron Works, built **Ringwood Hall**, **Chesterfield**. Inheriting on his brother's death in 1853 Richard Barrow laid out the gardens and erected glasshouses between 1853 and 1865. As well as a 70-ft (22 m) long conservatory attached to the house there was a magnificent conservatory, 220 ft (70 m) long, which dominated the formal gardens.

> The centre is also octagonal, surmounted by a dome supported by eight pillars of the same form… Under the dome is a large fountain of elaborate workmanship, and surrounded by foliage and flowering plants.[45]

This piece of conspicuous consumption was filled with carefully tended exotics including huge camellias and fuchsias '10–12 feet high'. An ironwork rose-arbour, 100 ft (30.5 m) long, with 'Roses of every shade and hue', led to it. The long terrace in front had central steps leading down to the flower gardens and an orchard.[46] There were also a peach house, vineries, an exotic fernery and many other greenhouses to supply the house with fruit and vegetables. With amazing and beautifully maintained displays, Mr Barrow could boast that Mr Prince, his second head gardener, had worked for dukes at Syon House and at Chatsworth.

Richard Barrow is an excellent example of a wealthy industrialist, 'one of the greatest of England's merchant princes, and "fine old English gentleman"' as a local paper gushingly enthused, who used his expensive garden (and parkland) for entertaining, to help establish his social status.[47] He exhibited flowers and fruit at local horticultural shows, together with the Duke of Devonshire.[48]

Barrow opened the gardens with their rare plants to small parties and to his workmen and their families on Sundays.[49] In 1873, after his death, the 'Grand Horticultural Show and Rural Fete' was held at Ringwood, with special trains running from Sheffield to Staveley.[50]

The estate was purchased in 1910 by Charles Paxton Markham (1865–1926). His father was a managing director of the Staveley Coal and Iron Company and Rosa, his mother, was a daughter

FIGURE 104.
Ringwood Hall, Garden Conservatory, illustrated in Journal of Horticulture and Cottage Gardener, 16 March 1876; demolished early twentieth century.

FIGURE 105. Ringwood
Hall, 1850s alcove
terminating the walk
below the conservatory.

COURTESY R. DAVIES

of Joseph Paxton. Markham was another wealthy businessman and generous local benefactor and dignitary, who also opened the grounds of Ringwood to his workmen and their families on Sunday afternoons, and he bequeathed the estate to his company for the benefit of the employees. In 1913 he donated the large fountain from his gardens to the new Eastwood Park, and probably demolished the large conservatory about the same time. Happily the attractive 1850s architectural alcove at the end of the terrace has survived, no doubt today a favourite background for wedding photos at the present hotel.

There was another of these high-status heated glasshouses at **Riddings House**, near Alfreton. James Oakes of Derby (1750–1828) purchased ironworks at Riddings in 1818 and then built a small villa, which he shielded from his coalmines with a 300 acre (121.5 ha) park.[51] His son James Haden Oakes continued as a highly successful and resourceful industrial entrepreneur (his firm erected the first ever oil refinery and produced paraffin oil in 1850), helping to create an estate village and model farm. The 1880 OS map shows the extent of the large range of greenhouses both attached to the house and in the gardens, as enthusiastically reported by the *Journal of Horticulture* in 1877:

> a dozen fruit houses, many of them of large dimensions, and nearly twice as many plant houses, besides numerous pits and other appendages, all filled to overflowing with choice collections of plants, many of them of recent introduction.[52]

The last phrase is significant, showing Haden Oakes' wealth enabled him to access and successfully cultivate the latest introductions with his head gardener, Mr Ward, who had the cachet of being Chatsworth trained. Attached to the house a 140 ft (42.7 m) long 'corridor' housed begonias, bougainvilleas and other colourful exotics. This led into an orchid house, greenhouse, stove-house with plants for 'dinner-table ornamentation' and for exhibiting. There was also an orchard house with peaches and nectarines and a palm house. On the other side of the house was the essential Fern House and Conservatory, both 40 ft long and 18 ft wide (12.2 × 5.5 m). The Conservatory almost overshadowed the house to which it was linked and was also used for evening entertainment. Lit by gas, 'the reflection among the Ferns and other plants has the appearance of very powerful moonlight.'[53]

Here again is the most up-to date technical innovation, much admired, though of doubtful help to the health of the plants. With its 'village of glasshouses' The Riddings is another example of the craze for exotic and fashionable plants, cared for by an expert gardener to flourish out of season and to impress visitors. The extensive pleasure grounds were of secondary importance.

As rock gardens became ever more extensive, from the 1850s Pulham and Sons could provide a highly convincing, man-made, hard wearing substitute, as at **Osmaston Manor**. Although the house was demolished in 1965 enough survives of the landscape to appreciate the scale and magnificence of this mid-nineteenth-century gem.

Francis Wright (1806–73) was a co-owner of Butterley Ironworks Company and consequently a very wealthy man indeed. In the mid-1840s he moved from Lenton Hall in Nottinghamshire and built a new home at Osmaston, on land he had inherited and added to, amounting to 34,000 acres (*c*.13,767 ha) by 1883.[54] His architect, Henry Stevens of Derby, designed a huge 70-roomed house with more than a few references to Tissington (family home of Mrs Wright), with neo-Jacobean facades and interiors. Appropriately the Butterley Company supplied the ironwork for the large stone classical conservatory, 77 ft long, 42 ft wide (23.5 × 12.8 m) and two storeys high. Inside delicate cast

FIGURE 106. Osmaston Manor, cast iron and stone Conservatory, photograph before demolition.

FIGURE 107. Osmaston Manor, interior cast iron Conservatory, photograph before demolition.

COURTESY SIR ANDREW WALKER-OKEOVER

iron pillars supported an enormous iron and glass roof. Linked to the house by a long picture gallery over an open loggia, this heated conservatory had an iron dolphin fountain in the centre and views over the garden terraces. Needless to say it was lavishly and expensively supplied with tender plants, many of which were fashionably brightly coloured.[55] A three-bay stone fernery was attached to it.

The heating system for house and conservatory was highly innovative, using under-floor pipes. The used air was carried underground, out to the kitchen garden, to escape through a chimney. Since this chimney had to be high – some 150 ft/45.7 m – the opportunity was taken to merge it with an Italianate tower, which could double as a belvedere. By the 1870s this ingenious new heating system was found to be deficient and standard fireplaces and chimneys were installed in the house. Ironically the tower, much lowered, remains as the only surviving building on the site.[56] Six acres (2.4 ha) of walled kitchen garden supplied vegetables, tender fruit in 18 glasshouses and large collections of plants for house and conservatory, including Mr Wright's favourite orchids.[57]

Below the house and conservatory a formal Italianate garden was designed by Joseph Paxton with Edward Milner. Long formal terraces were linked by flights of steps with 'Jacobean' balusters, which led down to the lowest terrace with its stone lined decorative pond. Flower-filled classical urns were placed on the retaining walls and on plinths.[58] Echoing eighteenth-century precedents the village was removed and rebuilt as a model village, while the valley below the house was landscaped with three lakes. From the house, over the terraces and down to the lakes, were stunning views over wooded countryside; views which survive unchanged today.

FIGURE 108. Osmaston Manor with attached picture gallery leading to the conservatory, aerial view before demolition in 1965.

Other features provided entertainment for family and guests. An aviary, about sixty by forty feet, was attached to the tennis court side of the stable block.

> It is enclosed by massively built walls about 15 feet high, and has an arched wire roof. The centre of the ground has been excavated and formed into a rugged and precipitous dell. Bold rocks jut out at every conceivable angle and with delightful irregularity. Trickling streams form tiny rivulets and gather into a glassy pool at the bottom where the Water Lily and kindred plants luxuriate. On the jutting rocks are alpine plants... The banks of the dell are turfed and planted with shrubs… But besides the water, rocks, shrubs and plants are 'birds, birds everywhere'.[59]

These were brightly coloured and exotic birds and there were yet more aviaries and an enclosed space for aquatic birds. The aviary was designed by Edward Milner, planted by the head gardener, Mr Booth, with rockwork made by the firm of James Pulham, who created the nearby rock garden complex using 'Pulhamite' artificial rockwork, which looks like authentic rock.[60] Designed by Edward Milner 1864–65, this area, reputedly costing several thousand pounds, was a *tour de force*. Each rock was carefully placed for effect with shapes and outlines shifted during construction to produce an apparently random positioning of rocks and boulders. Approached though a wide entrance:

> On either side the stony passage are fissures – yawning rifts, as if torn asunder by some superhuman power; passing these we enter the rock-bound dell. The rockery at Osmaston is not a huge pyramid of stones which we walk round to admire... It is an amphitheatre... In the centre of the enclosure is an irregular stream of water: at its edge are Sedges and water plants, massive boulders protrude through its sides covered with Lichens and half hidden by Ferns … and scattered about in apparent abandonment are mammoth stones, Heaths, Ferns, Azaleas and Conifers.

The sides of the amphitheatre are rugged rocks, clothed with foliage and draped with Alpine plants in great variety... We ascended from the dell by rough stone steps, and to look down on the scene below – the cascades, rocks and foliage chaotically intermingled, one is not surprised that Mr Parham [*sic* – Pulham] considers the work as one of his greatest triumphs, for this natural-looking and wild picture is entirely artificial.[61]

The naturalism and shade of the rockery/grotto/fernery with waterfalls must have been a welcome diversion on a hot summer's day from the formal, open terraces and a contrast to manicured lawns and flowerbeds. The sound of running water was an extra attraction, fed by pumps from a large reservoir on a hill above the house, which also fed the fountains.[62] In the central space of the rock gardens was a second glass roofed fernery (Pl. 25). It is still possible to follow the circular walks around the outside of the rocks, to enter via the stone arches and see the little pools, cascades, rustic pillars and mounds for fern, making enchanting surprises.

Edward Milner's work at Osmaston was his earliest Derbyshire commission. Milner (1819–84) was born at Darley Dale near Chatsworth where his father was a gardener. He became an apprentice of Paxton, who appears to have valued him, sending him to study at the Jardin des Plantes in Paris from 1841–45. Milner then became Paxton's assistant, helping at major public parks and at the Crystal Palace. With this experience behind him, he set up his own firm in 1858 and undertook private commissions throughout the country. In Derbyshire after Osmaston (1846–49, 1869–71), came Stancliffe Hall (1871), the Old Vicarage at Bakewell (1870–71), and most importantly, the Pavilion Gardens at Buxton (1871). Joined by his son Henry Ernest in 1870, the firm (later Milner-White) became a major influence on garden and landscape design, involved locally with Howard Park, Glossop (1887–88), Renishaw (1890–96 and later) and Kedleston (1920–22).[63]

Milner's increasing confidence, and ability with rockwork on a massive scale, was shown at the quarry gardens at **Stancliffe Hall**, purchased by a remarkable man, Joseph Whitworth (1803–87) in 1855. Whitworth was a brilliantly successful mechanical engineer, who invented the Whitworth screw thread and Whitworth rifle, and was also a generous philanthropist. The Whitworths did not move into Stancliffe until the 1860s, when work began on 'rock-gardens of the finest conceivable character utilising the gritstone quarries which had provided the stone for St. George's Hall in Liverpool'.[64] The acquisition of a baronetcy in 1869 further fuelled Whitworth's plans to aggrandise the house and grounds from a fairly modest start, to the extent that locals remarked that he 'turfed the slopes with banknotes'.[65] Milner designed the pleasure gardens which included curved circuitous paths as with his concurrent work at Buxton Pavilion Gardens.

Black's 1872 Tourist's Guide soon noted with approval:

The [new] mansion is erected on the site of the old hall, and is one of the noblest and most commanding in the country; and his grounds, which are now being formed, will be certainly the finest, most wildly picturesque, and most romantic of any in existence. The celebrated Darley Dale stone quarries … are all included in his pleasure grounds, and form natural rockeries of the most stupendous nature.[66]

'Stupendous' was, for once, an accurate description, for a bold concept transformed the quarry into a gigantic natural stone rockery. A cliff was excavated in the hillside, and the gritstone blasted with explosives to create spaces for planting.[67] The naturally picturesque scheme was embellished by ebullient Victorian planting of all that was newly fashionable, under the direction of Whitworth's gardener, Joseph Dawson, another pupil of Paxton 'whose zeal and intelligence have effected wonders'.[68] Sir Joseph Whitworth thought on a theatrical and grand scale, sparing:

> neither pains nor expense to clothe the barren sandstone rock, and to bring out in the most effective manner the contrast between the boldness and majesty of the rock, and the richness and variety of foliage and flowers.[69]

This commentator was particularly impressed by the rich colour of the luxuriant planting, with the typical Victorian enthusiasm for rhododendrons, azaleas, broom and conifers and a profusion of rock plants and alpines. The steep sides of the quarry rockeries had walks threading their way along between the large mill-stone grit rocks. Another writer (1884) fantasised whether or not the Matterhorn would appear:

> towering into the sky round the next corner, for, in truth, there is here much to remind the visitor of the lower slopes above Zermatt at the base of the Matterhorn, but the well-kept paths and easy gradients dispel the illusion.[70]

A little wooden bridge linked two huge quarried blocks (a 'chasm') and a small waterfall, to the designs of Milner and Son.[71]

FIGURE 109. Stancliffe Hall, a photograph of the outdoor and gardening staff in the 1890s taken in the Winter Garden (1885).

Whitworth, a brilliant man and a perfectionist, put as much imagination into his house and garden as into his various highly successful business ventures. He was well into his 60s, and semi-retired, when work started on the house and garden, but he insisted on the immaculate upkeep of the rockwork (15 acres/6.1 ha with the shrubberies) and the 20 acres (9.1 ha) of lawns and paths nearer the house. There were 2½ miles (4.1 km) of walks in all. As if this were not enough, Whitworth also commissioned a huge winter garden, 120 ft (36.9 m) long, attached to the house by a corridor, which was, of course, state of the art.[72] The estate was broken up after the death of Whitworth's widow and became a school from 1895 to 2001 and the Winter Garden was demolished.

In total contrast was the garden Milner designed at **The Vicarage, Bakewell**, for Edward Balston (1817–91), Vicar 1869–91. Clearly a man of some pretensions, Balston engaged the fashionable architect Alfred Waterhouse to build a large new vicarage in mildly Gothic style. Milner was commissioned to re-design the garden, with a large open lawn (for church fetes?). He added to the existing perimeter tree belts to provide privacy, placed a stylised formal parterre under the bay windows of the house and created a small enclosed circular flower garden to the rear of the house. The emphasis on trees and wide sweeps of grass on this steeply sloping site was reminiscent of a small country estate rather than a town garden.[73]

Milner did not include a rockery at The Vicarage, although by the 1870s modest rockeries were popular in smaller gardens, such as a town garden in Derby 'tastefully laid out with rockeries, rock arch, and rustic trellis, etc.' in 1879.[74] By then rockeries were often associated with ferns, which were also grown in Conservatories, Winter Gardens and in special Fern Houses, often supplied with rockwork and water. The fashion began in the 1840s, was at its peak 1850–90, to slowly die out after 1914.[75] From the 1850s James Pulham and Sons was the leading company constructing ferneries as fanciful, fashionable items. The finest examples were very elaborate with arches and ruins, while Grotto/Ferneries had dripping water and pools. At Shipley Hall, Alfred Mundy had two ferneries, one linking the mansion to the conservatory as:

> a curvilinear span-roofed corridor some 60 yards long; the side walls of this glass-covered way are in part clothed with Ferns planted in tufa, interspersed with Begonias of the Rex type.[76]

Tufa, a light and porous stone, was well suited for use in grottos and ferneries and Virginia cork was also widely used after the 1850s.[77]

In 1884 a local newspaper noted that men, women and children at Matlock railway station were selling large quantities of ferns and flowers to day trippers. The writer worried about the large scale loss of ferns in local habitats for 'a momento of their day's outing being generally the familiar basket of ferns taken from their rocky homes to perish in some smoky town'. His worries were proved correct. In 1886 a letter to the *Derby Mercury* berated 'Professional Fern Robbers', who had been so efficient:

that not a rare or choice fern is to be found in any of the dales through which the Midland line from Derby to Manchester passes, and the more distant dales are now being plundered in the same fashion.[78]

In 1898 'It was observed with much regret that, owing to the depredations of excursionists and others, the hartstongue and stagshorn fern, once so common [near Cromford] are now almost extinct'.[79]

Notes

All quotations from newspapers are © The British Library Board. All rights reserved. With thanks to the British Newspaper Archive (www.BritishNewspaperArchive.co.uk)

1.   *Yorkshire Gazette*, 13 July 1844, 6.
2.   Dr Darwin to Richard Lovell Edgeworth, 17 May 1802 quoted D. King Hele, *Erasmus Darwin, A Life of Unequalled Achievement* (1999), 341.
3.   Craven and Stanley, I, 51–53.
4.   Rev. J. C. Cox, 'The history of Breadsall Priory II', *Journal of Derbyshire Archaeology and Natural History* 27 (1905), 149.
5.   T. N. Redman, *An Illustrated History of Breadsall Priory*, (2009), 13–14; DRO: D1079/19/1 Plan of Breadsall Priory Estate 1860.
6.   Redman, *Illustrated History*, 14.
7.   Craven and Stanley, I, 53.
8.   SRO: D3272/6/4/2 Sale particulars Breadsall Priory, June 1884.
9.   Its changing shape can be seen on maps: DRO: D2275/M/71/14 (1761); D1079/11/1(1790); D1079/11/5 (1817); D1079/11/3 (1823); D1079/19/1 (1860); D1079/19/3 (1897); SRO: D3272/6/4/1(1884).
10. DRO: D1057/19/3 Sale of Breadsall Priory, July 1897.
11. Redman, *Illustrated History*, 19.
12. Craven and Stanley, I, 53.
13. B. M. Marsden, *The Early Barrow Diggers* (2011), 51–71.
14. *DM*, 25 Aug. 1847, 3; www.picturethepast.org.uk: ref DCHQ200009, a drawing of a room of Bateman's Museum shows row upon row of artefacts in wall cupboards and display tables.
15. L. Jewitt (ed.), *Black's 1872 Tourist's Guide to Derbyshire* (1999), 25, 135.
16. English Heritage, 'Images of England' nos 81139–40 note that surviving in the garden is a large stone garden seat with an early fourteenth-century blind arcade, cusped stone tracery on the back wall, and medieval gravestones embedded in the side walls; a sundial on a medieval column and a pair of medieval arches about ten ft (3 m) high, possibly also from Bakewell Church.
17. S. Glover and T. Noble, *The History of the County of Derby*, pt 2 (1829), 365.
18. *DM*, 16 Nov. 1859, 3: 'the last twelve years of his [Darwin's] life were spent at Breadsall'.
19. My thanks to Joan Webb who kindly guided me on site and discussed its history, including the possible Paxton connection, and its present restoration.
20. Information from Joan Webb. There is no known link with Repton, but he was working at Wingerworth, only ten miles/16 km) away, in 1809.
21. R. Barrow, who purchased the estate in 1858, added battlements and an attached castellated cottage.
22. DRO: D504/116/20 Sale catalogue for Sydnope estate, 1920.

23.   *JHCG*, 12 March 1874, 222–24; also 19 March 1874, 239.

24.   Glover and Noble, *History of the County of Derby*, 239–40.

25.   *Ibid.*, 240.

26.   S. Seligman, *Explore the Gardens at Chatsworth* (2008), 44. This has been a basis for this section.

27.   P. Boniface (ed.), *The Travel Journals of John Claudius Loudon and his wife Jane* (1987), 72–73.

28.   See K. Colquhoun, *A Thing in Disguise. The Visionary Life of Joseph Paxton* (2003), republished as '*The Busiest Man in England', A Life of Joseph Paxton* (2006).

29.   M. Woods and A. Warren, *Glass Houses, A History of Greenhouses, Orangeries and Conservatories* (1988), 123. It was paralleled by William Barron and Earl Harrington, at Elvaston.

30.   *DM*, 14 April 1830, 3.

31.   Glover and Noble, *History of the County of Derby*, 235; *Journal of Horticulture*, 1 Dec. 1870, 433.

32.   SRO: NLS 313/903 Georgiana, Lady Dover to Duchess of Sutherland, 11 June 1839. I thank Sue Gregory for this reference.

33.   *DM*, 3 Jan. 1838, 3.

34.   J. C. Loudon, 'Recollections of a Tour made in May, 1839', *Gardener's Magazine* n.s. 5 (1839), 458–59.

35.   SRO: NLS 313/907 Duke of Devonshire to Harriet, Duchess of Sutherland, 21 March [1843]. I thank Sue Gregory for this reference.

36.   SRO: NLS 313/907 Duke of Devonshire to Duchess of Sutherland, 21 March [1843].

37.   Woods and Warren, *Glass Houses*, 123–24.

38.   Seligman, *Chatsworth*, 14–15.

39.   *Black's 1872 Tourist's Guide to Derbyshire*, 101.

40.   R. A. Gaunt (ed.) *Unhappy Reactionary: The Diaries of the 4th Duke of Newcastle-under-Lyme, 1822–50*, Thoroton Society Record Series 43 (2003), 40–42.

41.   Colquhoun, *Busiest Man in England*, 129; M. F. Darby 'Joseph Paxton's Water Lily', in M. Conan (ed.), *Bourgeois and Aristocratic Encounters in Garden Art, 1550–1850* (2002), 267–70: accessed via www. onlinebooks.library.upenn.edu.

42.   Craven and Stanley, I, 60.

43.   Colquhuon, *Busiest Man*, 139, 231. Paxton's daughter Victoria married Allcard's youngest son in 1857.

44.   Colquhuon, *Bustiest Man*, 139–40; *DM,* 15 June 1870; N. Pevsner, *The Buildings of England, Derbyshire* (1979), 77–78. C. Beale, 'A forgotten greenhouse by Joseph Paxton: the conservatory at Hampton Court, Herefordshire', *Journal of Garden History* 30 (1) (Spring 2002), 74–83 for a discussion of the Burton Closes conservatory, with an 1846 photograph.

45.   *JHCG*, 16 March 1876, 215.

46.   *Ibid.*

47.   *DTCH*, 1 Aug. 1863, 2.

48.   For example the Clay Cross Horticultural Show, *Derbyshire Courier*, 16 Aug 1862, 3.

49.   *Derbyshire Courier*, 1 Nov. 1856, 3; 31 Jan. 1857, 2; 14 June 1862, 3; *DTCH*, 8 Nov. 1856, 3.

50.   *DTCH*, 23 July 1873, 1.

51.   Craven and Stanley, II, 302.

52.   *JHCG*, 57 (7 June 1877), 424–26. There is an illustration.

53.   *Ibid.*

54.   DRO: D1039/26 Osmaston Estate sale catalogue, 7 August 1883.

55. *JHCG*, 4 Nov. 1875, 403; DRO: D1039/26 Osmaston Estate sale details, 7 August 1883.

56. Craven and Stanley, II, 170–72; G. Worsley, *England's Lost Houses* (2002), 22; *JHCG*, 4 Nov. 1875, 403.

57. *JHCG*, 11 Nov. 1875, 428–29.

58. *Ibid.*, 4 Nov. 1875, 404; 11 Nov. 1875, 429; *CL*, 12 July 1902, 48–55; J. P. Craddock, *Paxton's Protégé, The Milner-White Landscape Gardening Dynasty* (2012), 5.

59. *JHCG*, 4 Nov. 1875, 403.

60. See English Heritage, *Durability Guaranteed: Pulhamite Rockwork – its Conservation and Repair* (2008), https://historicengland.org.uk/durability-guaranteed-pulhamite-rockwork; C. Hitching, *Rock Landscapes: The Pulham Legacy* (2012), 294.

61. *JHCG*, 11 Nov. 1875, 428–29. DRO: D1039/26 Osmaston sale catalogue 7 Aug. 1883.

62. 1883 sale catalogue; 'Osmaston Hall', *CL*, 12 July 1902, 48–55. My thanks to Sir Andrew Walker-Okeover for showing me the rock gardens at Osmaston.

63. Craddock, *Paxton's Protégé*; H. E. Milner, *The Art and Practice of Landscape Gardening* (1890).

64. *DM*, 5 Sept. 1866, 2.

65. Craven and Stanley, II, 204.

66. *Black's 1872 Tourist's Guide to Derbyshire*, 135.

67. Craddock, *Paxton's Protégé,* 25; B. Elliott, *Victorian Gardens* (1986), 176–77.

68. *GC*, 17 Dec. 1884, 808.

69. *GC*, 14 Aug. 1886, 210.

70. *GC*, 17 Dec. 1884, 808.

71. The Stancliffe bridge was the same design as Milner's at Buxton Pavilion Gardens.

72. *GC*, 17 Dec. 1884, 808 for a full description. Permission was not given to visit Stancliffe.

73. DRO: D2057 A/P1 34/88 Plan of Proposed Alterations, Bakewell Vicarage, Rev. E. Balston.

74. *DM*, 30 April 1879, 1. It was in Normanton Road, Derby.

75. See S. Whittingham, *The Victorian Fern Craze* (2009) for an excellent short account of this craze.

76. *JHCG*, 21 Sept. 1876, 265; *GC*, 18 Aug. 1883, 212.

77. E.g. *DM*, 7 June 1848, 3; 20 April 1898, 1; *Manchester Courier and Lancashire General Advertiser*, 17 May 1877, 3 and 18 Feb. 1881, 2.

78. *DM*, 16 June 1886, 6.

79. *DTCH*, 20 Sept. 1884, 8; 11 June 1898, 6.

CHAPTER NINE

A Victorian Miscellany, Including Designers from Loudon to Sitwell

To make a great garden one must have a great idea or a great opportunity.

Brandeth Bagshawe was a fine example of Victorian enterprise. A retired gardener living near Buxton, Bagshawe capitalised on the increased tourism to that town with the imaginative idea of opening his little garden to the public, with self-catering tea rooms. By the early 1840s **The Cottage of Content**, **Fern Road**, **Buxton**, was a well-known attraction just outside the town. 'A rare specimen of the genus homo – a contented man', his death in 1844, at the age of 78, was reported in national newspapers:

> His cottage was always neatly decked out, and his adjoining garden kept in excellent order; and being abundantly supplied with grottos [rockwork] etc. it was much resorted to in the season as a sort of tea garden by the visitors, to whom Brandeth was an object of interest.[1]

The full delight of this extraordinary cottage garden is revealed in William Adam's description:

> ...to the Cottage, situated under Grin-low. This belongs to a singular old man (Bagshaw Brandreth), who has followed the occupation of a gardener for many years, and chiefly inhabited this lone cottage, where, as time and opportunity permitted, he laid out and ornamented his little garden, building rustic and fanciful summer-houses, making tables, chairs and seats, in unison – all painted in harlequin colours. The diminutive, but elegant parterres, have a pretty effect, and altogether it presents an air of clean quiet beauty – in fact, all the externals of its significant name – 'The Cottage of Contentment.'… Here the Buxtonian or the stranger at times agreeably whiles away his hour – drinks his tea, or sips the sparkling glass, attended by the obliging host*
>
> *Parties take their own provisions.[2]

One feels that if only garden gnomes had been introduced in England by this date, Mr Bagshawe would have included them with enthusiasm.

Also out of the ordinary was the garden created on a challenging steep hillside at **Masson House** (or Lodge) near Matlock Bath, overlooking Masson Mill. The compact late Georgian house was purchased in 1832 by Charles Clarke (1788–1863), a Derby attorney, magistrate and small landowner with his wife Anne (1803–85), who soon became noted members of local society.[3] Erecting a massive retaining wall below the house the Clarkes then extended and developed the grounds above, allowing visitors by appointment. William Adam's report shows how the gardens combined modern features with picturesque views:

> Beginning with the fountain and conservatory, which is filled with beautiful things… [we] take our way up the walk, which leads, with many a turn, to a considerable height on the mountain side, with here and there a jutting crag, contrasting strikingly with the well-kept walks, and smooth lawns, and beautiful flowers and shrubs … as we ascend we are ever and anon arrested by some commanding or beautiful view… The finest, we conceive, both as to extent and power, is from the rustic summer-house near the top. Here the bold Cat Tor and Willersley Rocks, on which stand the [castle] gardens, are in our immediate front – the noble barrier of rocks, stretching on to Matlock, are on our left… But we must descend, and only notice in our way the Fernery, containing plants of the hardy British tribe; and the next is the rustic grotto* where we have one of the loveliest of 'peeps' we ever saw – the primitive and rocky character of the ground – the ample foliage, between which is seen, but far below, the river dashing over its stony bed, clear as the rock crystal in some places, but lashed into foam and spray in others – all which has a sublime effect.
>
> *a pair of very fine Eagles are caged here[4]

The house was sold after Mrs Clarke's death in 1886 and a plan of the garden shows the path winding up the hill past strawberry beds, flower beds and rose beds – an open ornamental kitchen garden. However the plan fails to convey how precipitous the site is and, although there are a few flights of steps shown, the paths criss-crossing its way up the hill must have been perilously steep. A summer house, ice house, two caves and a large urn on a hillock provide points of interest on the circuit, while deciduous trees and conifers form shrubberies and glades, with open areas.[5] Today the garden site is an inaccessible overgrown wood, although steep steps and half concealed paths, lined with stones, survive near the house.

There was another precipitous garden at **Vale House**, largely demolished in 2008. A mill owner, William Hollins (*c.*1820–1900), built his home on a hill, overlooking the source of wealth, the spinning mills and stream at Pleasley Vale. The house was placed high on a walled terrace with views down, and precipitous zigzag walks cut into the rocks. *The Journal of Horticulture* (1874) enthused about this high Victorian flower garden with ribbon borders in an old kitchen garden and elaborate colourful geometric circular flower beds with 'many thousands of plants'. There was an extraordinary feature one side of the terrace walk to the conservatory, parallel with the flower garden, where:

> a row of vases [urns], or instead of vases there were short lengths of trees with the middle scooped out, and placed on end to give the appearance of rustic vases, and these were planted round with dwarf yews kept closely cut; the dark green foliage of the Yews, and the bright magenta, pink, and crimson of the Geraniums with which they are filled, afforded a pleasing contrast.[6]

This Victorian love of brightly coloured mass bedding also appeared at the terraced gardens above **Hassop Hall**, where in 1844 a visitor praised a display of some 500 geraniums 'the eye may feast almost to intoxication with viewing these brilliant flowers resplendent with a thousand charms'.[7] At **Hardwick Hall** the scrolls and elaborate flowerbeds created in the 1830s (see Fig. 83) were admired as 'perfect sheets of the most varied and brilliant colours'.[8]

No consideration of Derbyshire gardens at this period could omit the first purpose-built public park in England, **Derby Arboretum**. Derby was an increasingly polluted town with some 35,000 inhabitants and Joseph Strutt (1765–1844), Mayor of Derby, wanted to provide a healthy green space, where people could afford to go for recreation. A member of a wealthy local textile family, whose members were also active nonconformist philanthropists, Strutt donated 11 acres (4.5 ha) of ground, including part of his own garden.[9] In 1839 John Claudius Loudon was commissioned to design a landscape, combining recreation with an educational experience. Over 800 species of shrubs and trees were arranged in family groups and labelled for identification, with added interest from flower urns, statues, seats, fountain and pavilions. There was a small admission fee to help pay for upkeep, but entrance was free on Sundays and Wednesdays (half day closing).

Loudon gave a lengthy account of the arboretum in *The Gardener's Magazine* October 1840, so that it, and his role in its creation, could be appreciated nationally as a bold new concept. Loudon designed an 11 acre (4.5 ha) arboretum as a long and irregular shape, surrounded by a belt of trees, with four wide straight walks crossing at a circular central point. This was to be marked by a statue surrounded by curved stone seats, but instead a fountain was substituted in 1845. Paths wound around the edge of the ground, with serpentine walks in between, providing a variant route round a series of raised mounds (6–10 ft/2–3 m high) which broke up and disguised the flatness of the ground and made it seem larger. Loudon reasoned:

> As a terminal object gives meaning to a straight walk leading to it, so it is only by creating artificial obstructions that meaning can be given to a winding walk over a flat surface. These obstructions may either be inequalities in the ground, or the occurrence of trees or shrubs in the line which the walk would otherwise have taken, so as to force it to bend out of that line.[10]

Joseph Strutt donated garden urns for ornamental features, but even here Loudon could not resist the urge to instruct and educate visitors. Bright red and orange flowers placed in them were to have their names 'written conspicuously on a card, and tied round the narrow part of each vase, and the kinds of flowers changed at least once a week, they will be instructive as well as ornamental'.[11] Even the placing of seats was subject to a written page of careful and earnest directions. Presumably it was as yet another part of the educational experience that the entrance lodges, (which doubled as picnic rooms), and the pavilions were different architectural styles of Tudor and Elizabethan. In all the cost came to £10,000.

The public opening on 16 September 1840 was celebrated by 6000 people. In his speech Joseph Strutt dedicated the gardens for public use to persuade the public 'from debasing pursuits and brutalising pleasures … by opening to them

FIGURE 110. Derby Arboretum, the central fountain of 1845. Early twentieth-century postcard.

new sources of rational enjoyment'.[12] Certainly Strutt would have approved the later installation of the elaborate cast-iron bandstand in 1899, for, as a sensible man, he had insisted on the inclusion of open areas within the grounds 'in which large tents might be pitched, a band of music places, dancing carried on etc'.[13] Sadly this jolly item went during the war.

Soon the arboretum was visited by thousands of people arriving by train excursions and temporary attractions were created such as 'a spacious "Crystal Palace" … in which flower-shows concerts, etc., are occasionally held, and which forms a delightful promenade in wet weather'.[14] In short it was a great success, with annual festivals to mark the original opening of the park. An estimated 30,000 people came in June 1876 to enjoy the park, musical entertainments and a balloon ascent, with organisers taking care that such events did not descend 'to ignorant buffoonery or coarse vulgarity'.[15]

Modern concern with health and safety is nothing new, as shown in a letter to the *Derby Mercury* 22 July 1846 which commented that the new central fountain was:

> a great acquisition and will add considerably to the general beauty of the scenery. The only objection to it is that the basin surrounding it is allowed to be open, whereby children are exposed to the danger of falling into it.

This danger could be avoided by adding 'a light iron palisade to surround the basin, which would afford sufficient security, and at the same time add to the beauty of the fountain.' The same Jeremiah then turned his attentions to a pool with rockery whose 'loose portions of spar ... become a continual temptation for children to endeavour to remove them, whereby they are exposed to the danger of falling into the water.' Again the provision of palisades was recommended, and a locked gate before the steps:

> I need not observe to you, Mr Editor, how important is the maxim that 'prevention' is better than cure. A striking illustration of this fact occurred at the Arboretum a few weeks since, when a poor boy lost his life by playfully leaping up to look into one of the vases, when, in consequence of its not having been properly fixed, it fell upon him and injured him so severely that on the following day he died. I am happy to say that since this fatal accident all the vases have been duly attended to.

He fails to say whether or not the vase was damaged.

The arboretum was extended and the town council took over the running in 1882 and provided free entrance. Ironically many specimen trees and shrubs were lost to pollution and replanted with more common hardier species, but a Lottery Grant in 2003 has helped to rectify this and to help overall restoration including the lodges and fountain (Pl. 26).

Edward Kemp (1817–91 had trained under Paxton, who perhaps recommended him as a designer for the gardens of **Cressbrook Hall**. Kemp went on to become a well-known garden designer. He explained his designs for Cressbrook and other gardens in *How to Lay Out a Garden* (1850). Some four miles (6.4 km) north-west of Bakewell, the hall is in an isolated position, approached by narrow steep roads and sited in a deep valley, providing truly spectacular views. It was built for Henry McConnel, a Manchester cotton merchant, who bought Cressbrook Mill near the river Wye in 1835 and then needed a home nearby. On the steeply sloping side of the valley, overlooking the mill, the architect Thomas Johnson of Lichfield designed the house in a fashionable Elizabethan style.[16] Soon this was found to be too small and was extended with a new wing and conservatory.

Although Kemp disliked 'the placing of terrace walls or other erections on a sloping bank', given the extreme slope of the site, massive bastion retaining walls were essential and became the dominating feature of Cressbrook's gardens.[17] In his book, Kemp describes this 'terrace garden' under 'Architectural Gardening' (gardening near a house), 'as an accompaniment to particular styles of architecture', with a consciously traditional garden matching the mock Elizabethan style of architecture, although modern plants were incorporated:

> The house stands almost on the edge of a steep declivity, clothed with old forest trees, the tops of which rise up and mingle with the ornamental parapet wall. This wall is built partly on the sloping bank, and the plateau between it and the house is valued as being the only level piece of ground anywhere in the neighbourhood... The object of the design was to produce such a combination of flowers and shrubs as would suffice to clothe and decorate the platform, without materially interfering with its size, or marring the picturesqueness of the outlying portions of the same; while at the same time, it was sought to give such an amount of regularity and symmetry to the arrangement of the beds, as the artificial character of the terrace, and the nature of its circumscribing wall appeared to demand.[18]

Kemp's plan shows four sections with fussy little formal beds of shrubs and flowers, so that the principal rooms looked out onto flower beds. Symmetrically dotted about were flowering shrubs including berberis, azaleas and hydrangeas. At the lower far end of the terrace, one square section had an elaborate parterre with symmetrical beds linked by standard roses, fuchsias and four-foot high Irish Yews. It also incorporated a popular new feature, the standard rose (Pl. 27). Perhaps in an attempt to provide some visual weight, the largest section was to have two symmetrically placed 'large vases or sculptured figures, on pedestals'. However, since they were to be placed each side of a circular bed of rhododendrons, soon the effect must have been lost. The enclosing buttress walls were topped with balustraded parapets – 'a very superior perforated parapet wall in the style of the house.' This was the uniting feature which pulled together the sections. The house is now a hotel and, bravely, the gardens have been restored to Kemp's layout.

The Nesfields were noted Victorian architects and landscapers. In 1852 William Andrews Nesfield (1793–1881) provided detailed plans for the gardens at **Sudbury Hall**. Little had happened there from 1780 until 1829, when the fourth Lord Vernon (1779–1835) inherited. By then the estate appears to have been rather neglected, with the church covered in ivy.[19] Although Lord Vernon was to have just 6 years at Sudbury, in 1829 there seemed every prospect of several years in which to improve the house and estate, not least because his wife Frances had just inherited a fortune from family estates in Cheshire. They turned to the elderly William Sawrey Gilpin (1761–1843) to redesign the garden, presumably having been impressed by his recently published (1832) *Practical*

FIGURE III. Cressbrook Hall, terrace garden layout based on Edward Kemp's original late 1840s plan, with more modern planting.

Hints upon Landscape Gardening. Gilpin's designs, still in the late Regency taste, are rather fussy to the modern eye.

Gilpin recommended formalising the open lawns from the lake up to the house. To suit the seventeenth-century house, he suggested a wide upper terrace with two elaborate parterres of over seventy small flower beds, 'characterized by ... precision and regularity'.[20] Below would be a longer parterre terrace with a circular central fountain.[21] Terraces were created, complete with the fountain, but with fewer flower beds. The pleasure gardens next to the church and kitchen gardens had been planted already as woodland and shrubbery with meandering paths.[22] Here Gilpin suggested clumps of trees and shrubs and, outside the kitchen gardens, yet more flower gardens and a rosary.

However the sudden death of Lord Vernon in 1835 bought unexpected changes to Sudbury as his son, George John Venables Vernon (1803–66), was a very different character. At first he intended to carry on with the transformation of the gardens below the hall. Paxton was invited to come over from Chatsworth to meet Gilpin and work continued on the gardens. The architect Anthony Salvin was invited to design drastic and dramatic 'improvements' to the house. Fortunately most were not put into effect.[23] In 1839 Lord Vernon decided that he had had enough of life in the English countryside, 'a compound of turnips, turnpikes and top-boots'. A fervent Dante scholar he decided to travel in Italy and produced at his own, considerable, expense a translation of Dante's *Inferno*.[24]

The house was advertised to let with 'Extensive FLOWER GARDENS and GROUNDS, Planted with every description of Herbaceous and American Plants; Terrace walk beautifully laid out, Fountain etc.'[25] It was leased by Queen Adelaide, widow of King William IV from 1840–42, and suddenly Sudbury became a royal home, visited by the great and the good while Mr Mitchell (head gardener since at least the early 1820s) unexpectedly found himself royal gardener. Later, abroad or not, Lord Vernon decided that the pleasure grounds at Sudbury needed attention and in 1852 he turned to W. A. Nesfield, recommended by his brother-in-law, Anthony Salvin, who was still making changes to the house.

Nesfield proposed a quite different garden behind the house, arguing for large terraces with elaborate French parterres *de broderie*, based on a design in d'Argenville's *Theory and Practice of Gardening*. This was in sympathy and scale with the seventeenth-century house, with statues, urns and clipped yews, but also having more modern planting such as standard roses and dense blocks of rhododendrons. Below, along the edge of the lake, was to be a straight formal walk or terrace, with end pavilions. The axial path from the house, through the gardens, would terminate visually with an existing island on the lake, having an open pavilion at its centre.[26] All this would have been vastly expensive to implement, so Gilpin's terraces remained, to be ever simplified over the years until they became little more than lawns. Currently the National Trust has implemented a modest improvement.

W. A. Nesfield's latest biographer has found references to Longford Hall, Osmaston Park, Shipley, Stancliffe and Wingerworth in Derbyshire, although there is no evidence that these commissions were implemented.[27] Nesfield's influence did provide his architect son, William Eden Nesfield (1835–88) with several commissions. W. E. Nesfield trained with his uncle Anthony Salvin, and although he admired Pugin his own designs tended towards the Arts and Crafts style, as at **Lea Wood Hall**, Holloway, near Cromford, 1872–77. Here he designed an early example of an Arts and Crafts house for the widow of wealthy William Walker, owner of a hat factory. In the 1850s Walker sold his business and bought land in Holloway on which to build a house. However he died in 1868 leaving his widow Mary to build the new house on behalf of their son William.

The chosen site was not without challenges, being a large, natural hollow, with slopes on all sides. The house was positioned on the rise of the south side, facing north, so the approach is up to the house with the ground beyond continuing to rise up to the south garden. As the ground falls from the east to the west, the Kitchen Garden on the east side of the house is higher than the garden on the west side. Consequently all the gardens had to have either slopes or terraces, or both. Fortunately the site is sheltered and has magnificent views to what are now splendidly wooded hills and countryside.

From the beginning Eden Nesfield considered house and surrounds as an entity, as revealed in a surviving informal letter to William Walker, Jnr.[28] The challenges of the site were such that Nesfield needed to refer his father, explaining that he had 'carefully considered the whole question of laying out your domain even once again and my Father has aided me with his valuable advice'. Another challenge for Eden Nesfield appears to have been the employment of William Barron to supply trees and plants. Barron, now in his early 70s, was very experienced in garden design and horticulture, and ran a successful business. Naturally he had his own suggestions for Lea Wood which worried Eden Nesfield, whose plans for the house are imaginative and highly original, but he was not confident about gardens. Presumably he received that part of the commission through the influence and reputation of his father. Eden Nesfield continually consulted his father, who did not always accept Barron's suggestions.

In his letter Eden Nesfield seems somewhat confused and on the defensive. For example, the entrance approach from the road up to the house was to be along a short avenue, but 'The only difficulty is getting an easy gradient from the steep road, onto [the] level drive of avenue'. It appears that Barron had suggested 'an ogee curve' to cope with gradient, which was rejected by Nesfield senior 'as much and even more than our original idea of entering at apex of triangle.' So carefully by-passing the problem for the moment, Eden Nesfield suggested an avenue up to the house and concentrated instead on the detail of planting: 'The avenue should be evergreen as being always cheerful and Lucombe oak is the best evergreen for this climate, and the most rapid grower'. He then condescendingly adds that 'Mr Barron should guarantee these if he supplies you with grown trees', and 'it is a pity if a little engineering on a humble scale and humouring cannot manage the difference between rise of

FIGURE 112. Lea Wood, garden bastion seen from park.

road and level of avenue and it shall'. In fact as the house was raised higher on a plinth, the gradient needed careful thought, but eventually it was achieved on a straight drive. Behind the house terracing was created on the rising ground, with flights of steps and thick retaining walls.

Eden Nesfield felt happier with the easier question of where to place the kitchen garden, although again he seems to have needed to turn to his father for advice: 'My Father quite agrees with Mr Barron as to position of Kitchen garden and on these points and all matters connected with planting says we could not obtain better authority'. It was placed above the east side of the house and again massive stone retaining walls were needed. Indeed over the whole garden the amount of earth moving must have been phenomenal.

A rough plan is included in Eden Nesfield's letter, with the west garden as a long terrace and a circular pond to mirror the bay window on the house. The sharp drop below to parkland and paddock is supported by a semi-circular bastion wall, which appears as a low wall when viewed from the house. Whereas, in the eighteenth century, a concealed ha-ha would have separated a garden terrace from the rural area beyond, 100 years later the dividing line is emphasised and made a feature in its own right. William Andrews Nesfield strongly disapproved of ha-has and insisted that obvious, and even ornate, fences should be used to clearly separate the formal and informal areas.[29] A press cutting 1877 noted:

> About the centre of the west point is a very large bay window [drawing room], concentric with which, at a distance of about 40 yards, is the boundary of a tastefully laid out garden, or terrace, from whence the view is one of pure sylvan beauty.[30]

The various levels meant flights of steps and the garden sections are separated by handsome stone walls, creating an interesting example of a romantic early Arts and Crafts garden to complement the house, although later additions have divided the original layout. No doubt planting details were left to the capable

William Barron, who must be responsible for the now magnificent specimens of a Copper Beech next to a huge Weeping Beech, which dominate the area where the south and west gardens join.

The full story of the debates and tensions behind the formation of the garden are hinted at in the letter and one regrets that more correspondence has not survived to give the full story of the differences between two noted and self-willed experts, William Andrews Nesfield and William Barron. It must have been a stressful commission for Eden Nesfield, who also had to contend with negligent contractors and workmen and apparently subsequent litigation.[31]

Arthur Markham Nesfield (1841–74) was the youngest son of W. A. Nesfield, who worked with his father and took over his garden design work by the mid1860s, but who died in an accident in 1874. He was involved at **Ogston Hall**, **Alfreton**, where from 1851 Gladwin Turbutt, whose family had owned Ogston since the early eighteenth century, enlarged and totally transformed Pickford's 1768 house into a 'Jacobethan' house. The architect was Thomas Chambers Hine, who in 1860 also designed the conservatory placed on a wide side terrace overlooking new formal gardens. Forty-six feet long and 24 high (14 × 7.3 m) this truly impressive structure dominates the gardens (Pl. 28). Constructed of ashlar sandstone it has large semi-circular headed windows between buttressed piers and originally was topped with an immense cast iron glazed dome.[32] As it was close to the house, both Turbutt and Hine wanted the conservatory to complement the house. Hine sent one of his working drawings asking 'if the alteration made in the detail is in accordance with your ideas of Jacobean architecture'.[33]

A little later Arthur Markham Nesfield submitted plans to rationalise the gardens to relate to the new facades of the house. He was only in his mid-20s and his survey and proposals are interesting, albeit a little muddled at times. He notes 'the irregular disposition of the [existing] slopes' and re-aligns them to form terraces at right-angles to the house, while at the same enlarging the terrace which runs along the garden façade of the house for greater effect and proportion. Influenced by his father he argued that the gardens should relate to the house and was disturbed by:

> the apparent disconnection between Conservatory and house, which although nearly connected by a terrace, are yet disjointed for want of the necessary link… As regards the character of the proposed treatment … it should be in strict accordance with the Architecture … and although part of Ogston is newly built, still being in an old style, the natural deduction is, that the treatment of the ground about it should be based on similar principles.

His solution for linking the lower house terrace to the higher conservatory terrace was radical and innovative, anticipating a feature later popularised by Lutyens. Instead of a straight flight of steps which 'would be centred on nothing' he suggested:

> A basin, which would be very useful in supplying the garden with water, with steps climbing round it to the upper level. A quaint figure spouting water into the subordinate basin would enhance the effect.[34]

This circular pool with steps round the sides would have been over 30 ft (9 m+) in diameter, and, although impressive viewed from the terrace, would have been over-scaled for the garden. Moreover, this new feature did not relate to the architecture of the house, as its proportions, design and inspiration were classical, although Nesfield may have intended 'Jacobean' balustrading to match the house. Expensive to excavate and construct this remained a paper plan only.

For the main pleasure garden below Markham Nesfield suggested a:

> parterre centred on dining room window, with compartment of flower beds… edged with box upon gravel with a grass plot and sundial or other interesting feature in its centre.

This was drawn on the plan as an oblong flower bed with concave corners without planting suggestions. As executed this parterre had a central central circular pond with fountain, surrounded by segmental-shaped colourful flower beds.[35] Beyond the conservatory a path leads up to the walled eighteenth-century kitchen garden, whose two arches are carved with the dates 1796 and 1798. The path is flanked by a length of crenelated wall, and leads under a stone wall enlivened with a thirteenth-century church window with gothic tracery, another example of Victorian reclamation from a local church.[36] These medieval 'ruins' by the kitchen garden still come as a complete surprise, which is after all one of the purposes of follies.

Today the gardens have been sympathetically restored but now, besides looking out to old parkland, there is also a large 'lake' created in 1957 when 200 acres (81 ha) of parkland next to the hall and gardens were submerged under a new reservoir.

The firm of William Barron and Son was involved in many gardens in Derbyshire, but other than Elvaston, only fragments survive. At some time in the 1880s Barron designed a garden for **Broomfield Hall**, **Morley**, the bones

FIGURE 113. Ogston 'parterre' now a simplified version of the original, with lawn replacing Derbyshire spa paths.

COURTESY D. WAKEFIELD

of which remain today, thoughtfully cared for by the current owners, Derby College. The house was built for Charles Schwind, a wealthy industrialist, who paid £8000 for the 107 acre (43.3 ha) estate in 1870.[37] Working with the lie of the land, Barron created terraced lawns surrounded by belts of specimen trees such as cedars, beech, oak, maples and sycamores, now impressively mature.

On the south side of the house terraces look over parkland and valley. The house terrace is supported by a sloping bank which Barron made into a rock garden of tufa and stones, probably planted with ferns. From this central stone stairs lead down to the main garden, a circle reflecting the curve of the upper terrace and rockery. Modern display in the flower beds, such as a mixture of colourful dahlias and ornamental grasses, nicely evoke the colourful displays of Victorian gardens. A further flight of steps lead down to another circular garden area with two flower beds set in manicured lawns and encircled with more of Barron's specimen trees. On one side sweeping lawns run parallel to the first lawn at the entrance front, again dominated by mature trees. On the other side former walled kitchen gardens are now used by the college as a training area for students, laid out as constantly changing small gardens. Hence the attractive box parterre, potager, gazebo and even a delightful stone ruin folly-William Barron would have approved.

In 1878 a wealthy Derby businessman Abraham Woodiwiss (1828–84), owner of a large construction company, purchased **The Pastures**, at Littleover, near Derby, a small estate of 88 acres (35.6 ha) with a compact late eighteenth-century house. Woodiwiss continued his social rise by becoming Lord Mayor of Derby in 1880–82 and was subsequently knighted in 1883. The gardens had probably been little altered since the house was built, with open lawns, and winding paths in shrubberies round two small lakes, and large kitchen garden. They would have been used for entertaining in the 1880s. We know that he added a

FIGURE 114. Broomfield Hall, Barron and Son's circular garden of the 1880s bought up to date with sympathetic modern planting.

COURTESY E. SWAN, DERBY COLLEGE

FIGURE 115. The Pastures, Derby, the 'modern rustic billiard room', 1880s.

COURTESY: R. PAINE, DERBY GRAMMAR SCHOOL

fashionable rockery, because it was robbed of ferns in 1887, by a thief 'who got his living by selling ferns etc.'[38] Sale details of 1893 provide more information, when ten acres of pleasure grounds, with two acres of lakes were 'most tastefully laid out in broad terraces and shrubbery walks.' There were:

> Rosary, Bowling Green, Lawn Tennis Grounds, Ferneries, and wide spreading lawns sloping to the two large ornamental lakes with miniature falls, island, rustic bridges and arbours. An iron lattice bridge connects the island with the mainland, and a boathouse is erected beside.

There was also a palm house fernery, ninety-six feet long vineries, and the usual range of hothouses.[39] A photograph shows the house, plain garden terraces and lawn down to the lakes. At the side, what looked like a summer house was actually a 'Modern Rustic Billiard Room, upholstered in crimson lush velvet, heated with hot water, containing lavatory and every convenience, including a very fine table'. Sadly this splendid interior has long gone but much of the building survives, although lacking the lantern which provided a top light for the billiard players. The craftsmanship of the billiard room is impressive with meticulous attention to detail. It may have been supplied by 'Garden Crafts Ltd of Staveley', in the Lake District, given its similarities with a smaller rustic summer-house at Little Onn, Staffordshire, probably supplied by that firm.[40]

With subsequent sales the estate had mixed fortunes, until the much enlarged house (now Rykneld Hall), and what remained of once extensive grounds, were acquired by Derby Grammar School in 1995. Modern housing developments now crowd around it.

When William Holden Drury (1802–77) inherited **Locko Park** in 1844 from his mother, daughter and heiress of William Drury Lowe, he changed his name to William Drury Lowe. As a great enthusiast of all things Italian he furnished the house with works of art purchased during frequent visits to Italy and added an Italianate bell-tower when the entrance front of the house was moved from the south to the east. House and approach were transformed. Visitors now came into the entrance forecourt under a classical arch, to face a new Italian wing and porch *cochère*. The original entrance front of the house was now the garden front, looking south down to Emes' lake, while the formal gardens lay to the west of the house, with shallow walled terraces, above which is the original kitchen garden, with a new vinery and conservatory.[41] His son inherited in 1877 and rather confusingly changed his name to William Drury Nathaniel Drury Lowe in 1884.

This William (1828–1906), and his wife Lucy, took an active interest in the design and furnishing of the gardens.[42] In the kitchen gardens another heated greenhouse was added in 1890, followed by four vineries and a central conservatory from Foster and Pearson in 1893, with a fashionable fernery.[43] The formal terraces below were italianised with great walls, entrance arches and flights of steps, urns and classical statues.[44] From all viewpoints in this large garden the vistas were (and are) formal, punctuated by classical features. The terrace below the huge retaining wall still has two series of flower beds laid out with a 'Union Flag' design, each with a central flower bed. They are shown in a photograph of 1893 with colourful bedding out plants.[45] Beyond are beautifully smooth clipped yew hedges with arched openings, also giving views through gates.

Particularly striking and original is the varied collection of statues ordered from the 1892 catalogue of the Parisian 'Val D'Osne', a foundry famous for its large cast iron fountains, large animal and other statues. Presumably Drury Lowe acquired this catalogue at the Paris Exhibition, and ordered from it over the next few years.[46] His choice included the somewhat fearsome, but magnificent, pair of griffins guarding the main entrance to the terraces, as well the terrifying eagle perched on rocks and the life-size lion and lioness nearby: all rather un-nerving (Pl. 29).

FIGURE 116. Locko Park, terracing and gardens. Griffin statues guard the kitchen gardens.

FIGURE 117. Locko
park, Flower garden
photographed in 1893.

COURTESY OF DERBY CITY COUNCIL
AND WWW.PICTURETHEPAST.
ORG.UK

At the same period a different approach was taken by another great enthusiast of Italy, Sir George Sitwell of **Renishaw Hall**. The estate had belonged to the Sitwells since the mid-sixteenth century, with the house built in the 1620s by George Sitwell (1600–67). The family wealth was based on nearby ironworks. By time that Sir Sitwell Sitwell, first baronet (1769–1811) inherited in 1793, the old formal seventeenth-century gardens, with their parterres, terracing and stone walls, bowling green and flowers beds had been replaced by newly fashionable open lawns, which reached up to the house.[47] Sir Sitwell enlarged the house and erected a (now ruined) gothick octagonal conservatory in 1808. This was converted into an aviary by the 1840s, when tame pheasants were stolen from it (Pl. 30).[48] Another gothick ornament was the entrance gatehouse, designed by Joseph Badger and Sir Sitwell, which eventually fell out of use once the drive was diverted, and instead became an eye-catcher, perhaps best known from John Piper's iconic painting.

Unfortunately Sir Sitwell and his son Sir George (1797–1853) were not wise with money and in 1849 many of the house contents were sold to pay the debts.[49] Then the house itself, with its 1200 acre (486 ha) estate, was put on the market in 1853–54. There were beds of coal and ironstone throughout the estate, but it failed to find a buyer, perhaps because of nearby ironworks and a railway going through the grounds.[50] Sir Reresby, the unfortunate third baronet, died at the age of 41 in 1862, having suffered the burden of inherited huge financial debts, leaving a two-year-old heir. His widow Lady Louisa Lucy then spent much of her life restoring the family fortunes, exploiting the coal seam in the park. She must have been interested in the gardens for the flower gardens were admired by selected worthy groups and local societies which were allowed access in the 1860s and 1870s.[51] Her son George Reresby Sitwell (1860–1943), fourth baronet, came of age in 1883, and with him came the most exciting phase for the gardens.

Sir George was to become a noted antiquary and talented eccentric He reacted to a childhood of enforced retrenchment with wild bursts of extravagance, yet also with his own periods of retrenchment and austerity. Both had a disastrous effect on his wife and children. Under his long ownership came a wonderful new garden for Renshaw, created in the spirit of the Italian gardens he admired so much. Sir George began by reinstating the destroyed seventeenth-century terracing, with two large wide terraces above a lawn, which sloped down gently towards two existing pools (shown on the 1854 sale plan). These were enlarged into irregular 30 acre (12.2 ha) lakes, one with an island, in 1892.[52] The terraces were linked by stone steps, the lower ones having stone statues on each side, which eventually looked down to a formal circular pool with a central fountain and a fish pond in the next section. Pyramids and columns of clipped yew punctuated and defined the outlines of the compartments of the terraces, with urns and statuary creating classical formality with constant surprises and vistas.[53] The eighteenth-century obelisks were moved around and ultimately placed in their present position. Flowers were permitted in beds at the sides, and woodland to the east was given three straight walks in eighteenth-century wildernesses.

The hall was let out between 1899 and 1904, and then Sir George continued work on his garden, influenced by his annual visits to Italy to look at gardens there. According to the principles he set out in his *Essay on the Making of Gardens* (1909) Sir George believed that his visits to 200 Italian gardens had given him a deep insight into their spirit and aesthetics. His genius was to transpose successfully the sunlit gardens of Italy, with their emphasis on shade and water to combat the heat, to chilly, industrial Derbyshire. The Renishaw garden was seen by Sir George as a formal introduction to the wider countryside and indeed four central statues look out towards the scenery beyond the garden. Later his son Osbert Sitwell felt that, visible in the distance, Bolsover Castle and Hardwick Halls resembled Italian hill towns.[54]

Sir George wrote that the garden must be considered as 'a gallery of foregrounds designed to set off the soft hues of the distance'. Within its bounds there must be elements of surprise, wonder and contrasts, while symmetry 'will be the law of

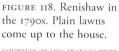

FIGURE 118. Renishaw in the 1790s. Plain lawns come up to the house.

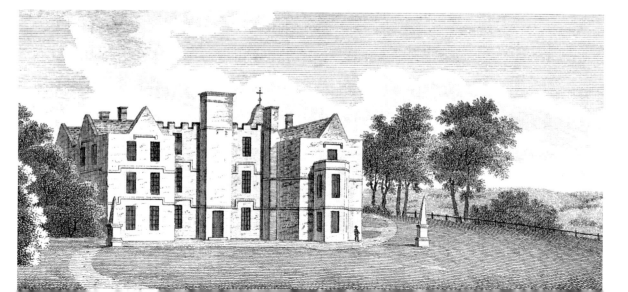

FIGURE 119. Renishaw
Hall, the obelisks
removed to Sir George
Sitwell's garden.
Photograph C. Beevers.

COURTESY MRS A. HAYWOOD

the garden' yet with some freedom to conceal faults of irregularity, while 'tricks
of technique' can lengthen the perspective and apparent size of the garden.[55] 'It
is not only that statues will set off the garden; we have to consider also that the
garden will set off the statues'. In a grand sweep Sir George incorporates sound
from birds, water and wind together with smell and touch. The garden is a work
of art and 'Art's highest appeal to emotion is in the region of sub-consciousness'.[56]

The design and inspiration was Sir George's although Francis Inigo Thomas
(cf. Drakelow), a cousin of Sir George, provided advice and Renishaw's agent,
William Hollingworth, was active in overseeing the ongoing changes.[57] The
Milner White partnership was called in for professional advice in 1890–92 and
1911, mainly for planting work outside the gardens, near the lakes.[58] With little
knowledge of flower planting, in 1909 Sir George did ask Gertrude Jekyll to
provide planting plans for his flower beds. Her recommendations provided
wonderful perfumes and colour.[59] Lutyens became a great family friend and
over the years provided Sir George with plans for his restless, ambitious and
expensive schemes, which, however, remained unexecuted whims.[60] Any plans
Lutyens might have provided for the garden were not used by Sir George
Sitwell, who really felt that Renishaw gardens were his own, sole, inspiration.

Sir George continued to embellish his much loved Italian gardens until his
death in 1943. Subsequent re-interpretations have added to the extraordinary
charm and complexity of the mature gardens with more colour and interest
including thousands of flowers, shrubs and trees. In his biography Osbert
Sitwell wrote with some bitterness about his father's obsession with the gardens,
resenting the huge sums and time spent on them. Yet later generations must
be grateful to Sir George, an amateur, for a masterpiece, whose design set a
standard for the Edwardian garden.

Notes

All quotations from newspapers are © The British Library Board. All rights reserved. With thanks to the British Newspaper Archive (www.BritishNewspaperArchive.co.uk)

1. *DM*, 21 Feb. 1844; repeated in *Stamford Mercury*, 23 Feb. 1844; *Norfolk Chronicle*, 9 March 1844; *Bury and Norwich Post*, 13 March 1844.
2. W. Adam, *Gem of the Peak* (1851), 305.
3. DRO: D170/1/11 lease of Masson House to Charles Clarke.
4. Adam, *Gem of the Peak*, 66–67.
5. DRO: D216 ES 1/3/12 Sale 'Particulars … of Masson House, Matlock Bath' 24 June 1886. See also *DTCH*, 19 June 1886, 4; *DM*, 16 June 1886, 1.
6. *JHCG*, 13 Aug. 1874, 144–46.
7. *DM*, 17 July 1844, 3.
8. *JHCG*, 30 Dec. 1875, 582–84; 1 Jan. 1876, 6.
9. T. Noble (ed.) and S. Glover, *History, Gazeteer and Directory of County of Derby*, pt 2 (1829), 574.
10. *Gardeners' Magazine* (Oct. 1840), 534; see M. L. Simo, *Loudon and the Landscape: from Country Seat to Metropolis 1783–1843* (1988), 191–205 for an excellent summary of the Arboretum. Long dividing mounds had been used by Lord Ongley at his Swiss Garden, Old Warden, in the 1820s.
11. *Gardener's Magazine* (Oct. 1840), 535.
12. S. Bagshaw, *History, Gazeteer and Directory of Derbyshire* (1846), 80.
13. *Gardener's Magazine* (Oct. 1840), 533.
14. Black's *1872 Tourist's Guide*, 164–66.
15. *Sheffield Independent*, 20 June 1876, 3.
16. Conservation Area Appraisal, Cressbrook and Ravendale September 2011: www.peakdistrict.gov.uk/date/Cressbrook-Ravenscroft CAA.pdf.
17. E. Kemp, *How to Lay Out a Garden* (1864), 176.
18. *Ibid.*, 193–5.
19. J. Britton and E. Wedlake Brayley, *The Beauties of England and Wales*, vol. III (1802), 408; J. Farey, *General View of the Agriculture and Minerals of Derbyshire*, vol. 2 (1815), 166.
20. W. S. Gilpin, *Practical Hints upon Landscape Gardening* (1835), 62.
21. I have been unable to access the original plan, but it is illustrated in G. Jackson Stops, *An English Arcadia 1600–1900* (1991), 132–33.
22. DRO: D5903/1- Map of Vernon estates 1794; D5903/2 map of 1823.
23. G. Jackson Stops, *An English Arcadia*, 132–33.
24. *DM*, 2 Jan. 1895, 2
25. *DM*, 6 Nov. 1839, 3.
26. See Jackson Stops, *English Arcadia*, 133–35 for an illustration of the proposals and full explanation. I was not able to access the original designs and correspondence. The island in the lake is not shown on the 1823 estate map but is shown as an irregular island on the 1845 tithe map (DRO: D2360/3/260a) which also mentions 'Pleasure Ground and Walks adjoining the flower garden and Churchyard'.
27. S. R. Evans, *Masters of their Craft: The Art, Architecture and Garden Design of the Nesfields* (2014), 167. The Nesfield archives are in Australia.
28. DRO: D1263/1/2 – photocopy of letter from Eden Nesfield, 3 April 1875. I am most grateful to Mr Stephen Taylor for showing me around the house and gardens at Lea Wood and explaining much of their background and development.
29. See Evans, *Masters of their Craft*, 52.
30. DRO: D1263/1/4 Press cutting? dated 22 Dec. 1877.

31. Letter from Eden Nesfield, June 1885, in Evans, *Masters of their Craft*, 160–61.
32. *JHCG*, 5 March 1874, 205.
33. DRO: D37/11/7xiv Thomas Hine to G. Turbutt, 28 July 1860.
34. DRO: D37MP/124. Plan and accompanying notes, signed by Markham Nesfield.
35. *JHCG*, 5 March 1874, 205.
36. I thank Mr Wakefield for his advice on Ogston gardens.
37. Craven and Stanley, II, 259. OS map 1881 does not show the upper and lower circles and rockery, which appear on the 1900 OS map.
38. *DM*, 20 July 1887, 8; *Derby Daily Telegraph*, 16 July 1887, 3.
39. DRO: D216/ES1/3/55 Sale of the Pastures, 16 May 1893; *DM*, 3 and 10 May 1893. A postcard of the Footbridge *c.*1910 – www.picturethepast.org.uk, ref. DRBY001382; this shows a rustic arbour alongside the lake.
40. J. Wymark, *Thomas Mawson – Life, Gardens and Landscapes* (2009), 84–85.
41. Nottingham University Archives DrE 130/44 letter A. Buchanan to Drury Lowe, 22 July 1854; Dr E 130/45 payment of casting for new vinery 5 Feb. 1859; Dr E 130/48 bills for new conservatory 5–21 Feb. 1859.
42. *E.g.* Dr E 165/18/23 and 24 W. Drury Lowe to Li[Lucy] 1880 asking her to 'put into shape' his sketched idea for a circular classical summer house, which was not built.
43. Dr E 174/2 letter 25 Sept. 1890; Dr E 174/38 contract 31 Oct. 1893.
44. Dr 2 P7-15 (1892); Dr P 140 plans by Architects Stevens and Robinson, 1892.
45. www.picturethepast.org.uk. DRBY007894; the west archway entrance and formal garden is photographed: *ibid.,* DRBY007892.
46. I am grateful to Mr Marshall, head gardener at Locko for this information and to Nina Grant at Locko. In 1893 Lowe enquired about the price of two bronze frogs from A. Durene, maître des forges, Paris: Dr E 174/46. 9 Jan. 1894.
47. D. Kesteven, *Renishaw Hall Gardens, Guidebook* (2010). D. Seward, *Renishaw Hall, The Story of the Sitwells* (2015), 35, 54, 57. I thank Chris Beevers, archivist at Renishaw for the information that the formal gardens had gone by 1782.
48. *Sheffield Independent*, 1 Feb. 1845, 8; 18 April 1846, 2.
49. See the excellent guidebook by Sir Reresby Sitwell, *Renishaw Hall and the Sitwells* (2009); Seward, Renishaw Hall; *Sheffield Independent*, 21 July 1849, 4; 29 Dec. 1849, 6.
50. *Sheffield Independent*, 15 Oct. 1853, 4; 12 Aug. 1854, 4; *DTCH*, 23 Sept. 1854, 5. DRO: D6573/Box128/6 Sale Particulars.
51. *Sheffield Daily Telegraph*, 14 July 1869, 8; *Sheffield Independent*, 27 June 1871, 6.
52. *Sheffield Independent*, 18 Sept. 1893, 8.
53. *CL*, 3 Nov. 1900, 560–68 show the garden with formal planting and small flower beds in the terrace garden.
54. O. Sitwell, *Great Morning* (1948), 60.
55. Sir G. Sitwell, *An Essay On the Making of Gardens* (1909), 39, 71–73, 89.
56. *Ibid.*, 75, 56–58.
57. I thank Chris Beevers for the information about the involvement of Thomas and Hollingworth.
58. O. Sitwell, *Left Hand, Right Hand* (1945), 25, quoting a letter from Sir George that 'White the landscape gardener' had spent several days at Renishaw. J. P. Craddock, *Paxton's Protégé, The Milner White Landscape Gardening Dynasty* (2012), 133. Milner received payments 1890–92. Chris Beevers notes that their work was largely the Milner Plantation near the lakes, which screened the railway.
59. Sitwell, *Great Morning*, 60.
60. *Ibid.*, 19–25.

CHAPTER TEN

The Spas: Matlock Bath, Matlock Bank, Bakewell, Buxton, Derby, Ilkeston

....

A haven of rest and refreshment.

Spas in Derbyshire flourished in the eighteenth and nineteenth centuries. Visitors took the water treatment and then needed amusing, hence the development of public gardens and promenades. The social aspect became increasingly important, as noted in a poem (1762):

> *On Going to Matlock Bath*
> Herein join the Men of *Business*, *Birth*, and *Wealth*
> In numerous Crowds; for *Pleasure*, or for Health:
> Here *Health*, and *Friends*, and *Entertainment* meet
> And all the Grandeur of a *rural* Seat.[1]

Matlock Bath spa began modestly in 1698 with a small bath where people could bathe and also drink the waters. From the early eighteenth century, taking full advantage of mineral waters with a constant temperature of 20°C, enterprising hoteliers developed a small spa.[2] They transformed an unlikely backwater into a spa to rival Bath and Tunbridge Wells by also advertising the picturesque richly wooded valley. When Lady Sophia Newdigate visited Derbyshire in 1747 she was not impressed by Chatsworth but loved Matlock as 'extreamly Romantick and agreeable … The walks about this place are excessively delightfull'. She was rowed up the river by moonlight and enthused:

> On one side of the [Bath] House is a Grove of lofty Trees, on the other a delightful shady Lawn, called *The lovers Walk*. In short, the whole Place is surrounded with agreeable Landscapes, fine Wood, pleasant Walks, high Rocks, steep Hills, and romantic views; which, together with the constant rolling of the *Darwent* Streams, render it a perfect Paradise.[3]

After a healthy dip visitors could socialise, take a gentle walk, play bowls and admire the scenery down to the Derwent. In 1755 Resta Patching and his company went one evening to a nearby inn, 'The Boat-house', with its:

> neat Assembly-room, where Company from the Bath frequently come to drink Tea, and a have Concert; there being a handsome Orchestra… Sometimes the Company go in the Pleasure-boat on the River and have a Concert of French Horns etc.
>
> [Returning] we found sufficient Amusement till Supper-time, by observing the different Employments of the Company: Some were loitering on the Terras, some frolicking on the Green, some sauntering in the Grove, and some amusing themselves in the Lovers Walk. In the Great Room some Ladies were employ'd at the Needle, while others were as busy at Cards.[4]

The **Lovers' Walk** was a riverside walk on the eastern side of the Derwent, accessed by ferryboat. From the early 1740s trees had been cleared to create winding paths for three-quarters of a mile (1.2 km) along the river bank and up the steep and thickly wooded cliffs (Pl. 31). The focal point was a natural cascade falling from a thermal spring and, near the viewing point for the Cascades, a path led 200 ft (61 m) up and along the Cliff, from where there were spectacular views. The paths were enlivened with urns and ornaments and two benches from which to admire the views (and presumably regain your breath).[5] Although The Walks were purchased by Richard Arkwright in 1782 as an annex to Willersley Castle, they remained accessible, but separated by a wall from the Castle's landscaped grounds, so positioned that the Cascade could be seen from both sides. By 1785 Birdcage Walk, another path to the top of the cliff, was provided with rustic alcoves top and bottom.

A hundred years later these walks were just as popular, with *Black's Tourist Guide* (1872) noting that 'the path winds slowly in a zig-zag direction up the face of the thickly-wooded and almost perpendicular rock, the distance of the ascent being relieved by alcoves and rustic seats.'[6] By 1787 Robert Marsden's Hotel and Hot Bath boasted a Bowling Green, gardens and 'twelve acres of Pleasure Ground', and the Temple Hotel at the Old Bath included 'large Gardens and Pleasure Grounds' when sold in 1806.[7]

As part of the Matlock experience visitors could walk or drive to nearby Cromford for the modern equivalent of afternoon-tea, *vide* this little verse printed in the *Derby Mercury*, 25 August 1780:

FIGURE 120. 'View of the Beautiful Cascade, near Matlock Bath', from *The Modern Universal British Traveller* (1779) after T. Smith (1743).

AUTHOR'S COLLECTION

An Extempore, *on seeing the* Thatch'd-House* under the Hill,
at Cromford near Matlock

> This cot a Name more fam'd can boast,
> Than ought e'er rais'd by Adams'** Skill;
> It oft creates this Bumper Toast –
> *'The Thatch'd House under the Hill.'*

*A Place frequently visited by private Tea-Drinking Parties from Matlock Bath
**Great Architects

As Matlock Bath went from strength to strength a further attraction was added, taking advantage of the enthusiasm for the Picturesque. The '**Heights of Abraham**' (Masson Tor), was said to be so named because of its resemblance to the Heights in Quebec, Canada, scaled by General Wolfe to defeat the French in 1759. This would appeal to the patriotic traveller, no longer free to undertake the European Grand Tour by the 1790s. Created in 1787 by the Simpson family who had opened a third Bath, 'Fountain Bath' in 1786, these 33 acres (13.4 ha) of commercial pleasure grounds were part of their estate, on the western side of the Derwent opposite Lovers' Walk. They took full advantage of the dramatic scenery of the Valley, planting a bare steep hill with fir trees placed along a zigzag walk, again giving wonderful views.[8] Later the ground became more varied:

> covered with a rich variety of wild flowers, mosses and lichens, and from the midst of them, and of the ferns and brackens with which they are intermixed, tall pines and firs spring up, and masses of projecting rock jut out in every direction.[9]

In 1810 a new owner, Dr Jonathan Gilbert, opened Rutland Cavern, the first show cavern, excavated from former lead mines. The rugged picturesqueness of the estate was enhanced by two Gothic Tower houses: stuccoed sham castles, which doubled as eye-catchers.[10] The original zigzag walk and a thatched tufa

FIGURE 121. Matlock Bath, rustic seat below Lovers' Walk based on an original eighteenth-century alcove and seat.

FIGURE 122. Matlock
Bath, Mawe's Museum
next to Vallance's shop.
Vallance's garden is
hidden behind the
caption.

COURTESY OF MISS FRANCES WEBB
AND WWW.PICTURETHEPAST.
ORG.UK

alcove survive, though today's visitor often prefers to take the cable car to the summit, where modern visitor attractions have been added.

Another of the growing number of visitor attractions at Matlock Bath was the **Royal Museum**, a spar shop on Museum Parade, established by John Mawe (1764–1829), a well-known mineralogist and businessman, who also had shops in London and Cheltenham. The Museum displayed and sold high-quality jewellery, ornaments, minerals and sculpture, made in Mawe's workshops. His widow Sarah continued to run the business as 'Mawe's Original Royal Museum', under the patronage of the Duke of Devonshire, extending the range of stock and cleverly adding a subscription Library supplied with local and national newspapers.[11] Then, in 1831, Mawe's former manager John Vallance (1781–1853) set up a rival establishment next door, unsurprisingly leading to tense relations between the two.[12] Besides being an expert petrifactioner Mr Vallance was clearly a man of enterprise, persuading both the Duke of Devonshire and the Duke of Rutland to be patrons, and his business was extremely successful.

> Besides a wonderful array of often expensive items for sale, Mr Vallance embellished an outside attraction, the small garden next to his manufactory and opposite the shop.
>
> Mr Vallance has retained for the use and recreation of company the finest part of the Museum Garden, with its tasteful embellishments of rock and spar work, enriched with some rare species of the botany of the Peak.[13]

The enterprising Vallance used it as publicity to keep his shop in the public eye and encourage visitors and buyers, apparently with considerable success. Next to the river, the garden was:

tastefully laid ... the rock-work which he has so judiciously introduced proves him to be a man of good taste in such matters; and we were pleased to hear that he had received commissions from several noblemen for tuffa etc. for the purpose of ornamenting their gardens in a similar manner ... we believe there are very few persons who have visited Matlock Bath, who have not, as a matter of course, lounged an hour or two away in this lovely garden.[14]

Since Mr Vallance also sold 'spars and tuffa for rockwork, grottos, gardens etc.' this was an astute move.[15] One publicity stunt was an evening entertainment:

a wandering minstrel, whose melodious notes, vocal and instrumental, are nightly heard in Vallance's museum garden... He assumes a no less poetical cognomen than "Leander", and dresses in the costume of an ancient Spanish minstrel; and certainly his execution, both with voice and guitar, aided by his singularly romantic appearance and gentlemanly demeanour, pleased ... Mr Vallance ... deserves praise for his liberality in allowing his beautiful little garden to be thus nightly appropriated.[16]

As part of Matlock's celebration of the first anniversary of Queen Victoria's coronation, Mr Vallance fired small cannon in his garden. One wonders what other entertainments were offered by this enterprising man, who also donated a life-size figure of an African chief in full costume to the Derby Museum in 1840.[17]

In 1849 the railway came to Matlock Bath and with it day trippers, necessitating more diversions and entertainments. One was a new commercial pleasure grounds, **Derwent Gardens**, sited on flat ground by the river Derwent, whose spring fed water gardens had rustic grottoes and alcoves. Two grottos and a fountain in a base of tufa are now beautifully restored. An early fun-fair switchback was added in the 1890s, while nearby, a bandstand and rockeries were added to the riverside path at Lovers' Walk in 1893.

In 1882–83 The Pavilion and Gardens Company Ltd was formed to acquire 14 acres (5.7 ha) of land above the Royal Hotel. Here they built a Pavilion, (Palais Royal), with attached gardens designed and laid out brilliantly by Edward Speed (1834–92). He transformed the rough steep terrain, using soil excavated from digging foundations for the Pavilion, to create three formal promenade terraces, 100 yards (*c.*91 m) long with a huge rockery garden, a grotto with spar work above the Victoria Cavern, alcoves, ornamental water and thick planting.[18] The steepness of the site necessitated massive retaining walls, (one nearly 45 ft/13.7 m high) for the terraces, which were linked by wide flights of steps. Other attractions included tennis courts, croquet and bowling greens.

Opened in July 1884, the glass pavilion provided indoor facilities for the thousands of visitors to Matlock Bath, offering refreshments, reading room and concert hall. The cost of laying out the grounds came to over £17,000 but within two months over 50,000 people passed through the entrance gates.[19] Further improvements followed with ornamental ponds and two grottos using spar from the grounds. The parterres were 'laid out most tastefully with flowers' and views from the terraces were stupendous. Admission cost 6d (2.5p), 'while day excursionists are admitted at fourpence each, on shewing their railway tickets. No extra charges

FIGURE 123. Matlock
Bath, Derwent Gardens
grotto, late nineteenth
century.

are made when once inside the wonderful grounds'.[20] Soon the Pavilion and
gardens were at the centre of the town's tourism and established the reputation
of Edward Speed. Proving too expensive to run profitably, ultimately they were
replaced by *Gulliver's Kingdom,* more suited to the needs of the modern tourist.

In contrast **Matlock Bank** developed as a spa in the nineteenth century,
based on the hydo, an organised and scientific regime for invalids, and a quite
different experience to the relaxed water cures at Matlock Bath:

> ...there are several large and excellently conducted hydropathic establishments.
> Among these may be mentioned Mr Smedley's, one of the largest and best conducted
> establishments of its kind in the kingdom. It is capable of accommodating some
> hundreds of patients, and no greater proof of its excellence can be adduced than to
> say it is always full and constantly enlarged.[21]

The splendidly named Smedley's Hydropathic Establishment was developed
by John Smedley (1803–74), a successful local textile mill owner. In Yorkshire
he had benefited from a cold water cure (a combination of drinking water
and bathing), and decided to bring the benefits of this treatment to the small
settlement at Matlock, which had a ready supply of mineral water and a railway
from 1849. Smedley was a serious, moral and religious man, hard-working and
with high standards suited to the era, and his hydro quickly developed into a
successful large scale operation, establishing Matlock Bank as a popular new spa
town, with other smaller hydros also flourishing there. His initial building (1853)
was on a hillside dominating the town and by the 1860s some 2000 people came
each year, encouraged by an extended rail service. The building was enlarged
in 1867 and 1885, with a splendid winter garden added in 1900. Although with

rigid rules, serious regimes, communal meals and no alcohol, Smedley's Hydro also offered, as part of the treatment, the relaxation of enjoying the local scenery behind the large plate glass windows so beloved of the Victorians. The Winter Garden with ballroom:

> also provides a conservatory and promenades, lighted with electricity. On the right side from the entrance is the fernery ... [which] runs nearly the whole side of the right side of the hall, and the tufa used weighs 70 tons, the very best specimens Derbyshire could produce... Here are about 200 different varieties [of ferns].[22]

FIGURE 126. Riber Castle brooding on the skyline over the town of Matlock Bank.

The acquisition of more land permitted the laying out of formal terraces, planted with flowers and trees, and a row of covered wooden shelters from which to admire the view and watch people playing on the lower tennis courts and bowling green. Following closure in the 1950s, the Country Council purchased the site and buildings in 1955 and only vestiges of the grounds remain.

Riber Castle (1862–68), a grim and forbidding fantasy castle on top of a hill above the town, was designed and built by John Smedley as his home. A brooding presence, it continues to dominate as an eye-catcher and reminder of Smedley's consequence. The castle is enclosed within its own embattled walls, within which were once large pleasure grounds, summer houses, kitchen gardens and greenhouses. This white elephant was sold after Smedley's death, followed by a chequered history including a spell as a school and later a zoo. It is currently under restoration for conversion into apartments.[23]

Walking around the market town of **Bakewell** today there is little to show that in the late eighteenth century this was an aspiring Spa, under the aegis of the Dukes of Rutland at nearby Haddon Hall. The first duke built a Bath House here in the late seventeenth century, but little happened once the family moved to Belvoir Castle in Rutland as the main family home. Indeed, in 1792, the Duchess of Rutland and her young family preferred to stay at Buxton for the waters as 'her favoured Summer retreat'.[24] Perhaps this was what challenged the young fifth Duke of Rutland to develop Bakewell as spa town to rival Buxton, currently being developed by the Duke of Devonshire. He failed, not least because the waters were nowhere near as warm as those at Buxton. Although helped by the creation of Rutland Square (1804), *The Rutland Arms*, Rutland House and Rutland Terrace, and even a small Botanical Garden, Bakewell was never developed on the grandiose scale of Buxton.

Probably, in the early nineteenth century, a greater attraction than the waters was the famous geologist, 'the ingenious and intelligent Mr White Watson,

FLS, a gentleman highly distinguished for his geological researches, and whose collection of fossils attracts many visitors from Matlock and Buxton'.[25] Watson (1760–1835), a local man who lived most of his life in Bakewell, was a stone-carver, geologist and botanist who formed a notable collection of fossils and marbles, selling specimens from a shop in the town. He lived at the Bath House in Bakewell, acting as superintendent of the baths. In 1805, as an attraction for promenading visitors, Watson laid out a small botanic garden adjoining the bath, with two grottos. The Duke rebuilt the baths in 1829, but 100 years later the spring supplying the Bath House dried up. Today just fragment of the gardens remain, somewhat municipal but cheerfully planted, with the rather sad remains of one surviving grotto.

From Roman times **Buxton** has been known for the benefits of its warm water for both bathing and drinking. Its proximity to Chatsworth led the Earl of Shrewsbury to bring the captive Mary Queen of Scots here in 1573 to stay at Buxton Hall (now the Old Hall Hotel), a house he had just completed as lodgings for important visitors to the bath. The Hall gardens developed over the years and at the end of the seventeenth century had a bowling green and walks. In 1734 a visitor noted 'new gardens with planting and several curious walks'.[26] What were probably three fish ponds belonging to the hall were to be altered by Joseph Paxton into irregular shapes, converted to lakes when the land passed to the new Pavilion Gardens in 1871. Later Dukes of Devonshire continued to take an active interest in the town acquiring land as an investment, but compared with Bath, it failed to come up to the rising expectations of eighteenth-century visitors.

FIGURE 127. Buxton, The Hall Hotel and Fountain Gardens with Paxton's pools, engraving 1850s.

AUTHOR'S COLLECTION

In 1755 Resta Patching was disappointed:

> the dirty Village of Buxton; the publick Baths are at a publick Inn, which, by Way of Preheminence is dignified and distinguished by the Name of *the Hall*: It is a large commodious House and a great Deal of good Company resort to it in Summertime and stay a month or two for the Benefit of Bathing, or the Pleasure of the Country for Air and Exercise.

He was scathing about the garden walks in the town, which covered about an acre (0.4 ha):

> almost circular, bounded on one Side by a pretty River, on the other, by the aforesaid dirty Lane; The walks are not Grass or Gravel, but of pure natural Earth, strew'd over with fine Ashes to prevent the Soil from sticking to the Ladies Shoes … we returned to our Inn, disappointed in our Expectations of finding Buxton a grand and brilliant Place.[27]

However visitors continued to arrive, some combining the health treatment with a holiday, visiting nearby attractions. The town expanded, helped by its position on a main turnpike road by the 1760s and served by regular coaches by the 1770s. By then there was a 'Buxton Season' from April to August, with races held nearby. The links with the Duke of Devonshire were carefully stressed, with those staying at his hotel, *the Hall*, having priority (and reduced prices) at the Baths. His new hotel, the *Eagle and Child* advertised in 1774 that residents had complementary use of a Sedan and Bathing Chair, as did those staying at Buxton Hall.[28] After he inherited in 1764 the wealthy fifth Duke of Devonshire (1748–1811) systematically purchased land and enlarged the visitor attractions as speculative ventures, with the avowed aim of transforming Buxton into the Bath of the North. John Carr of York was engaged to design the elegant Crescent (1780s) with its shops, lodgings, hotels; Assembly Room; huge stables (1785–90), and, later, the Square. By 1790 *The Topographer* could declare that 'the greater part of the company flock hither rather for the dissipation of their time than the restoration of their health'.[29]

By the late 1780s the *Derby Mercury* was reporting new arrivals at Buxton in its weekly 'Intelligence' section, listing the many socially important visitors, actively promoting and drawing attention to the Spa as 'Buxton Wells' or 'Buxton Spa', on a par with Bath. 'The adjacent Country forms a pleasing landscape – there are many pleasant rides and walks.' These included the four mile (6.4 km) 'Duke's Drive' through Ashwood Dale created by the Duke in 1795.[30] By now there were card assemblies and balls in the Crescent, a theatre, coffee shops, and the social cachet of links with the Duke, who stayed there with his family in 1788 'for the Benefit of the Waters'. This led other members of the nobility to patronise the Baths, and in 1792 the *Mercury* went as far as to intimate (erroneously) that the Prince of Wales would stay.[31] Many of the hotels and lodgings had their own garden as Lady Hester Newdigate noted in 1781: 'enjoyed our quiet dinner in a neat pretty room looking into beds [of] flowers and flowering shrubs.'[32]

The impetus was continued by the sixth Duke, who laid out 'The Slopes', open hilly gardens facing the Crescent, *c.*1818, using Wyattville, who was working

FIGURE 128. Buxton, 'The Slopes', early nineteenth-century etching showing the area before it became dominated by trees.

COURTESY OF MISS FRANCES WEBB AND WWW.PICTURETHEPAST. ORG.UK

at Chatsworth house. Visitors were suitably impressed by the changes:

> The present noble Duke, following the example of his illustrious father, is continually adding to the rides, walks, and plantations in the vicinity. The serpentine walk commences opposite the square, winding beautifully on each side of the Wye. The walks are well laid out, the cascades and bridges have a good effect, and the trees, which are shooting into beauty, render it a delightful spot. The more recent improvements on St. Anne's Cliffe [The Slopes] ... render the hill a highly ornamental pleasure ground, harmonising with the classic architecture of Carr. A series of terrace walks, one above another, sweep in a circular direction, to agree with the convex form of the hill, and communicate with each other by flights of steps at each end and in the centre of the different walks. Numerous seats are placed on the walks for the accommodation of the company, and beautiful vases [urns] ornament the whole.[33]

Later the Duke used Paxton to modify the Slopes *c.*1840 and alter the Wye, adding artificially created pools and cascades, enlivened with rustic bridges and edged with serpentine walks with seats and summer houses.[34] Following the arrival of the railway in 1863, special excursion trains bought thousands of visitors to enjoy massed bands, Morris dancing and to admire the hotels and buildings decorated with flags and garlands.[35] However the *piece de resistance* came in 1871 with the **Pavilion and Public Gardens** complex, laid out on land at Buxton Hall, given by the seventh Duke of Devonshire. Financed by the Buxton Improvements Company, Ltd, this was specifically created to increase the attractions and prosperity of the town, with a Music Hall and ornamental gardens and walks, utilising Paxton's serpentine walks with two lakes and fountains. As its designer Edward Milner later explained 'The principal object was to create an attraction to Buxton, that visitors might be induced to frequent the place, and prolong their stay.'[36]

The new public Gardens were enthusiastically described in *Black's Tourist Guide* in 1872:

> The Pavilion, a light iron and glass structure, 400 feet in length, rising from a stone base, is warmed, for a winter covered walk, by four rows of hot-water pipes going round the whole building, and is also lighted with gas in the evening. [It] contains a central hall for concerts and assemblies, flanked by two conservatories, with waiting rooms. From a terrace running the whole length of the Pavilion the ground slopes beautifully down to the river Wye, which is crossed by a handsome cast-iron bridge, over which the principal walk passes from the centre of the terrace to the band-stand, whence the walks diverge in various directions... Two miles of walks and five bridges have been constructed; and the two lakes, which will be remembered by visitors to Buxton, have been joined, two new waterfalls have been made, and the grounds have been thickly and artistically planted with evergreens and trees. Statuary also is not wanting.[37]

FIGURE 129. Buxton
Pavilion Gardens and
bandstand. engraving
*c.*1875.

AUTHOR'S COLLECTION

Milner had worked with Paxton at the Crystal Palace and with public parks in Lancashire, thus Buxton incorporated by now standard curving paths, serpentine water, bridges and cascades, plentiful supply of greenery and a bandstand. The initial nine acres (3.6 ha) were extended to 23 acres (9.3 ha) and Pulham and Sons laid out rockwork. Then with the addition of the Concert Hall (Octagon, 1875), Theatre (1899) and Opera House (1903) Buxton provided elegant Spa facilities and accommodation, shops, extensive pleasure grounds and varied entertainment, as it continues to do today.

Not all Spas were successful. In 1733 Dr Chauncey uncovered a suitable spring in **Derby** and established a cold bath with rooms over it, but died shortly afterwards.[38] New owners added attractions, but by 1739 the venture was to let advertised as 'A SPAW with Cold BATH, and two Rooms to dress in, also a large long room over the Whole; and Pleasant Walks'. Within a year it was for sale again and Derby's spa had failed.[39] The original bath house became an inn, and is now the *Old Spa Inn*, Abbey Street.

After the discovery of warm springs in 1829, **Ilkeston**, a small market town on the Nottinghamshire border, ventured into the spa market. Baths opened and the mineral water was also sold for consumption, advertised as helpful to an amazing assortment of ailments. In 1832 the enterprising Thomas Potter, a local coalmaster, created a bath house close to the *Rutland Hotel* 'for the accommodation of the higher classes of patients'. Lodgings and facilities sprang up to cater for visitors, with the obligatory pleasure-grounds for the entertainment of visitors. 'Vauxhall Gardens' were created between the Baths and the Rutland Hotel: 'tastefully laid out in walks, bowling green, archery ground, etc. and afford every facility for a variety of amusements.'[40]

They were the work of Thomas Hives, proprietor of the *Rutland Arms Hotel* (and the *Railway Hotel* by 1849), who took advantage of the new railway station to encourage special excursion trains. The enterprising Mr Hives then arranged spectacular entertainments with dancing, ballooning, fireworks and tight-rope walking. In 1851, following a cricket match, there was a 'Grand Gala and Fete Champêtre'.[41] The spa was popular until the late 1890s when pollution from nearby mining led to the closure of the baths about 1900. They and the Rutland Hotel were demolished and so ended Ilkeston's brief popularity as a spa town.

Notes

All quotations from newspapers are © The British Library Board. All rights reserved. With thanks to the British Newspaper Archive (www.BritishNewspaperArchive.co.uk).

1. *DM*, 9 July 1762, 3.
2. See excellent www.derbyshiredales.gov.uk Matlock Bath Conservation Area Appraisal (July 2006).
3. WRO: CR 1841/7 Diary of Lady Sophia Newdigate's Tour 1747, 45.
4. R. Patching, *Four Topographical Letters, Written in July 1755, Upon a Journey thro' Bedfordshire … Derbyshire etc.* (2011), 43–45.
5. W. Bray, *A Sketch of a tour into Derbyshire and Yorkshire* (1778), 77–78.
6. E. Jewitt (ed.) *Black's 1872 Tourist's Guide to Derbyshire* (1999), 249. See Watercolour by G. Robertson (1798) of this seat (Derby Museum and Art Gallery).
7. *DM*, 10 May 1787, 4; 30 April 1789, 1; 11 Sept. 1806, 1.
8. J. Britton and E. Wedlake Brayley, *The Beauties of England and Wales*, vol. III (1802), 510; *DM*, 31 July 1833, 2.
9. *Black's Tourist's Guide*, 246.
10. DM, 13 June 1838, 2.
11. *DM*, 25 Aug. 1824, 3; 4 Nov. 1829, 2; 13 Aug. 1831, 3; 3 Oct. 1838, *1ff.*
12. *DM*, 8 June 1831, 3; 27 March 1833, 2: court case over a quarrel about an advertising board.
13. *DM*, 2 Sept. 1829, 4; 25 May and 8 June 1831, 3; An additional attraction was a live falcon. DRO: D2360/3/28 Tithe map for Matlock 1848; D1331 tithe award.
14. *The Matlock Tourist and Guide Through the Peak* (1838), 45.
15. *Ibid.*, 5, 9.
16. *DM*, 29 July 1835, 3.
17. *DM*, 10 July 1839, 3; 9 Dec. 1840, 3.
18. *DTCH*, 21 Jan. 1882, 5; 10 May 1884. *Nottinghamshire Guardian*, 10 Feb. 1882, 5; *DM*, 22 Feb 1882, 7; *Leeds Mercury*, 7 May 1883, 8. www.picturethepast.org.uk image DCHQ001974.
19. *DTCH*, 10 May 1884, 6; 1 Nov. 1884, 3; *Leeds Mercury*, 29 July 1884, 8.
20. *DTCH*, 6 June 1885, 9; 4 July 1891, 2.
21. *Black's Tourist's Guide*, 251.
22. *DTCH*, 17 Nov. 1900, 6. www.derbyshiredales.gov.uk Matlock Bank Conservation Area Appraisal 6. Landscape Appraisal. Accessed 2012.
23. Craven and Stanley, II, 185–86; G. Headley and W. Meulenkamp, *Follies* (1990), 280; (1999 edn), 185.
24. *DM*, 12 July 1792, 4.
25. T. Noble (ed.) and S. Glover, *The History, Gazetteer, and Directory of the County of Derby*, pt 2 (1829), 66.

26. Quoted in English Heritage Listing, Pavilion Gardens, Buxton II* List No. 1000675.

27. Patching, *Topographical Letters*, 37, 40, 42.

28. *DM*, 22 April 1774, 4; 29 May 1778.

29. *The Topographer* 18, Sept. 1790, 188.

30. *DM*, 13 Sept. 1787, 4; 3 July1788, 4; *Black's Tourist's Guide*, 59.

31. *DM*, 15 May 1788, 4; 12 July 1792, 4.

32. WRO: SR136/B2733 Lady Hester to Sir Roger Newdigate July 1781.

33. Noble and Glover *The History, Gazetteer*, pt 2, 179.

34. *Journey Book of England, Derbyshire* (1841), 122; W. Adam, *Gem of the Peak* (1851), 285, 291, 310. *Manchester Courier and Lancashire General Advertiser*, 18 June 1853, 7; *Black's Tourist's Guide*, 59.

35. *DM*, 1 July 1863, 2; 31 May 1865, 8; 15 June 1878, 1; 28 April 1886, 3.

36. E. Milner, *The Art and Practice of Landscape Gardening* (1890), 95–97.

37. *Black's Tourist's Guide*, 46–47, based on an article in *The Illustrated London News*, 30 Sept. 1871.

38. R. Simpson, *A Collection of Fragments illustrative of the History and Antiquities of Derby* (1826), 531.

39. *DM*, 6 April; 3 May 1739, 4; 15 May 1740, 4; 26 March 1741, 4.

40. *DM*, 21 Oct. 1829, 3; 23 June 1830, 3; 20 April 1831, 3; 18 April 1832, 3;' 4 July 1832, 2. *Black's 1872 Tourist's Guide*, 226.

41. *Nottinghamshire Guardian*, 28 June 1849, 2; 5 July 1849, 3; 21 May 1850, 3; 18 July 1850, 5; 12 Sept. 1850, 5; 21 Aug. 1851, 4.

CHAPTER ELEVEN

Edwardian Gardens

…the Revival of garden craft is the work of English architects.

Architectural structure featured strongly in the late nineteenth-century garden, with its increased emphasis on formality. The influential *The Formal Garden in England* (1892) by Reginald Blomfield and Francis Inigo Thomas celebrated surviving formality citing Bolsover, Eyam, Haddon Hall, Melbourne Risley, Swarkeston and Tissington. They went on to work together at Drakelow in 1900. Also, leading architects Edwin Lutyens, Reginald Blomfield, Herbert George Ibberson and Walter Tapper were involved with gardens in Derbyshire.

In *Gardens for Small Country Houses* (1912) Gertrude Jekyll and Lawrence Weaver illustrated fashionable key features in contemporary gardens, both for established gentry and the successful aspiring businessman. Now clipped, evergreen hedges divided the garden into different areas, which could be square, rectangular and even circular, and include sunken areas. Terraces near the house, with stone and brick paving or the new 'random' paving, often had alpine plants in joints to create a degree of informality. Retaining walls for terracing might also planted with alpines and linked by flights of brick or stone steps, often semi-circular. An integral part of the design was a small formal pond, often a lily pond, surrounded by a stone kerb. Space would be made for a tennis court. A pergola, with brick or stone piers, could be covered with climbing roses with a central path through. By 1907 the commercially astute nursery of William Barron and Son advertised 'laying out of Rose Gardens and the construction of Pergolas.'[1] Luxuriant herbaceous borders and rock gardens broke-up the formal shapes, while urns, terracotta pots, statues, sundials provided interest and ornament. Benches provided seating and an open summerhouse was popular for afternoon tea.

An architect who featured several times in this book was Charles Edward Mallows (1864–1915), a noted architect and landscape gardener, who had worked with Thomas Mawson and who favoured the Arts and Crafts style.[2] In 1913 Mallows designed **The Green**, **Eckington** for Sir George Sitwell. In his autobiography Osbert Sitwell resentfully recalled some of the extravagancies of his father, Sir George, including the expenditure of £8000 or £10,000 at Eckington:

> on making a fantastic garden, with enormous stone piers, and monoliths … within the grounds of a little house that had been built as a school for the village by an ancestor of ours in 1720, but for the past hundred years had been a farm.[3]

His book includes a 'Sketch Design for Terrace East Side of "The Green" Eckington for Sir George Sitwell Bart', signed 'C. E. Mallows 1913'.[4] Happily several of Mallow's working drawings for The Green survive, dated between 1913 and his death in 1915.[5] A newly discovered (2009) plan by Edwin Lutyens for the 'The Green' is dated 1916, which must be for additional work, but it has led to the assumption that the whole concept and design was by Lutyens.[6] He was a frequent visitor to Renishaw, but his many building proposals for Sir George came to nothing.[7]

The rectangular 1 acre (0.4 ha) garden at The Green occupies a corner plot facing the village green, with one side sharply curved to follow the existing road. A stone-paved terrace with double herbaceous borders runs the width of the house. In front of the entrance door there is a classic Arts and Crafts feature of a millstone-grit circle set into a semi-circular step, as sketched by Mallows. From here the garden is seen as a carefully composed set piece of architectural features and colourful planting. A long pergola leading to the iron entrance gate is seen over a cast-iron balcony, (a cheaper option to Mallows' suggested stone balustrade). First there are steps down to a circular pond with a fountain head in the rear wall.[8] Then, at this lower level, comes the pergola walk beyond which is Mallows' decorative iron-work gate, which doubles as an eye-catcher and also permits a glimpse into the garden from outside, as with a traditional garden *claire voyée* (Pl. 33).[9] Stone 'windows' on the boundary wall either side of the gate allow glimpses in and out of the garden.[10]

The pergola's stone piers support large oak beams. Both sides have a rill, while the little semi-circular lily pools half-way along are perhaps Lutyens' idea. The sound of running water adds to the pleasure of exploring the gardens. Mallows proposed several water rills and ponds in the garden- more than are currently there, such as a bridge over a water rill parallel to the entrance gate, which led to dipping well near the boundary wall.[11] Like his suggestion of curved stone walls under the terrace, with rusticated stone niches having semi-circular shell detailing, several expensive suggestions were not followed.

It is problematic to work out exactly what is Lutyens' contribution to the garden given that Mallows had submitted so many detailed sketches. Perhaps Lutyens suggested planting dwarf apple trees either side of the long pergola walk and placing yew hedges which separate the other part of the garden with its tennis court and exedra hedge.[12] Irrespective of who designed the gardens, the overall effect is charming and intimate, exemplifying Sir George Sitwell's enthusiasm for Italianate gardens. Recently the gardens have been restored beautifully and the informal, colour-themed planting of whites, blues and purple acknowledge the contemporary influence of Gertrude Jekyll.[13]

The kudos of a putative Lutyens connection can be seen at the gardens of **Morley Manor**, a large, handsome 'Jacobethan' mansion built by G. F. Bodley in 1894 for Hugh Alleyne Sacheverell Bateman (whose family lived at nearby Breadsall).[14] Bateman died following a riding accident in 1896, when only 36 years old, and the house and garden were completed by his widow Anna (1866–1946), based on a garden surviving from an earlier house.[15] When the house was sold in 1938 the sale particulars describe the garden compartments of a typical Edwardian country-house garden, 'tastefully laid out' with terraced lawns, picturesque rose gardens, yew hedges, 'avenue of Yews terminated by old world thatched Summer Arbour', herbaceous borders and rock gardens. There was also the ubiquitous tennis lawn or bowling green.

Emphasis was put on the 'Stone Artistic Pergola Walk, Designed by Sir Edwin Lutyens'.[16] This was destroyed sometime between 1956 and 1997 while the hall was a Dr Barnado's home. This attribution to the prestigious name of Lutyens is probably just an estate agent's wishful thinking. Today all that remains are immaculately kept upper and lower lawns and a long yew hedge in which are set two original plain ashlar seats with arms. At its centre wrought-iron gates lead to the fashionable semi-circle of wide stone steps down to the lower gardens.

FIGURE 131. Morley Manor, Upper garden with gate piers and steps to lower garden and lost pergola. Stone seat in hedge.

COURTESY P. MARPLES

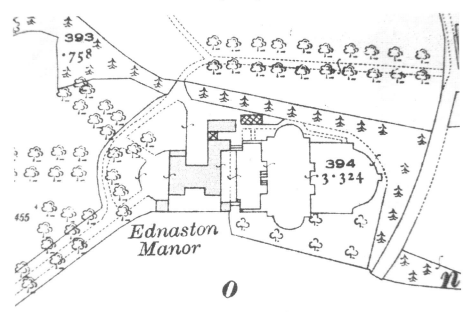

FIGURE 132. Ednaston Manor, Lutyen's plan as shown on 1920 OS map.

On the other hand there is a proven Lutyens connection at **Ednaston Manor**, built for William Goodacre Player (1866–1959), joint Managing Director of the Nottingham tobacco firm John Player and Sons founded by his father. In 1912 Player purchased a farm at Ednaston, adding a small country house while retaining two homes in Nottinghamshire. Lutyens designed the new house and garden and a replacement farm. However with the First World War intervening, work was not completed until 1919 and the next year the gardens were planted out by William Barron and Son.[17]

At the entrance (west) three avenues of chestnuts formed a *patte d'oie* from the enclosed forecourt, a design sympathetic to the 'Queen Anne' architectural style of the house. The south façade has a terrace with herringbone brick paths and small formal flower beds edged with Derbyshire Hopton stone flags, enclosed at each end by walls to an open summer house with steep hipped roofs and Tuscan Doric columns.[18] The main (east) garden has a balustraded terrace with steps down each side to a lower terrace, which in turn leads down to a large lawn with apsidal ends. Further steps then lead to another area terminating in a central apse. There is a confident play of curves and angles, walls and ornamental steps linking different levels, and stress on symmetry, formal yew hedges and controlled planting.[19]

For these gardens Lutyens designed a delightful 'wheelbarrow' bench, with plain wooden slats and a solid wooden wheel attached at one end and two barrow handles at the other: a reminder of his attention to detail and his inventive humour.

If ever a lost garden site was haunted, it would be **Drakelow**. The house was demolished in 1938 to make way for a power station, ironically itself now demolished with much of the huge site an industrial wilderness. When an enthusiastic security guard escorted me round what survives of the 'sunken garden', even on a sunny September day, the atmosphere was tangible.[20] All that remain are the retaining walls of a sunken Edwardian garden by the river, yet these were enough to evoke the charm of the lost gardens. Now completely lost under tons of industrial spoil are the other walled gardens with their luxuriant planting, flower beds and a multitude of flower-filled urns, statues and architectural features.[21]

These were commissioned by Sir Robert Gresley (1866–1936), eleventh baronet, who inherited the estate in 1868 and lived there after he came of age in 1887. His marriage to the eldest daughter of the Duke of Marlborough in 1893 no doubt influenced his decision to remodel and improve the house and pleasure grounds *c.*1900–02. He turned to the architect and garden designer Sir Reginald Blomfield, who remodelled the house and designed a new entrance lodge and gate piers (still *in situ*), while his collaborator Francis Inigo Thomas designed new gardens.

By now the area between the house and river was simply lawn.[22] This was transformed by creating a plain formal walled garden. The terrace next to the house was given emphasis with a classical balustrade and urns. New central Italian steps swept down either side of a classical 'arch', in front of a grotto-like space, inspired by Italian gardens. Along each length of the garden is a high brick wall with four oval niches for busts (a seventeenth-century fashion), and near the house an oblong recess cut into the wall takes a bench. The central lawn is viewed from long side terraces, while, at the bottom of the garden, a

FIGURE 133. Drakelow, terrace and steps *c.*1903.

© LOOK AND LEARN

FIGURE 134. Drakelow, remains of terrace and garden today.

COURTESY VAL FARREN, DRAKELOW DEVELOPMENTS

waterside terrace along the river Trent had a long classical balustrade with urns, echoing the balustrade on the house terrace. At each end of the riverside terrace handsome brick gateways, with large double keystones, provided exits.

In an existing circular walled garden, a central pond was given a mermaid fountain. Eight path 'spokes' were reduced to four, each leading to a vine-covered tunnel out into the wooded 'Wilderness'. Flower filled urns on plinths were positioned at intervals between flower beds and around the circumference. The nearby walled kitchen garden was also given a central fountain. To terminate a long formal walled rose garden, enclosed on one side by a high wall, Blomfield designed a classical temple with three arches. It was doubtless he who encouraged the placing of classical statues in the gardens. Tragically, this totally private world of elaborate walled gardens with their mass of colourful flowers and shrubs, fountain, urns and statues was destroyed after the Gresleys sold Drakelow in 1933. Soon the house was demolished and the gardens lost to the power station.[23]

There is just a possibility that Sir Reginald Blomfield made a contribution at **Netherseal Old Hall**, which was transferred to Derbyshire from Leicestershire in 1899. Confusingly there were two Netherseal Halls in Netherseal village, but one was demolished in 1933, while the Old Hall, a wonderful mix of periods, survived. It belonged to the Gresley family from the seventeenth century, who rented it out until their estates were broken up in the 1920s.[24] Lying close to the road at the end of the village, the Old Hall is enclosed behind brick walls with some 15 acres (6.1 ha) of gardens and pools, whose outer shape is defined by a meandering stream. A brick alcove in the long stone boundary wall on the north-west side is probably late seventeenth or early eighteenth century and looks onto the walled ornamental kitchen gardens. The pleasure gardens are terraced with ponds below.[25] At the end of the garden stone-revetted little streams, controlled by sluices, must have been very picturesque when created, but clumsy twentieth-century repairs have rather dulled their charm. However the sound of falling water still delights as you walk around this informal wooded area beyond the hall lawns.

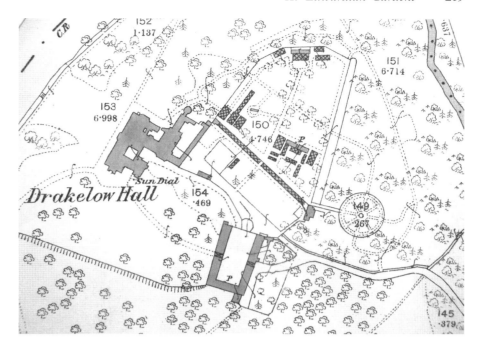

FIGURE 135. Drakelow Hall and gardens from 1882 OS map, pre-Edwardian alterations. Circular rosary on right next to walled garden; lawn from house to river on left.

OS MAP COPY AT DRO

Much of the present garden dates from the period when the house was greatly extended in the early twentieth century and again in 1933. Stone edged paths lead into picturesque woods, and elaborate water garden rockeries are currently being restored after years of neglect. As you leave the kitchen garden through a gateway, at right angles to the wall, there is a totally unexpected building façade, which conceals a utilitarian brick shed. Also acting as a garden feature, this unusual façade, made of crisp machine made bricks, has a doorway with a moulded arch, a small window with a semi-circular architrave and decorative brickwork (Pl. 34). Behind this, the gardeners' shed and store has a plain wooden door, but its metal window is an Arts and Crafts delight of three joined casements, resting on a shelf of moulded terracotta bricks, which in turn rest on another angled row of bricks. A stone over-door plaque has the date 1915. This remarkable little garden shed, for really it is no more, is attached to gardeners' sheds or bothies. It is so accomplished that it is tempting to ascribe it to Blomfield who undertook work next door in 1914.[26] At this period Netherseal Old Hall was tenanted by the wealthy William Worthington of Worthington's Brewery in Burton-on-Trent.[27] This is a garden that could well repay further research.

Another well-known contemporary architect, Herbert George Ibberson (1866–1935), designed the attractive Arts and Crafts house and gardens at **Raenstor Close**, Youlgreave for the Misses Melland between 1909 and 1911.[28] The house is partly hidden from the road by attractive gritstone walls with niches. Each side of the gate piers of the curving entrance wall has carved panels, depicting stylised foliage and animals in flat relief. It is no surprise to learn that Ibberson had worked in the same London office as Ernest Gimson and Ernest Barnsley.

FIGURE 136. Raenstor
Close, decorated wall to
entrance gates, 1909–11,
H. G. Ibberson,

An iron gate permits glimpses of the house, its overthrow a worthy successor to
Robert Bakewell with elegant and sinuous leaves. The garden was given the usual
features of the period, a long pergola, flagstone paths, tennis lawn and rose beds.
To the side of the house is a large semi-circular exedra with rows of planting:
an almost architectural feature, backed by trees, to conceal the road which runs
along the house and side garden. Sale details in 1953 still mention terraced walks
edged with lawns and flower beds, bowling green or tennis lawn adjoining the
house 'screened by Pergola covered flagged paths on two sides'.[29]

The architect Sir Walter Tapper (1861–1935) was involved with two gardens
in Derbyshire: Parwich and Shipley. Known for his ecclesiastical work, Tapper
designed the rood screen, pulpit and font cover for St Peters church at Parwich
for its vicar, Rev. Claud Lewis, who lived at **Parwich Hall**. Situated in the village
some five miles (8 km) north of Ashbourne, the hall was built *c*.1747, by Sir
Richard Levinge (1723–86) as an austere handsome five-bay, three-storey brick
house.[30] The steepness of its site is shown by the approach from the road, up to
the front door via three flights of steep steps, then a further nine steps. Creating
a garden on such a hilly site would be challenge.

The original eighteenth-century garden was a double terrace to the side of the
house, surrounded by brick walls which provided shelter on this exposed position.
A lower strong stone retaining wall made a boundary wall from the village. To the
side beyond this was an irregularly shaped kitchen garden. On the steep hillside
above the hall and gardens was a natural landscape of fields and trees. The whole
ensemble was restrained yet impressive, dominating the village. In 1814 the estate
was purchased by William Evans of Darley Abbey, and thereafter the house was

used as a summer residence and so remained comparatively unaltered until the early twentieth century when the family estates were split. The hall became the home of the Rev. Claud Lewis (vicar at Parwich, 1904–11), who enlarged the house in 1905–06 and asked Walter Tapper to transform the simple garden layout into a series of linked garden rooms, surrounded by strong dry stone walls.

An architect who specialised in ecclesiastical Arts and Crafts Gothic, Tapper had worked at Shipley Hall and garden (below) in a rather different style. At Parwich he doubled the size of the gardens to 5½ acres (8.8 ha), added more terraces and created irregularly shaped garden rooms which are strongly architectural and approached through stone archways. Originally approached by a row of walnut trees, an attractive Arts and Crafts stone summer house at the top of the formal gardens has a heavy stone roof, long mullioned windows with leaded panes, and is heated by a fireplace, hence the large chimney stack to the side. It looks over a large tennis court separated by a stone wall from a

FIGURE 137. Parwich Hall, Sir Walter Tapper's summer house (1906).

COURTESY A. AND R. SHIELDS

FIGURE 138. Parwich Hall, Upper Garden with rockwork and path overlooking the gardens.

COURTESY A. AND R. SHIELDS

formal rose garden, whose original layout survives. The original 400-foot long herbaceous border and the rose pergola have gone.

Long paths and tantalising glimpses through arches make the garden seem larger than it is. Above the formal areas, precipitous narrow flights of stone steps lead up through the wild garden on the hillside above to an avenue of trees at the top. This provides splendid views down over the garden, village and countryside. Among these higher gardens, informally planted and carpeted with wild garlic, are scattered several rockeries on the west side, apparently at random on the steep slopes. Some are semi-circular rock lined retreats, provided with seats for resting after the climb up and down the steep paths which cut across the area. Rock outcrops and boulders are incorporated and this semi-woodland area is curiously dis-orientating with its winding paths, low dry stone walls criss-crossing, and views down to the maze of small walled-garden rooms below.

Besides the building of hundreds of metres of beautifully made dry-stone-walling, there was the massive job of digging into the hillside to create both the garden and informal gardens above the existing terraces. The ground is full of huge rocks, with solid rock outcrops and it becomes increasingly steep towards the top of the hillside. Parwich is unusual in that the standard Edwardian features of herbaceous borders, rose pergola, rose garden, croquet and tennis lawn and summer house were added to wooded hillside walks with rock gardens.[31] The result is still a delight of varied surprises and highest craftsmanship. The gardens are beautifully and lovingly maintained (and enhanced) by the current owners, Alice and Robert Shields.

Sir Walter Tapper is also associated with the gardens at **Shipley Hall** (*qv*). From the 1820s and '30s these were known for their exotic fruit, prestigious and expensive to grow, with orange and lemon trees seasonally displayed in the garden.[32] Over the years were added even more hothouses and greenhouses, a conservatory and adjoining fernery and vineries.[33] Alfred Miller Munday (d. 1877) inherited in 1850, and in 1860 he commissioned W. E. Nesfield to build a delightful model farm, complete with turrets. His nearby water tower doubled as a tall ornamental eye-catcher and also a practical feature for the walled kitchen gardens. William Barron was responsible for moving large trees, both as specimens and for clumps, as part of the redesigning of the lawns and park 1872–74.

Alfred Edward Mundy (d. 1920) inherited in 1877, and encouraged his brilliant head gardeners, William Elphinstone (1880–99) and John Cragoe Tallack (1900–09). The lawns with their specimen trees became part of wider gardens with herbaceous borders and roses, surrounded by well-established groves including splendid beeches. Tapper remodelled the house in 1895, designed the attractive entrance lodges *c.*1910 and must be the designer of that favourite Edwardian feature, a rose covered pergola. Here this strongly architectural feature linked the lawn with a fine beech avenue:

> The pergola is furnished with an arched roof and four domes placed at equal distance apart. The wood used is oak, and the supports consist of slender pillars of brick in cement. Instead of the usual grass or gravel walk underneath of ornamental York flagstones are used.[34]

FIGURE 139 *(opposite).* Shipley Hall, Sir Walter Tapper's Nottingham Lodge and gatepiers *c.*1910.

There was also a tufa-edged lily pond surrounded by flowering plants and fountain on the terrace.

However the family's coal mines were creeping too close to the house and in 1922 the estate was sold to the Shipley Colliery Company. This led to the inevitable demolition of the house in 1943 once acquired by the National Coal Board, who mined under it.[35] In the 1970s, 700 acres (283 ha) of reclaimed land and opencast quarries were converted into a country park, and at its centre the foundations of the demolished hall have been marked out with bricks and surrounded by lawn. Looking at the interpretation boards and seeing what has been lost, it is hard not to be depressed.

Having looked after **Sutton Scarsdale** from 1882, William Arkwright (1857–1925) inherited it from his cousin in 1915. He created a garden from the lawns and specimen trees noted in an earlier chapter and incorporated the Octagon kitchen garden into the new pleasure gardens. However, at the end of the war Arkwright sold the 5000 acre (2024.5 ha) estate, with its 'well planned terraced pleasure gardens with Archery Ground, Croquet and Tennis Lawn, Octagon Garden, Cedar Garden, Gold and Silver Borders, Italian Yew Pergola'.[36] Also for sale were seventeenth- and eighteenth-century garden ornaments and wrought iron gates.[37]

A photograph in the sale brochure shows the terrace to the south of the house as a long walk, terminating with an arch. Its retaining wall was topped with a stone parapet in curves, decorated with small urns. Four huge Carrara

FIGURE 141. Sutton Scarsdale, remains of terrace and retaining walls but without its urns and summer house.

marble urns spaced along its length migrated to Thorn House, Wembury, Devon, purchased by William Arkwright when he left Sutton Scarsdale. There he transformed the gardens into imitations of those he had created, and abandoned, at Sutton Scarsdale.[38]

In the 1920s new owners dismantled the house and only Sir Osbert Sitwell's last minute intervention saved the shell in 1946. He hoped to restore the house and even commissioned Milner White and Sons to propose a planting scheme. The firm suggested rather basic shrubberies and perimeter planting which would at least have given the ruined house a civilised setting.[39] Post-war was not a good time for such plans and Sir Osbert had to admit defeat and to hand over to the Department of the Environment in 1969. The house is now stabilised as a safe and evocative ruin, but lacks a garden and the parkland with its numerous trees and ponds has vanished.

On many counts **Thornbridge Hall,** near Bakewell is a remarkable garden, not least for the joyous profusion of architectural ornament strewn throughout. The story of Thornbridge from 1900 to 1945 is that of two owners, whose considerable entrepreneurial wealth embellished house and gardens as a suitably impressive setting for their social aspirations. In 1896 George Jobson Marples, a Yorkshire businessman, bought the 185 acre (57 ha) Thornbridge estate and its Jacobean style house for £25,000.[40] He promptly enlarged the house, decorated it opulently and fitted modern electricity. It stands on a high plateau with extensive views over the park, which he extended. Garden terraces were created, with impressive retaining walls on the slopes of the south and east sides below the house, using spoil from the huge new cellars and new ornamental pond. The estate was further improved with a large gatehouse, lodges, cottages and new stable block and Marples' own private railway station nearby: Mr Marples was out to impress.

Money was thrown at the gardens for quick results.[41] As early as September 1898, *The Gardeners' Chronicle* admired the landscaping of a park with new

FIGURE 142. Thornbridge Hall, rock archway between terrace and kitchen gardens by J. Backhouse and Son of York, *c.*1900.

lake, the large scale planting of mature trees 'for immediate effect', and a pinetum. Most amazing was a, now lost, Winter Garden under construction 'with underground caves, cascades, and a miniature lake. This conservatory is about 50 feet by 40 feet and 20 feet in height'.[42] The gardens and park were designed by Simeon Marshall of J. Backhouse and Son's Nursery at York, famous for its alpine plants and rock gardening on a grand scale. Marshall designed the attractive water garden at the pool with its rockwork banks covered with masses of alpines and shrubs, stream fed cascades and pools, tufa grottos and massive stone slab bridge. The main 'promenade' or terrace under the house continued under an impressive rockwork tunnel or arch to the 'terraced fruit garden in three tiers, [which] promises to become a most useful as well as an ornamental garden.' This 'naturalistic' feature made a strong contrast to the more formal terraces below the house, which had replaced the former kitchen gardens (Pl. 35).

The next phase came after the death of George Marples in 1929 when the estate was sold to Charles Boot, who owned a Sheffield based international firm, Henry Boot Construction. Again house and garden were used for social and business entertaining. With pretensions to embellish his superbly terraced garden Charles Boot had the perfect occupation: construction and demolition contractor. A contract to work on Clumber Park, demolished in 1938 after fire damage, gave the ideal opportunity to acquire an eclectic collection of temples, statuary, urns and balustrading. Of variable quality, but with an impeccable provenance, these were placed strategically round the gardens within the existing layout and planting. In fact so many objects were acquired from Clumber and other houses that Mr Boot seems to have run out of suitable sites, and rather desperately piled them around. Mismatched urns line walls along a drive near the entrance façade and large statues are scattered around borders. A statue of Handel (?) is placed within coping from a flower bed, and Atlas towers on the

FIGURE 143. Thornbridge Hall, two tiers of the Sydnope Hall fountain with quatrefoil basin added; in the background, a late nineteenth-century temple, another of Mr Boot's acquisitions.

COURTESY J. AND E. HARRISON

side-lines. Others are placed more strategically in formal gardens, accompanied by a large variety of urns and assorted benches. However, no doubt several have travelled round the grounds to new sites over the past 70 years. Much of the extensive classical stone balustrading came from Clumber Park, but this fits effortlessly onto the earlier terracing walls.

To Mr Marples' formal terrace garden, with its clipped yew hedges and specimen clipped green and golden yews and hollies, and grass 'beds', Mr Boot added an eclectic subject range of Clumber park statues and urns.[43] Another huge stone fountain, or more accurately two tiers of the five tiered fountain from Sydnope Hall, (also owned by Mr Boot), is sited in a new basin in the centre of the 1930s orchard, with classical statues of the four seasons on one side. These were not from Clumber but a gift from the Greek government to Mr. Boot in the 1930s, partly in return for his gift of Chantry's statue of George Canning removed from Thornbridge's Winter Garden.[44]

Given the excess of disparate ornament throughout the gardens, the result should be daunting, but one soon adapts, especially as the gardens are divided into so many varied compartments. So the temples, benches, fountains and urns provide focal points, places to sit, talking points and a *leitmotif* throughout this unpredictable and rather magical garden. It comes as little surprise to learn that Charles Boot set up the Pinewood Film Company in 1934 on his estate in Buckinghamshire, for the Thornbridge gardens might be a film set.[45] After the death of Mr Boot in 1945 the house was sold to Sheffield City Council who used it as a teacher-training college until 1997. It was then purchased by Mr and Mrs Hunt, who restored the garden, followed in 2002 by Jim and Emma Harrison who have continued the tradition of truly imaginative embellishment of house and garden. Today it is beautifully and lovingly restored and maintained while new planting, both modern and traditional, has given yet another, modern, layer of interest.

Sir Francis Burdett, eighth baronet (1869–1951), inherited **Foremark Hall** in 1892, although it was not until his marriage in 1908 that he turned his attention to the gardens, little changed during the previous century. Between 1909 and 1919 several plans were proposed, even during the war. An unsigned sketch plan dated September 1909 shows a proposal for the west side of the gravel forecourt, with two long grass walks separated by a balustrade from a shrubbery. This has a circular summer house marked 'pagoda' at one side and a circular rose garden nearby.[46] This has the hallmarks of a Milner-White partnership design, much of which was adapted, with the circular garden and fountain, shown on the 1923 OS map. This family firm was London based, run by Henry Ernest Milner, son of Edward Milner (*cf.* Bakewell, Buxton, Omaston and Stancliffe) and then by Edward White, his partner and son-in-law, from the early twentieth century.

To complicate matters, in 1912 Locksheath Nurseries of Southampton were approached for plans and recommended that essential for Edwardian gardens:

> a Pergola be erected on the south side of the tennis lawn, occupying the straight level stretch of ground between the suggested western exit to the bottom of the sloping ground approaching the church … [it] should be of good proportions and of an imposing character, massive rather than otherwise in appearance and sufficiently high to allow the shoots of plants growing over it to trail two or three feet from the overhead cross beams.
>
> I also suggest that clipped evergreen trees be placed in the alcoves on the east and west [garden] wings of the house, which would be in character with the design of the garden in front. An alternative scheme to the foregoing would be to fill the alcoves with trained scented-leaved geraniums.[47]

FIGURE 144. Foremark Hall and pavilions; Edwardian quatrefoil pond.

COURTESY R. MERRIMAN, FOREMARK SCHOOL

FIGURE 145. Foremark Hall, under restoration: the remains of small, enclosed Arts and Crafts garden, probably *c.*1915–18.

COURTESY R. MERRIMAN, FOREMARK SCHOOL

The surviving accounts are not complete but it would seem that, more sensibly, the experienced local landscape gardeners and nurserymen, William Barron and Son, were engaged. In 1913 the firm quoted to level ground on the old carriage drive in front of the house using 'soil from the sunk fence near the Temple (leaving an even slope) and relay with turf cut from flowers beds and round [the] Temple'.[48] They planted rhododendrons round the late eighteenth-century Temple on the perimeter of the pleasure grounds: a popular and colourful planting scheme:

> We will undertake to plant 129 Named Rhododendrons in groups of 7 or 8 of one colour, either white, scarlet, crimson, pink or purple, on beds round Temple, and guarantee for twelve months, for the sum of Fourteen pounds ten shillings.[49]

The overall design plan went to Milner Son and White. A delightful, but unexecuted, plan (1914) for the garden proposed a long, irregular pond crossed by a bridge, a waterfall at one end and semi-circular seat at the other.[50] Their bill for 1915–16 came to the tidy sum of £1008 12s 3d, for 'preparing plans and superintending the work under the management of an expert foreman'. It included £80 15s 9d to Barron and Son 'for planting'.[51] Labour totalled £533 13s 0d and there were sums for rock plants, tulips and grass seed, on all of which Milner and White charged 10% commission. It is not known what was involvement of the head gardener Mr Thrule, but the firm charged 5% for supervision on £78 'work done by Estate'.

The bill included £14 for a seat from Castles and £53 5s for a 'Figure' by Crowther and Son which may be the lead statue of 'Boy and Swan' purchased in June 1916 but damaged in transit by rail.[52] If it was a statue fountain, it may have been placed in a quatrefoil shaped pond in the enclosed garden next to the kitchen garden. This was a compact Arts and Crafts style garden with central water rill, cascade and pond, with areas for herbaceous borders (or rockeries) at the side. It must have been most attractive when planted out, perhaps with some of the rock plants, which totalled £23 1s in the bill. This little garden has a deep tiled open summer house with overhanging eaves in one corner and could be the work of Milner and White. The garden is being restored by Repton School, who have owned Foremark since 1947. Although now school buildings cover most of pleasure grounds, the Edwardian gardens by the house survive in outline and are well maintained.

William Barron and Son's gardens at **Tissington Hall** *c.*1913 reflect the contemporary interest in hedged enclosures, terracing and linking steps, and the importance of relating gardens to the house. Home of the FitzHerbert family since the early seventeenth century, the stone built hall, with its large walled forecourt and stone entrance archway, dates from *c.*1609. Robert Bakewell ironwork gates were inserted into the entrance arch and allow picturesque views into the forecourt.

Little is known about the original gardens. When the house was offered to let for 3 years in 1774, the not entirely helpful details simply mention gardens and fish ponds, with the manor abounding with 'fish, game and rabbits'.[53] However the addition of a large 'Jacobethan' attached library wing and service wing in 1910, for Sir Hugo Meynell FitzHerbert (1872–1934), encouraged enlargement of the garden in a traditional style.

The 1880 and 1899 OS maps simply show a terrace behind the house with central flight of steps up to a lawn, set within a wooded plateau having what appear to be mounts at two corners.[54] The 1920 OS map shows the new library wing, creating an L-shaped garden façade to the house, and the present garden layout. The terrace has been widened to accommodate the length of the new

FIGURE 146 *(left)*. Tissington Hall, early twentieth-century 'castellated' yew hedge at top of the garden.

COURTESY SIR RICHARD FITZHERBERT.

FIGURE 147 *(right)*. Tissington Hall, Edwardian terraces and rose parterre sympathetic to the early seventeenth-century house.

COURTESY SIR RICHARD FITZHERBERT

FIGURE 148. Kings
Newton Hall, bastion on
garden boundary stone
walls.

wing, still with the lawn above. However the garden has now been lengthened with a second, narrower, terrace beyond which is another lawn area (tennis court?) enclosed by the 'crenellations' and 'buttresses' of a magnificent formal clipped yew hedge. Much of this hedge has gone, so it is somewhat difficult to gauge the original enclosed effect of the top garden, which is now open to the hills beyond. There is now an attractive rose garden on the lowest lawn. The FitzHerbert family still live there and it is regularly open to the public.[55]

Another commission for Barron and Son was at **Kings Newton Hall**, behind its high garden walls on the main street of the village, The Elizabethan house passed by marriage to the Coke family of nearby Melbourne, who thereafter let it out to tenants. The rubble sandstone garden walls survived the landscaping movement and a two storey brick summer house still survives on a perimeter garden wall. From its upper floor there would have been views over the garden and out over the park. The gardens may have been improved by William Speechly (1735–1819), a well-known horticulturist, expert on pineapple and vines, who lived here after his retirement as head gardener at Welbeck.[56]

Following a disastrous fire in 1859 the gutted house was left unoccupied for 50 years and as a romantic ivy-covered ruin it even became a tourist attraction, the gardens 'now used for pleasure parties, and being only so short a distance from Derby, are much frequented'.[57] Then in the early twentieth century the house was rebuilt by the forceful Cecil Paget (1874–1936), General Superintendent of the Midland Railway and later second baronet Paget (1923). His (unknown) architect sympathetically incorporated what survived from the ruined house into a replacement Jacobean style house. With active involvement from Sir Cecil, William Barron and Son created a new garden behind the house as series of linked spaces.[58] A long rose garden terrace, with irregular flag stones separating the beds, overlooked a small formal tripartite sunken garden with another rose garden and lily pond.[59]

Barron and Son could be responsible for two semi-circular bastions in the perimeter garden wall. The larger is aligned on Barron's new garden behind the house, while the smaller is on the side wall, where there was once an early twentieth-century wrought iron screen. Bastions were quite fashionable in the 1730s, but also appear in the early twentieth century (*vide* Lea Wood), so they could be a deliberate revival.

Not all gardens had professional designers. In 1911 Philip Robinson (1882–1978), a Chesterfield manufacturer, purchased **Park Hall**, **Walton**, an old farm house, which he transformed into a small country house with newly created gardens between 1913 and 1935. Year by year his note-book of 'Park Hall Improvements' laconically lists the *ad hoc* main improvements to house and garden, including such modern features as a garage and swimming pool.[60] Work started with a rose garden, fruit trees and hedges and a woodland walk with seats. Not everything succeeded as noted in 1918: 'Greenhouse stove connected to house hot water pipes (a failure)'.

Robinson's sketchbook (1933) includes drawings dated November 1918 for possible alterations to house and garden.[61] In sympathy with the date of the house (1664) one sketch suggests an enclosed walled garden, with raised terrace walks and steps down to central grass parterres. There would be a 'moat' outside one buttressed wall crossed by a little bridge into the garden through a gate with stone piers. On the 'moat' corner would be a raised square viewing platform or bastion. Of these ideas a 'look-out 'and bridge over a dry moat were built in 1914–15.[62] Work in the 1920s continued to extend, embellish and redesign the garden, with the 'drawing room terrace' (1920), roses to the pond garden and levelling the 'Old Rose garden to create a tennis court' (1921). The croquet lawn was renovated, '2 garden vases bought' in 1922; a sundial was moved into the pond garden and a 'seat made round the Sycamore Tree on the lower Tennis lawn' in 1923; the lower pond and bog garden was finished, the croquet lawn enlarged and a balustrade erected at the end of the sunken walk. Modern Improvements included 'town water laid on to kitchen garden and fountain' in 1925, town electricity bought to the house in 1927 and electric pumps for the water.

Up-to-date in 1929, a garage nick-named 'Tuts Tomb' [Tutankamun] was erected at a cost of nearly £46. 'Mayoral seats' were put up to celebrate Philip Robinson's year as Lord Mayor of Chesterfield, and the gardens were increasingly used for social entertaining.

Expensive to lay out with the varying levels and generous use of stone and water, the two acres (0.8 ha) of gardens were clearly intended to look traditional, with nothing ostentatious or *nouveau riche* but with quietly up-to-date facilities. Here Robinson could entertain family and friends in a traditionally hospitable manner with tennis, swimming and garden walks. The bowling green was provided with a delightful timber-framed tea pavilion with interior pargetting. Open on two sides it was built from ten tons of reclaimed oak timbers from the fourteenth-century Old Priests' Cottage near Walton, demolished in 1933 (Pl. 36).[63]

FIGURE 149. Park Hall, corner 'look out' at end of terrace, 1914/5.

COURTESY K. AND M. STANIFORTH

The main garden has three crazy paving terraces linked by central steps up to a stone alcove, all with luxuriant side planting. The lowest terrace has a simple Lutyens style central apse with small pool and wall fountain, while at the side of the next terrace there is a stone seat facing an open 'Pergola on the Terrace' made in 1933. Along the complete length of this garden runs a little stream, crossed by with small stone bridges. By the 1930s the gardens had the standard 'crazy-paved paths', tennis lawn, fish pond and lily pond, rose garden, rock garden, swimming pool and even a 'Garden Sleeping House'.[64] A rather nice touch was the conversion of the children's playground, no longer needed, into a rockery in 1920.

Within enclosed walls and hedges, the gardens are self-contained and inward looking, except at the one corner where the 'look-out' can still be climbed to give views out, although now instead of open countryside the view is over encroaching housing development. The gardens have been restored brilliantly by the current owners Kim and Margaret Staniforth, who have respected and enhanced the Arts and Crafts features. Imaginative modern additions work coherently with traditional planting, held together by the stone walls, architectural features and a variety of eye-catchers, seats and benches: a charming and delightful garden.

Belper River Gardens were developed 1905–07 as a welcoming little public park, now in the shadow of the East Mill at Belper (1912), one of a complex of cotton mills on the site owned by the Strutt family. George Herbert Strutt, (great-nephew of Joseph, founder of Derby Arboretum), largely paid for the creation of these gardens next to the river, for the benefit of local people, who paid a small entrance fee. The narrow site ran along the river on a former osier bed, which was cleared and widened into the river to create broad promenade walks. Along with rustic arches and shrub bordered walks was a rather jolly

FOUNTAIN & BANDSTAND BELPER RIVER GARDENS.

FIGURE 150. Belper River
Gardens, Bandstand and
Pulham's fountain.

bandstand with a copper roof. The gardens were so successful that Strutt further
enlarged them and commissioned Pulham and Sons to decorate the gardens
with rockwork. A high curving rockery hid the boathouse, a small circular
rockwork pool had a fountain and rockwork features, while the mill lode was
converted into a formal water garden with islands.

A Swiss-style tea room was enlarged with a verandah as the gardens became
popular, although its original thatched roof was soon replaced with more
practical tiles. *The Belper News* regaled its readers with the delights of the
Gardens' attractions including 'Grand evening fete', 'sparkling music', and
that perennial favourite, the 'gorgeous firework display'.[65] Fairylights, music
and fireworks were regular attractions and the *News* even felt, rather too
optimistically, that the river gardens made Belper 'the modern Mecca of Mid-
Derbyshire … quickly outrivalling the many charms of Matlock'.[66] In 1966
ownership passed to Belper Urban District Council and currently Amber Valley
Borough Council cares for the site and has spent much on it. Sadly the Swiss
Tea Rooms are boarded up, but as an Edwardian time-warp, albeit now a little
municipal, these gardens are still an oasis of calm and charm.[67]

Notes

All quotations from newspapers are © The British Library Board. All rights reserved. With
thanks to the British Newspaper Archive (www.BritishNewspaperArchive.co.uk).

1. *DDT*, 12 Oct. 1907, 2.
2. G. Jeckyll and L. Weaver, *Gardens for Small Country Houses* (1912), i–ii, 64, 666–68,
    76–77, 96–97, 134, 144–45. For examples of his work see J. Brown, *The Art and
    Architecture of English Gardens* (1989), 144–53. He illustrated T. H. Mawson's *The Art
    and Craft of Garden Making* (1907).
3. O. Sitwell, *Great Morning* (1948), 280–81.

4. *Ibid.*, illustration opp. p. 40. Its reference to p. 110 is an error as this refers to a new house for the gardener Ernest de Taeye in an unused kitchen garden.

5. O. Sitwell, *Laughter in the Next Room* (1949), 263–65; DRO: D6573/Box 104. Sitwell estate records. Sketches include an interior design.

6. Copy ground plan by Lutyens at DRO: D6281/3/11, dated March 1916 (original at Renishaw Hall). www.imagesofengland.org.uk IoE number 79604 (1985).

7. Sitwell, *Great Morning*, 25.

8. DRO: D6573/104/15 plan of July 1914. DRO: D6573/104/19 'railing round pool, Barbers garden.'

9. DRO: D6573/Box104/17, 23 Sitwell estate papers, sketch for entrance from road.

10. DRO: D6573/Box104/17, 23; 104/31/2 is a variant design for the iron work of the gate and side balustrades.

11. DRO: D6573/104/14 (1914).

12. DRO: D6281/3/11/uncoloured plan1916 by Lutyens.

13. My thanks to Alex Styan for providing information about the restoration of the gardens and to Mr and Mrs North for allowing access.

14. Craven and Stanley, II, 293–94.

15. See Ordnance Survey maps for 1881, 1900, 1914. Accessed via www.maps.nls/os/6inch-england-and-wales.

16. DRO: 6852; D302/ES26. Auction Sale catalogue, 11 Oct. 1938. See www.picturethepast.org.uk DCCS0002234, photo of Morley Hall and gardens in the 1930s.

17. Craven and Stanley, I, 90.

18. Description based on English Heritage Register of Parks and Gardens, List entry 1000678; www.imagesofengland.org.uk number 81362.

19. 1920 OS map, XLIII.16.43.16

20. My thanks to Val Farren of Roger Bullivant Ltd for permission to visit and to Simon Baxter for sharing his knowledge of the site on a guided walk.

21. *CL*, 22 March 1902, 368–74; 16 March 1907, 378–85; 17 Feb. 1934, 161–64, 257, 338.

22. Georgian Group, Pardoe collection DERB8017a, Drakelow Hall from the North-West engraving from a drawing by Lady Penelope Gresley, 1855; there is another copy DRO: Zsp 023/30. *CL*, 22 March 1902, 368–75. *CL*, 16 March 1907, 378–84 shows the terrace.

23. Some idea of the quality of the garden ornament can be seen with the lead Drakelow urn, purchased by Lord Fairhaven for Anglesey Abbey in 1934, and still *in situ* by the Quarry garden there (National Trust).

24. Craven and Stanley, I, 156–57; II, 294–95.

25. www.south.derbys.gov.uk/NethersealConservationAreaCharacterStatement, 2010. The ponds are not shown on two early maps: DRO: D77/8/17 (1785); D77/8/18: map of the estate of William Nigel Gresley (1829), but lower pools appear on the 1843 tithe map. On the 1881 OS map these two long pools have become the present large pool, with a strangely shaped, angular pool above.

26. Craven and Stanley, I, 157; R. A. Fellows, *Sir Reginald Blomfield, An Edwardian Architect* (1985), 169.

27. 1911 census; my thanks to Sue Gregory for accessing this information.

28. N. Pevsner, *Buildings of England, Derbyshire* (1979), 57; www.imagesofengland.org.uk no. 81100.

29. DRO: D302 Z/ES 38 Sale of Raenstor Close, April 1953.

30. see Craven and Stanley, II, 176–77 for the history of the house and its owners.

31. DRO: D504/116/41 sale of Parwich estate, 1915.

32. J. C. Loudon, *Encylopaedia of Gardening* (1822), item 7524; RHS *Horticultural Transactions* 2 (1822), 295; vol. I, 306 – my thanks to Sue Gregory for this reference. *DM*, 7 Nov. 1838, 3. The gardener was Richard Ayres, from a family of influential local gardeners.

33. *GC*, 18 Aug. 1883, 211–12. *The Gardens of Shipley Park*, booklet on sale at Shipley Park – no date or author.

34. *GC*, 17 Jan. 1903, 44; DRO: D1834/383 contemporary photograph from collection of N. V. Cowlishaw; RIBA library catalogue, ref. A317, 'Album of the work of Sir Walter Tapper'.

35. B. Taylor, 'The Gardens of Shipley Hall' in *Shipley Country Park Studies in History Research Papers* (1985–87) ed. P. Ibbotson and B. Taylor. accessed: http//"Shipley/studhistory1.htm".

36. DRO: D6704/1/1 Sale catalogue for Sutton Scarsdale estate, 6 Nov. 1919. The catalogue can be viewed online – see www.richardsbygonetimes.co.uk sutnscar.pdf.

37. *DTCH*, 25 Sept. 1920, 4.

38. I am grateful to Dr Jane Bradney for the story of urns; see also http://thornhouse.co.uk/history.htm accessed May 2012.

39. DRO: D6573/Maps 135, signed Edward White, July 1948.

40. DRO: D4719/7/41 has a photograph of a map of the estate in 1896 and a drawing of the Georgian hall in 1871.

41. Craven and Stanley, II, 221–22. *Derby Daily Telegraph*, 11 March 1897, 3; *DTCH*, 24 May 1903, 9 puts the sum expended at £160,000.

42. *GC*, 17 Sept.1898, 221–23.

43. It is difficult to be accurate about the timing of the arrangements, but an idea is shown by the photograph of the 'Dutch' terrace in 1898 (*GC*, 17 Sept. 1898, p. 221) and later photographs: www.picturethepast.org.uk refs DCHQ000062;DCHQ003726.

44. *DTCH*, 14 June 1930, 7; 25 October 1930, 10; *Derby Daily Telegraph*, 7 April 1931, 4.

45. *DTCH*, 13 Sept. 1935, 10.

46. DRO: D5054/20/7 working sketch dated 10 Sept.1909, 'estate Office Ingelby.' This may have been an unexecuted suggestion to reposition an existing eighteenth-century circular temple in the woods nearby.

47. DRO: 5054/20/2 2 May 1912. W. J. Middlebrooke 'Suggestions for laying out Garden and grounds on the South Front of Foremark House'. The plan is missing.

48. DRO: D5054/22/4/10(xviii) W. Barron to L. C. Picton, 18 June 1913.

49. DRO: D5054/22/4/11(iii, iv) W. Barron to L. C. Picton, 14 and 24 Feb. 1913.

50. SRO: D5054/20/12 endorsed 'White's plan for a garden'. Signed 'Edward White 12/2/14'.

51. DRO: D5052/22/4/1(iv) Milner Son and White's bill 27 July 1915 for 'professional services'.

52. DRO: D5054/22/4/1 series of bills.

53. *DM*, 24 June 1774, 3.

54. See also *CL*, 4 Feb.1899, 144–47.

55. Craven and Stanley, II, 223–25.

56. *DM*, 20 April 1859, 5.

57. Craven and Stanley, I, 130–31; South Derbyshire District Council, *Kings Newton Conservation Area Character Statement, Consultation Draft* (2010); E. Jewitt (ed.), *Black's 1872 Tourist's Guide to Derbyshire* (1999), 256.

58. *Ibid.*, 15 Dec. 1936, 6.

59. *DDT*, 15 Dec. 1936, 6; 24 Aug. 1938, p. 6. DRO: D2190/13/12 – two photographs of the rose terrace, 1924.

60. DRO: D5395/22/1/1/43 Notebook of Philip Robinson.

61. DRO: D5395/22/1/7/3 'sketchbook of Park Hall when owned by Philip M. Robinson' 1933.

62. DRO: D5395/22/1/1/43. Illustrated in 1937 sale brochure (DRO: D5395/22/1/7/4) as 'A Stone-built TOOL or GARDEN HOUSE with flat roof forms a place of vantage'. The 'look out' steps were provided with 'pillars from rose hill house' in 1935: DRO: D5395/22/1/1/4, notebook entry.

63. DRO: D5395/22/1/7/5: Notes on Park Hall from a report on a garden party given by Philip Robinson in the *Derbyshire Times* 3 June 1934, 14; DRO: D5395/22/1/7/4 Park hall Sale 1937.

64. DRO: 5395/22/17/4 sale particulars for Park Hall 1937.

65. *Belper News*, 21 September 1906, 5.

66. *Belper News*, 24 May 1907, 5.

67. www.derwentvalleymills.org/history/communities/178-the-river-gardens-belper; Amber Valley Borough Council, Belper River Gardens Management Plan 2010–2015 – accessed opengov.ambervalley.gov.uk.

CHAPTER TWELVE

A Miscellany of Gardeners and Nurserymen

....

How many flowery realms there are yet to conquer.

Skilled gardeners are the unsung heroes of gardening history yet most are anonymous. Information, particularly before the nineteenth century, is disappointingly elusive and they are rarely mentioned by name. An early exception is Leonard Wheatcroft (1627–1706), known through his autobiography.[1] Polymath (or jack of all trades), tailor, carpenter, schoolmaster, inn-keeper, parish clerk, gardener and poet, Wheatcroft sourced and planted trees, working in orchards and gardens of several Derbyshire gentry in the 1660s and '70s, and he may have designed simple layouts. Occasionally a name appears when there was a problem, as with William Marriot, aged 37, 'bred a gardener' who deserted his wife and three children in 1787. 'He has been lately employed as a director of Workmen in laying out grounds under Mr [William] Emes, whose service he has deserted.' (7 June 1787: to avoid a tediously long reference section single references from *Derby Mercury* are noted in the main text of this chapter simply by a date).

Yet the position of head gardener was a very responsible one. Much was expected and increasingly demanded were the special skills to raise exotics and then, in the nineteenth century, huge numbers of bedding plants. The job of gardener (and nurseryman) often ran in families, but finding a reliable and satisfactory gardener could be a problem. Appointments were often made from other estates, whose owner or head gardener could recommend one of their trainees. The Rev. Thomas Calton, vicar of Duffield wrote to an unknown correspondent in 1726:

> I sent immediately to our Gardiner upon ye receipt of yours and met with one yt was formerly an Apprentice to him. He is willing to serve you but insists upon £12 per annum and will serve no Gentleman under[.] they say he writes and accounts well and is a Plaisterer as well as a Gardiner.[2]

Another recruitment source was a nursery, whose owner had often been a former gardener and who trained his own men. In 1838 the nurseryman Joshua Wilson advertised that he could recommend experienced gardeners, while the *Derby Mercury* has several examples of gardeners advertising for posts and providing local nurserymen as contacts and referees.[3] An example of the often close link between gardeners and nurserymen is John Scott from Yorkshire, who became head gardener to the Duke of York at Oatlands Park, Surrey. He then returned to Yorkshire and became a nurseryman. Later he became head gardener at Chatsworth and trained his son Adam (1790–1891), who worked at Kedleston as a young gardener and afterwards went to Chatsworth to work with his father. About 1825 Adam moved to Bakewell and set up as a successful market gardener and farmer.[4]

Between 1800 and 1850 a handful of advertisements in the *Derby Mercury* from those seeking employment, show little change over that period. Most offered skills in the kitchen, fruit and flower gardens, providing a suitable 'unexceptional character'.[5] There were many more would-be employers advertising and they expected miracles of multi-tasking, combined with excellent references and total sobriety. Owners of smaller properties expected their gardener to combine work in the garden with other work, such as groom or coachman.[6]

> Wanted a steady single man, as a Kitchen Gardener, whose character for Industry, and Sobriety, will bear the strictest inquiry, such a person may meet with a Place of constant employ…
>
> N.B. If he can wait at Table, it will be more agreeable (15 June 1781)

An advertiser near Chesterfield wanted his gardener to take care of his greyhounds and wait occasionally at the table, for £25 *per annum* and clothes (14 Oct. 1784). An advert from Mr Trubshaw, cabinet maker in Derby in 1771, sought a man aged between 20 and 40, who would wait on the table, look after the garden, and also the horses. 'He must also understand the Nature of keeping Accounts, and write a good Hand'. Naturally he had to be honest and truthful, while in return he would be well paid (22 Nov 1771). Even this sounds slightly less onerous than the advert for a married couple in 1812: 'middle aged active persons, the Man as GARDENER, and his wife as COOK and HOUSEKEEPER', in a large household, who had lived with 'Families of Distinction' where references could be provided for ability, honesty, sobriety and industry:

> the Gardener having a general knowledge of Planting, Draining, and all kinds of new Ground, and Water Works, with a perfect knowledge of establishing old gardens, so as to resume their former vigour - Emolument not so much the object as a Comfortable Situation.
>
> No objection to superintend a small farm. (1 Oct. 1812)

A reminder of the young age at which work started is shown in an advertisement of 1847 for a married man to be a gardener near Matlock Bath. 'If he has a family of two or three children above 12 years of age, they would be employed also' (23 June 1847). For the under-gardeners and apprentices the work was hard, hours long and pay small, which may be why the 17-year-old James Wigley, apprentice to Samuel Smith, a gardener at Bonsall, ran away from his master, in 1773 (26 Aug. 1773). Yet apprenticeships at larger establishments were sought after, as with the hopeful parents of another 17-year-old who advertised in 1844:

wish[ing] to engage him in the GARDENS of a NOBLEMAN, GENTLEMAN or NURSERYMAN, where he would have the opportunity of learning the whole process of GARDENING in all its branches. (17 Jan. 1844)

Unsurprisingly given the long hours and harsh working environment, drink was a problem and sobriety was stressed. In 1769 Robert Wilmot of Osmaston Hall, gave somewhat optimistic instructions for employing a new garden labourer:

Pray endeavour to get a proper lad [man] that has been used to a Garden. You'll enquire his Character – If he be an Impudent, Whoreing, Drinking Fellow he won't do. He must have had the Small Pox and Measles and not be a Papist or Methodist.[7]

In 1813 there was a rather prescriptive advert for which one would not imagine a rush of applicants:

a steady active Man Servant, to manage a kitchen garden, and take care of a Horse and Gig, also to clean knives and shoes etc. … A middle aged single Man would be preferred, and as he must conform to strict family orders, and regularly attend a dissenting place of worship, none need apply but such as can bring an unexceptionable character for sobriety and good behaviour. (25 March 1813)

In 1821 Mr Wilson, Nurseryman of Derby optimistically advertised:

Wanted a gardener who understands forcing and the management of Fruit Trees in general, and who would have no objection to wait at Table *occasionally*, milk a cow, and assist in the care of Horse and Gig.

N.B. None need apply whose character will not bear the strictest investigation for sobriety and honesty. (14 Nov. 1821)

Samuel Smith, joint owner of Tansley Nurseries, Matlock even appeared in court charged with drunkenness in 1885, with damning words from the Bench:

The defendant ought to know better than to behave in that way, there were several previous convictions and he would have pay 10s costs... Police Constable Hadfield said he found the above defendants lying together on the road, they were both very drunk and using a lot of bad language.[8]

The term 'Gardener' covered both the highly skilled and the jobbing labourer, such as the local man who took a rather extreme measure to obtain extra income by fighting a boxing-match. These were brutal affairs but lucrative for the winner. The match took place in 1829 between one Hardy from Ripley, a frame-worker turned gardener, and Gas, a touring pugilist. The *Mercury* noted rather ominously that Hardy had 'acquired in his neighbourhood considerable notoriety as a fighter', but he was knocked senseless at the thirty-fourth round, and so failed to win the £100 prize (13 May 1829). Many were gardeners cum seedsmen, owning or renting fields and gardens to grow their produce and selling at a shop or stall at the local markets.

We know names of several head gardeners though reports of their winning prizes in Horticultural and Florist Shows. For example Thomas M'Lauren/ M'Laurin (1798–1856), head gardener at Renishaw Hall, displayed exotics at the Horticultural Society Show at Sheffield Botanical Gardens in 1839. Then, following the financial problems and retrenchment of the Sitwell family in the late 1840s, he became a grocer and assistant overseer of the poor at Eckington, next to the Renishaw estate.[9] He was well educated and an intellectual man, noted for growing rare tropical plants.[10] Of course Derbyshire did have two nineteenth-century 'celebrities' of the gardening world, Joseph Paxton and William Barron, both of whom were expert self-publicists.

Suppliers

In the seventeenth and eighteenth centuries at the larger country estates trees, shrubs and flowers were usually grown by the head gardener at the estate nursery. Extra trees might be obtained from local landowners who had a surplus or who sold for profit. However obtaining stock could be an *ad hoc* arrangement. In 1750 Leake Okeover, of Okeover Hall, acquired Scotch firs from an acquaintance in Leicestershire. His agent reported back that [Mr Mason] 'sends his humble service and will spare you one hundred in exchange for 4 or 5 couple of hounds'.[11]

Local merchants and seedsmen supplied gardeners of small estates, who also supplied one another with surplus stock. In the 1660s–80s Leonard Wheatcroft, the freelance gardener (*supra*), sourced trees for small estates, probably from several small suppliers.[12] By the eighteenth century there were several small commercial nurseries scattered over Derbyshire and nearby counties. Some can be traced by adverts in local newspapers, including Charles Basseldine, near Bolsover, who sold limes and elms together with standard (clipped) yews, hollies and bay 'all with fine balls' for the fashionable formal gardens of town and country (19 Aug. 1736). John Smith at Duffield Bridge, Derby, offered a variety of trees, fruit trees, standard yews, striped hollies, and cherry and apples trees for espaliers (1 Sept. 1737; 6 Sept. 1745). Mr Godkin at Melbourne, used a Derby shopkeeper as an agent to sell walnut and elm trees (3 Dec. 1741). George Beastall sold trees, fruit trees and shrubs from his nursery at Alfreton (13 Nov. 1783).

There were large scale suppliers such as the Perfect family at Pontefract (from 1717) and the Pope family at Birmingham from the 1770s and of course the big London nurseries.[13] Probably people in north Derbyshire bought from Robert Turner at Kersall Moor, just north of Manchester. Turner, noted as gardener and nurseryman in 1754, developed a large nursery which in the 1760s and 1770s advertised a large and varied stock of trees, shrubs, fruit bushes and

FIGURE 151. Sir Joseph Paxton: a portrait pose as successful gardener and glasshouse designer, 1860s.

flowers for the garden, selling both wholesale and retail. He appears to have set up business in the late 1720s and sold up in the early 1780s, 'Being old, and not able to follow so large a Business', and died 'at an advanced age' in 1785.[14] The account books of Sir Robert Burdett of Foremark Hall for the 1740s–60s reflect the range of suppliers upon which local gentry could call. He bought from a 'Mr Williamson, the nurseryman' in 1742, 1749 and 1753, whose bills came to nearly £32, suggesting sizable orders. He also purchased consistently from a local gardener/nurseryman Hodgkinson of Derby and Ann Sandys of Ashbourne (see below). In 1761 200 rose trees were purchased from 'Stevenson ye Gardiner in London'.[15] Many county families spent time in London each year, which would allow visits to nurseries there.

The raising and sale of flowers was on a smaller, more specialised scale. Most prestigious were the valuable auriculas, carnations and tulips much prized in the eighteenth and into the nineteenth century. This is a topic in its own right, so here one will just note that they were grown by enthusiasts and exhibited at specialist Florist Feasts and shows at various towns by the 1750s. Whole collections might come on the market following the death of a collector, as in 1744 when Sir Theophilus Biddulph of Elmhurst (near Burton-on-Trent) died and 'all his curious collection of Flowers, consisting of a great variety of choicest sort of Auriculas and Carnations' was sold at auction.[16] Derbyshire enthusiasts may have purchased tulips from Nottingham, from where specialists advertised from the 1740s, often using the advertising ploys of 'final sales' and 'moving premises'.[17]

By the 1830s Derby had yearly specialist auctions of imported Dutch bulbs (known as 'roots'), and by 1837 there were also local auctions at Ashbourne, Belper, Melbourne and Wirksworth, indicating just how popular bulbs had become and how much easier to obtain.[18] By then florists and nurseries such as Sadler and Wilson of Derby were selling them in their standard stock. On the other hand, if you could not afford to buy, or if you coveted a specific prize winning 'root', theft seemed another option, and was regularly reported in the local newspaper. The *Derby Mercury* reported a theft of tulips and auriculas from Leonard Fosbrooke at Shardlow Hall, who offered the large reward of 10 guineas for a conviction (8 June 1750). Amateur enthusiasts in Derby were regularly targeted, including Cornelius Flint who lost polyanthuses (7 April 1824). Mr Robinson lost his 'choice tulips' within a few days of planting in 1837, perhaps just having bought them 3 weeks previously at Eyre's annual auction of Dutch bulbs, which included hyacinths, jonquils, narcissus, tulips, ranunculi and anemones (25 October; 15 November 1837).

These were carefully targeted thefts as the *Mercury* remarked in 1835, when Mr Cliff, gardener and seedsman at Stapenhill, was robbed of 'valuable prize tulip roots… There is no doubt the robbery was committed by some-one who knew their value, and had marked them when in flower'. A little earlier it had commented that 'no doubt is entertained of there being receivers of stolen flower roots, who retail them at a distance from the town'. A reward of two guineas was offered and the reporter noted (to discourage other would-be thieves), that if caught the punishment was a minimum of six months in prison, or up to £20 fine (15 July 1835; 28 April 1830). This may have been the official line but a court case suggests caution. In 1833 Mr Potter on Kedleston Road, Derby had 16 auriculas and an earthen flower-pot stolen from his garden. He suspected a William Johnson of Mackworth so, with Constable Potter, he went to Johnson's garden and, indeed, found his flowers freshly planted together with the pot. Yet Johnson was acquitted with a good character reference and Potter was said to have been mistaken, which must have infuriated him (6 Feb. 1833). There must be other fascinating stories of local rivalries and obsessions behind many reported robberies, which cut across the social classes and involved those who seemed law-abiding citizens.

Nurserymen

Some small-scale nurserymen ran their nurseries in tandem with other work, such as gardening, farming and publican, depending on their skills and financial acumen. Unfortunately bankruptcies were not infrequent as with William Bradley, who lived near Chesterfield, 'farmer, labourer and nurseryman' and was declared bankrupt (15 March 1837). John Stott of Buxton was listed as nurseryman, florist and 'beerhouse keeper' when he became bankrupt (4 Sept. 1889). Enforced sales of stock must have affected other local nurseries when plants were sold off cheaply. As many were to find, running a nursery was a skilled and risky business, with inclement weather, disease and competition. Since most could not afford to buy enough land, enforced moves might follow when leases expired.

By the mid-nineteenth century the number of nurserymen had grown considerably with better road and rail transport, and there were dozens of small seedsmen and nurserymen in the county. Advertising was expensive and therefore erratic. For example James Brailsford announced that he was setting up as a nurseryman at Ashover, on old established nursery grounds (17 Nov. 1841). Thereafter he did not advertise. Did he prosper or did he fail? The sheer size of nursery stock is impressive. Even smaller nurseries stocked hundreds of thousands of trees, as when Robert Bromley at Wirksmoor Moor Nursery announced the sale of 400,000 forest trees 2–4 ft (0.6–1.2 m) high (21 Jan. 1824). It does not appear that any Derbyshire nurseries specialised in rare and exotic plants, but that they supplied everyday needs, with trees, fruit trees, shrubs, bulbs and bedding out plants.

Running a nursery was frequently a family affair over several generations, often involving women. The Sandys family were gardeners and nurserymen with members at Kedleston, Melbourne and Ashbourne. With a nursery near Ashbourne, in 1758–9 Charles Sandys advertised as a nurseryman, offering a large variety of fir trees, evergreens, flowering shrubs *etc.* for sale.[19] In 1760, he supplied many of the flowering shrubs for Kedleston Hall, where his brother was head gardener. Okeover's head gardener informed his employer, that from Sandys' nursery 'you may be fitted with as good plants as [you] can have in the Nurseries near London'.[20] When Charles died in 1761 his widow Anne, left with at least three young children, continued the business:

> She begs leave to assure those Gentlemen, or Ladies, who will do her the Honour to encourage her, they may depend upon her constant Endeavours to serve them in the best Manner, at the most reasonable rates.[21]

Ann Sandys ran the business successfully and by 1773 had the confidence to describe herself as 'Nursery and Seeds-woman', offering a wide range of trees, shrubs and bulbs 'which are all included in my printed catalogue.' She drew attention to the fact that: 'The situation of my Nursery being in a cold Country [county], consequently the Plants are much hardier, and will flower better than those drawn out of warmer Nurseries' (5 and 12 February and 13 November 1773) Ann died in 1793, having run a successful nursery for 25 years. She must have been a very astute business woman, having her own pew in the organ loft of Ashbourne parish church, a mark of respectability and status.[22] Her son and grandson ran a nursery at nearby Mayfield (15 September 1796; 15 July 1829).

It was inevitable that some nurserymen should decide to offer a design or planting service, following in the steps of the famous, and highly successful, George London and Henry Wise of Brompton Nursery. Thomas Ayres (1775–1825) was head gardener to Lord Scarsdale at Kedleston while his brother Richard was gardener at Shipley (14 July 1814). Thomas went on to establish a nursery business at nearby Duffield which his son Thomas (1804–38) then took over, running the firm during his father's long illness. They sold a wide variety of evergreen and deciduous flowering shrubs, fruit trees and forest trees. At the time of his death in 1825 Thomas Ayres senior was called 'Landscape Gardener' in his will.[23] Thomas junior then continued the landscape design work ambitiously advertising as:

> Landscaper Gardener, Nurseryman etc,:
>
> Solicit[ing] a continuation of that patronage he has hitherto experienced viz.
>
> In the Planning, Designing and Laying out of Parks, Lawns, Lakes, Pleasure Grounds, Parterres, Kitchen Gardens etc.
>
> The Designing and executing on the most improved Principles, Hot-houses, Green-houses, Conservatories, and every other kind of Horticultural Buildings, and The Planting, and general Management of Woods and Plantations, by Contract or otherwise. (25 May 1825)

He advertised in newspapers in Leicestershire, Birmingham and Sheffield, offering to meet possible clients for consultation. In Yorkshire and near Sheffield he had worked 'beautifying the mansions and grounds of gentlemen', with the design and planting of grounds, managing woods and planning and construction of horticulture buildings and grottos.[24] Appealing to 'new money' Thomas drew attention to his success in transplanting trees 10–20 ft (3–6 m) high 'which at once produces that immediate effect, so desirable round any new house or grounds'.[25]

As a family business, while Thomas junior concentrated on his landscape gardening practice, his brother John and Thomas (a relation) ran the nursery, which had been left to Mary Ayres, wife of Thomas senior, for her lifetime.[26] After Thomas junior died in 1838, aged just 34, his brother John sold the remaining stock and the Ayres vanish from print after just two generations (17 October 1838; 17 February 1841).

An example of a highly successful family nursery which supplied many of the roses for Victorian gardens in Derbyshire was Godwins' Collycroft Nursery, Ashbourne. William Godwin (1769–1853) established the nursery, which was flourishing by the 1820s. Archibald Godwin (1809–82) took over the business in 1847 and boasted that, with his brother at Market Drayton, he was 'one of the most extensive and successful rose growers in the Kingdom'. A 12-page catalogue was available.[27] Not satisfied with just local trade, in 1852 Godwin advertised a mail order service in Birmingham and travelled there to meet prospective clients.[28]

By 1861 Archibald Godwin was employing seven men and four boys. An excellent businessman, he offered ladies a 'splendid collection of all the leading varieties, kept in pots'. Indeed container grown plants were used extensively by Godwin for ease of transport, in what we are apt to think is a modern idea (2 May 1849; 10 July 1850; 29 June 1870) Another successful marketing strategy was a separate Rosarium and nursery, created in 1852, which adjoined Ashbourne Railway station. As reported in *White's Directory of Ashbourne* (1857), this hillside rosarium was open to all without charge. With views down over the town of Ashbourne, it was a noted and popular resort for visitors. Here Mr Godwin could display a choice selection of his rose stock to be admired, and hopefully purchased. The roses were surrounded by trees and shrubs in what must have been a very attractive site. Free annual exhibitions of roses were held in the 1850s, and Mr Godwin's 1865 advertisements in the *Mercury* were directed at 'visitors to Ashborne and Dove Dale', suggesting that they might like to view the Rosarium where the best sorts of roses were kept in pots for easy transit, close to the railway station.[29]

By the 1870s Archibald Godwin's sons, Archibald and John, had joined the business, now Godwin and Sons, and the firm also appealed to the lower end of the market:

> cheap plants for bedding and window decoration … [which] are very healthy and fine and will be sold 10 per cent cheaper than they can be bought at Derby or elsewhere, and delivered FREE OF CARRIAGE in quantities. (1 May 1872)

In 1879 sheds and a greenhouse were seriously damaged by a fire started by the overheating of a fire needed to protect the plants from frost. The Godwins were not insured – a reminder of one of the many hazards of running a nursery business.[30] By 1890 the business was in other hands.

The Coolings, father and son, built up a respected family business in Derby by the 1870s, but competition and lack of financial acumen led to failure, another illustration of just how risky the nursery trade could be. Edwin

Cooling, Nurseryman, Seedsman and Florist, specialised in greenhouse and bedding-out plants of 'beautiful luxuriance' (28 April 1841). He bred the bright colours loved by the Victorians, including verbenas, petunias, heliotropes, geraniums, fuchsias, lobelias, ageratums, salvias and calceolarias, which he sold at his nursery and Derby market. By the 1860s his stock extended to include ornamental trees, rhododendrons, fruit trees and roses and his 1868 catalogue offered 'Rosariums laid out and planted on advantageous terms'. With over 30 years' experience 'in the Art of Landscape Gardening' Cooling was 'very happy to undertake the laying out and planting of New Grounds, by contract or otherwise, also the erection and furnishing of every description of Horticultural Buildings.' These he could stock with 'collections of plants to produce an effect at once, on very liberal terms.'[31]

When Cooling died in 1885 it was immediately apparent that his financial liabilities almost equalled his assets of £4129. Edwin Cooling junior tried to protect the estate to provide for his step-mother and sister, paying off creditors bit by bit for three years and was partially successful. However the unfortunate man seems to have been out of his depth 'the clerical work and business was rather beyond him'. In 1888 and 1889 the court agreed that Cooling junior appeared to be an honest man, who 'acted in perfect good faith' but had not been prudent, just over-optimistic in thinking that he could salvage an income for the family, particularly when trade had been poor for 12 months. It sounds as if the position was impossible given that the greenhouses were so dilapidated that they had to be rebuilt and the grounds restocked, for which he used up his own capital (16 May 1888; 13 November 1889). Cooling hung on for a while, exhibiting at local floral shows but finally had to sell.

Joseph Yates (1735–86) was head gardener at Foremark Hall.[32] He resigned in 1763 to take over his uncle's nursery business in Derby, as gardener, seedsman and nurseryman.[33] On Yates' death in 1786 his sister Lydia Yates announced that, as sole executor, she intended to continue the Derby nursery and seed business with a Joseph Wilson (30 November 1786). Wilson (d. 1830), or his son, another Joseph (1791–1832), gained a reputation for not only selling, but also for setting out plants in the landscape. 'Wilson' laid out and planted a new winding hilly walk at the Heights of Abraham, Matlock Bath (23 July 1818). When Wood Villa, Uttoxeter was advertised to let in 1824, it boasted 'Pleasure grounds tastefully laid out by Wilson' (4 February 1824). A skilled nurseryman, he advertised 500 pineapple plants for sale in 1825 (31 August 1825). These were difficult and expensive to grow, so this was also a statement of professional skill.

After Joseph Wilson senior's death his wife Mary and sons continued the nursery business as 'Joseph, Joshua and Thomas Wilson', usually referred to as 'Messrs Wilson'. Joseph junior died in 1832 and in August 1838 Mary Wilson sold the business to her son William (1791–1841), his wife Mary and William Sadler (8 Aug. 1838). This prompted Joshua Wilson to branch out on his own, with ambitious aspirations as 'Landscape and Ornamental Gardener', announcing that:

Joshua Wilson Nursery and Seeds-man, and Landscape Gardener, Green Lane, Derby [thanked past customers] ... for the extensive and liberal patronage with which his Mother, Brothers and Sisters, and himself, have been honoured during the superintendence of the old-established concern, since the decease of his father.

With 13 years' experience he was extending his own gardening business to include:

Grounds laid out in the most approved modern style – combining the artificial in conformity with the natural beauties of the situation. All kinds of garden Architecture, as Vineries, Greenhouses, Stoves, Alcoves, Verandas, Trellis-work Grottoes etc. tastefully designed on the most improved principles. Ground-work and Planting executed on the most reasonable terms... (29 Aug. 1838)

This was rather ambitious and he may not have been successful as the following year Joshua was advertising more prosaically as a seed merchant in St Peter's Street, Derby (25 March 1839). At some period he went into partnership with Nathaniel Bryan, a shiftless character who ended up in court for debt in 1850, when it was noted that his numerous previous employments included 'for a short time ... carrying on business in co-partnership with one Joshua Wilson as Nurserymen and Landscape Gardeners'. Bryan's many other jobs including junk dealer, assistant superintendent at a lunatic asylum, commercial traveller, licensed victualler, farmer, game keeper but more frequently out of work. Any partnership with such a feckless, but persuasive man inevitably must have ended in tears.[34]

However, returning to the main firm, William Wilson died in 1841 as a 'highly respected' nurseryman and his widow Mary moved out of the business leaving it to their business partner William Sadler.[35] Sadler then ran the business with his son-in-law, Joseph Wilson (16 November 1842). The firm of Wilson and Sadler seems to have lurched from crisis to crisis until in 1849 there was complete financial collapse of 'one of the oldest established concerns in the Midland Counties', with the sale of the entire nursery stock of all remaining nursery grounds and shop fixtures (19 September, 24 October 1849). Upon which Joseph Wilson (1827–56), rather rashly announced that he had purchased the stock and business formerly carried on by his grandfather, and lately by Mr W. F. Sadler.[36] Within 2 years the business was sold again.

William Henry Holmes (1783–1855), nurseryman and florist of Sudbury, was a man of true Victorian enterprise and respectability. His first career was as 'Music and Drawing Master' and, with the patronage of the Vernons of Sudbury Hall, he organised a very successful annual subscription concert and ball at Uttoxeter between 1818 and 1830. In 1824 he was joined by his eldest son, also William Henry Holmes (1812–85), a musical prodigy who became a Professor of Music at the Royal Academy of Music at the age of 21 and, later, a nationally known pianist. Holmes senior became Clerk to the Trustees of the Ashbourne–Sudbury Toll Road from 1836 to 1854 and was clearly a pillar of local society.

It appears that Mr Holmes decided to set up a small nursery business while continuing to teach musical pupils and singing at local concerts.[37] In 1835 he advertised for a manager for his 'small Florist and Nursery Establishment', suitable for a single young man of 'steady habits and content with moderate wages'.[38] By 1837 he advertised as Nurseryman and Florist, but significantly stressed that he bought in the plants 'from several first-rate florists'.[39] The next year he advertised that he had on show all the latest varieties exhibited at the 'Metropolitan Flower Shows', which he had visited to select the newest plants: the 1830s equivalent of the influence of the modern Chelsea Flower Show.[40]

Since Mr Holmes was exhibiting successfully at local shows by 1840, including a prize at the Birmingham Dahlia Exhibition, he must have had a sound knowledge of plants well before this.[41] The most likely explanation is that his father James was the 'Mr Holmes' who won prizes at the Derby Florists' Feasts in the 1790s.[42]

From 1837 Mr Holmes opened his gardens at Sudbury for visitors to stroll around, and see flowers in bloom, which could be purchased from the nursery. His specialities were carnations and dahlias, with fashionably brightly coloured flowers such as pansies, mimulus, geraniums, petunias, salvias and calceolarias, all for sale in the adjoining nursery.[43] Quickly the *Derby Mercury* gave him editorial space, such as:

> [Mr Holmes] had a brilliant assemblage of Company on Saturday last at his show of carnations and picotees. The Gardens (which are now in high beauty) were crowded with persons of rank and fashion. (14 Aug.1839)

Then, in an adroit move, Mr Holmes persuaded Queen Adelaide, who lived at Sudbury Hall from 1840–43, to become the patron of his nursery, thereby allowing him to put the royal coat of arms at the top of his advertisements. This also gave him the excuse to celebrate her birthday and to attract the local gentry to his gardens. On 17 August 1842 the *Derby Mercury* reported:

> Festoons of dahlias and laurel were hung from a semi-circular line of pillar roses, facing the public road. The words 'Long live Queen Adelaide' were formed with dahlias, and placed along the front of Mr Holmes's house, and had a very pleasing effect. A rustic temple in one of the gardens was covered with dahlias, and made the building appear to be formed entirely of flowers … and a military band played at intervals… In the evening the gardens were beautifully illuminated with variegated lamps and were thronged with visitors.

The same summer he extended his show of flowers to include roses and in 1842 introduced a 'Grand Dahlia Show', offering handsome prizes for exhibitors who had to be 'amateur growers and Gentlemen's Gardeners only'. There was an entrance charge of 7s 6d (37p) for exhibitors and 1s (5p) for the general public (31 Aug. 1842). Then he offered a prize of a silver cup worth 10 guineas 'to be competed for by those Persons (or their Gardeners) who have purchased Dahlias this year from W. H. Holmes' (6 September 1843). His next coup was to obtain the patronage of Queen Victoria and Prince Albert in 1844, allowing him to celebrate three royal birthdays each year and to display three royal names with the Royal Coat of Arms above his advertisements.

In 1842 a military band played with free entry to the gardens, so presumably this venture paid for itself by extra publicity and sales. By 1846 the nursery had been in business for nine years and W. H. Holmes, 'Landscape Gardener, Nurseryman and Florist', felt it was time for a more sophisticated musical entertainment. So his loyal celebration of Prince Albert's birthday in August was dignified by an afternoon piano recital by Professor W. H. Holmes (his son) on 'one of Messrs Broadwood's New Repetition Grand Piano Fortes' (26 August 1846). The next celebration in August 1847 was described by the *Derby Mercury* in words which must have gratified Mr Holmes and done wonders for his business:

FIGURE 152. Sudbury churchyard, gravestones of William Holmes and his family.

> [the gardens] were crowded with fashionable company ... the village bells rang merily[sic] through the day. In the afternoon a delightful concert was given in the open air, and was a great musical treat...Between the instrumental pieces Mr Holmes senr. sang several fine tunes (8 September 1847)

These Horticultural Fetes gained wider recognition and lengthy enthusiastic reports of one in August 1848 give a glimpse of what the 300 visitors found.

> The ornamental parts of the grounds were laid out in grass terraces, and in box and gravel terraces geometrically disposed, and the curiosity of the visitors was attracted by a remarkably beautiful specimen of artificial ruins. This was constructed by Mr Holmes from fragments of the windows and other parts of a church which was taken down in the neighbourhood some time ago ... and being placed in a favourable site forms a highly picturesque and interesting object. (6 September 1848)

Today we might not enthuse quite so much about the very bright colours of the flowers including a 'gorgeous company of dwarf antirhinums which absolutely fatigued the eye with the contrasts of their colours'.

It may have been the death of his wife and a daughter in 1853 that led Mr Holmes to retire. By then he was over 70 and rather ominously a notice appeared in the *Mercury* which suggests that Holmes was in debt. He died in March 1855 and with him the nursery business at Sudbury.[44]

More nurserymen/landscape gardeners

Thomas Ayres and Joseph Wilson were not alone in offering landscaping services. John Parry, foreman to William Emes, became a partner with George Rogers, 'Nurseyman, Seedman and Gardener', in 1789. He offered to design and layout pleasure grounds and plantations, with 'his long and extensive experience in ornamental improvements'.[45] More ambitious were the multi-tasking claims of T. Baynton of Heanor:

> lays out Villa Grounds, Parks, Lawns, Water and Approaches in the newest taste. Planting done to give immediate effect to Home and Park Scenery, Designs furnished

for Gardens, Horticultural and Rural Buildings, and for Draining, Irrigating, and improving Domains Lands.

Undertakes the general Management of Woods, Plantations, Roads, Rail-Roads, Canals, Ornamental and useful Hydraulic Devices…

N.B. Analysis of Soils and Manures, with directions for the improvement of steril Lands. (4 March 1829)

James Jackson, 'Landscape Gardener and Ornamental Ground workman', purchased Wilson and Sadler's business in 1851 (30 April 1851). By now the term 'landscape gardener' appears to have been used more loosely, for Mr Jackson (1807–*c.*1860) was a nurseryman who had spent 25 years as an ornamental planter, and invited people to inspect the quality of his work by visiting:

his MODEL GARDENS at the Spa [Derby] where every description of Geometrical Flower Gardens etc. may be seen... His system will be found to combine great utility with strict economy… Gardens laid out, and kept in repair, by the day, the month or the year. (7 May 1851)

Perhaps it was 'landscape gardeners' like Jackson, with their fussy 'geometrical flower gardens', who were in the mind of the author of a newspaper article in 1851 about Haddon Hall, the harmony of whose gardens layout he compared with the

too common practice of … setting a landscape gardener or a nurseryman to surround [a house] with twisted gravel walks and clumps of shrubs, arranged without the slightest reference to the lines, colour or expression of the building. (3 September 1851)

More successful was Edward Speed (1834–92) a Cambridgeshire man who became a gardener, after a spell as wine merchant and nurseryman. By 1868 he had a hollyhock named after him – 'French white with deep purple'.[46] His elder brother Thomas (1831–82) was head gardener at Chatsworth from 1868, and it was probably he who secured an important commission for Edward, to lay out the new pavilion gardens at Matlock Spa in 1882–84. Uniformly enthusiastic accounts in local newspapers agree that Edward Speed was a very talented and imaginative man who transformed a rocky, bare precipitous hill-side into an attractive series of immense terraces, with clever planting, seats, fish ponds, grottos and views (see Fig. 124). Gaining confidence as work progressed Speed also designed an Italianate ticket office at the entrance.[47] By 1890 he was noted as the 'well known landscape gardener at Matlock Bath', became a pillar of the community as Surveyor of the Local Government Board and died 'a much respected inhabitant of Matlock Bath.'[48] He was also a publican at the Old Vaults on North Parade in Matlock, from at least 1890, an occupation he shared with another brother.[49]

Of course interesting as they are, none of these can compete with the brilliant William Barron (*qv*), landscape gardener and nurseryman, for whom there is, as yet, no biography.

Notes

1.   D. Riden (ed.), 'The Autobiography of Leonard Wheatcroft of Ashover, 1627–1706' in *A Seventeenth-Century Scarsdale Miscellany*, Derbyshire Record Society 10 (1993), 84, 88–89, 93, 94.

2.   DRO: D1881/BoxD/15. Copy letter book of Rev Thomas Calton, Vicar of Duffield *c*.1717–25. n/d but the next letter refers to the death of Sir John Curzon (1727).

3.   *DM*, 29 Aug. 1838, 3; 23 Nov. 1853, 2; 4 March 1863, 4.

4.   *DTCH*, 24 Jan. 1891, 5ff., 'Death of the Chesterfield Centenarian'.

5.   *DM*, 5 July 1792, 1; 27 Aug. 1812, 1; 12 Aug. 1835, 3; 29 May 1839, 3; 25 July 1849, 2.

6.   *DM*, 8 April 1768, 4; 10 Feb. 1803, 1; 12 Dec. 1832, 3; 16 Feb. 1842, 2; 20 Nov. 1850, 2.

7.   DRO: D3155-WH 1780 – loose papers; Robert Wilmot to Robert Garner, 11 Sept. 1769.

8.   *DTCH*, 31 Jan. 1885, 9.

9.   *Sheffield Independent*, 17 Aug. 1839, 5; 13 Sept. 1856, 5 (obituary). Information from Sue Gregory, who notes that a Thomas McLaren was born in 1798 at Blair Atholl.

10. O. Sitwell, *Two Generations* (1940), 63.

11. DRO: 231M/E4682 Thomas Green to Leake Okeover, Oct. 1750.

12. Autobiography of Leonard Wheatcroft, 88, 93.

13. J. Harvey, *Early Gardening Catalogues* (1972), 30; *Early Nurserymen* (1974), 95; Brunton Forbes of Perry Hill, nr Birmingham advertised in the *DM*, 5 Feb. 1789, 1. K. Clark, 'What the Nurserymen did for us: the roles and influence of the nursery trade on the landscapes and gardens of the eighteenth century', *Garden History* 40 (2012), 17–33.

14. *Manchester Mercury*, 30 April 1754, 4; 8 March 1768, 1; 15 Feb. 1774, 4; 2 Dec. 1777, 3; 26 Feb. 1782, 1; 16 Aug. 1785, 4.

15. DRO: D5054/13/2, the rental Account Book for Burdett estates 1741–60; entries 13 July 1742; 25 Sept. 1749; 4 Aug. and 15 Oct. 1753. D5054/13/9 entries 11 Feb. and 29 July 1761.

16. *Aris's Birmingham Gazette*, 19 March 1744. There were similar sales of private collections of tulips over the years: *DM*, 26 April 1776, 4; 7 May 1828, 3; 31 Mar. 1830, 1; 22 May 1833, 3.

17. *DM*, 2 May 1746; 17 April 1747 ;15 April 1748; 28 April 1749; 19 Sept. 1755; 11 Sept. 1761; 23 Oct. 1778.

18. *DM*, 5 Oct. 1825, 2; 19 Oct. 1831, 2; 20 Nov. 1833, 2; 10 Sept. 1834, 2; 4 Nov. 1835, 2; 7 Dec. 1836, 2; 20 Sept. 1837, 3; 27 Sept. 1837, 2; 11 and 25 Oct. 1837, 2; 1 Nov.1837, 2; *etc.*

19. *DM*, 27 Oct. 1758, 4; 26 Oct; 2 and 24 Nov. 1759, 4.

20. DRO: 231/M/E/4836. Martin Leggett, head gardener to Leake Okeover, 28 Jan. 1761.

21. *DM*, 28 Aug. and 4 Sept. 1761, 4. Anne had six children between 1754 and 1761: John (1754); John (1755–96) – the first son must have died; William (1757), who became a gardener; Ann (1757 – alive 1793); Charles (1759); and Charlotte (1761). My thanks to Sue Gregory for compiling a Sandys family tree.

22. Lichfield Joint RO: LRO B/C11 1793 Will of Ann Sandys. I thank Sue Gregory for this reference. For a fuller account of Ann Sandys and other nurserywomen see D. Barre, 'Entertaining Women: shaping the business of gardening in the Midlands' in M.

Dick and E. Mitchell (eds) *Landscape and Green Spaces: Gardens and Garden History in the West Midlands* (2017).

23. LJRO B/C11/1825 will of Thomas Ayres, 'Landscape Gardener', 28 June 1825. Probate was granted for £600: information kindly supplied by Sue Gregory.

24. *DM*, 29 Oct. 1828, 3; 26 Oct. 1831, 3; 20 March 1833, 3. *Birmingham Gazette*, 29 Nov. 1830, 3; 7 March 1831, 1. *Sheffield Independent*, 1829–30; *Leicester Journal*, 13 Sept. 1833, 1.

25. *Sheffield Independent*, 18 Sept. 1830, 1.

26. S. Glover, *Directory of the County of Derbyshire* (1829), 65, lists Thomas as ornamental gardener, and Thomas and John as nurserymen and seedsmen. Mary described herself as 'Mary Ayres, Gardener' *DM*, 22, April 1835.

27. *DM*, 20 Oct. 1847, 2; *Staffordshire Advertiser*, 6 Nov. 1847, 1.

28. *Aris's Birmingham Gazette*, 11 Oct. 1852, 2; 7 Feb. 1853, 3.

29. *DM*, 29 June, 1853, 3; 6 July 1859, 4; 28 June 1865, 4; 29 June 1870, 4. The 1882 OS map suggests a formal layout with hillside terraces.

30. *Staffordshire Sentinel and Commercial & General Advertiser*, 11 Jan. 1879, 5.

31. DRO: D773 Catalogue of Edwin Cooling, Mile Ash Nurseries, 1868.

32. DRO: D5054/13/15/1 Burdett account book, entries 1739–61; D5054/13/9 Sir Robert's Account book – Yates was paid £31 10s including board wages when he left in 1762.

33. *DM*, 1 Feb. 1763, 4; LJRO B/C/11 Will of William Hodgkinson, 10 Feb. 1763. He died unmarried and left over £800 in cash bequests to family members plus property.

34. www.londongazetter.co.uk/issues/21122/pages/2129. Accessed 2014.

35. *Leicester Chronicle*, 14 May 1841, 3.

36. Joseph Wilson 'formerly of Derby, nurseryman' died at Sydenham (*DM*, 27 Feb. 1856, 5); W. F. Sadler died early in 1850 (*DM*, 29 March 1850, 2).

37. for example *DM*, 15 April 1835, 3; Pigot's *Commercial Directory for Derbyshire* (1835) lists William Henry Holmes as teacher of music and organist, but this was probably Holmes Junior.

38. *Staffordshire Advertiser*, 19 Dec. 1835, 2.

39. *Staffordshire Advertiser*, 13 May 1837, 2; *DM*, 31 May and 16 Aug. 1837, 3.

40. *Staffordshire Advertiser*, 14 April 1838, 2; 25 May 1839, 1.

41. *Aris' Birmingham Gazette*, 5 Oct. 1840, 1.

42. My thanks to Sue Gregory for the information that William Henry Holmes was the son of James and Sarah who married 19 March 1782 at All Saints Derby. He was baptised at St Werburgh's Derby 1 April 1783.

43. *Staffordshire Gazette and County Standard*, 21 Sept. 1839, 2; 10 Oct. 1840, 2; *DM*, 31 May and 16 Aug. 1837, 3; 11 April 1838, 3; 30 May 1838, 3; *Staffordshire Advertiser*, 14 April 1838, 2; 25 Aug. 1838, 2; 12 June 1839 *etc.*

44. *DM*, 10 and 23 Aug. 1853; 26 April 1854; 19 July 1854, 1.

45. *Chester Chronicle*, 25 Dec. 1789, 1. He was based at Llafdulas and Rogers was based at Chester.

46. *Lloyds Weekly Newspaper*, 18 Oct. 1868, 11.

47. *DTCH*, 10 May 1884, 6; 13 Sept. 1884, 3; 2 Aug. 1884, 6; 12 Jan. 1895, 6; *Leeds Mercury*, 29 July 1884, 8.

48. *DTCH*, 13 Dec. 1890, 6. Obituary 14 May 1892, 8.

49. *DDT*, 13 Nov. 1890 – application for licence of Old Vaults, Matlock. I am grateful to Sue Gregory for providing information from the censuses.

Three Modern Gardens

Travelling around Derbyshire researching for this book it was a delight to see ongoing restoration and enhancement of gardens in the spirit of the originals. Although outside the time-scale set for the book, three modern gardens in particular reflect earlier influences.

The Burrows was developed by the late Craig Dalton with 'Garden Rooms' as separate areas of interest, with hidden surprises and variety of shapes, plants and trees, colours and atmosphere. The whole is pulled together by a skilful use of vistas, statues and wrought ironwork. A high-point is the enclosed 'Italian' white garden with its wide central walk culminating in the Tuscan temple, which reflects in a pool. Happily this garden cannot be pinned down to any one style.

At **Thornbridge**, the Harrisons have created a 'Scented Garden' in tune with the other sections of the gardens, blending in, yet self-contained and complementing the Orangery and greenhouse.

The brilliant work of Mr and Mrs Gerrish at **Herbert Lodge**, **Bonsall** seemed an appropriate conclusion to this work. I visited in search of a mid-nineteenth-century tufa rock arch which had been transferred there from the gardens of

FIGURE 153. The Burrows Gardens, the Roman white garden created in 2005 by Craig Dalton and Julian Dowle.

COURTESY MRS N. DALTON

FIGURE 154. Thornbridge Hall, the Scented Garden Terrace created in 2011.

COURTESY J. AND E. HARRISON

Mill Hill House in Derby, when that house was demolished.[1] I did indeed find a tufa arch which was an entrance to a rockwork passage which wound its way across the garden. I confess to being fooled into thinking that all this was an original feature and only a small, circular rock fernery leading off it, caused some doubt. In fact, not only was the rockwork passage and archway new, but the hillside garden itself was newly created as a modern interpretation of a classical formal garden, combined in true eighteenth-century spirit with informal woodland walks.

Attached to the house itself is a grotto summer house with a little cascade next to it. Only rockwork 'crenellation' above it, and the entrance arch (not quite gothic and not quite classical), suggest that it is not as old as first seems. Inside, the spirit of original grotto builders has been followed, with colourful decorative shell work and mottos (Pl. 37). Beyond the grotto a path winds up behind the house to a formal long terrace walk, approached under a wrought iron arch. The eye-catcher at the end is an open classical temple, whose rear wall facing the viewer has a *trompe l'oeil* scene with classical obelisks and a rotonda. One side wall has a delightfully whimsical painted interpretation of the garden itself. At the centre of the terrace steps lead to another grotto, this time built on a curve with a large central opening and side entrances, again made from rubble stone with dressed quoins, a mixture of classical and rustic gothic, and the focal point of the garden. The Mill House tufa had been incorporated seamlessly here. Above this, and across the garden, is the rockwork open tunnel, with huge blocks of stone.[2]

Work was still in progress on the upper levels (2013), but an eighteenth-century style statue of a huntsman with his dog, placed among the trees, suggested that there were yet more interesting interpretations to follow as the garden develops. On the other side of the house a classical garden room had been created, with urns, statue and a pool with steps and terracing dictated by different level of the site. In short this is a truly imaginative new garden, whose details are influenced by the eighteenth century but which has an independently modern feel. As work in progress continues, the gardens at Herbert Lodge promise to be ever more enticing.

Notes

1.   *Derbyshire Life*, 29 April 2010.
2.   Mr and Mrs Gerrish worked with Andy Land to design the garden rockwork, incorporating huge stones transported from Bonsall moor.

Bibliography

Archives

Chesterfield Library
A387: William Emes's plan of Wingerworth, 1777.

Derby County Record Office
D37/M/H13: Estate map of Ford House, c.1780.

D37/11/7: Ogston correspondence, 1860.

D37MP/124: Ogston Plan and notes, Markham Nesfield, 1860s.

D77/8/17-18: Netherseal maps, 1785, 1829.

D157MT/3037: SE View of Snelston Hall by Cottingham, 1827.

D157MT/3042: Design for a Gothic Seat, Snelston Hall.

D157M/T4094: Plan of Snelston by Robert Bromley, 1824.

D216 ES1/3/12: Masson House sale particulars, 1886.

D216/ES1/3/55: Sale catalogue The Pastures, 1893.

231M /E/4682 and 4836: Okeover correspondence, 1750 and 1761.

D302/ES9: Sale particulars for Longford estate, 1920.

D302/ES26: Sale catalogue Morley, 1938.

D302 Z/ES 38: Sale catalogue Raenstor Close, 1953.

D307/1/8/16-17: Plan of proposed carriage road Hassop Hall, 1829.

D393/1: Riseley estate map, 1722.

D504/116/19: Sale catalogue Darley House, 1923.

D504/116/20: Sale catalogue Sydnope estate, 1920.

D504/116/41: Sale catalogue Parwich estate, 1915.

D504/149/2/13: Sale catalogue Snitterton, 1932.

D505/72/8: Map of Barlborough estate, 1723.

D517 Box A-7 1:1 William Emes's calculations for Shipley grounds, 1772.

D518M/E27: Elvaston account book, 1713–14.

D518M/F150: Elvaston, C18 accounts.

D518 M/F492: Plan of parterre and canal c.1700, perhaps Elvaston.

D593/2: Wingerworth sale brochure, 1920.

D773: Catalogue of Edwin Cooling, Mile Ash Nurseries, 1868.

D804/A/P1 48a: Longford tithe map, 1840.

D1039/26: Osmaston sale brochure, 1883.

D1079/11/-- Breadsall Priory estate maps: 11/1 (1790); 11/5 (1817); 11/3 (1823).

D1079/19/1-3 Breadsall Priory sale catalogues, (1860), 1884, 1897.

D1263/1/2: Lea Wood, photocopy letter from Eden Nesfield, 1875.

D1263/1/4: Lea Wood, press cutting? Dec. 1877.

D1306 A/PP1: Wingerworth estate map, 1758.

D1881/Box D/15: Letter book of Rev. Calton, Vicar of Duffield c.1717–25.

D1881 Box A: D'Ewes Coke's Sketchbook, early nineteenth century.

D1881/Box D: Eighteenth century papers, Coke family of Brookhill.

D2057 A/P1 34/88: Edward Milner's plan for the gardens, Bakewell Vicarage.

D2190/13/12: Two photos of rose terrace, Kings Newton Hall, 1924.

D2275/M/71/14: Breadsall Priory map, 1761.

D2293/1/1: Sale particulars Newton Park estate, 1836.

D2360/3/28: Matlock tithe map, 1848.

D2360/3/260a: Sudbury tithe map, 1845.

D2360/3/369: Alderwasley tithe map, 1841.

D2375/296/4: Calke estate map, 1857.

D2375M//76/122: Calke, Lady Caroline Harpur's Expenses, 1750.

D2375M/296/2: Calke estate map, 1761.

D 2535/M/19/1: Wm Emes's plan for Alderwasley, 1784.

D2554: Alfreton Park estate map, 1822.

D3155 WH1779 & 1780: Osmaston, Wilmot correspondence 1769–70.

D3249/3: Longford estate map, 1834.

D4719/7/41: Thornbridge, drawing of old hall, 1871; estate map, 1896.

4996/6/66: Photocopy of 1770s map of Elvaston gardens.

D5054/13/5/1: Burdett Accounts Book 1695–1708.

D5054/13/9: Personal Account Book of Sir Robert Burdett, 1750s/60s.

D5054/20/2: Middlebrooke's plan for garden at Foremark, 1912.

D5054/20/7: Foremark gardens working sketch, 1909.

D5054/20/12: Edward White's plan for a garden at Foremark, 1914.

D5054/22/4/series: Bills for Foremark grounds, 1913–15.

D5054/26/1: Map of prosed improvements for Foremark landscape, *c*.1737.

D5395/22/1/7/3: Sketchbook of Park Hall, 1933.

D5395/22/1/7/4: Park Hall sale brochure, 1937.

D5395/22/1/1/43: Notebook of Philip Robinson, Park Hall.

D5395/22/1/7/5: Notes on Park Hall, 1934.

D5430/12/6/1-3: Auction of Stoke Hall, 1839.

D5557/9/1: Radburne map, 1711.

D5557/9/2: William Emes's plan for Radburne, 1790.

D5780: Riseley accounts, 1681–83.

D5903/1 & 2: Sudbury estate maps 1794 and 1823.

D6104/59: Plan of The Pastures estate, 1841.

D6272/66/1: Shipley estate plan, early nineteenth century.

D6281/3/11: The Green, Eckington. Copy of Lutyens' plan, 1916.

D6430/2/8: Howard Colvin's working papers on Calke Abbey, 1980s.

D6573/Maps 135: Edward White's Plan for Sutton Scarsdale gardens, 1948.

D6573/Box104: The Green, Eckington. C. E. Mallows' plans 1914/5.

D6704/1/1: Sutton Scarsdale estate sale catalogue, 1919.

D7107/4/1: Wigwell Grange sale particulars, 1892.

D7676/Bag C/247: Hassop estate map, 1831.

D7676/Bag C/261: Joshua Major's plan for Derwent Hall gardens, 1833.

D7676/Bag C/314: Hand written poem about Holme Hall, late seventeenth century.

D7676 Bag C/307 & 309a: Sale details Derwent, 1841, 1851.

D7676 Bag/C779/23: Misc. C17 plans and drawings, Holme Hall.

Derby Local Studies Library

LSL 6303B W. Mugliston, Monody written at Matlock Bath

LSL 6303 C. W. Mugliston, A Contemplative Walk with the Author's Wife and Children in the Parks of George Morewood, Esq. at Alfreton

Lichfield Joint Record Office

LJRO B/C11/1763: Will of William Hodgkinson, 1763.

LJRO B/C11 1793: Will of Anne Sandys, 1793.

LJRO B/C11/1825: Will of Thomas Ayres, 1825.

National Gazeteer of Great Britain and Ireland (1868)

Royal Horticultural Society, Horticultural Trans. 2 (1822)

Switzer, S. Practical Kitchen Gardener (1727)

Staffordshire County Record Office

D1287/18/10 (P/831): Bridgeman letters 1789.

D(W)1733/C/3/129, 137, 143, 144, 148, 190, 290–91: Sutton Scarsdale Hall, 1775–1830s.

D1788 parcel 57: Letter June 1804 re John Webb.

D3009/2: Plan of Newton Solney, 1827.

D3272/6/4/2: Sale particulars Breadsall Priory, June 1884.

NLS 313/903 & 907: Sutherland family letters 1839 and 1843.

University of Nottingham, Manuscripts and Special Collections

Drury-Lowe: Dr E 130/44-5, 48; 165/18/23-4; 174/2; 174/38; 174/46: Contracts, letters, payments 1850s and 1890s.

Dr 4 P1/2: Map of Locko park, 1763.

Dr P 140: Plans of Locko by Architects Stevens and Robinson, 1892.

Dr P 72: Plan of the intended Park by Wm Emes, 1792.

Manvers Collection: Ma 2 P.238 Map of 'Old coats' 1659, altered 1688.

Warwickshire County Record Office (WRO)

CR136/B1419: Letter to Sir Roger Newdigate, 1705.

CR136/B/2668: Travel Journal of Mary Conyers, 1747.

CR136/B2717: Lady Hester to Sir Roger Newdigate, 1780/1.

CR 1841/7: Travel Journal of Lady Sophia Newdigate, 1747.

William Salt Library, Stafford

WSL/2/42/42 Journal of James Reading of Derby.

Staffordshire Views: J. Buckler's water colour of Hardwick New Hall (1813) *et al*. Accessed via 'Gateway to the Past' website: https://www.staffordshire.gov.uk/leisure/archives/collections/OnlineCatalogues/GatewaytothePast/home.aspx.

Printed Primary Sources

Adam, W. *Gem of the Peak* (1851; 5th edn, Derby; rep. Buxton, 1973).

F. White and Co. *A History, Gazetteer and Directory of the County of Derby* (Sheffield, 1857).

Bagshaw, W. *History, Gazetteer and Directory of Derbyshire* (Sheffield, 1846).

Barron, W. *The British Winter Garden* (London, 1852).

Bateman, C. *A Descriptive and Historical Account of Alfreton* (Alfreton, 1812).

Blomfield, R. and Inigo Thomas, F. *The Formal Garden in England* (London, 1892).

Bray, W. *A Sketch of a Tour into Derbyshire and Yorkshire.* (1778; ECCO print edition).

Britton, J. and Brayley, E. W. *The Beauties of England and Wales, or, Delineations, Topographical, Historical, and Descriptive, of each County*, vol. 3 (London, 1802).

Broadley, A. M. (ed.) *Doctor Johnson and Mrs Thrale , including Mrs Thrale's Journal of a Welsh Tour made in 1774* (London, 1910).

Byng, J. *The Torrington Diaries* vol. 2, ed. C. Bruyn Andrews (1935; USA, 1970 edn).

Chesterfield, Lord *Letters of Philip, 2nd Earl of Chesterfield to Several Celebrated Individuals* (London, 1835).

Cibber, T. and Shiels, R. *Lives of the Poets of Great Britain and Ireland,* vol. 2 (London, 1753).

Cotton, C. *The Wonders of the Peake* (2nd edn 1683, ECCO print edition).

Cunningham, P. *Chatsworth or the Genius of England's Prophecy* (Chesterfield, 1783).

Deacon, D. Jnr. *Poems* (London, 1790, ECCO print edition 2011).

Defoe, D. *A Tour Through the Whole Island of Great Britain* (1724), eds P. N. Furbank, W. R. Owens and A. J. Coulson (New Haven and London, 1991).

Durant, D. and Riden, P. (eds) *The Building of Hardwick Hall, part 2: The New Hall, 1591–98* (Chesterfield, 1984).

Fane, W. D. (ed.) The Coke Papers at Melbourne Hall, *Derbyshire Archaeological and Natural History Society* 11 (1889), 54–67.

Farey, J. *General View of the Agriculture and Minerals of Derbyshire,* vol. 2 (1815; repr. General Books USA, 2010).

Furness, R. *Medicus-Magus A Poem in Three Cantos* (Sheffield, 1836).

Gaunt, R. A. (ed.) *Unhappy Reactionary: The Diaries of the 4th Duke of Newcastle-under-Lyme, 1822–50.* Thoroton Society Record Series 43 (Nottingham, 2003).

Gibbs, J. *Book of Architecture, Containing Designs of Buildings and Ornaments* (London, 1728).

Gilpin, W. S. *Practical Hints upon Landscape Gardening* (2nd edn, London, 1835).

Glover, S. and Noble, T. *The History, Gazeteer and Directory of the County of Derby, Pt II* (Derby, 1829).

Hardinge, N. Knoll Hills, written in 1735, in *Poems, Latin, Greek and English: to which is added an historical Enquiry and Essay* (1818; Google e-book).

Historical Manuscripts Commission, 12th Report, Appendix. Pt III, *MSS of the Earl Cowper, preserved at Melbourne House*, vol. 3 (1889).

Historical Manuscripts Commission, MSS of Rye and Hereford Corporations, 13th Report, App. IV, appendix E (1892), letter, Rev. John Nixon to Miss Mary Bacon, Sept. 1745.

Hobbes, T. *The Moral and Political Works of Thomas Hobbes of Malmesbury* (London 1750). Accessed via www.openlibrary.org.

Jewitt, A. (ed.) *The Northern Star*, or *Yorkshire Magazine* vol. 1, (July 1817), 95

Jewitt, L. *Illustrated Guide to Haddon Hall* (London, 1871).

Jewitt, L. (ed.) *Black's 1872 Tourist's Guide to Derbyshire,* (Edinburgh 1872; rep. Bakewell 1999).

Johnson, S. *The Letters of Samuel Johnson*, vols 1 and 2 ed. R. W. Chapman (Oxford, 1952).

Kelly's Directory of the Counties of Derby, Notts, Leicester and Rutland (London, 1891).

Kemp, E. *How to Lay Out a Garden* (3rd edn, London, 1864).

Kerry, C. The Autobiography of Leonard Wheatcroft, *Journal of Derbyshire Archaeological and Natural History Society* 21 (1899), 26–60.

Kip, J. and Knyff, L. *Britannia Illustrata or views of Several of the Queens Palaces also of the Principal Seats of the Nobility and Gentry of England* (London, 1707).

Langley, B. *New Principles of Gardening* (London, 1728).

Lawson, W. *A New Orchard and Garden* (1618; fascimile of 1635 edn, Totnes, 2003).

Lees, K. Maddocks R. and Southall, S. *Extracts from the Personal Diary Between the Years 1817–1862 of Edward Walhouse Littleton, Afterwards the First Lord Hatherton 1791–1863* (Trowbridge, 2003).

Levey, S. A. and Thornton, P. K. (eds) *Of Household Stuff: the 1601 Inventories of Bess of Hardwick* (London, 2001).

Llanover Lady (ed.) *The Autobiography and Correspondence of Mrs Delany*, vol. 1. (2nd ser., London, 1862; revised S. Chauncey Woolsey, Boston, 1879).

Loudon, J. C. *Encylopaedia of Gardening* (London, 1822).

Loudon, J. C. Recollections of a Tour made in May, 1839, *Gardener's Magazine* n.s. 5 (1839), 458–60.

Loudon J. C. (ed.) *The Landscape Gardening and Landscape Architecture of the Late Humphrey Repton* (1840; reprint 2012).

Loudon, J. *Plain Instructions in Gardening* (11th edn, London, 1874).

Lysons, D. and Lysons, S. *Magna Britannia, Being a Concise Topographical Account of the Several Counties of Great Britain,* vol. 5 (London, 1817).

Macky, J. *A Journey Through England,* vol. 2 (2nd edn, London, 1724).

Major, J. *The Theory and Practice of Landscape Gardening* (Leeds, 1852).

Markham, S. *John Loveday of Caversham 1711–1789: The Life and Tours of an C18 Onlooker* (Salisbury, 1984).

Mason, W. *The English Garden A Poem in Four Books,* Book 3, ed. W. Burgh (London, 1783).

Mawson, T. H. *The Art and Craft of Garden Making* (4th edn, London, 1912).

Milner, H. E. *The Art and Practice of Landscape Gardening* (London, 1890).

Morris, C. (ed.) *The Journeys of Celia Fiennes* (London, 1947).

Morris, C. (ed.) *The Illustrated Journeys of Celia Fiennes 1685–c.1712* (London, 1982).

Neale, J. P. *Views of the Seats of Noblemen and Gentlemen,* vol. 6 (London, 1823).

Patching, R. *Four Topographical Letters, Written in July 1755, Upon a Journey thro Bedfordshire, Northamptonshire, Leicestershire, Nottinghamshire Derbyshire, Warwickshire etc.* (London, 1757, ECCO print edition).

Pigot's Commercial Directory for Derbyshire (London, 1835).

Pilkington, J. *A View of the Present State of Derbyshire,* vol. 1 (London, 1789).

Pococke, R. *The Travels Through England of Dr Richard Pococke during 1750, 1751 and later years,* ed. J. J. Cartwright. Camden Society 42 (London, 1888).

Radburne Garden Accounts, 1697–98 in *Derbyshire Miscellany* 1(i) (1956); 2(vii) (1961/2).

Rayner, S. *The History and Antiquities of Haddon Hall Illustrated by 32 Highly Finished Drawings with an Account of the Hall in its Present State* (1836). Transcribed by D. Trutt. Accessed via www.haddon-hall.com.

Repton, H. *Fragments on the Theory and Practice of Landscape Gardening* (London, 1816).

Riden, D. (ed.) 'The autobiography of Leonard Wheatcroft of Ashover, 1627–1706', in *A Seventeenth-Century Scarsdale Miscellany.* Derbyshire Record Society 20 (Derby, 1993).

Seward, A. *Letters of Anna Seward, Written Between the years 1784 and 1807,* 6 vols (Edinburgh, 1811).

Simpson, R. *A Collection of Fragments Illustrative of the History and Antiquities of Derby* (Derby, 1826).

Sitwell, Sir G. *An Essay on the Making of Gardens* (London, 1909).

Shaw, S. *History and Antiquities of Staffordshire,* vol. I (London, 1798).

Switzer, S. *Ichnographia Rustica: or, The Nobleman, Gentleman, and Gardener's Recreation,* vols 1 and 2 (London, 1718).

The Gentleman's Magazine 14 (1744), Poem on Lady Curzon's grotto.

The Matlock Tourist and Guide Through the Peak (Matlock, 1838).

The Topographer, nos 10 (January 1790), 39–40; 18 (September 1790).

Watson, W. *A Delineation of the Strata of Derbyshire* (Sheffield, 1811).

Winthrop Sargent, H. *Skeleton Tours through England, Scotland and Ireland, Wales ... with some of the Principal Things to see, Especially Country Houses* (New York, 1871).

Woolley, W. *History of Derbyshire* (1712), (eds) C. Glover and P. Riden, Derbyshire Record Society 6 (Derby, 1981).

Young, A. *The Farmer's Tour Through the East of England,* vol. I (London, 1771).

Other references

Adveno Brooke, E. *The Gardens of England* (1857).

Anon. *Kedleston Hall Guidebook* (Swindon, 2010).

Armstrong, P. *The English Parson-Naturalist: A Companionship between Science and Religion* (Leominster, 2000).

Ashbourne Local History Group, *A Georgian Country Town Ashbourne, 1725–1825,* vol. 2, Architecture (Nottingham, 1991).

Barnatt J. and Williamson, T. *Chatsworth, A Landscape History* (Macclesfield, 2005).

Barre, D. Entertaining women: shaping the business of gardening in the Midlands. In M. Dick and E. Mitchell (eds) *Landscape and Green Spaces: Gardens and Garden History in the West Midlands* (University of Hertfordshire, forthcoming 2017).

Batey, M. *Regency Gardens* (Princes Risborough, 1995).

Beale, C. A forgotten greenhouse by Joseph Paxton: the conservatory at Hampton Court, Herefordshire, *Journal of Garden History* 30(1) (Spring 2002), 74–83.

Bennett, S. *Five Centuries of Women and Gardeners* (London, 2000).

Bickerstaffe, D. The chamber at Knowle Hill, *Grampian Speleogical Group Bulletin* 4th ser. 5(1) (Oct. 2011), 13–14. Accessed via www.gsg.org.uk.

Boniface. P. (ed.) *In Search of English Gardens: The travel journals of John Claudius Loudon and his wife Jane* (Wheathampstead, 1987).

Bradley Hole, K. *Lost Gardens of England from the Archives of Country Life* (London, 2004).

Brighton, T. Chatsworth's C16 House and Gardens, *Garden History* 23(1) (1995), 29–25.

Brighton, T. The Ashford Marble Works and Cavendish patronage, 1748–1905, *Bulletin of the Peak District Mines Historical Society* 12(6) (1995), 64.

Brogden, W. A. *Stephen Switzer, Garden Design in Britain in the Early C18* (PhD thesis, University of Edinburgh, 1973). Accessed via www.era.lib.ed.ac.uk.

Brown, J. *Gardens of a Golden Afternoon* (London, 1982; repr. Penguin Books, 1985).

Brown, J. *The Art and Architecture of English Gardens* (London, 1989).

Campbell, G. *The Hermit in the Garden, From Imperial Rome to Ornamental Grove* (Oxford, 2013).

Chandler, J. (ed.) *Travels Through Stuart Britain: The Adventures of John Taylor, the Water Poet* (Stroud, 1999).

Charlesworth, M. *The English Garden, Literary Sources and Documents*, vol. 2 (Robertsbridge, 1993).

Clark, K. What the nurserymen did for us: the roles and influence of the nursery trade on the landscapes and gardens of the eighteenth century, *Garden History* 40(1) (2012), 17–33.

Colquhoun, K. *'The Busiest Man in England', A Life of Joseph Paxton, Gardener, Architect and Victorian Visionary* (rev. edn, Boston MA, 2006).

Colvin, H. Calke Abbey, Derbyshire I, *Country Life*, 20 October 1983.

Colvin, H. *Calke Abbey, A Hidden House Revealed* (London, 1985).

Colvin, H. *A Biographical Dictionary of British Architects 1600–1830* (3rd edn, London, 1995).

Cowell, B. Hardwick Hall in the Eighteenth Century, *Georgian Group Journal* 16 (2008), 43–58.

Cox, Rev. J. C. The history of Breadsall Priory II, *Journal of Derbyshire Archaeology and Natural History* 27 (1905), 138–49.

Craddock, J. P. *Paxton's Protégé, The Milner White Landscape Gardening Dynasty* (York, 2012).

Craven, M. Willersley: An Adam Castle in Derbyshire, *Georgian Group Journal* 22 (2014), 109–22.

Craven, M. and Stanley, M. *The Derbyshire Country House*, 2 vols (Ashbourne, 2001).

Darby, M. F. Joseph Paxton's water lily. In M. Conan (ed.), *Bourgeois and Aristocratic Encounters in Garden Art,* *1550–1850* (Washington DC, 2002), 267–70. Accessed via www.doaks.org/extexts.html.M.Conan.

Daniels, S. *Humphry Repton, Landscape Gardening and the Geography of Georgian England* (New Haven CO and London, 1999).

Derbyshire County Council, *Elvaston Castle Country Park* (guidebook, n.d.).

Dixon Hunt, J. *William Kent, Landscape Garden Designer* (London, 1987).

Dixon Hunt J. and Willis, P. (eds) *The Genius of the Place: The English Landscape Garden 1620–1820* (London, 1975).

Drury, P. *Bolsover Castle*, English Heritage guidebook (Swindon, 2014).

Edwards, D. G. *The Hunlokes of Wingerworth Hall*, (2nd edn, Chesterfield, 1976).

Edwards, P. The gardens at Wroxton Abbey Oxfordshire, *Garden History* 14(2) (1986), 50–60.

Elliott, B. *Victorian Gardens* (London, 1986).

Elliott, B. From arboretum to the woodland garden, *Garden History* 35 suppl. 2 (2007), 71–83.

Elliott, P., Watkins, C. and Daniels, S. William Barron (1805–91) and C19 British Arboriculture, *Garden History* 35 suppl. 2 (2007), 129–48.

English Heritage, *Durability Guaranteed: Pulhamite rockwork – its conservation and repair* (2008). Accessed via www.historicengland.org.uk/durability guaranteed.

Evans, S. R. *Masters of their Craft: The Art, Architecture and Garden Design of the Nesfields* (Cambridge, 2014).

Eyres, P. (ed.) The Blackamoor and the Georgian garden, *New Arcadian Journal* 69/70 (2011), 52–62.

Faulkner, P. A. *Bolsover Castle*. English Heritage Guidebook (London, 1972).

Fellows, R. A. *Sir Reginald Blomfield, An Edwardian Architect* (London, 1985).

Francis, J. 'My Little Gardine at Dassett Paled'. Sir Thomas Temple and his garden at Burton Dassett in Warwickshire, *c*.1630, *Garden History* 41(1) (2013), 21–30.

Gent, N. D. *Patterns and Shapes of the Pinxton China Factory, 1796–1813* (Pinxton, Notts., 1996).

Girouard, M. *Robert Smythson and the Elizabethan Country House* (New Haven CO and London, 1983).

Girouard, M. Early drawings of Bolsover Castle, *Architectural History* 27 (1984), 510–18.

Girouard, M. *Hardwick Hall*. National Trust Guidebook (London, reprint 1996).

Gomme, A. *Smith of Warwick* (Stamford, 2000).

Hagglund, E. Cassandra Willoughby's visits to country houses, *Georgian Journal* 11 (2001), 185–202.

Harris, E. and Laing, A. No fishy tale: a true account of the Fishing Room at Kedleston, *Apollo* 1 (2006). Accessed via www.freelibrary.com>Arts,visualand performing>Apollo>April 1, 2006.

Harris, J. *William Talman* (London, 1982).

Harris, J. The Duchess of Beaufort's observations on places, *Georgian Group Journal* 10 (2000), 36–42.

Harris, L. and Jackson-Stops, G. When Adam delved, Robert Adam and the Kedleston landscape, *Country Life*, 5 March, 1985.

Haslam, C. Knowle Hill, notes on its history and restoration (Typescript, Landmark Trust, n.d.).

Hart, W. H. Proceedings in the Court of Exchequer respecting the Chatsworth Building Accounts, *Journal of the Derbyshire Archaeological and Natural History Society* 3 (1881), 7–55.

Harris, L. *Robert Adam and Kedleston. The Making of a Neo-Classical Masterpiece* (Wisbech, 1987).

Harvey, J. *Early Gardening Catalogues* (London, 1972).

Harvey, J. *Early Nurserymen* (London, 1974).

Hayton, D., Cruickshanks, H. and Handley, S. (eds) *The History of Parliament: The House of Commons 1690–1715* (London, 2002).

Heath, P. *South Derbyshire District Council, Heritage News* 21, Winter 2005–06; 26 (February 2008); 28 (Autumn 2008); 30 (Sept. 2009). Accessed via www.south-derbys.gov.uk/heritage-news.

Heath, P. Sealwood Cottage Derbyshire: an early *cottage orné* by 'Dr Syntax'. *Georgian Group Journal* 18 (2010), 105–14.

Headley, G. and Meulenkamp, W. *Follies. A Guide to Rogue Architecture in England, Scotland and Wales* (London, 1990).

Headley, G. and Meulenkamp, W. *Follies, Grottoes and Garden Buildings* (London, 1999).

Henderson, P. *The Tudor House and Garden* (New Haven CO and London, 2005).

Hitching, C. *Rock Landscapes, the Pulham Legacy* (Woodbridge, 2012).

Hussey, C. *English Gardens and Landscapes 1700–1750* (London, 1967).

Jackson Stops, G. Restoring the garden at Calke, *Country Life,* 18 May 1989.

Jackson-Stops, G. *An English Arcadia, 1600–1990. Designs for Gardens and Garden Buildings in the Care of the National Trust* (London, 1992).

Jarvis, S. Gothic rampant: designs by L. N. Cottingham for Snelston Hall. *V&A Album* 3 (1984), 322–31.

Jeckyll, G. and Weaver, L. *Gardens for Small Country Houses* (London, 1912).

Jones, B. *Follies and Grottoes* (London, 1979).

Keay, A. and Watkins, J. *The Elizabethan Garden at Kenilworth Castle* (Swindon, 2013).

Kerr, V. *Melbourne Hall Gardens* Guidebook (Derby, 1984).

Kerry, C. Leonard Wheatcroft of Ashover, *Journal of Derbyshire Archaeology and Natural History Society* 18 (1896), 29–80.

Kesteven, D. *Renishaw Hall Gardens* Guidebook (2010).

Kettle, P. *Oldcotes, The Last Mansion Built by Bess of Hardwick* (Cardiff, 2000).

King Hele, D. *Erasmus Darwin, a Life of Unequalled Achievement* (London, 1999).

Kirke, H. The Peak in the days of Queen Anne, *Journal of Derbyshire Archaeological and Natural History Society* 26 (1904), 205–18.

Kowsky, F. R. *Country, Park and City: The Architecture and Life of Calvert Vaux* (London, 2003).

Laird, M. *The Flowering of the Landscape Garden* (Pennsylvania, 1999).

Marsden, B. M. *The Early Barrow Diggers* (2nd edn, Stroud, 2011).

Mayer, L. *Humphry Repton* (Oxford, 2014).

Meir, J. *Sanderson Miller and his Landscapes* (Chichester, 2006).

Mowl, T. *Elizabethan Taste, Jacobean Style* (London, 1993).

Mowl, T. *Gentlemen and Players: Gardeners of the English Landscape* (Stroud, 2000).

Mowl, T. *Historic Gardens of Gloucestershire* (Stroud, 2002).

Mowl, T. *The Historic Gardens of England, Oxfordshire* (Stroud, 2007).

Mowl, T. and Barre, D. *The Historic Gardens of England, Staffordshire* (Bristol, 2009).

Mowl, T. and Earnshaw, B. *Architecture without Kings* (Manchester, 1995).

Mowl, T. and Hickman, C. *The Historic Gardens of England, Northamptonshire* (Stroud, 2008).

Mowl, T. and James, D. *The Historic Gardens of England, Warwickshire* (Bristol, 2011).

National Trust, *Calke Abbey.* Guidebook (London, 1996).

National Trust, *Of Household Stuff: The 1601 Inventories of Bess of Hardwick* (London, 2001).

National Trust, *A Short Guide to Calke Abbey Garden* (London, 2007).

Newton, S. C. The gentry of Derbyshire in the

seventeenth century, *Derbyshire Archaeological Journal* 86 (1966), 1–30.

Pendleton, J. *A History of Derbyshire* (London, 1886).

Pevsner, N. *The Buildings of England, Derbyshire* (Harmondsworth, reprint 1979).

Raeburn, M., Voronikhina, L. and Nurnberg, A. *The Green Frog Service, Wedgwood and Bentley's Imperial Russian Service* (London, 1995).

Redman, T. N. *An Illustrated History of Breadsall Priory* (Breadsall, 2009).

Riden, P. and Fowkes, D. *Hardwick. A Great House and its Estate* (Chichester, 2009).

Rolf, V. *Bathing Houses and Plunge Pools* (Princes Risborough, 1988).

Saunders, E. *Joseph Pickford of Derby, a Georgian Architect* (Stroud, 1993).

Seligman, S. (ed.) *Explore the Garden at Chatsworth, Maps, Guidebook and History* (Bakewell, revised 2008).

Seward, D. *Renishaw Hall, The Story of the Sitwells* (London, 2015).

Simo, M. L. *Loudon and the Landscape, From Country Seat to Metropolis* (New Haven CO, 1988).

Sitwell, O. *Two Generations* (London, 1940).

Sitwell, O. Left Hand, Right Hand (1945)

Sitwell, O. *Great Morning – being the Third Volume of Left Hand, Right Hand!* (London, 1948).

Sitwell, O. *Laughter in the Next Room* (London, 1949).

Sitwell, Sir R. *Renishaw Hall and the Sitwells* (Wymondham, Suffolk, 2009).

Sleigh, J. Sir John Statham of Wigwell, *Journal of the Derbyshire Archaeological and Natural History Society* 4 (1882), 38–39.

Sotherby's Chester, *Catalogue Hopton Hall Sale*, 5–6 September 1989.

Stamper, P. *Historic Parks and Gardens of Shropshire* (Shrewsbury, 1996).

Strong, R. *The Renaissance Garden in England* (London, 1979).

Strong, R. *The Artist and the Garden* (New Haven CO and London, 2000).

Taylor, B. The gardens of Shipley Hall. In P. Ibbotson and B. Taylor (eds) *Shipley Country Park Studies in History Research Papers* (1985–87) Accessed via http//"Shipley/studhistory1.htm".

Taylor, T. *A Life of John Taylor, LLD of Ashbourne* (London, 1910).

Tinniswood, A. *The Polite Tourists. A History of Country House Visiting* (London, 1998).

Trubshaw, S. *Trubshaw Family Records 1285–1876* (Stafford, 1876).

Usher, H. *Knowle Hill Ticknall, and the Burdetts* (Ticknall, 2006).

Wain, H. J. *The Story of Drakelow* (Birmingham, 1966).

Warner, T. 'Combined Utility and Magnificence' Humphry Repton's commission for Wingerworth Hall in Derbyshire: the anatomy of a missing Red Book, *Journal of Garden History* 7(3) (1987), 271–301.

White, R. (ed.), *Georgian Arcadia: Architecture for the Park and Garden* (London, 1987).

White, R. Robert Adam's rustic designs, *Georgian Group Journal* 23 (2015), 167–68.

Whittingham, S. *The Victorian Fern Craze* (Oxford, 2009).

Willis, P. *Charles Bridgeman and the English Landscape Garden* (London, 2002).

Wilson, P. K., Dolan, E. A. and Dick, M. (eds), *Anna Seward's Life of Erasmus Darwin* (Studley, 2010).

Wiltshire M. and Woore, S. *Medieval Parks of Derbyshire* (Ashbourne, 2009).

Woods, M. and Warren, A. *Glass Houses: A History of Greenhouses, Orangeries and Conservatories* (London, 1988).

Worsley, G. *England's Lost Houses from the Archives of Country Life*, (London, 2002).

Worsley, L. *Bolsover Castle* English Heritage guidebook (London, 2001).

Worsley, L. Bolsover Castle in the eighteenth century, *Georgian Group Journal* 11 (2001), 169–84.

Worsley, L. *Cavalier* (London, 2007).

Wymark, J. *Thomas Mawson – Life, Gardens and landscapes* (London, 2009).

Country Life (CL) early articles

(The Country Life Pictures Library website has a selection of old photographs).

Barlborough Hall: 27/10/1900.

Chatsworth: 23/6/1900, 5/1/1918.

Drakelow Hall: 22/3/1902, 16/3/1907.

Elvaston Castle: 4/1/1899, 21/1/1899.

Etwall Hall: 27/05/1899.

Eyam Hall: 7/7/1900.

Haddon Hall: 1/6/1901.

Hardwick Hall: 13/10/1910.

Kedleston Hall: 24/08/1901, 20/12/1913, 27/12/1913.

Longford Hall: 6/5/1905.

Melbourne Hall: 7/04/1928.

Osmaston: 12/7/1902, 16/3/1907, 17/2/1934.

Renishaw Hall: 3/11/1900.

Sudbury Hall: 15/6/1935.

Sutton Scarsdale Hall: 15/2/1919.
Thornbridge Hall: 4/2/1899.
Tissington Hall: 18/4/1911.
Wingerworth Hall: 29/1/1910.

Gardener's Magazine
Accessed via Biodiversity Heritage Library website
www.biodiversitylibrary.org.
Elvaston: May 1839, pp. 458–89; Derby Arboretum:
    Oct. 1840, p. 533–35.

Gardeners' Chronicle
Accessed via Biodiversity Heritage Library website.
Elvaston: 8, 15, 22, 29 Dec. 1849; 5, 12, 19 Jan. 1850; 23
    Dec. 1876; 25 April 1891.
Shipley: 18 Aug. 1883, 17 Jan. 1903.
Stancliffe: 17 Sept. 1898; Tissington: 17 Dec. 1884.

Journal of Horticulture and Cottage Gardener
Accessed via Biodiversity Heritage Library website.
Elvaston: 1 Dec. 1870; 9 Sept. 1875; Hassop: 30 Dec.
    1874; 1 Jan. 1876.
Ogston: 5 March 1874; Osmaston: 4 and 11 Nov. 1875.
Ringwood: 16 March 1876; Shipley: 21 Sept. 1876.
Sydnope: 12 and 19 March 1874; The Riddings: 7 June
    1877.
Vale House: 13 Aug. 1874.

Newspapers
Accessed via www.British Newspaper Archive.co.uk

Aris's Birmingham Gazette
Belper News
Birmingham Gazette
Chester Chronicle
Derby Daily Telegraph
Derby Mercury (DM)

Derbyshire Courier
Derbyshire Times and Chesterfield Herald (DTCH)
Leeds Mercury
Leicester Journal
Lloyds Weekly Newspaper
Manchester Courier and Lancashire General Advertiser
Manchester Mercury
Morning Post
Norfolk Chronicle
Nottinghamshire Evening Post
Nottinghamshire Guardian
Sheffield Daily Telegraph
Sheffield Independent
Stamford Mercury
Staffordshire Advertiser
*Staffordshire Sentinel and Commercial & General
    Advertiser*
Staffordshire Gazette and County Standard
Yorkshire Gazette

Council Websites consulted online
www.derbyshiredales.gov.uk/ Ashbourne Conservation
    Area Appraisal: 5
www.info.Ambervalley.gov.uk/ Belper River Garden
    Management Plan 2010–2105
www.south-derbys.gov.uk/ Bretby Conservation Area
    Character Statement, 2010
www.peakdistrict.gov.uk/ Cressbrook and Ravendale
    Conservation Area Appraisal, 2011
www.south-derbys.gov.uk/Kings Newton Conservation
    Area Character Statement, Consultation Draft, 2010
www.derbyshiredales.gov.uk/ Matlock Bath Conservation
    Area Appraisal 6, July 2006
www.south-derbys.gov.uk/ Netherseal Conservation
    Area Character Statement, 2010
www.chesterfield.gov.uk/ Staveley Conservation Area
    Character Appraisal, 2010